Archives and Libraries in the Ancient Near East 1500–300 B.C.

Olof Pedersén

CDL Press
Bethesda, Maryland

Pedersén, Olof, 1946–
Archives and libraries in the Ancient Near East, 1500–300 B.C. /
Olof Pedersén.
p. cm.
Includes bibliographical references and index.
ISBN 1-883053-39-0
1. Archives—Middle East—History—To 400. 2. Libraries—Middle East—History—To 400. 3. Middle East—Antiquities. I. Title.
Z722.7.P42 1998
027.0394—dc21 98-4337
CIP

The cuneiform on the front and back cover is the beginning of the colophon to a tablet from the library of the Assyrian king Asshurbanipal, published in H. C. Rawlinson, *A Selection from the Miscellaneous Inscriptions of Assyria*, 2nd ed., London 1891, pl. 48.

Contents

Abbreviations

The bibliographical abbreviations used in this work are listed below. In addition, each excavation has its own set of abbreviations for the designation of areas, houses, excavation numbers, etc. I have, as much as possible, tried to avoid these special abbreviations, and when they occur in this work, they are in most cases self-explanatory—detailed explanation of these special abbreviations can be found in the archaeological publications of the appropriate site.

AA	*Archäologischer Anzeiger*. Berlin.
AAAS	*Les Annales Archéologiques Arabes Syriennes*. Damaskus.
AASOR	The Annual of the American Schools of Oriental Research. Cambridge, Mass.
Abr-Nahrain	Abr-Nahrain: An Annual published by the Department of Middle Eastern Studies, University of Melbourne. Leiden.
ADFU	Ausgrabungen der Deutschen Forschungsgemeinschaft in Uruk-Warka. Deutsches Archäologisches Institut Abteilung Baghdad. Berlin.
ADOG	Abhandlungen der Deutschen Orient-Gesellschaft. Berlin.
AfO	*Archiv für Orientforschung*. Berlin, Graz, and Horn.
AfO Beih.	Archiv für Orientforschung, Beiheft. Berlin, Graz, and Horn.
AJA	*American Journal of Archaeology*. Princeton, N.J.
Akkadica	*Akkadica*. Musées royaux d'art et d'histoire. Bruxelles.
ALA I–II	O. Pedersén. *Archives and Libraries in the City of Assur: A Survey of the Material from the German Excavations* I–II. Acta Universitatis Upsaliensis, Studia Semitica Upsaliensia 6. Uppsala 1985. Studia Semitica Upsaliensia 8. Uppsala 1986.

ALASPM	Abhandlungen zur Literatur Alt-Syrien-Palästinas und Mesopotamiens. Münster.
AnSt	*Anatolian Studies: Journal of the British Institute of Archaeology at Ankara*. London.
AOAT	Alter Orient und Altes Testament. Kevelaer, and Neukirchen-Vluyn.
AOATS	Alter Orient und Altes Testament, Sonderreihe. Kevelaer, and Neukirchen-Vluyn.
AoF	*Altorientalische Forschungen*. Berlin.
APAW	Abhandlungen der Preußischen Akademie der Wissenschaften. Berlin.
Archéologia	*Archéologia: revue mensuelle*. Paris
ASAW	Abhandlungen der Sächsichen Akademie der Wissenschaften zu Leipzig, Philologisch-historische Klasse. Berlin.
Assur	*Assur: A Publication of the International Institute for Syro-Mesopotamian Studies*. Malibu, Calif.
AuOr	*Aula Orientalis: revista de estudios del Proximo Oriente Antiguo*. Sabadell, Barcelona.
AUWE	Ausgrabungen in Uruk-Warka, Endberichte. Deutsches Archäologisches Institut, Abteilung Baghdad. Mainz am Rhein.
BA	*Biblical Archaeologist*. Cambridge, Mass. and Atlanta, Ga.
BaF	Baghdader Forschungen. Deutsches Archäologisches Institut, Abteilung Baghdad. Mainz am Rhein.
BaM	*Baghdader Mitteilungen*. Deutsches Archäologisches Institut, Abteilung Baghdad. Berlin.
BaM Beih.	Baghdader Mitteilungen Beiheft. Deutsches Archäologisches Institut, Abteilung Baghdad. Berlin.
BASOR	*Bulletin of the American Schools of Oriental Research*. Missoula, Mont., etc.
BATSH	Berichte der Ausgrabung Tall Šēḫ Ḥamad/Dūr-Katlimmu 1. Berlin 1991–.
BCH	*Bulletin de correspondence hellénique*. Athens.
BE	The Babylonian Expedition of the University of Pennsylvania. Philadelphia, Pa.
Belleten	*Belleten*. Türk Tarih Kurumu. Ankara.

Berytus	*Berytus: Archaeological Studies*. Beirut.
BiOr	*Bibliotheca Orientalis*. Nederlands Instituut voor het Nabije Oosten. Leiden.
BoSt	Boghazköi-Studien.
CDAFI	*Cahiers de la Délégation Archéologique Franšaise en Iran*. Paris, and Teheran.
CPOP	Civilisations du Proche-Orient II: Philologie. Neuchâtel and Paris 1992–.
CRRAI	Compte rendu de la ... Rencontre Assyriologique Internationale.
CRRAI 30	*Cuneiform Archives and Libraries: Papers read at the 30e Rencontre Assyriologique Internationale, Leiden, 4–8 July 1983*, ed. K. L. Veenhof. Uitgaven van het Nederlands Historisch-Archaeologisch Instituut te Istanbul 52. Istanbul 1986.
CRRAI 32	*Keilschriftliche Literaturen: Ausgewählte Vorträge der XXXII. Rencontre Assyriologique Internationale Münster, 8.–12.7.1985*, eds. K. Hecker and W. Sommerfeld. Berliner Beiträge zum Vorderen Orient 6. Berlin 1986.
CRRAI 35	*Nippur at the Centennial: Papers Read at the 35e Rencontre Assyriologique Internationale, Philadelphia, 1988*, ed. M. deJong Ellis. Occasional Publications of the Samuel Noah Kramer Fund 14. Philadelphia, Pa. 1992.
CRRAI 36	*Mesopotamie et Elam: Actes de la XXXVIème Rencontre Assyriologique Internationale, Gand, 10–14 juillet 1989*, eds. L. De Meyer and H. Gasche. Mesopotamian History and Environment, Occasional Publications I. Ghent 1992.
CRRAI 39	*Assyrien im Wandel der Zeiten: XXXIXe Rencontre Assyriologique Internationale, Heidelberg 6.–10. Juli, 1992*, ed. H. Waetzoldt and H. Hauptmann. Heidelberger Studien zum Alten Orient 6. Heidelberg 1997.
CTH	E. Laroche. *Catalogue des textes hittites*. Paris 1971.
CTN	Cuneiform Texts from Nimrud. British School of Archaeology in Iraq. [London].
DaM	*Damaszener Mitteilungen*. Deutsches archäologisches Institut Station Damaskus. Mainz am Rhein.
EAEHL	*Encyclopedia of Archaeological Excavations in the Holy Land*, ed.

	M. Avi-Yonah. London and Oxford 1975–1978.
Ex oriente lux	*Jaarbericht van het vooraziatisch-egyptisch genootschap "Ex oriente lux."* Leiden.
FS Alp	*Hittite and Other Anatolian and Near Eastern Studies in the Honor of Sedat Alp*, eds. H. Otten, H. Ertem, E. Akurgal, and A. Süel. Ankara 1992.
FS Boehmer	*Beiträge zur Kulturgeschichte Vorderasiens: Festschrift für Rainer Michael Boehmer*, eds. U. Finkbeiner, R. Dittmann, and H. Hauptmann. Mainz am Rhein 1995.
FS Dussaud	*Mélanges syriens offerts à Monsieur René Dussaud par ses amis et élèves* 1–2. Paris 1939.
FS Houwink ten Cate	*Studio historiae ardens: Ancient Near Eastern Studies Presented to Philo H. J. Houwink ten Cate on the Occasion of his 65th Birthday*, eds. T. P. J. van den Hout and J. de Roos. Uitgaven van het Nederlands Historisch-Archaeologisch Instituut te Istanbul 74. Istanbul 1995.
FS Koschaker	*Symbolae ad iura orientis antiqui pertinentes Paulo Koschaker dedicatae*, eds. T. Folkers, et al. Studia et documenta ad iura orientis antiqui pertinentia 2. Leiden 1939.
FS Lipinski	*Immigration and Emigration within the Ancient Near East: Festschrift E. Lipinski*, eds. K. Van Lerberghe and A. Schoors. Orientalia Lovaniensia Analecta 65. Leuven 1995.
FS Reiner	*Language, Literature, and History: Philological and Historical Studies Presented to Erica Reiner*, ed. F. Rochberg-Halton. American Oriental Series 67. New Haven, Conn. 1987.
FuB	*Forschungen und Berichte*. Staatliche Museen zu Berlin. Berlin.
HAHE	J. Renz and W. Röllig, *Handbuch der althebräischen Epigraphik* I, II/1, and III. Darmstadt 1995.
HdO	Handbuch der Orientalistik. Leiden.
HSS 1–21	Harvard Semitic Series. Cambridge, Mass. 1912–1970.
HSS 22–	Harvard Semitic Studies. Atlanta, Ga. 1977–.
IEJ	*Israel Exploration Journal*. Jerusalem.
Iraq	*Iraq*. British School of Archaeology in Iraq. London.
JAOS	*Journal of the American Oriental Society*. New Haven, Conn.
JCS	*Journal of Cuneiform Studies*. New Haven, Conn., Cambridge, Mass., and Philadelphia, Pa.

JEN	*Joint Expedition with the Iraq Museum at Nuzi.* American Schools of Oriental Research, Publications of the Baghdad School, 1–6. Paris, Philadelphia, Pa., and New Haven, Conn. 1927–1939. *Joint Expedition with the Iraq Museum at Nuzi.* 7 (=*SCCNH* 3). Winona Lake, Ind. 1989.
JKlF	*Jahrbuch für Kleinasiatische Forschung.* Heidelberg.
JNES	*Journal of Near Eastern Studies.* Chicago, Ill.
KBo	*Keilschrifttexte aus Boğazköy.* Berlin.
KTU	M. Dietrich, O. Loretz, and J. Sanmartín. *The Cuneiform Alphabetic Texts from Ugarit, Ras Ibn Hani and Other Places (KTU: second enlarged Edition).* ALASPM 8. 1995. 2nd edition of M. Dietrich, O. Loretz, and J. Sanmartín. *Die keilalphabetischen Texte aus Ugarit,* Einschließlich der keilalphabetischen Texte ausserhalb Ugarits. AOAT 24/1. 1976.
KUB	*Keilschrifturkunden aus Boğazköi.* Berlin.
LTBA I	L. Matouš. *Die lexikalischen Tafelserien der Babylonier und Assyrer in den Berliner Museen* I. Berlin 1933.
Materialien	J. Oelsner. *Materialien zur babylonischen Gesellschaft und Kultur in hellenistischer Zeit.* Assyriologia 7. Budapest 1986.
MDAIK	Mitteilungen des Deutschen archäologischen Instituts. Abteilung Kairo. Mainz am Rhein 1930–.
MDOG	*Mitteilungen der Deutschen Orient-Gesellschaft zu Berlin.* Berlin.
MDP	*Mémoires [de la] Délégation en Perse / Mémoires de la Mission Archéologique en Iran / Mémoires de la Délégation Archéologique en Iran.* Paris.
Museum Journal	*Museum Journal.* University Museum Philadelphia. Philadelphia, Pa.
MVAG	*Mitteilungen der Vorderasiatischen Gesellschaft / Mitteilungen der Vorderasiatisch-ägyptischen Gesellschaft.* Berlin.
N.A.B.U.	*N.A.B.U.: Nouvelles Assyriologiques Brèves et Utilitaires.* Paris.
NR	M. E. L. Mallowan. *Nimrud and its Remains* I, II, and foldings. London 1966.
NEAEHL	*The New Encyclopedia of Archaeological Excavations in the Holy Land* 1–4, ed. E. Stern. Jerusalem and New York, N.Y. 1993.
OEANE	*The Oxford Encyclopedia of Archaeology in the Near East,* ed. E. M. Meyers. New York, N.Y., and Oxford 1997.

OIC	Oriental Institute Communications. The University of Chicago. Chicago, Ill.
OIP	Oriental Institute Publications. The University of Chicago. Chicago, Ill.
OLA	Orientalia Lovaniensia Analecta. Leuven.
OrAnt	*Oriens Antiquus*. Rome.
Orient Express	*Orient Express: Notes et Nouvelles d'Archéologie Orientale*. Paris.
OrNS	*Orientalia. Nova Series*. Rome.
PBS	Publications of the Babylonian Section. University of Pennsylvania, The University Museum. Philadelphia, Pa.
RA	*Revue d'Assyriologie et d'Archéologie Orientale*. Paris.
al-Rāfidān	*al-Rāfidān: Journal of Western Asiatic Studies*, Tokyo.
RGTC	*Répertoire Géographique des Textes Cunéiformes*, Beihefte zum Tübinger Atlas des Vorderen Orients, Reihe B 7. Wiesbaden.
RLA	*Reallexikon der Assyriologie (und Vorderasiatischen Archäologie)* 1–. Berlin and New York, N.Y., 1932–.
SAA	State Archives of Assyria. Helsinki.
SAAB	*State Archives of Assyria Bulletin*. Padova.
SAAS	State Archives of Assyria Studies. Helsinki.
SAU	W. H. van Soldt. *Studies in the Akkadian of Ugarit: Dating and Grammar*. AOAT 40. 1986.
SCCNH	*Studies on the Civilization and Culture of Nuzi and the Hurrians* 1–5. Winona Lake, Ind., 1981–1995. *Studies on the Civilization and Culture of Nuzi and the Hurrians* 6–. Bethesda, Md. 1994–.
Semitica	*Semitica: cahiers*. L'Institut d'études sémitiques. Paris.
SGKAO	Schriften zur Geschichte und Kultur des Alten Orients. Zentralinstitut für Alte Geschichte und Archäologie Berlin. Berlin.
StBoT	Studien zu den Boğazköy-Texten. Herausgegeben von der Kommission für den Alten Orient der Akademie der Wissenschaften und der Literatur Mainz. Wiesbaden.
Sumer	*Sumer: A Journal of Archaeology and History in Iraq / Arab World*. Baghdad.
Syria	*Syria: Revue d'Art Oriental et d'Archéologie*. Paris.
TCL	*Textes cunéiformes. Musée du Louvre*, Département des Antiquités Orientales. Paris.

THeth	Texte der Hethiter. Heidelberg.
TTKY	Türk Tarih Kurumu Yayınlarından. Ankara.
UF	*Ugarit-Forschungen: Internationales Jahrbuch für die Altertumskunde Syrien-Palästinas*. Kevelaer and Neukirchen-Vluyn.
UVB	*Vorläufiger Bericht über die von dem Deutschen Archäologischen Institut (und der Deutschen Orient-Gesellschaft) aus Mitteln der Deutschen Forschungsgemeinschaft unternommenen Ausgrabungen in Uruk-Warka*. Berlin.
VAB	Vorderasiatische Bibliothek. Leipzig.
VS	Vorderasiatische Schriftdenkmäler der Staatlichen Museen zu Berlin. Berlin.
WO	*Die Welt des Orients*. Göttingen.
WVDOG	Wissenschaftliche Veröffentlichung der Deutschen Orient-Gesellschaft. Leipzig and Berlin.
ZA	*Zeitschrift für Assyriologie und Verwandte Gebiete / Zeitschrift für Assyriologie und Vorderasiatische Archäologie*. Berlin and New York, N.Y.
ZÄS	*Zeitschrift für ägyptische Sprache und Altertumskunde*. Berlin.

Preface

Despite an increasing interest in archival studies and the appearance during the last decades of several studies concerned with individual archives or libraries in the Ancient Near East, there has not been an overview presenting the main finds and reaching general conclusions about the occurrence and use of archives and libraries. This work presents such an overview for the period 1500–300 B.C. It deals with the cultures using cuneiform script and those using other scripts, especially the alphabet.

Most of the large findings of texts from this period had originally been preserved in archives or libraries. In the main parts of this study, the remains of these archives and libraries are presented in their archaeological context. The material is divided according to major geographical area, city, building, and room of origin. Several general questions about the material will be considered to the extent the available data will allow. There will be an attempt to reach preliminary conclusions about the use of archives and libraries.

The material presented here is the result of more than a century of archaeological activity in the Near East. During changing political circumstances, archaeologists have been allowed by the different governments and state antiquities authorities to proceed with their investigations. Without these countries deep interest into their history and the hard work of numerous archaeologists, the material used for this work would not have been available. During the decades, many have deciphered and studied the excavated texts. The names of many of these scholars or institutions can be found in the presentation of the material.

Acknowledgments

I thank a number of colleagues for their contributions to this work through their readiness to answer questions, freely offering information, or allowing me the use of unpublished or published material. The following colleagues were kind enough to read and comment on sections of the manuscript in an earlier form: M. Dandamaev, K. Deller, V. Haas, M. P. Maidman, and G. Wilhelm.

Several scholars were extremely generous in sharing with me information about new excavations or previously unavailable data. I thank P. M. M. G. Akkermans (Tell Sabi Abyad), R. M. Boehmer (Uruk), G. Bunnens (Til-Barsip), S. Dalley (Til-Barsip), R. Dittmann (Kar-Tukulti-Ninurta), E. Klengel-Brandt (Babylon), H. Kühne (Dur-Katlimmu), C. Kühne (Ḫarbe), J. Margueron (Emar), P. A. Miglus (Assur), L. Sassmannshausen (Nippur), W. Sommerfeld (Sippar), and P. Åström (Idalion). I also express my gratitude to J. Renger for permission to utilize the institute library in Berlin—an important accommodation considering the problematic library situation within the field in Sweden.

I express my appreciation to the Swedish Research Counsel of Humanities and Social Sciences, which has provided financial support for my research and its publication.

Important for the presentation of the archives and libraries are the plans of cities and houses. The basic material has been taken from a large number of different publications, made uniform in scale, rotated with north at the top, and supplied with indications of the findspots of the archives and libraries.

For the courtesy to use the plans of cities and houses in order to illustrate the placement of archives and libraries, I am grateful to a number of institutions and individuals:

Y. M. Al-Khalesi (Kurruḫanni, figs. 9–10), P. M. M. G. Akkermans (Tell Sabi Abyad, figs. 46–47), American Schools of Oriental Research (Ta'nak, fig. 15), L. Bachelot (Burmarina, fig. 86), D. Bahat (Jerusalem, fig. 109), R. M. Boehmer (Tell Imlihiye, Uruk, figs. 56, 98–100), British Institute of Archaeology in Ankara (Ḫuzirina, figs. 87–88), The British Museum (Alalakh, Nineveh, Sippar, Ur, figs. 13–14, 55, 75–76, 94, 96–97), British School of Archaeology in Iraq (Dur-Kurigalzu, Imgur-Enlil, Kalḫu, Nineveh, Tell Rimah, figs. 39–40, 49–50, 66–71, 74, 77–78), G. Bunnens (Til-Barsip, figs. 84–85), E. Carter (Anshan, Susa, figs. 60, 101), Deutsche Orient-Gesellschaft (Assur, Babylon, Kar-Tukulti-Ninurta, Šarišša, figs. 25, 35–37, 52–53, 62–65, 90–91), Deutsches Archäologisches Institut (Babylon, Dur-Šarrukin, Uruk, figs. 51, 73, 89, 99–100), R. H. Dornemann (Azu, figs. 11–12), Harrassowitz Verlag (Elephantine, fig. 103), Harvard University Press and Harvard University (Nuzi, figs. 2–8), Israel Exploration Society (Arad, Lachish, figs. 106–108), H. Kühne (Dur-Katlimmu, figs. 41–42, 80–81), J. Margueron (Emar, figs. 26–29), P. Matthiae (Tell Fray, fig. 48), Max-Freiherr-von-Oppenheim-Stiftung (Guzana, figs. 82–83), The Metropolitan Museum of Art (Susa, fig. 101), L. de Meyer (Sippar, figs. 93–94), P. A. Miglus (Assur, figs. 35–36, 62–63), E. O. Negahban (Kabnak, figs. 57–58), P. Neve (Ḫattuša, figs. 18–19, 21), The Oriental Institute of the University of Chicago (Dur-Sharrukin, Idalion, Nippur, Persepolis, Tell Fekhariya, figs. 43, 54, 72, 95, 102, 110), W. Orthmann (Ḫarbe, figs. 44–45), T. Özgüç (Tapigga, figs. 23–24), Palestine Exploration Fund (Samaria, figs. 104–105), Dr. Ludwig Reichert Verlag (Kalḫu, fig. 66), W. Schirmer (Ḫattuša, fig. 20), R. P. Sobolewski (Kalḫu, figs. 68–69), M. W. Stolper (Anshan, fig. 60), W. M. Sumner (Anshan, fig. 59), A. Süel (Šapinuwa, fig. 22), Undena Publications (Kurruḫanni, figs. 9–10), University of Pennsylvania Museum of Archaeology and Anthropology (Šibaniba, Anshan, Ur, figs. 38, 55, 60, 79, 96–97), D. Ussishkin (Lachish, fig. 106), Yale University Press (Akhetaten, figs. 16–17), and M. Yon (Ugarit, figs. 30–34).

Chapter 1
Introduction

Writing was invented ca. 3200 B.C. The oldest script seems to be the Mesopotamian pictographic script, which after a short time developed into cuneiform writing, which remained in use until the first century A.D. (the latest dated cuneiform text dates to A.D. 75). Writing systems soon developed in Egypt and Elam, and eventually other writing systems came into use in some areas. The simplest writing system, the alphabet or consonantal writing, was invented after 1700 B.C.[1]

This study concentrates on archives and libraries from 1500–300 B.C., although a few archives and libraries that continued the cuneiform tradition in the following centuries have also been included. The period 1500–300 B.C., the second half of the history of cuneiform writing, saw the increasing acceptance of the alphabet, which eventually was to replace the cuneiform script completely. Cuneiform script was normally written on clay tablets, whereas papyri, leather, or ostraca were, as a rule, used for alphabetic writing. Other writing materials and scripts are also attested, though less frequently, in the periods and areas of interest here.

From approximately 1500–1200 B.C. cuneiform script had its widest geographical distribution as the written means to express different languages, and Akkadian, written in cuneiform, served as the *lingua franca* for international communication. Of limited use, until ca. 1200 B.C., was the so-called "Ugaritic" script, an alphabetic system written with cuneiform signs.

1. For introductions to writing systems, cf., e.g., I. J. Gelb, *A Study of Writing*, 2nd ed. (1963), and later reprintings, and P. T. Daniels and W. Bright, eds., *World's Writing Systems* (1995), with further bibliography. Cf. also H. Günther and O. Ludwig, eds., *Schrift und Schriftlichkeit / Writing and Its Use: Ein interdisziplinäres Handbuch internationaler Forschung / An Interdisciplinary Handbook of International Research* 1, Handbücher zur Sprach- und Kommunikationswissenschaft 10:1 (1994).

Ca. 900–450 B.C. was the last important period of cuneiform writing; thereafter use of cuneiform script was rather limited, both geographically and in the type of text in which it was employed. During this period, the alphabet became the dominant script in the Levant, and was increasingly used alongside cuneiform in all other geographical areas, so that by 450 B.C. it had become the dominant system everywhere.

There has been a growing awareness during the last decades that the large number of clay tablets with cuneiform writing (as well as ostraca and papyri with alphabetic script) , in most cases, had belonged to collections, which have been called "archives" or "libraries." During recent years there has been a large number of studies of individual archives or of parts of archives, but only a few studies dealing with libraries. There have also been some analyses of archives or libraries in individual cities. A limited number of studies have dealt with general issues relating to archives and libraries.[2]

The terms "archive" and "library" may refer either to a collection of texts or to the room or building in which the collection was stored. This study focuses on collections of texts found in or next to their original place of storage. Also collections of texts in secondary archaeological context are analyzed, as well as a few empty rooms previously used for storing texts. On the other hand, no systematic attempt is made to discuss text collections without known findspots. Texts not known to have been found together but which on the basis of their contents have been grouped into what has sometimes been called "archives" are, as a rule, not treated in this work.

2. For overviews and works addressing general issues, cf. M. Weitemeyer, *Babylonske og assyriske arkiver og biblioteker* (1955), which is a short, rather dated, survey of archives and libraries in Babylonia and Assyria. K. R. Veenhof, ed., *Cuneiform Archives and Libraries*, CRRAI 30 (1986), despite the title, almost exclusively deals with archives, and not libraries. It contains an important introduction by K. R. Veenhof, as well as descriptions of a selection of archives by different scholars. General introductions to the history of archives and libraries are E. Posner, *Archives in the Ancient World* (1972), and F. Milkau and J. Shawe, "Der alte Vorderorient," in *Handbuch der Bibliothekswissenschaft* III/1: Geschichte der Bibliotheken, eds. F. Milkau and G. Leyh (1955), 1–55. Both studies are good from the point of general archival and library study, but weaker from the point of knowledge of the material from the Ancient Near East. Cf. also G. Goossens, "Introduction à l'archivéconomie de l'Asie antérieure," *RA* 46 (1952), 98–107; A. A. Kampman, *Archieven en Bibliotheken in het Oude Nabije Oosten*, Handelingen van het Zesde Wetenschappelijk Vlaamsch Congres voor Boek- en Bibliotheekwezen (1942), 182–211; and J. L. van der Gouw, *Archiefwetenschap* (1973).

For studies of individual archives or libraries, as well as archives and libraries in individual cities for the period under consideration here, see almost all references to Chapters 2 and 3.

The term "archive" here, as in some other studies, refers to a collection of texts, each text documenting a message or a statement, for example, letters, legal, economic, and administrative documents. In an archive there is usually just one copy of each text, although occasionally a few copies may exist. "Library," on the other hand, denotes a collection of texts normally with multiple copies for use in different places at different times, and includes, e.g., literary, historical, religious, and scientific texts. In other words, libraries may be said to consist of the texts of tradition. With rather broad definitions of the terms "document" and "literary text," it may be simplest to say that archives are collections of documents and libraries are collections of literary texts. Before the invention of the printing press the difference between texts in archives and those in libraries had more to do with content than physical appearance, even if it was not exclusively so. The division could be reformulated in the modern world as one between libraries housing printed books and archives where single copies of documents are stored.[3]

Occasionally a few library texts have been found in an archive and a few archive texts in a library. This does not change the overall designation of the collection as "archive" or "library." But when library texts are found in an archive, the designation "archive with library" (or "archive with library section") is used, and when archive texts are found in a library, the designation "library with archive" (or "library with archive section") is used. Choosing an accurate designation becomes even more difficult when the number of archive and library texts in a collection are almost equal; the terms "library and archive" or "archive and library" are intended to convey this situation.

It is not easy to set a required minimum size in order for a group of texts to be categorized as an archive or a library. Any limit will always exclude a number of candidate text collections from consideration. Alternatively, were we to include all collections having the same placement and function as larger archives and libraries, the smallest (and most frequently attested) size of an archive or library would be just one text. Considering these problems and the lack of information about several of the smallest text collections, there is a practical, floating lower limit to the size of archives and libraries in this work. When there is available information concerning small text groups, they have been included as archives and libraries. On the other hand, some-

3. Definitions of archives and libraries have already been formulated, e.g., in the works referred to in n. 2. In some modern countries, there are somewhat varying local definitions and limitations applying to archives and libraries, as can be found in some modern handbooks of archival and library sciences; I have found no reason to discuss such matters here.

what larger text groups may not be included, because there is not enough information about them.

It is often possible to subdivide archives on the basis of content, for example, by individual, family, or subject. Such subdivisions are here called "dossiers." (In some other studies such subdivisions are also called "archives." But in order to maintain more consistent and refined terminology such a definition is not used here.)

The archives and libraries discussed in this work are those for which there is external evidence of being collections of texts. In most cases this means that the texts were found together in one identifiable location. However, there are individual exceptions to this rule. For example, groups of texts with different findspots within the same site may be treated as a single archive or library if the content of the texts and the archaeological circumstances make it probable that originally it was a single collection stored in one place. Remains of archives or libraries without known findspots will not be discussed systematically. No attempt will be made to create artificial "archives" by means of combining individual texts found in different findspots, for example, texts which mention the same persons, although there are other, seemingly unrelated texts from the same findspots. Such reconstructed "archives" may have been dossiers if they ever existed as collections.

Considering the thousands of texts and the diverse archaeological matters referred to in the discussed archives and libraries, full documentation of all details cannot be provided here; such additional bibliographic information is often to be found in the cited works or in standard handbooks.[4]

There are several factors that can make the identification and analysis of an archive or library difficult. These problems may concern the excavation itself: the methodology employed, documentation of the excavation, and publication of the results. Many excavations, especially those during the nineteenth century, were not carried out according to what is now considered to be acceptable scientific principles, and texts from different archives or libraries were frequently mixed with each other during or after the excavation. The documentation of the excavations is often not of a standard suitable for a study such as ours, and the documentation is often not available to all scholars. Publication of the texts and the archaeological background are incomplete for many sites. Often only the texts (or a selection of texts), but not the archaeological details, is available, or only the archaeological information but not the

4. For cuneiform texts, cf. especially R. Borger, *Handbuch der Keilschriftliteratur* I–III (1967–1975), and the year bibliographies in *OrNS* and *AfO*.

texts. Despite these shortcomings, an attempt has been made here, often with incomplete data, to create as complete a picture as possible.

In Chapters 2 and 3, the presentation and preliminary analysis of the archives and libraries is divided into two main historical periods, 1500–1000 B.C. and 1000–300 B.C., a division to be found in many historical surveys of the Ancient Near East.[5] When considering the distribution of the excavated archives and libraries within these main periods, it is practical for this study to analyze archives and libraries according to a main area, this "area" defined according to major historical, geographical, and cultural categories. The areas used for the period 1500–1000 B.C. are the Mitannian and Egyptian areas, the Hittite area, the Middle Assyrian area, the Middle Babylonian area, and the Elamite area. For the period 1000–300 B.C., the divisions are the Neo-Assyrian area, the Neo-Babylonian area, the Persian area, and the Western Alphabetic area (the Western Alphabetic area includes the Levant and surrounding areas using West Semitic languages with an alphabetic script). For the centers of cuneiform writing in southern Mesopotamia old archival traditions will be followed to their end, even past the lower time limit. Archives and libraries outside these geographical or chronological limitations, for example, in the Mediterranean area, have not been included here.[6]

5. For basic historical information, cf. standard historical textbooks, e.g., A. Kuhrt, *The Ancient Near East c. 3000–330 BC* (1995); P. Garelli, *Le Proche-Orient Asiatique: des origines aux invasions des peuples de la mer*, Novelle Clio 2 (1969); P. Garelli and V. Nikiprowetzky, *Le Proche-Orient Asiatique: les empires Mésopotamiens, Israël*, Novelle Clio 2 bis (1974); E. Cassin, J. Bottéro, and J. Vercoutter, eds., *Die altorientalischen Reiche* I–III, Fischer Weltgeschichte 2–4 (1965–1967); *The Cambridge Ancient History* 1–6, 3rd or 2nd revised ed. (1970–1994); and M. Liverani, *Antico Oriente: Storia società economia* (1988).

Among historical studies of periods discussed in this work, note especially G. Wilhelm, "Mittan(n)i, Mitanni, Maitani. A. Historisch," *RLA* 8 (1994), 286–296; D. Stein, "Mittan(n)i. B. Bildkunst und Architektur," *RLA* 8 (1994), 296–299; E. Carter and M. W. Stolper, *Elam: Surveys of Political History and Archaeology*, University of California Publications: Near Eastern Studies 25 (1984); and J. A. Brinkman, *A Political History of Post-Kassite Babylonia 1158–722 B.C.*, Analecta Orientalia 43 (1968), all of which contain further bibliographical references.

6. Information about archives and libraries from earlier periods in Mesopotamia may be found in the works cited in note 2; in J. N. Postgate, *Early Mesopotamia: Society and Economy at the Dawn of History* (1992), fig. 2:12; or in recent publications of text-groups. For archives and libraries outside the geographical boundaries of this book, general references are: for Egypt, cf. W. Helck, "Archive," *Lexikon der Ägyptologie* I (1975), 422–424, and J. von Beckerath, "Bibliothek," *Lexikon der Ägyptologie* I (1975), 783–785, both with further references; for archives of clay tablets in the Bronze-Age Mediterranean area, cf. S. Hiller and O. Panagl, *Die frühgriechischen Texte aus mykenischer Zeit: Zur Erforschung der Linear B-Tafeln*, Erträge der Forschung 49 (1976).

Several often large collections of bullae, once fastened to no longer preserved archival documents written on papyri, have been found from the Hellenistic period. From mainland Greece, some 2,500

Within these areas, each city in which archives or libraries have been excavated is presented with a brief summary of the results of the excavations, concentrating on the period of interest for this study. Palaces, temples, and other official buildings, as well as private houses, and especially rooms that may have served as a place for storing an archive or a library, receive a summary description as background to the presentation of the archive or library. In addition to the maps (*Plans 1* and *61*) showing the locations of the cities with archives and libraries, general city plans, whenever possible, show the findspots of archives or libraries, and more detailed plans of the houses are provided to give further information about the archive or library rooms.

Chapter 4 is a comparison and general analysis of the archives and libraries presented in Chapters 2 and 3. The distribution of the archives and libraries in the areas discussed, buildings and rooms wherein collections were found, size, writing materials, scripts, languages, type of texts, chronology, and lifetime are considered. There is an attempt to identify the owners of official and private archives and libraries.

The methodology, items noted, and issues examined in the discussion of each archive and library are consistent, as much as possible.

The distribution of archives and libraries in the excavated cities within the two main periods and the defined geographical areas will be the starting point for the analysis. The houses and the types of rooms in which archives and libraries were found will be considered, and the placement of these rooms within the houses, as well as the possibility of archives or libraries on upper floors, will be examined. An attempt will also be made to study the method of storage of texts in the archive or library room.

I will try to provide the number of texts belonging to each archive and library. This is, unfortunately, not always possible due to the often extensive destruction of texts, resulting either in the disappearance of remains, thus yielding a count that is too low, or, quite opposite, in its division into a number of fragments, thus yielding a count that may far exceed the original number of texts. In many cases the excavated number of texts or fragments is not available. I will try to provide the count of texts originally in the archives and libraries (missing pieces will be reconstructed or broken pieces will be joined to the original complete texts). However, this is often not possible, and many numbers given should be understood only as approximations.

bullae have been found in Titani and 600 bullae in Kallion. Some 14,000 bullae were unearthed in Delos, on the island with the same name, and 11,000 bullae in Nea Paphos on Cyprus. Some 8,000 bullae have been found in Artaxata in Armenia. The largest collection, some 25,000 bullae, was unearthed in Seleukia on the Tigris. Cf. also Uruk below (chapter 3.2). References to these collections of bullae can be found in, e.g., M.-F. Boussac, "Sceaux déliens," *Revue archéologique* 1988 (1988), 308–340, especially 308–309.

The various writing materials, scripts, and languages will be considered whenever possible. It can be expected that most of the preserved writing material consists of clay tablets due to their rather imperishable nature. There were various formats of clay tablets, often depending upon the specific function of the text. But this aspect will not be considered systematically here due to lack of availability of so much of the material.[7] Other more perishable writing materials will be accounted for whenever possible. This may be in the form of minor remains of collections of writing boards, papyri, leather, ostraca, or lead rolls. There are a large number of references to, for example, writing boards in numerous texts from the Hittite, Middle Assyrian, Neo-Assyrian, and Neo-Babylonian areas.[8]

Letters and documents with obligations may have seal impressions in addition to the text. If the text was written on a clay tablet, the seal impressions were placed directly on the tablet (or on the enclosing envelope). If materials like writing boards, papyri, or leather carried the text, sealings had to be made on dockets or bullae of clay fastened by means of strings to these script carriers. Dockets are tablet-formed, often triangular shaped, hanging on the strings, and in most cases carrying inscriptions. Bullae are smaller pieces of clay, often fastened directly onto the object and often without inscription. Many of the dockets and bullae were used to seal objects other than writing materials, and collections of clay dockets or bullae will only be considered here if there is a possibility that they were fastened to now missing perishable writing material.[9]

The different scripts and languages will be noted. On clay tablets, the script, in most instances, is cuneiform, but various alphabetic writing systems and other scripts are attested. The languages in the different archives and libraries will be indi-

7. The form and size of clay tablets have, e.g., from archives in the Middle Assyrian and Neo-Assyrian areas been surveyed by J. N. Postgate, "Middle Assyrian to Neo-Assyrian: The Nature of the Shift," *Assyrien im Wandel der Zeiten*, CRRAI 39 (1997), 159–168.

8. Cf., e.g., H. Hunger, "Holztafel," *RLA* 4 (1972–1975), 458–459; M. San Nicolò, "Haben die Babylonier Wachstafeln als Schriftträger gekannt?" *OrNS* 17 (1948), 59–70; and D. Symington, "Late Bronze Age Writing-Boards and Their Uses: Textual Evidence from Anatolia and Syria," *AnSt* 41 (1991), 111–123.

For findings of preserved writing boards, cf. R. Payton, "The Ulu Burun Writing-Board Set," *AnSt* 41 (1991), 99–106, which is dated to the Late Bronze Age next to the south coast of Turkey; as well as below, Chapter 3, for the libraries Kalḫu 10 (section 3.1.2.2), Kalḫu 14 (section 3.1.2.4), and Assur 20 (section 3.1.1.2), from the Neo-Assyrian period.

9. Studies of the use of seal impressions can be found in, e.g., D. Collon, *First Impressions: Cylinder Seals in the Ancient Near East* (1987 and later reprints); McGuire Gibson and R. D. Biggs, eds., *Seals and Sealing in the Ancient Near East*, Bibliotheca Mesopotamica 6 (1977); and S. Herbordt, *Neuassyrische Glyptik des 8.–7. Jh. v.Chr.: Unter besonderer Berücksichtigung der Siegelungen auf Tafeln und Tonverschlüssen*, SAAS 1 (1992), all of which include additional bibliographical information.

cated, the Semitic languages: Akkadian with Babylonian and Assyrian dialects, Ugaritic, Aramaic, Hebrew, and Phoenician; the Indo-European languages: Hittite, Luwian, Palaic, and Greek; as well as the different agglutinative languages: Sumerian, Hurrian, Hattic, and Elamite. Due to frequent problems with the availability of the materials a complete listing of languages is often not possible.

The ability to place archives and libraries in correct chronological order and to place texts in chronological sequence within an individual archive or library depends on the chronology in use during that period and its synchronization to absolute dates. The most elaborate dating systems are in the Assyrian areas that used an eponym dating system and in the Babylonian areas that employed regnal years for dating. Other geographic areas discussed in this work did not maintain as elaborate a dating system and datings are, therefore, more problematic. The possibilities and problems with the dating system(s) are briefly discussed in the introductory remarks for each area.

An attempt will be made to investigate the distribution of the archives and libraries over the centuries considered in this work. I will also try to examine the lifetime of different archives and libraries, despite the difficulties resulting from the dating systems and the unavailability of much of the detailed chronological information.

Palaces, temples, and other public buildings are, in the following chapters, defined as official buildings, whereas living quarters are termed private houses. The definition of the types of buildings is essentially an archaeological matter and has, in most cases, already been correctly established during the excavation. Whenever possible, the owners of and the persons responsible for the archives and libraries will be identified and attempts will be made to demonstrate the relationship between the owner of the collection and the type of building housing the texts. The validity of the hypothesis that official archives and libraries were housed in official buildings and private archives in private houses will be examined and, when appropriate, alternate hypotheses offered.

The division of the collections of texts into archives and libraries according to the types of excavated texts will be considered. The frequency of archives, as well as of libraries, will be discussed. We will examine the extent to which the division of text collections into archives and libraries corresponds to the excavated material, and how often and to what extent archival material can be found in libraries or library material in archives. Due to the large amount of often inaccessible, unpublished texts, the classifications of texts belonging to an archive or library used in this work are quite rough and preliminary. Nonetheless, all available information will be used in order to get a preliminary idea as to the content of common types of archives and libraries.

In the final section, general principles governing archives and libraries will be discussed. Main trends within the analysis of the archives and libraries will be identified.

Only a limited number of the archives and libraries presented here are well published and studied. In order to reach some uniformity in the presentation of the rather diverse material, the presentation has concentrated on the main issues from an archival point of view. For this reason, other aspects, such as more advanced social and economic interpretations of the institutions or the families concerned, have, as a rule, not been discussed in this study.

1500–1000 B.C.

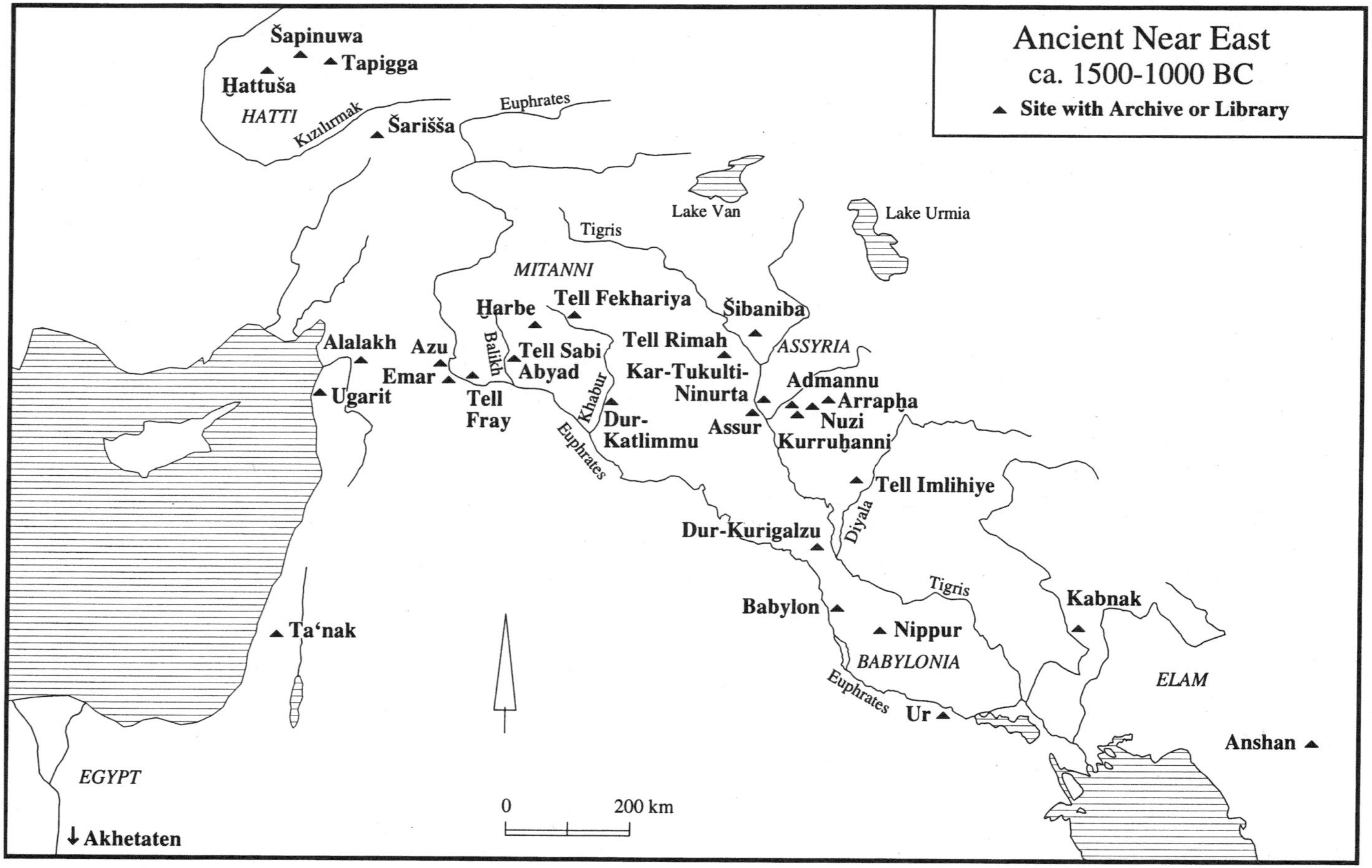

Plan 1. Ancient Near East.
Map showing cities with archives and libraries ca. 1500–1000 B.C.

Chapter 2

Archives and Libraries in the Near East 1500–1000 B.C.

The period 1500–1000 B.C., which has been called the Late Bronze Age and the beginning of the Iron Age, was dominated by the Mitanni, Hittite, Middle Assyrian, Kassite, Middle Babylonian, and Middle Elamite powers. The presentation of the cities in which archives or libraries have been found is divided on the basis of cultural and political criteria into: (1) Mitannian and Egyptian areas; (2) Hittite area; (3) Middle Assyrian area; (4) Middle Babylonian area; and (5) Elamite area. A few basic historical points may underline this division.

After the end of the Old Babylonian period, before the period of interest here, several smaller states continued the cultural tradition in various parts of the Near East. In the Mitannian area, in northern Mesopotamia and Syria, the Mitanni state came to dominate the political scene ca. 1500–1350 B.C. Around 1350 B.C., in the Anatolian highland, in the northwest, the Hittite area had been strengthened under the king Suppiluliuma, who incorporated the western half of Mitanni. The Hittite empire remained a leading power until its end around 1180 B.C. In the center of the Middle Assyrian area, in the northeast, the Assyrians had during the middle of the fourteenth century B.C. taken up an independent position in the previously eastern part of Mitanni. Especially during the thirteenth century and around 1100 B.C., Assyria was the important Middle Assyrian state. The Middle Babylonian area, in southern Mesopotamia, was first an important state governed by the Kassites. Later, in the middle of the twelfth century B.C., indigenous kings ruled over the area. The Elamite area, in the southeast, experienced a period of Mesopotamian dominance, which was followed by a stronger Elamite state during the thirteenth and twelfth centuries B.C.[1]

1. For general historical information, cf. Chapter 1, n. 5.

The great majority of preserved written documentation found in archives or libraries from this period consists of clay tablets with cuneiform script used to express several languages and dialects. Alphabetic script had recently been invented in the Canaanite area in the southern Levant. It may have been used on a perishable writing material. But at Ugarit a cuneiform alphabetic system has been preserved on clay tablets.

2.1 Mitannian and Egyptian Areas

The archives and libraries with cuneiform texts from the Mitannian and Egyptian areas date to the period ca. 1500–1350 B.C. The Hurrian state of Mitanni, centered in the upper Khabur area, and, possibly, led by some Indo-European groups, dominated the northern part of Mesopotamia. Neither its capital, Waššukkanni (cf. however for later periods 2.3.7), nor any other of the central, more important cities such as Taidu, has been extensively excavated for this period. Therefore, archives or libraries from the center of Mitanni have not yet been discovered. But when extensive excavations there do occur, large collections of Hurrian and Akkadian clay tablets may be expected.

Presently the main evidence of archive is from the periphery of Mitanni. In the east, there is Nuzi (2.1.1) with a large number of archives, nearby Kurruḫanni (2.1.2) with two essentially unpublished archives, as well as Arrapḫa, the unexcavated capital of this area, where one archive has been found (2.1.3). In the west, Alalakh (2.1.5) has a number of archives and the remains of a library; one archive has been discovered in Azu (2.1.4) and another in Ta'nak (2.1.6).

In Egypt an archive combined with a small library has been unearthed in Akhetaten (2.1.7). (Archives with domestic Egyptian scripts will not be discussed here.) At Akhetaten the use of clay tablets with cuneiform writing is documented for the correspondence with Canaanite viceroys, as well as with the great powers of the time: Mitanni, the Hittite state, Babylonia during Kassite rule, Alašiya (Cyprus), and, during the final phase, Assyria. This Egyptian archive indicates that in these other areas there should be cuneiform archives during this period.

The preserved texts are written in cuneiform script on clay tablets. Most texts are written in the Akkadian language, in principle in the Babylonian dialect, often with local influences. Some Hurrian texts, such as letters from the central Mitanni area, indicate the use of the Hurrian language, even though no Hurrian archive has as yet been excavated. The Akkadian used at Nuzi reflects a strong Hurrian influence.

In contrast to well-established Assyrian and Babylonian dating practices, the archives from Mitanni and Egypt do not have any standardized method of dating.

This fact and the general unsecured absolute dating for this period in this area have resulted in several problems in dating the archives and libraries. Dates are, therefore, normally not expressed in exact absolute years, but in approximate years, often related to the reigns of named kings.

The archives found in Ekalte (Tall Munbaqa)[2] and Terqa (Tell Ashara)[3] are here considered to represent the end of the previous period, and are therefore not discussed; study is needed to clarify the chronological details concerning these sites. In addition to the archives and libraries discussed below, individual tablets or small remains of archives have been found at a number of other sites in these areas.[4]

2.1.1 Nuzi (Yorgan Tepe)

Nuzi (modern Yorgan Tepe) is situated ca. 16 kilometers southwest of modern Kirkuk. E. Chiera, R. H. Pfeiffer, and R. F. S. Starr directed American (and partly joint Iraqi) expeditions to the site in 1925–1931. Nuzi was, during Level II, an important provincial capital in the kingdom of Arrapḫa (cf. below 2.1.3), which belonged to the state of Mitanni. One major trench was excavated below this level: Levels XII–X are the lowest levels, and date to the Ubaid period; Levels IX–VII date to the Uruk period; and Level IV to the Early Dynastic period. Level III, when the city was called Gasur, is dated by the existence of Old Akkadian tablets. Level IIB dates to the Ur III period and Level IIA to the Old Assyrian period. Above Level II is a later Level I, with limited remains.

The presentation here is limited to Level II. The central tell (here called the citadel), with palace, temple, and private houses, measured somewhat more than 200 × 200 meters. The palace is situated in the middle of the citadel with the temple northwest of the palace. These buildings are surrounded by private houses except in the

2. Cf. W. Mayer, "Munbāqa, Tall. A. Philologisch," *RLA* 8 (1993–1997), 417; and D. Machule, "Munbāqa, Tall. B. Archäologisch," *RLA* 8 (1993–1997), 418–419, both with further bibliography.

3. Cf. G. Buccellati and M. Kelly-Buccellati, "Terqa," *OEANE* 5 (1997), 188–190, with further bibliography; for the problems with the dating of the so-called Ḫana texts, cf. A. H. Podany, "A Middle Babylonian Date for the Ḫana Kingdom," *JCS* 43–45 (1991–1993), 53–62.

4. For Nawar (modern Tell Brak), cf. G. M. Schwartz, "Brak, Tell," *OEANE* 1 (1997), 355–356, with further bibliography; I. L. Finkel, "Inscriptions from Tell Brak 1984," *Iraq* 47 (1985), 187–201; I. L. Finkel, "Inscriptions from Tell Brak 1985," *Iraq* 50 (1988), 83–86; N. J. J. Illingworth, "Inscriptions from Tell Brak 1986," *Iraq* 50 (1988), 87–108; G. Wilhelm, "A Hurrian Letter from Tell Brak," *Iraq* 53 (1991), 159–168; as well as D. Oates and J. Oates, "A Note on the Date of the Fragmentary Tablet TB 11021," *Iraq* 53 (1991), 158; for Kumidi (modern Kamid el-Loz), cf. R. Hachmann, "Kumidi (Tell Kāmid al-Lōz)," *RLA* 6 (1980–1983), 330–334, with further bibliography; and for Hazor, cf. A. Ben-Tor, "Hazor," *OEANE* 3 (1997), 1–5, with further bibliography.

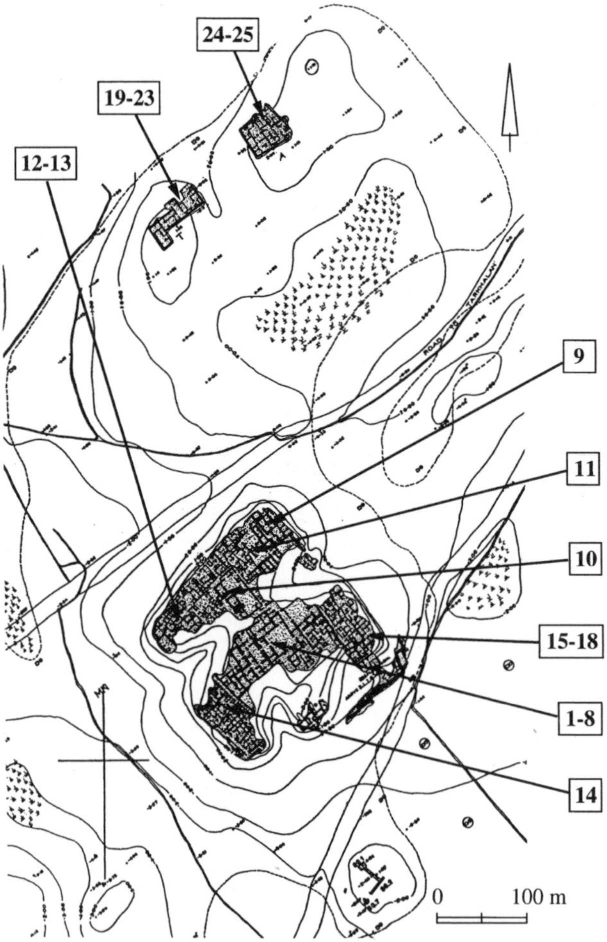

Plan 2. Nuzi.
General plan with archives **Nuzi 1-25**.
From R. F. S. Starr, *Nuzi* II (1937), plan II.

northern corner of the tell, where an official building (the arsenal) was excavated. Below the citadel, to the north, are areas of private houses, which probably formed a lower city, the extent of which has not been clearly established. Two such areas ca. 300 meters north of the citadel were excavated and have been named the Western Suburban area and the Eastern Suburban area.[5]

The texts are written in the Middle Babylonian dialect of Akkadian, but with a strong Hurrian influence, indicating that Hurrian was the spoken language. A time span of ca. 85 years for the Nuzi archives is generally accepted among scholars. The absolute chronology is more complicated to establish. An impression of the seal of Sauštatar, king of Mitanni during the second half of the fifteenth century, occurs on a tablet from Nuzi; but it is unclear whether this text was written during the reign of Sauštatar or during that of a successor. A final destruction of the city by the Assyrians, possibly by Aššur-uballiṭ I (1363–1328 B.C.), is probable, but has so far not been proved. Legal documents reflect special Nuzi types, which have undergone extensive study. There is sometimes an uncertainty in the assignment of findspots of the clay tablets. Therefore, in some cases there may exist alternative solutions to some of the difficulties concerning their division into archives.[6]

2.1.1.1 Archives in the Palace

The palace was surrounded on three sides by streets; the fourth side is not preserved. There were two large courtyards in the palace complex. Courtyard M94

5. For short surveys of Nuzi, cf. D. L. Stein, "Nuzi," *OEANE* 4 (1997), 171–175; and M. A. Morrison, "Nuzi," *The Anchor Bible Dictionary* IV (1992), 1156–1162, both with further bibliographies. R. F. S. Starr, *Nuzi* I (1939) and II (1937) are the basic archaeological publications. A short preliminary review of the archives can be found in the "Preface" in E. R. Lacheman, *Economic and Social Documents,* Excavations at Nuzi 7, *HSS* 16 (1958), v–viii. The basic bibliography is M. Dietrich, O. Loretz, and W. Mayer, *Nuzi-Bibliographie,* AOATS 11 (1972), with a continuation in A. Fadhil, *Studien zur Topographie und Prosopographie der Provinzstädte des Königreichs Arrapḫe,* BaF 6 (1983), 346–350. Main text publications are E. Chiera and E. R. Lacheman, *Joint Expedition with the Iraq Museum at Nuzi* (=*JEN*) 1–6 (1927–1939), as well as E. Chiera, Excavations at Nuzi 1, *HSS* 5 (1929); R. H. Pfeiffer, Excavations at Nuzi 2, *HSS* 9 (1932); T. J. Meek, Excavations at Nuzi 3, *HSS* 10 (1935); R. H. Pfeiffer and E. R. Lacheman, Excavations at Nuzi 4, *HSS* 13 (1942); E. R. Lacheman, Excavations at Nuzi 5, *HSS* 14 (1950); E. R. Lacheman, Excavations at Nuzi 6, *HSS* 15 (1955); E. R. Lacheman, Excavations at Nuzi 7, *HSS* 16 (1958); and E. R. Lacheman, Excavations at Nuzi 8, *HSS* 19 (1962). Several important studies and publications of more texts can be found in the series *Studies on the Civilization and Culture of Nuzi and the Hurrians* (=*SCCNH*) 1 (1981); *SCCNH* 2 (1987) contains Excavations at Nuzi 9/1; *SCCNH* 3 (1989) =JEN 7; *SCCNH* 4 (1993) contains Excavations at Nuzi 9/2; *SCCNH* 5 (1995) contains Excavations at Nuzi 9/3; *SCCNH* 6 (1994); and *SCCNH* 8 (1996) contains Excavations at Nuzi 10/1.

6. Cf., e.g., G. Wilhelm, "Mittan(n)i A. Historisch," *RLA* 8 (1994), 286–296; and A. H. Friedmann, "Towards a Relative Chronology at Nuzi," *SCCNH* 2 (1987), 109–129.

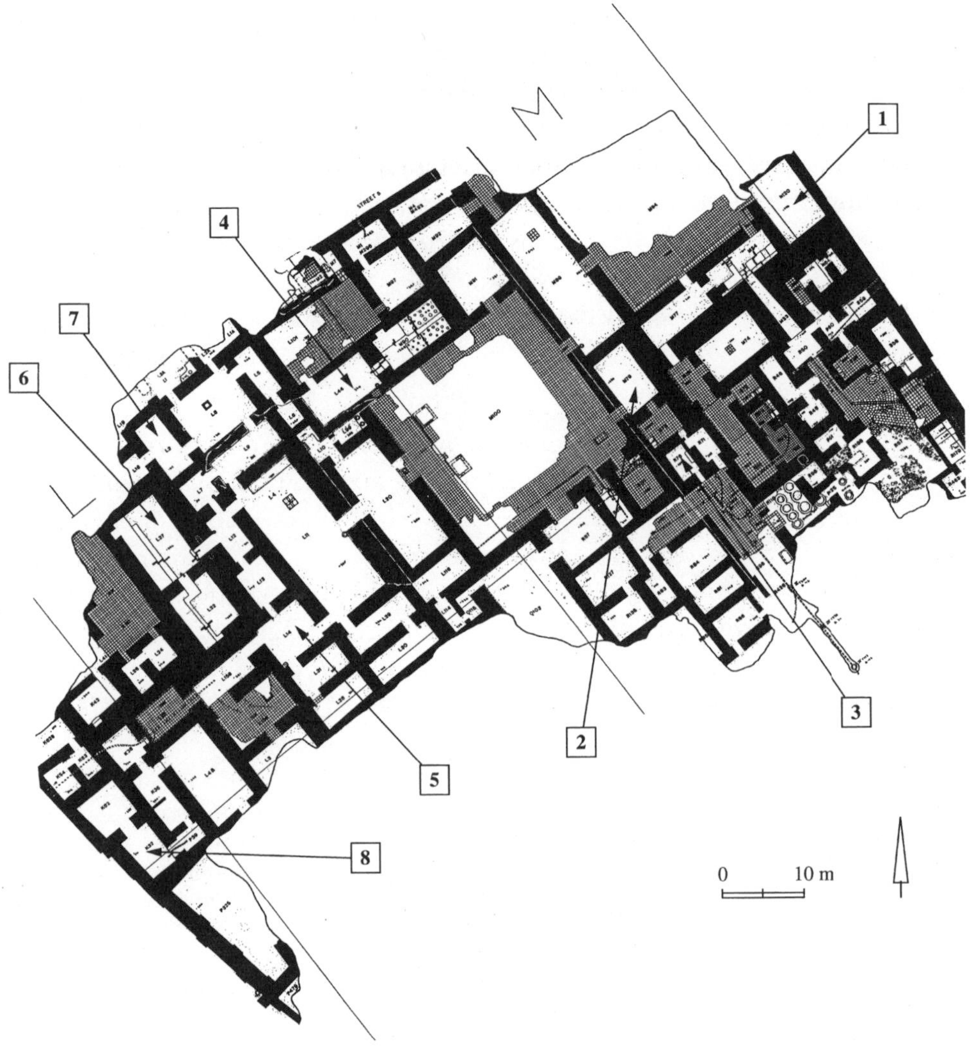

Plan 3. Nuzi.
Plan of palace with archives **Nuzi 1-8**.
From R. F. S. Starr, *Nuzi* II (1937), plan III.

(also called C94 in some publications) was situated in the north corner of the palace, probably at the main entrance to the palace in a no longer preserved part of the northwestern or northeastern outer wall. Room N120 (or C120 in some publications) in the east corner of this courtyard contained an archive (**Nuzi 1**) with 175 clay tablets. Among the 129 published tablets from this group, more than 60 concern military matters, many of which are lists of horses, chariots, and weapons. This archive also contains a group of 34 tablets, which seems to be the personal dossier of the woman Tulpun-naya. Her connection with the military administration is unclear. A group of eight tablets belonging to Ar-tura and his son may either form a separate sub-group or be misplaced from the archive in his private house (discussed below).

The Central Courtyard M100 is situated southwest of Courtyard M94, with a room between them allowing for communication. In the east corner of Courtyard M100 is Room M79, where an archive (**Nuzi 2**) with 54 clay tablets has been excavated. This archive concerns Elḫip-Tilla and Ewri-šarri, *šakin bīti*, "palace managers," and deals with the administration of palace property. Half of the texts are delivery notes concerning metals and other materials for the production of arrows. There are also a number of administrative lists of persons and objects, as well as some receipts.

The section of the palace southeast of Courtyard M94 is part the domestic area. The main kitchen is situated in Room R118 with the Kitchen Courtyard R95–R96 to the southwest. In the small Room R76 (C76 in some publications) beside this courtyard, an archive (**Nuzi 3**) with 152 clay tablets was found. The 135 published texts are various types of administrative documents, especially lists and delivery notes. The largest group concerns corn for the royal family, but there are several other types of texts, including some dealing with the distribution of oil for various gods. In the west corner of Courtyard M100, Room L44 (also called C44) contained 11 clay tablets (**Nuzi 4**); seven concern the administration of textiles, the others concern women.

Southwest of the Central Courtyard M100, inside the Main Room L4–L11, seem to be the more private areas of the palace. Room L14 (also called C14), which is central to communication in this area, contained 29 clay tablets (**Nuzi 5**), dealing with deliveries of food. Although Room L27 should contain a considerable number of clay tablets (**Nuzi 6**), only 12 have as yet been found. They are inventories of furniture and other objects, possibly, once stored in this room. Some remains of such objects seem to have been excavated in the room. Room L2 (called C2 in some publications) contained 48 clay tablets (**Nuzi 7**) of which 42 are published. Fourteen of these texts concern allegations against the mayor, Kušši-ḫarpe.

In the innermost part of the palace, in Room K32, bordering the southwestern outer wall, eight clay tablets (**Nuzi 8**) are reported to have been found. There are some problems with the correct assignment of texts to this group, but two of the tablets may concern queen Tarmennaya, daughter of Teḫip-Tilla.[7]

2.1.1.2 Archive in the Arsenal

The Arsenal (or Treasury, according to the interpretation of the excavators) was probably a two-story building. An administrative archive (**Nuzi 9**) consisting of 280 clay tablets was excavated in Rooms D3–6, with a few similar texts in Room D21 (or according to the archaeological publication in Rooms D2, D5, D7, and D21, D20, D12). The texts are mainly receipts of grain for the king's horses, officers, the queen, and the gods.

2.1.1.3 Archive in the Temple Area

The temple area was surrounded by Streets 5, 6, 7 and 8; Street 5 separated the temple from the palace. The northern cella, G29, was probably dedicated to the goddess Ištar-Šawuška, the southern cella, G53, possibly to the god Teššup. An archive (**Nuzi 10**) of clay tablets was unearthed in G73 and G29, with a few additional tablets in G53. Room G73 was a small archive room or alcove in the east corner of cella G29, from which it was partially blocked by a wall. Also a collection of glazed pots were found in the archive room. Due to the looting of the temple, many of the tablets were spread out in the section of the cella bordering the archive room. The 60 clay tablets so far published constitute the archive of Kirip-šeri and some other persons. Most of the texts are private contracts.

2.1.1.4 Archives in Private Houses around the Palace

2.1.1.4.1 Archives in Houses Northwest of the Palace

North of the temple, at the corner of Streets 7 and 8, House[8] 31 was situated with its entrance facing the street corner. The family archive was divided between two inner rooms. The excavators unearthed 75 clay tablets in Room C19 and about 80 clay tablets in Room C28. This was the archive (**Nuzi 11**) of Zike, his son Artimi, and his grandson Šar-Teššup. In Room C28 there were legal and business documents of the

7. W. Mayer, *Nuzi-Studien I: Die Archive des Palastes und die Prosopographie der Berufe*, AOAT 205/1 (1978); and E. Heinrich, *Die Paläste im Alten Mesopotamien* (1984), 82–86.

8. In the Nuzi publications the individual private houses in the city area were called "Group." Here such a complex is called "House."

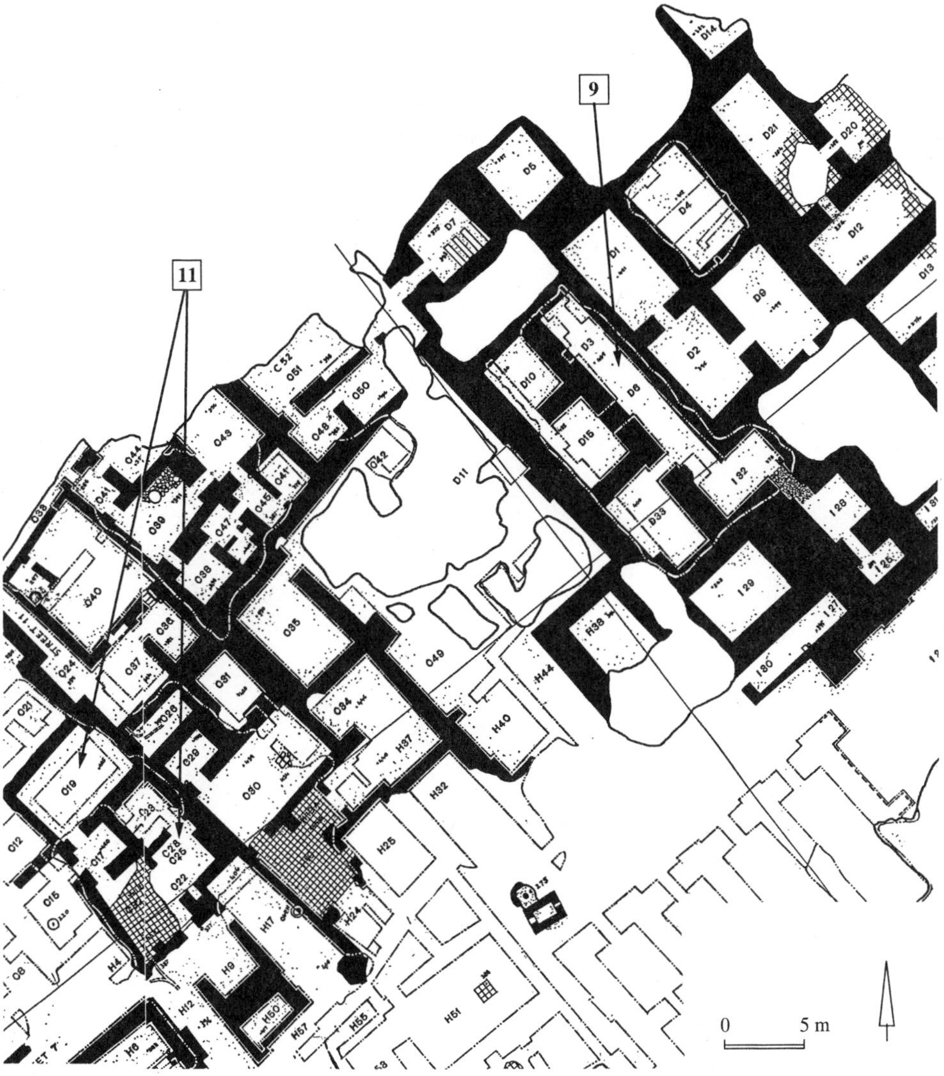

Plan 4. Nuzi.
Plan of area with private houses and the arsenal north of the palace, with archives **Nuzi 9** and **Nuzi 11**.
From R. F. S. Starr, *Nuzi* II (1937), plan III.

family; in Room C19 most of the texts were grain receipts, often mentioning the palace and the queen.

In the western part of the preserved private houses there were entrances to Houses 24 and 25 from Street 15. In House 24 clay tablets were found in Room F24. This was the archive (**Nuzi 12**) of Teḫip-šarri and Ṣill-apuḫe, as well as the latter's son. Most of the texts are contracts. In addition to the clay tablets, there was a bronze tablet. It has not been possible to prove if Room F25 belonged to the house and the tablets there to the archive. House 25, nearby, had clay tablets in Room F19 and in Rooms F16+26 (if the assignment of the latter group to this house and not to House 22 or 24 is correct). The tablets in Rooms F16+26 may be the archive (**Nuzi 13**) of Ḫutanni. In House 23, whose entrance was on Street 10, the clay tablets in Rooms F4 and F6 may also constitute an archive.

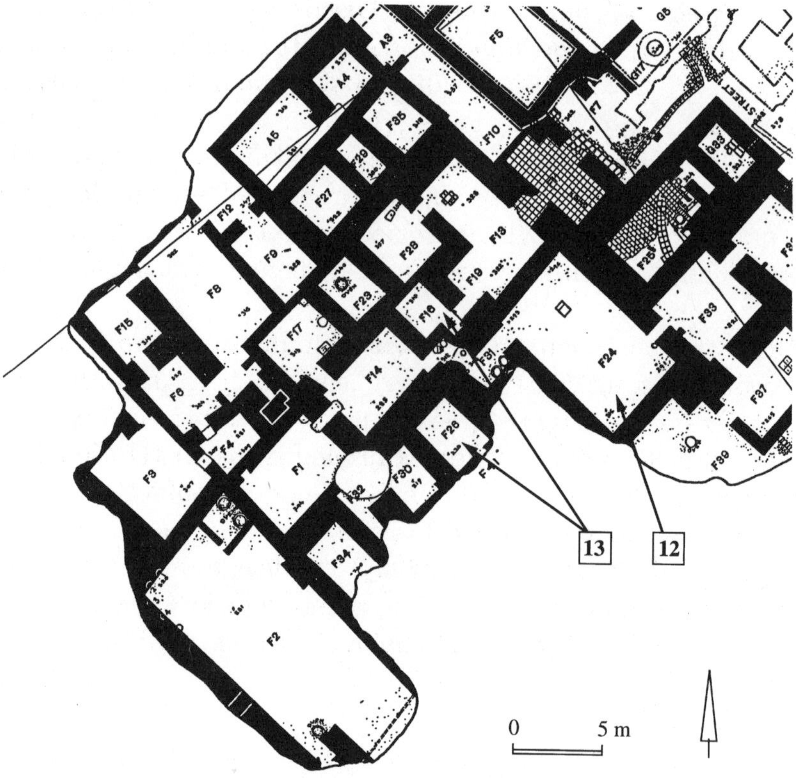

Plan 5. Nuzi.
Plan of area with private houses northwest of the palace, with archives **Nuzi 12-13**.
From R. F. S. Starr, *Nuzi* II (1937), plan III.

2.1.1.4.2 Archives in Houses Southwest of the Palace

Southwest of the palace, separated from it by Street 4, was an area with private houses, accessible through Streets 1, 2, and 3 as well as Street 4. The archaeological reports indicate the excavation in some of the houses of groups of clay tablets that seem to be archives. In House 2 clay tablets were excavated in Rooms P401, P400, and P382; in House 3 clay tablets were found in Rooms P470 and P486; in House 6 in Room P357; in House 8 a total of 70 tablets in Rooms P466+P460, P456, P467 and K465; and in House 10 there were 10 clay tablets, of which 5 are school tablets, in Room P313.

Upon analysis of the published information on the provenances of the tablets, it seems that all or most of the houses in this area of the city contained documents from one large family archive (**Nuzi 14**), in which other families are also attested. The owner of several of the texts was Eḫli-Teššup, son of Taya. His daughter, Šarum-elli, married Zikanta, son of Ḫampizi, which may explain why the texts of these two families are found together. The reasons for the texts concerning a few other families being placed together with these cannot, as yet, be determined. However, the distribution of mixed texts from this archive in at least Houses 2, 3, and 8 along Street 2 and possibly also in Houses along Street 4 raises the possibility that this does not reflect the original storage locations, but rather may be a result of the ancient destruction and looting of the city or careless treatment during the excavation or thereafter. A rearrangement of clay tablets has been attempted, but is for the time being only (an attractive) speculation.[9]

2.1.1.4.3 Archives in Houses Northeast of the Palace

Northeast of the palace, separated from it by Street 12, was an area with private houses, accessible through Street 12 and another, no longer preserved street northeast of the area. At the southeast end of Street 12, House 19 was situated. In Rooms S112, S124, and S129, in the northeasternmost part of the house, 60 clay tablets were found. This archive (**Nuzi 15**) was kept by Puḫi-šenni and his father Muš-apu. Puḫi-šenni served as a representative (*amumiḫḫuru*) of Urḫi-kušuḫ, who bore the title "prince" (*mār šarri*); also a few documents of Urḫi-kušuḫ are preserved, as well as several texts belonging to other persons. Most texts are legal documents, for example, sale adoptions, but there are also a number of loan documents, a few administrative lists, and a letter. In Rooms S132 and S133, in the northwestern half of the house, 70 clay tablets were unearthed. Pašši-Tilla, sometimes his son, his brother, or his father

9. M. A. Morrison, "The Southwest Archives at Nuzi," *SCCNH* 2 (1987), 167–201.

Pula-ḫali the merchant (*tamkāru*), kept this archive (**Nuzi 16**). It is not known whether these texts belong to another family and are a separate archive or whether they belong to the family attested in the first-mentioned group of rooms of the house. Twenty texts are loan documents; several legal texts; a few administrative lists; and three letters.

From the no longer preserved street northeast of this area with private houses, were the entrances to Houses 17 and 18A. In House 17 the excavators unearthed eight clay tablets in Room S110 and 24 clay tablets in Room S113. These are the two parts to the archive (**Nuzi 17**) of the family of Kuššiya. In Room S110, texts of Utḫap-tae, son of Ar-tura, were found (cf. the texts in N120 of the palace mentioned above), and in Room S113 the texts of Šeḫal-Teššup, first cousin once-removed of Utḫap-tae, and others. In House 18A, approximately 65 clay tablets (42 tablets and 34 identified fragments) were found in the corridor S151, probably originally stored in the small Room S307 nearby. This is the archive (**Nuzi 18**) of the family of Ḫuya. Most of the texts belonged to Ḫuya's sons Šukriya and Tarmiya; also a few belonged to their sons.[10]

2.1.1.5 Archives in Private Houses in the Suburban Areas

2.1.1.5.1 Houses with Archives of Teḫip-Tilla and His Family

Two suburban areas were excavated ca. 300 meters north of the main tell. In the western suburban area, the southwestern half of the excavated area, were some of the houses belonging to the family of Teḫip-Tilla. In the southwesternmost part of this half, eight rooms of the probably much larger house of Enna-mati, son of Teḫip-Tilla, were unearthed. The excavators reported unearthing more than 1,000 clay tablets in this house. Most of the tablets were found in Rooms T.T. 15 and 16 (also called T15 and T16) and some tablets in Room T.T. 19 (also called T19) nearby. Room T.T. 15 was built as a bathroom, but was later replastered without the water installations and then used as the main archive room of the family. The archive (**Nuzi 19**) spanned five generations of the family, of which the best attested are Teḫip-Tilla and Enna-mati. Also there are documents of Puḫi-šenni, the father of Teḫip-Tilla; Takku, son of Enna-mati; and Tieš-urḫe, son of Takku. A main objective of the archive seems to have been to document the family real estate holdings. There are a large number of sale-adoption documents of Teḫip-Tilla and litigation documents of Enna-mati, recording, respectively, the acquisition and keeping of their real estate.

10. M. A. Morrison, "The Eastern Archives of Nuzi," *SCCNH* 4 (1993), 1–130.

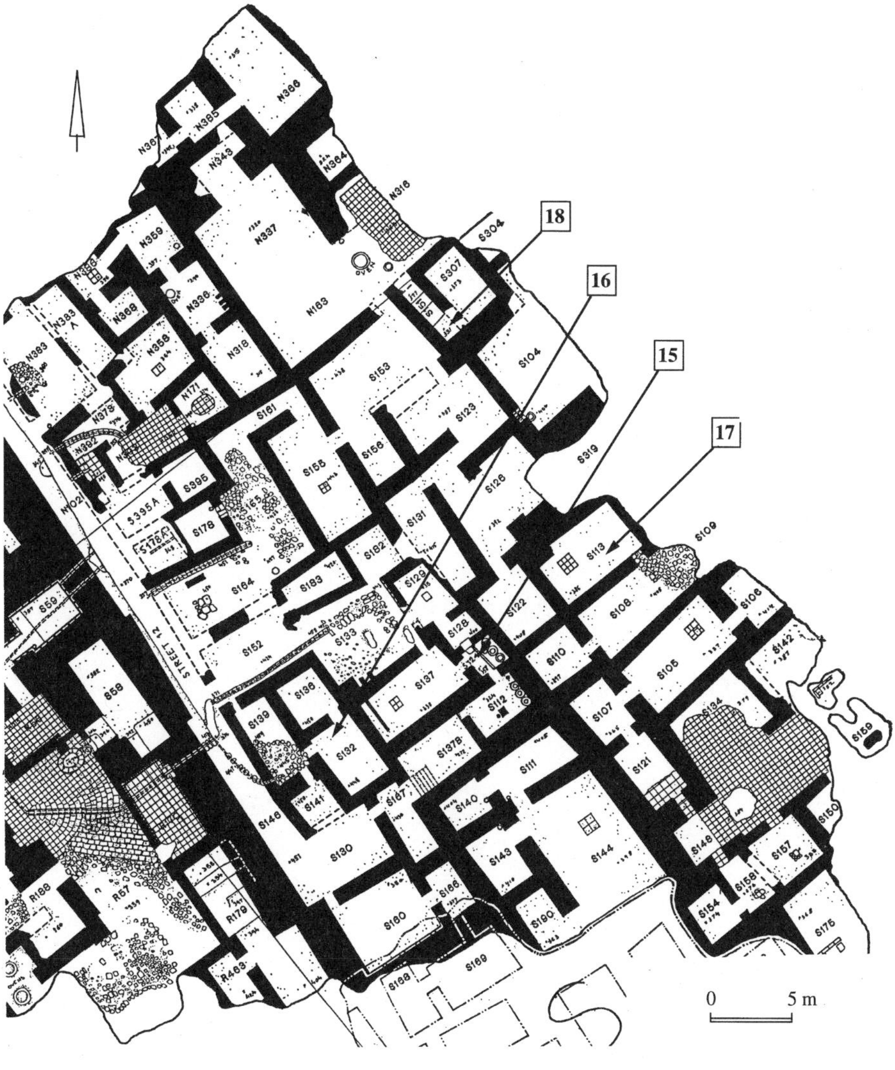

Plan 6. Nuzi.
Plan of area with private houses northeast of the palace,
with archives **Nuzi 15-18**.
From R. F. S. Starr, *Nuzi* II (1937), plan III.

The house immediately to the northeast of the house of Enna-mati was the house of Tarmi-Tilla, son of Šurki-Tilla and grandson of Teḫip-Tilla. In Room Sh.T. 13 (also called T13), the excavators unearthed 63 clay tablets, the archive (**Nuzi 20**) of Tarmi-Tilla. Most of the tablets are legal documents, but there is also a group of loan documents, an administrative list, and a letter.[11]

2.1.1.5.2 Houses with Archives of Other Families

The northeastern half of the excavated part of the houses in the western suburban area contained archives of other persons. Rooms Sh.T. 10, 11, and 12 seem to be part of one family's house. In Rooms Sh.T. 11 and 12 (also called T11 and T12), the excavators unearthed more than 70 texts, which seem to have been the archive (**Nuzi 21**) of Kel-Teššup and his father Ḫutiya, who worked for Šilwa-Teššup. Most of the tablets are legal documents, but there are also administrative lists and some letters. In Room Sh.T. 10 (also called T10) 12 clay tablets belonging to the archive (**Nuzi 22**) of Kurpa-zaḫ, son of Ḫilpiš-šuḫ, of another wing of the same family, were found. These tablets include legal documents and a letter. The eastern part of the western suburban excavation area was a separate house. In Rooms Sh.T. 1 and 4 (also called T1 and T4) of this house, an archive (**Nuzi 23**) of 40 clay tablets was unearthed. The 21 tablets in Room Sh.T. 1 concern Ḫui-te and other family members. In Room Sh.T. 4, most of the tablets concern Mušeya and Ḫašiya, the father and grandfather of Ḫui-te. Almost all are legal documents.[12]

2.1.1.5.3 House with Archives of Šilwa-Teššup, the Prince

The large, palatial house of Šilwa-Teššup, *mār šarri*, "prince," occupied most of the eastern suburban excavation area, excluding the north corner. More than 700 clay tablets belonging to his archive (**Nuzi 24**) were excavated in several of the rooms in the northeastern part of this house. The main archive rooms were Rooms 23 and 26, but groups of tablets were also found in Rooms 14 and 13 (rooms in the eastern suburban area are also called A23, A26, etc.).

In Room 23 the excavators found about 330 clay tablets, often dealing with Šilwa-Teššup's herds. Among them are 131 records of animals; 34 records of animal hides,

11. M. Maidman, *A Socio-Economic Analysis of a Nuzi Family Archive* (University Microfilms 1976); and M. Maidman, "A Nuzi Private Archive: Morphological Considerations," *Assur* 1/9 (1979), 179–186.

12. G. Dosch and K. Deller, "Die Familie Kizzuk, Sieben Kassitengenerationen in Temtena und Šuriniwe," *SCCNH* 1 (1981), 91–113.

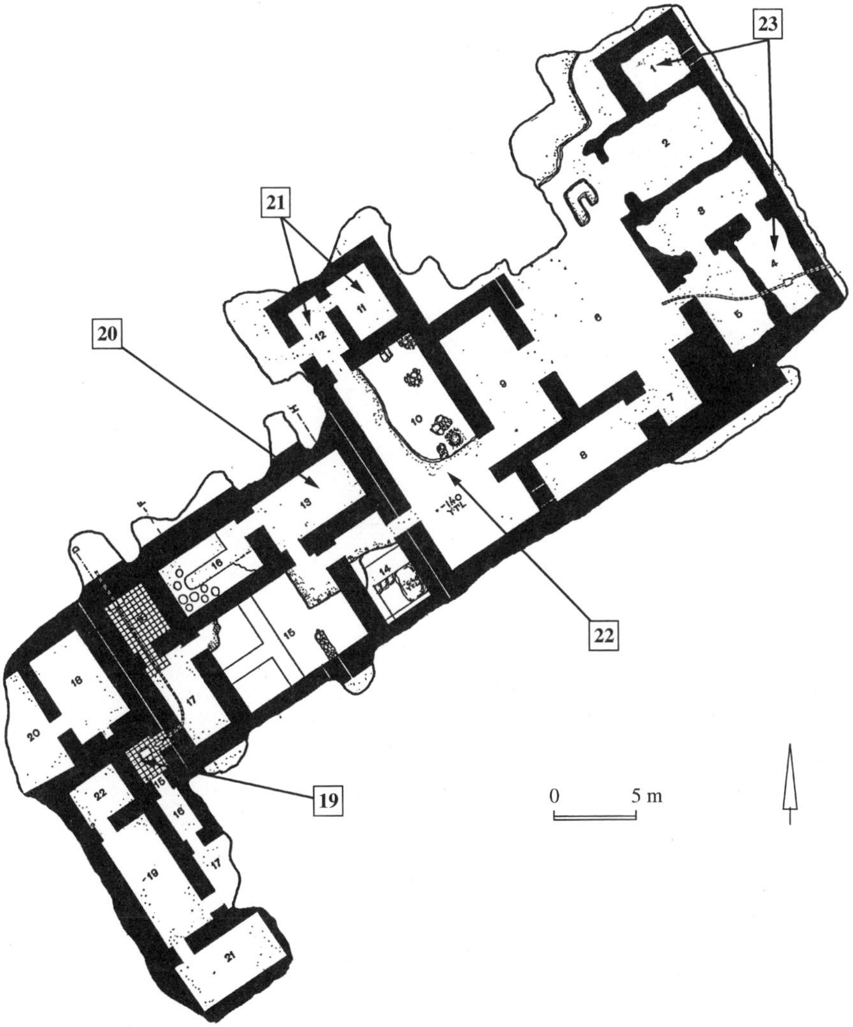

Plan 7. Nuzi.
Plan of area with private houses in northwest suburban area,
with archives **Nuzi 19-23**.
From R. F. S. Starr, *Nuzi* II (1937), plan 30.

wool, and hair; 80 records of grain; and 23 lists of servants. Among the approximately 195 tablets in Room 26 were business contracts of Šilwa-Teššup and several royal documents. The large number of loan documents (actually a majority of all such documents found at Nuzi) recording loans given by Šilwa-Teššup are characteristic of this archive. Among the royal documents are a letter from the Mitannian king Sauštatar; documents of the kings Itḫi-Teššup and Kipi-Teššup, as well as of the latter's son Ḫišmi-Teššup; and tablets of the woman Amminaya, the recipient of the Mitannian king's letter.[13]

2.1.1.5.4 House with Archive of Akkuya and Zike

The northern corner of the eastern suburban area was part of another house. About 190 clay tablets were excavated in Room 34, and some 20 additional in Rooms 30 and 35 (also called Rooms A34, A30 and A35). The tablets are the archive (**Nuzi 25**) of Akkuya, his son Zike, the sons of Zike, sometimes even grandson, as well as some other individuals who, at present, cannot be shown to be related to this family. Most of the texts are legal documents of the types found at Nuzi, for example, sale-adoption. But there are also four letters. In addition, there are 29 lists of persons and materials in connection with war chariots; these lists may have entered the archive due to the activities of Akap-šenni, son of Zike.[14]

2.1.2 Kurruḫanni (Tall al-Fakhar)

Kurruḫanni (modern Tall al-Fakhar) was situated ca. 28 kilometers southwest of Nuzi. Y. M. al-Khalesi led an Iraqi excavation there from 1967 to 1969. The tell is a low, sloping mound measuring approximately 200 × 135 meters. The clay tablets

13. M. A. Morrison, *Šilwa-tešup, Portrait of a Hurrian Prince* (University Microfilms 1974), and M. A. Morrison, "The Family of Šilwa-Tešub mār šarri," *JCS* 31 (1979), 3–31. A new edition of the texts has started with G. Wilhelm, *Das Archiv des Šilwa-Teššup*, Heft 2, Rationenlisten I (1980); G. Wilhelm, *Das Archiv des Šilwa-Teššup*, Heft 3, Rationenlisten II (1985); G. Wilhelm, *Das Archiv des Šilwa-Teššup*, Heft 4, Darlehensurkunden und verwandte Texte (1992); D. Stein, *Das Archiv des Šilwa-Teššup*, Heft 8, Seal impressions, Texts (1993); D. Stein, *Das Archiv des Šilwa-Teššup*, Heft 9, Seal impressions, Catalogue (1993). Textgroups still to be published are G. Wilhelm, *Das Archiv des Šilwa-Teššup*, Heft 5, Texte zur Viehhaltung, Heft 6, Rechtsurkunden und Briefe, and Heft 7, Die Vorläuferarchive; in addition G. Wilhelm has planned Heft 1, Gesamtdarstellung, Heft 10, Prosopographisches Namenverzeichnis, and Heft 11, Glossar und Indices.

14. G. Dosch, *Die Texte aus Room 34 des Archivs von Nuzi*, (Heidelberg: Magisterarbeit, 1976).

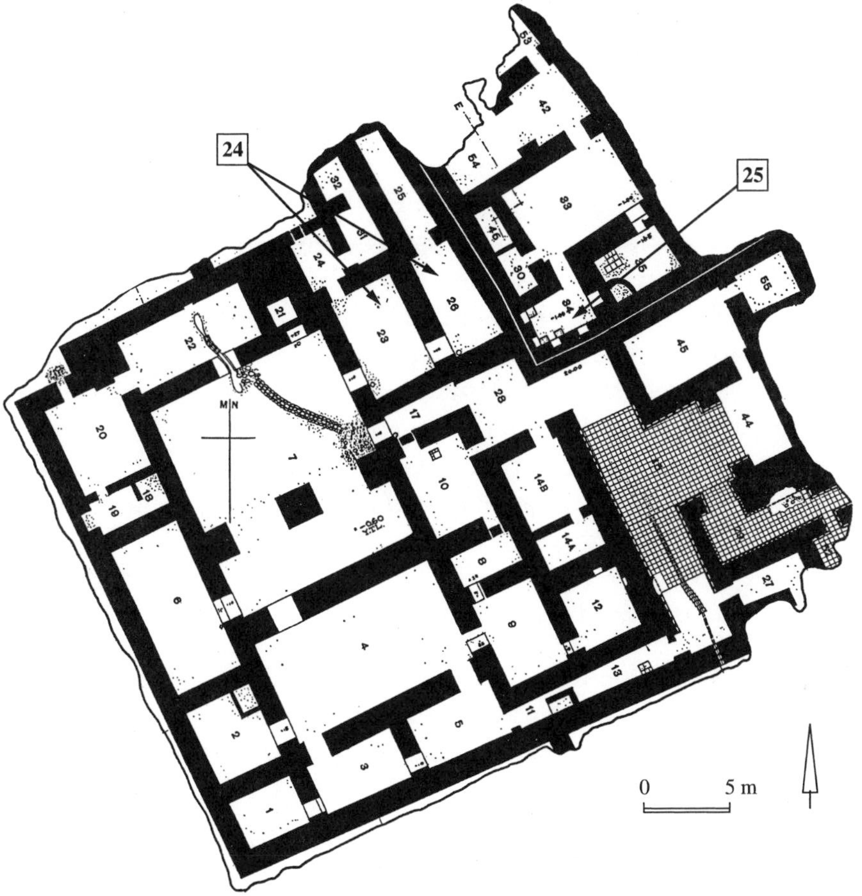

Plan 8. Nuzi.
Plan of area with private houses in northeast suburban area,
with archives **Nuzi 24-25**.
From R. F. S. Starr, *Nuzi* II (1937), plan 34.

excavated on the site are composed in the Middle Babylonian dialect of Akkadian, with Hurrian influence, just as at nearby Nuzi.[15]

2.1.2.1 Archives in the Palace

The Green Palace, so-called because of blue-green walls and floors, occupied ca. 60 × 30 meters, a large part of Level II of the tell. The entrance was from the southeast, with a Reception Room 10 inside Courtyard 13. Room 11, northeast of Room 10, was one of the archive rooms (**Kurruḫanni 1**). Room 4, in the inner northern part of the palace, housed the main archive (**Kurruḫanni 2**). Clay tablets were unearthed on the floor together with broken pottery. It is possible that the tablets had been kept in these jars, and that the jars were placed on the brick bench along the northwestern wall of the room. A total of about 1000 clay tablets were found in the palace and in secondary positions outside the building; only about 200 of these texts are complete or almost complete. A division into archives cannot be made here, because the contents of very few tablets have been reported and it is not known from which of the archive rooms the individual tablets came. I can mention only the main types of texts, viz. legal documents of the common types from Nuzi and Arrapḫa, administrative documents and letters. The texts date approximately to the same period as the Nuzi archives.[16]

2.1.3 Arrapḫa (Kirkuk)

Arrapḫa (modern Kirkuk) is near the foothills of the Zagros, 16 kilometers northeast of Nuzi. There has been no scientific excavation of the tell, locally called Qal'a, on the eastern bank of the Khasa river, because the modern city Kirkuk covers the ancient tell, as well as large areas around it on both sides of the river. In the period of the Nuzi tablets, Arrapḫa was the capital of a state that included both Nuzi and Kurruḫanni. The tablets found at Arrapḫa are of the same types as those from Nuzi.

15. G. Wilhelm, "Kurruḫanni," *RLA* 7 (1980–1983), 371–372, is a general introduction with bibliography. Preliminary publications of the archaeological material can be found in Y. Mahmoud [Al-Khalesi], "Tell al-Fakhar: Report on the First Season's Excavations," *Sumer* 26 (1970), 109–126, pls. 2–27; and Y. Mahmoud Al-Khalesi, "Tell al-Fakhar (Kurruḫanni), a *dimtu*-Settlement: Excavation Report," *Assur* 1/6 (1977).

16. A. Fadhil, *Rechtsurkunden und administrative Texte aus Kurruḫanni* (Heidelberg: Magisterarbeit, 1972); F. N. H. Al-Rawi, *Studies in the Commercial Life of an Administrative Area of Eastern Assyria in the Fifteenth Century B.C., Based on Published and Unpublished Cuneiform Texts* (Ph.D. Theses, University of Wales, 1977); some of the texts from a planned publication by B. K. Ismail and M. Müller have been presented in "Einige bemerkenswerte Urkunden aus Tell al-Faḫḫār zur altmesopotamischen Rechts-, Sozial- und Wirtschaftsgeschichte," *WO* 9 (1977–78), 14–34.

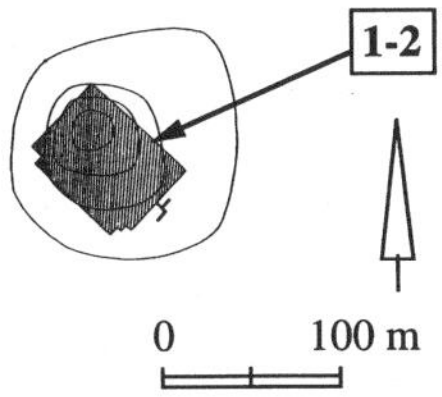

Plan 9. Kurruḫanni.
General plan with archives **Kurruḫanni 1-2**.
From Y. M. Al-Khalesi, *Assur* 1/6 (1977), 20.

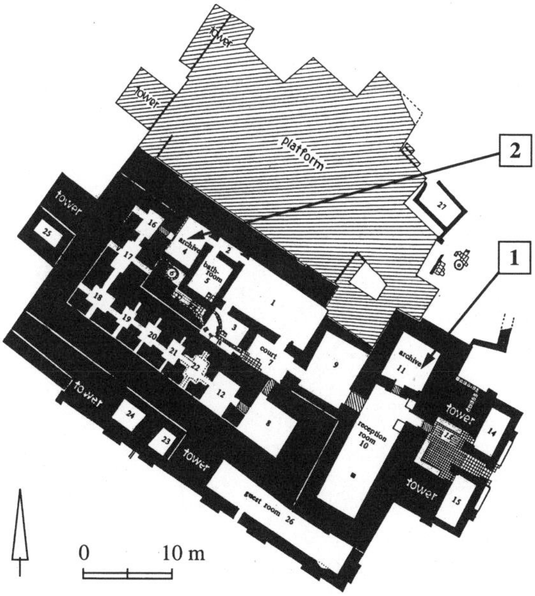

Plan 10. Kurruḫanni.
Plan of palace with archives **Kurruḫanni 1-2**.
From Y. M. Al-Khalesi, *Assur* 1/6 (1977), 21.

2.1.3.1 Archive Probably from Private House

Around the year 1912, clay tablets were found as a result of earth collapsing on the side of the mound. The findspot was at first kept secret, but was revealed several years later. However, excavations were not possible, because it posed a danger to the foundations of modern buildings higher up on the tell. In a reconstruction, 144 tablets have been assigned to the archive (**Arrapḫa 1**). At least 72 of these texts can be shown to have belonged to the archive, since they concern five generations of the family of Wullu. The texts, contemporary with the Nuzi tablets, concern land tenure, movable property, and private legal matters.[17]

2.1.4 Azu (Tell Hadidi)

Azu (modern Tell Hadidi) is situated on the west bank of the Euphrates about 30 kilometers north of Emar. After the Dutch excavation of 1973–1974, an American expedition led by R. H. Dornemann continued the explorations from 1974–1978. The site consists of a western High Tell and an eastern Low Tell. Occupation is attested from at least 2300 B.C. Whereas only the High Tell, some 500 × 300 meters, was occupied during the Middle Bronze Age, both the High and the Low Tells were inhabited during the Early Bronze Age and again during Late Bronze Age I under Mitannian domination, indicating a city of approximately 500 × 1000 meters. Its decline coincided with the decline of Mitanni, the Hittite conquest of the area, and, later on, the leading role of Emar.[18]

2.1.4.1 Archive in Private House

In area H, in the western part of the High Tell, the excavators unearthed the lower level of a large house, which consisted of a courtyard surrounded by rooms on the west, north, and south sides. An archive consisting of 14 clay tablets was found in this house. A jar in the northwestern room contained eight of the tablets; the remaining tablets were discovered in this room and other rooms and in the courtyard nearby. Most of the tablets remain unpublished, but they have been reported to be the archive

17. K. Grosz, *The Archive of the Wullu Family* (1988).

18. For a short survey of the site, cf. R. H. Dornemann, "Hadidi, Tell," *OEANE* 2 (1997), 453–454, with further bibliography. Cf. the preliminary reports by R. H. Dornemann, "Tell Hadidi: A Millennium of Bronze Age City Occupation," in Excavation Reports from the Tabqa Dam Project - Euphrates Valley, Syria, *AASOR* 44 (1979), 113–151; and R. H. Dornemann, "Salvage Excavations at Tell Hadidi in the Euphrates River Valley," *BA* 48 (1985), 49–59, with further bibliography.

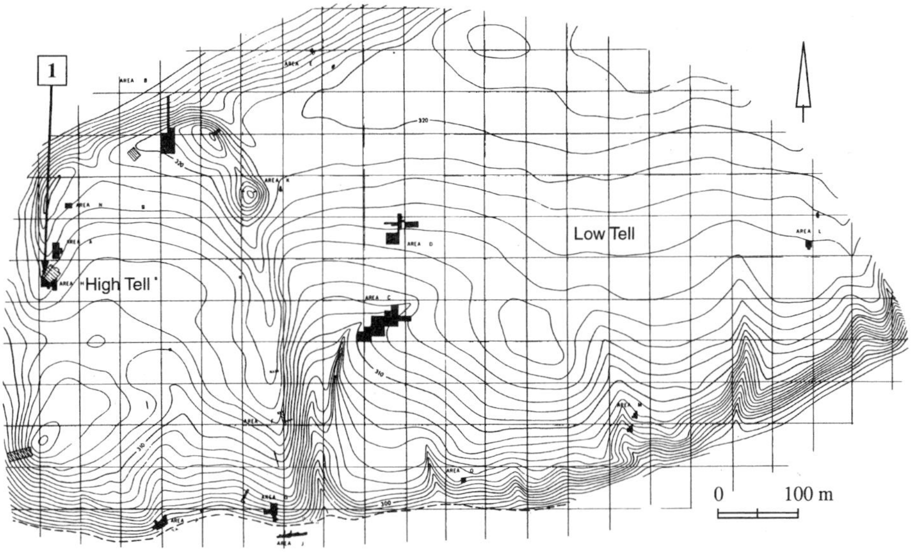

Plan 11. Azu.
General plan with archive **Azu 1**.
From R. H. Dornemann in J. C. Margueron, ed., *Le Moyen Euphrate* (1980), 217–234, plate I.

(**Azu 1**) of Ḫuziru and his son Yaya, dating approximately to the fifteenth century B.C., during the period of Mitannian domination. Among the texts are six purchase documents, a will, four other legal documents, two administrative lists, and a letter.[19]

2.1.5 Alalakh (Tell Açana)

Alalakh (modern Tell Açana) is situated in the southern part of the Amuq plain, 400 meters east of the Orontes river in the area where the river makes a large swing and changes its northward direction southwestward to the sea. L. Woolley directed the English excavations during 1937–1939 and 1946–1949. The tell measures 750 × 300 meters, with its axis running roughly northwest by southeast. The highest part of the

19. Cf. R. H. Dornemann, "Tell Hadidi: A Millennium of Bronze Age City Occupation," in Excavation Reports from the Tabqa Dam Project - Euphrates Valley, Syria, *AASOR* 44 (1979), 144–147; and R. H. Dornemann, "Salvage Excavations at Tell Hadidi in the Euphrates River Valley," *BA* 48 (1985), 56–57, based on the work of the epigraphist R. Whiting.

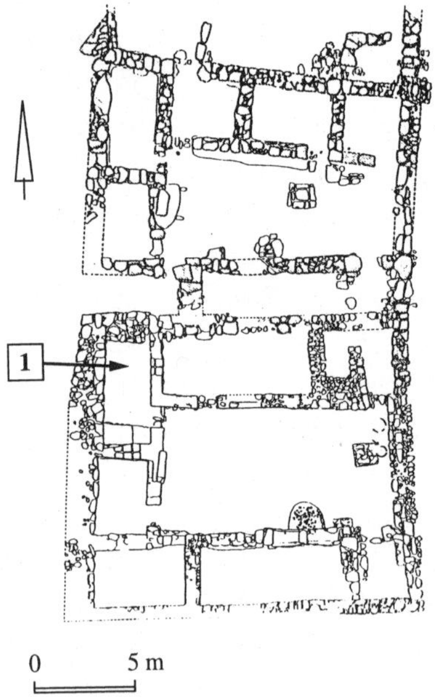

Plan 12. Azu.
Plan of private house with archive **Azu 1**.
From R. H. Dornemann, *BA* 48 (1985), 56.

mound is its northwestern third; it is here the excavations were concentrated. Occupation is attested from Level XVII, at the beginning of Middle Bronze Age, to the destruction of Level I, around 1200 B.C. Level VII, with palace, temple, and town wall with gate, produced Old Babylonian clay tablets. Level IV, with palace, temple, and several private houses, as well as remains of a town wall, dates to the Mitanni period. Following the destruction of Level IV, the Hittites rebuilt the city in Levels III–I. There are several chronological problems connected with the material, but the archives from Level IV, discussed below, are here considered to be from the fifteenth century B.C. The texts are written in the Middle Babylonian dialect of Akkadian with Hurrian influence.[20]

20. For short surveys of Alalakh, cf. D. L. Stein, "Alalakh," *OEANE* 1 (1997), 55–59; and E. L. Greenstein, "Alalakh Texts," *OEANE* 1 (1997), 59–61, both with further bibliographies. L. Woolley, Alalakh: *An Account of the Excavations at Tell Atchana in the Hatay, 1937–1949*, Reports of the Research Committee of the Society of Antiquities of London 18 (1955), is the main publication of the archaeological material. For the chronological problems, cf., e.g., M.-H. Gates, *Alalakh – Tell Atchana, Levels VI and V: A Re-Examination* (Diss. Yale 1976); and M.-H. Gates, in P. Åström, ed., *High, Middle or Low?* (1987), 60–86.

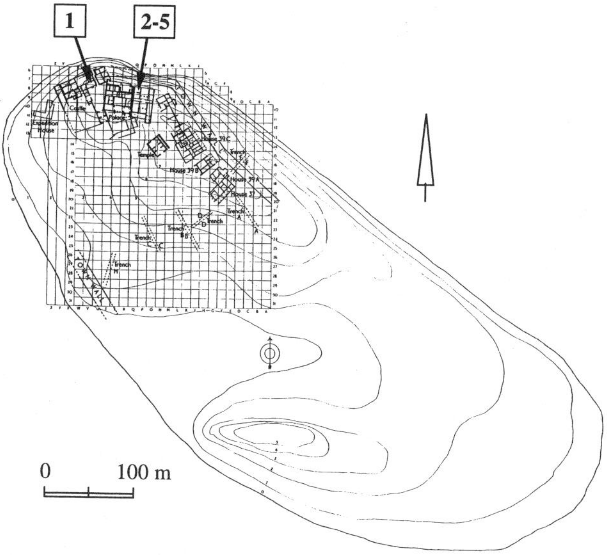

Plan 13. Alalakh.
General plan with archives
Alalakh 1-5.
From L. Woolley,
Alalakh (1955), plate XXII.

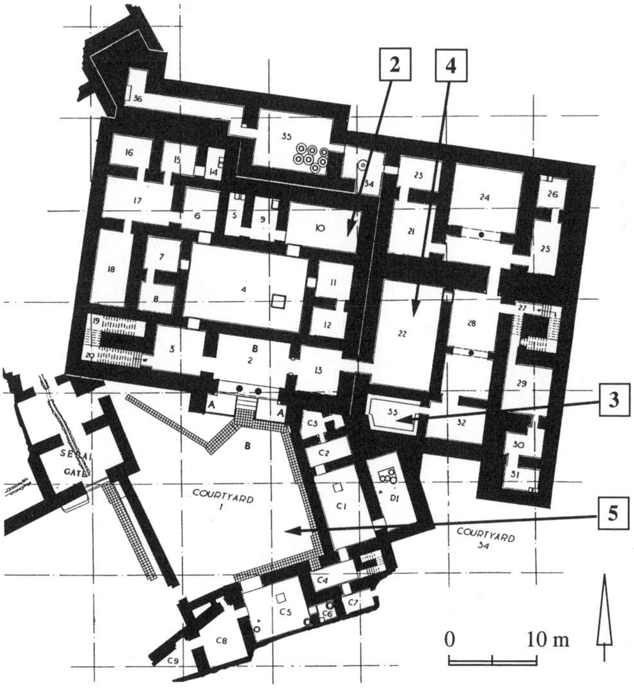

Plan 14. Alalakh.
Plan of palace with archives
Alalakh 2-5.
From L. Woolley,
Alalakh (1955), 113 fig. 44.

2.1.5.1 Administrative Archives and Remains of Small Library in the Palace Area

The palace is situated in the northern part of the city next to the town wall. Immediately northwest of the palace is a town gate through which it was possible to enter the city, thereby passing through an area with administrative buildings, called by the excavators the "Castle" or the "Fortress." The fortress and an older palace from Level V had a northwest to southeast direction. It was possibly Idrimi who built the new Level IV palace in a north to south direction, and his son Niqmepa who expanded it. After the reign of Ilim-ilimma, the son of Niqmepa, the palace was destroyed by fire, but the fortress and the other parts of the city continued until Level IV was destroyed, possibly by the Hittites under Suppiluliuma.

When entering through the northwestern town gate, people had to pass a large courtyard before reaching the inner gate. On the western side of this courtyard, the fortress is situated, on the eastern side is the palace. In Room W1 northwest of this courtyard, the excavators unearthed 140 clay tablets or fragments. From the evidence of the 83 identified tablets, this seems to have been an administrative archive (**Alalakh 1**), possibly under the responsibility of Ballanuwa and Enḫuta, both with the title *šatam šarri* (ŠÀ.TAM LUGAL), "royal administrator." Most of the texts are administrative lists or notes, listing persons, houses, animals, foodstuffs, and other materials. There are also six legal documents, often before Niqmepa. Among them are three documents recording purchases by Enḫuta, and a receipt. There is also a letter to Ballanuwa and even a treaty composed for Idrimi.

The palace entrance was from a courtyard on the southern side. To the west of the entrance room, which had two pillars at the front, was a staircase to the upper floor where the royal apartment was located. Inside the entrance was the central courtyard (Room 4), which in the northeast corner had a door to Room 10. Here 26 clay tablets and fragments were unearthed. It is not clear whether the archive (**Alalakh 2**) was placed in this room or in a room on the upper floor. Among the 15 identified tablets are 11 administrative lists or notes. In addition, there are two letters, one of them to Niqmepa, a surety before Niqmepa, and even a purchase of a slave by Idrimi.

East of the entrance room it was possible to pass through a room into an expansion unit of the palace with an inner courtyard (Room 22). In the southern part of this section of the palace, inside Room 32, where a number of jar stoppers with seal impressions were found, was the archive (**Alalakh 3**) in Room 33. Around the walls were mudbrick benches, possibly for placement of the 44 clay tablets and fragments found there. Most of the 28 identified tablets are administrative lists, sometimes administrative notes dealing with persons, foodstuffs, animals, textiles, and weapons. There is also a letter, a legal statement concerning Niqmepa, and a purchase document. In the already mentioned Courtyard 22, the remains of a small archive (**Alalakh 4**) with at least nine clay tablets were found. They were legal documents, often issued before Niqmepa, Ilim-ilimma, or the Mitanni king and they concerned members of the royal family or related persons. Among the texts are loan and purchase documents, marriage documents, and a legal settlement. A few clay tablets was also excavated in some of the other rooms of the palace; at least some of them may have belonged to archives mentioned here.

In the courtyard south of the main entrance to the palace, fragments of seven large clay tablets were unearthed. The excavators considered the tablets to be the contents of a basket that someone had tried to save at the time of the fire. The tablets seem to be the few remains of a library (**Alalakh 5**), and consist of incantations, omens, and Sumerian-Akkadian hymns.[21]

2.1.6 Ta'nak (Ta'annach)

Ta'nak (or Ta'annach, modern Tell Ti'innik) is situated on the southwest side of the Plain of Jezreel, some eight kilometers southeast of Megiddo. The site measures ca. 320 × 150 meters. E. Sellin directed Austrian excavations on the site between 1902 and 1904; P. Lapp directed an American expedition 1963–1968; and A. E. Glock worked there from 1985 to 1987. The best-known periods are Middle Bronze Age III to Late Bronze Age IIA, ca. 1700–1350 B.C., but the excavations have revealed occupation during the Early Bronze Age, ca. 2700–2300 B.C., and from the Iron Age through the Persian Period, ca. 1200–400 B.C., as well as from the Roman and Byzantine periods.[22]

2.1.6.1 Remains of an Administrative Archive

The early excavations unearthed an archive consisting of 12 clay tablets in or near a clay chest in a room east of a subterranean chamber in the center of the northern half

21. The texts have been published in D. J. Wiseman, *The Alalakh Tablets* (1953); supplemented by D. J. Wiseman, "Supplementary Copies of the Alalakh Tablets," *JCS* 8 (1954), 1–30; several of the texts have received new treatments, e.g., by M. Dietrich and O. Loretz in *UF* 1 (1969), 37–64; *WO* 5 (1969–1970), 57–93; and *ZA* 60 (1970), 88–123. The seal impressions have been published by D. Collon, *The Seal Impressions from Tell Atchana/Alalakh*, AOAT 27 (1975).

22. For short surveys of the site, cf. A. E. Glock, "Taanach," *The Anchor Bible Dictionary* VI (1992), 287–290; A. E. Glock, "Taanach," *OEANE* 5 (1997), 149; and A. E. Glock, "Taanach," *NEAEHL* 4 (1993), 1428–1433, all with further bibliographies. The first expedition has been published in E. Sellin, *Tell Ta'annek*, Denkschriften der Kaiserlichen Akademie der Wissenschaften in Wien, Philosophisch-historische Klasse 50, 4 (1904); and E. Sellin, *Eine Nachlese auf dem Tell Ta'annek in Palästina*, Denkschriften der Kaiserlichen Akademie der Wissenschaften in Wien, Philosophisch-historische Klasse 52, 3 (1905).

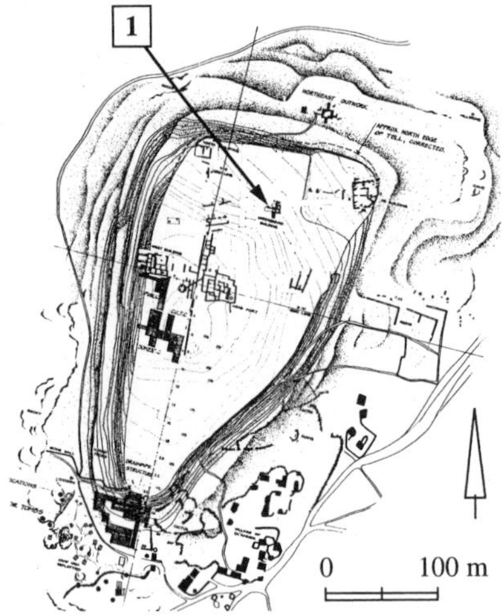

Plan 15. Ta'nak.
General plan with archive **Ta'nak 1**.
From P. Lapp, *BASOR* 195 (1969), 3 fig. 1.

of the tell. The tablets, dating to the middle of the fifteenth century B.C., after the Egyptian victory at Megiddo during the reign of Thutmose III, are the remains of an archive (**Ta'nak 1**) of Talwašur (the name has sometimes been read Rewašur), who was the local ruler. They consist of seven letters and five lists of individuals. Talwašur is the addressee in all the letters in which the addressee's name is preserved. The language used is Babylonian with a West Semitic influence. In a twelfth-century context in another part of the site, the archaeologists unearthed a clay tablet written in alphabetic cuneiform (cf. 2.2).[23]

2.1.7 Akhetaten (el-'Amarna)

Akhetaten (modern el-'Amarna) is situated approximately 300 kilometers south of Cairo, on the east bank of the Nile. The city was founded by Amenophis IV, also known as Akhenaten, and served as the capital of Egypt in the middle of the fourteenth century B.C. In 1887 a number of clay tablets were discovered by peasants; this led to the English excavations of 1891–1892 directed by F. Petrie. Then followed the German excavations of 1911–1914 led by L. Borchardt and the English and American excavations of 1921–1924 and 1926–1937 by E. Peet, L. Woolley, H. Frankfort, and J. D. S. Pendlebury. Beginning in 1977 the last-mentioned excavations resumed under the direction of B. J. Kemp. The city is one of the few relatively well-preserved cities of

23. F. Hrozny, "Keilschrifttexte aus Ta'annek," in E. Sellin, *Tell Ta'annek* (1904), 113–122, pls. X–XI; F. Hrozny, "Die neugefundenen Keilschrifttexte von Ta'annek," in E. Sellin, *Eine Nachlese auf dem Tell Ta'annek in Palästina* (1905), 36–41, pls. I–III; and A. E. Glock, "Texts and Archaeology at Tell Ta'annek," *Berytus* 31 (1983), 57–66.

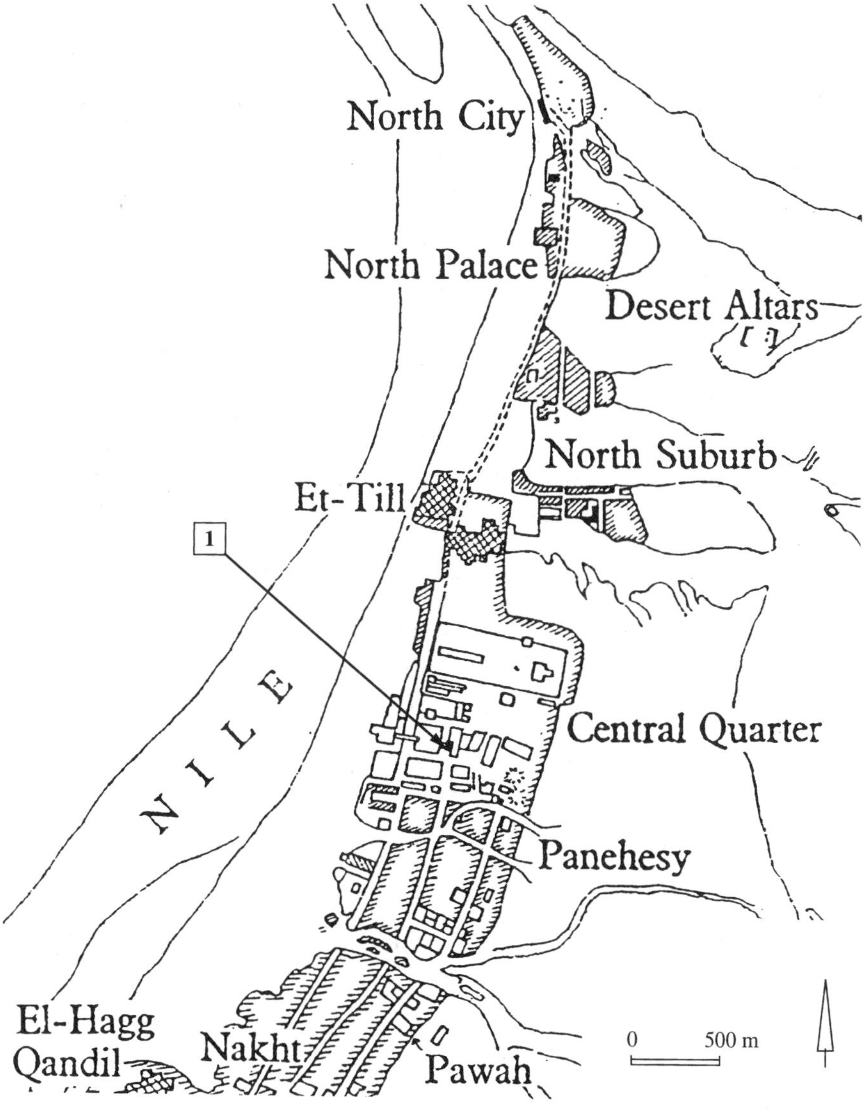

Plan 16. Akhetaten.
General plan with archive **Akhetaten 1**.
From W. Stevenson Smith, *The Art and Architecture of Ancient Egypt* (1958), fig. 63.

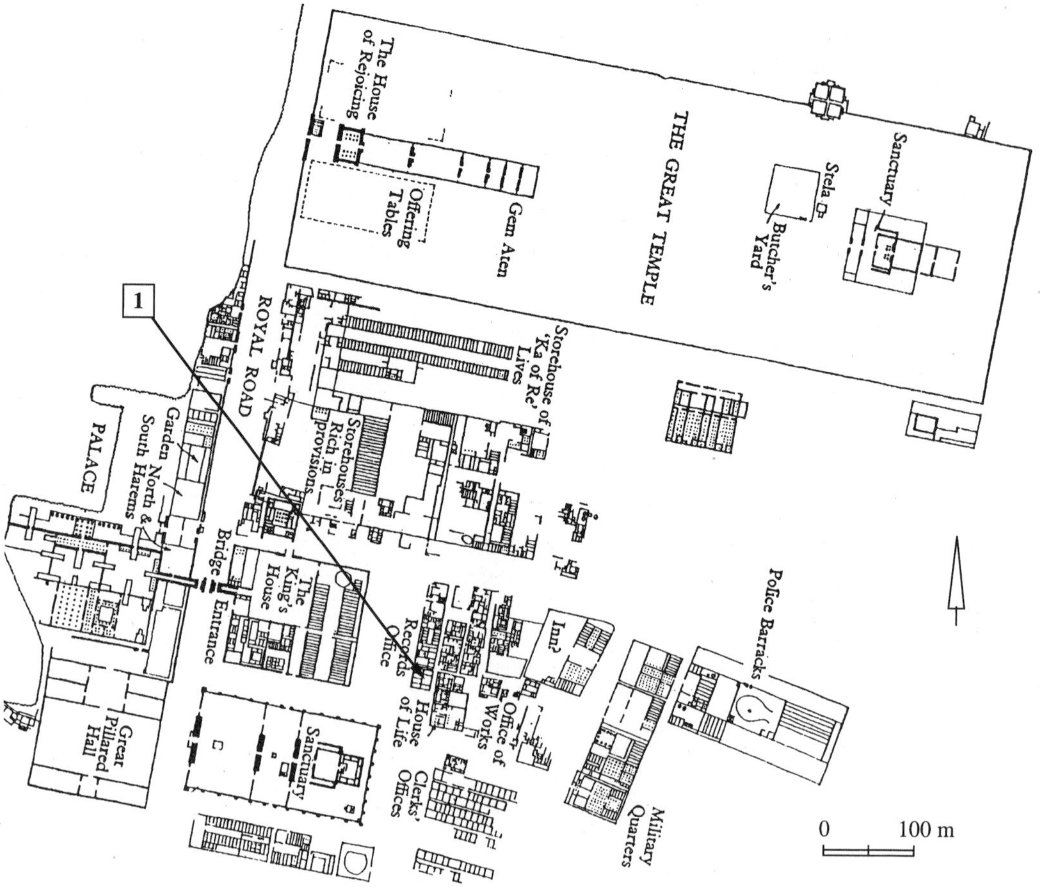

Plan 17. Akhetaten.
General plan of center with archive **Akhetaten 1**.
From W. Stevenson Smith, *The Art and Architecture of Ancient Egypt* (1958), fig. 65.

ancient Egypt. Palaces, temples, and areas with private houses have been excavated. The administrative center was in the Central Quarter, south of the Great Temple of Aton and east of the Palace. The Records Office (House Q 42 21, previously House 19), with the remains of an archive of clay tablets in cuneiform script, was situated in this quarter beside similar administrative buildings just east of the King's House and northeast of the Smaller Temple.[24]

24. As short introductions to the site, cf. B. J. Kemp, "Tell el-Amarna," *Lexikon der Ägyptologie* VI (1986), 309–319; B. M. Bryan, "Amarna, Tell el-," *OEANE* 1 (1997), 81–86; and S. Izre'el, "Amarna Tablets," *OEANE* 1 (1997), 86–87, all with further bibliographies. Main archaeological publications are F.

2.1.7.1 Administrative Archive with Small Library in the Palace Area

The Records Office was a house measuring 19 × 22 meters. It seems to have had a staircase leading to an upper floor. Inscriptions on bricks from this house describe it as "the place of Pharaoh's letters." Among the 376 preserved clay tablets from the city, all except four probably come from this house—one tablet was found in a house east of the Records Office, another one in the Clerks' House No. 43 (Q 43), and two in houses more than a kilometer to the south. Many more, perhaps 150 to 200 tablets, were found together with the preserved tablets, but were destroyed due to careless treatment after the excavation. Most of the tablets seem to have been preserved in the southwest room of this house. It has been claimed that at least some of them were found in a broken clay pot. A few tablets were discovered in other rooms of this house, including two pits under the floor. Far more numerous hieratic letters of the king must have existed. They may also have been placed in the same house, or, as has often been assumed, in the building immediately north of it.[25]

The tablets are the remains of an administrative archive combined with a library division (**Akhetaten 1**), and date to a period of, at most, thirty years, perhaps only some fifteen years during the reigns of Amenophis III and Amenophis IV in the middle of the fourteenth century B.C. The archive division consists of 349 cuneiform texts: 344 are letters and five are inventories attached to letters. On 19 of the letters there are traces of ink notes in hieratic script made by the archivist when the letters were received.

Petrie, *Tell el Amarna* (1894); L. Borchardt and H. Ricke, *Die Wohnhäuser in Tell el-Amarna*, WVDOG 91 (1980); T. E. Peet and C. L. Woolley, *The City of Akhenaten* I, Memoir of the Egypt Exploration Society 38 (1923); H. Frankfort and J. D. S. Pendlebury, *The City of Akhenaten* II, Memoir of the Egypt Exploration Society 40 (1933, 1972); J. D. S. Pendlebury, *The City of Akhenaten* III, Vols. 1–2, Memoir of the Egypt Exploration Society 44 (1951); and B. J. Kemp, *Amarna Reports* 1–6 (1984–1995).

25. F. Petrie, *Tell el Amarna* (1894), 23–24, 34–37, pl. XLII; and J. D. S. Pendlebury, *The City of Akhenaten* III, Vols. 1–2, Memoir of the Egypt Exploration Society 44 (1951), 120, 130, pls. XIX, XX.

For the number of tablets given here, the following has been taken into account. Today 382 El-Amarna tablets (EA) have been counted. One of the tablets (EA 333) in J. A. Knudtzon, *Die El-Amarna-Tafeln*, VAB 2 (1915), was not from Amarna but from Tell el-Ḥasî in southwestern Palestine. Several of the lexical fragments in the library division may join according to P. Artzi, "Observations on the 'Library' of the Amarna Archives," *Cuneiform Archives and Libraries*, CRRAI 30 (1986), 210–212, thereby reducing the number of tablets.

The groundplan of the house is ca. 400 sq m, not just 40 sq m as claimed in C. Kühne, *Die Chronologie der internationalen Korrespondenz von El-Amarna*, AOAT 17 (1973), 2 n. 12; therefore some of the reasons given there against the placement of at least some hieratic letters in the same building are not valid.

The international correspondence consists of 44 tablets: 40 are international letters from, or sometimes to, major kings in Babylonia, Mitanni, Alašia, Hatti, Arzawa, and Assyria; four tablets are inventories sent along with letters. Most of the texts are written in the Middle Babylonian dialect of Akkadian, two in Hittite, one in Hurrian, and one in Middle Assyrian.

The correspondence with rulers, who were often vassals, in Syro-Palestine consists of 305 tablets; all except one are letters, the only exception being an inventory attached to a letter. The letters are written in Middle Babylonian, sometimes heavily influenced by the local Semitic languages of the area.

The library division consists of 27 texts, which are not of the archival types just described. Among the texts, which have to date been identified, are six myths and epics, four syllabaries and lexical texts, as well as one god-list belonging to the Mesopotamian tradition. One text is an Akkadian version of the Hittite-Hurrian Kešši story. A unique text lists Egyptian words written in syllabic cuneiform with Babylonian translations.[26]

2.2 Hittite Area

The archives and libraries with cuneiform texts from the area of Hittite rule date, in most cases, ca. 1350–1180 B.C. This is the best-attested period of the Hittite empire, from the expansionist period during the reign of Suppiluliuma until the final days of the empire.

Large excavations have been conducted in the capital Ḫattuša (2.2.1), which has produced several large archives and libraries. Among the cities in the Hittite homeland, Tapigga (2.2.3) has an archive, and in Šapinuwa (2.2.2) and Šarišša (2.2.4) libraries and archives have been found. In Hittite-dominated Syria, the excavators have unearthed a library and several archives in Emar (2.2.5), and several archives and libraries in Ugarit (2.2.6). There must have existed important archives and libraries in other, not yet excavated cities, particularly the residence city of the Hittite viceroy,

26. The standard edition of the texts is still J. A. Knudtzon, *Die El-Amarna-Tafeln*, VAB 2 (1915, later reprints), with some more texts in A. F. Rainey, *El Amarna Tablets* 359–379, Supplement to J. A. Knudtzon, *Die El-Amarna-Tafeln*, AOAT 8, 2nd rev. ed. (1978). The latest translation with commentary on the letters, but unfortunately without transliteration, is W. L. Moran, *The Amarna Letters* (1992), and the latest edition of the literary texts is S. Izre'el, *The Amarna Scholarly Tablets*, Cuneiform Monographs 9 (1997). For a bibliography, see J.-G. Heintz, et al., *Index documentaire d'El-Amarna, I.D.E.A.* 1: Liste/Codage des textes, Index des ouvrages de référence (1982). The library part is discussed in P. Artzi, "Observations on the 'Library' of the Amarna Archives," *Cuneiform Archives and Libraries*, CRRAI 30 (1986), 210–212. Cf. also C. Kühne, *Die Chronologie der internationalen Korrespondenz von El-Amarna*, AOAT 17 (1973).

Karkemish, where levels from this period have not been extensively examined. Only one Hittite archive (2.2.3) from the period before 1350 B.C. has so far been discovered, possibly due to a lack of excavation at deeper levels. However, texts from older periods have often been found in later archives or libraries.

Cuneiform script on clay tablets was used for most preserved texts. In addition, wooden writing boards seem to have been used, for example, in Ḫattuša, even though no writing boards have been preserved in this area. The Middle Babylonian dialect of Akkadian language was used throughout the entire area dominated by the Hittites. Use of the Indo-European Hittite language was limited essentially to the Hittite homeland. Hurrian was used throughout the entire region, but limited mainly to religious texts. Together with the adoption of the cuneiform script, came a knowledge of Sumerian; but generally its use was restricted to scholarly matters. In Ugarit the use of the local alphabetic cuneiform, the so-called "Ugaritic script," on clay tablets is well attested for both the Ugaritic and Hurrian languages. For monumental inscriptions and seals, hieroglyphic Luwian is attested, especially in the main Hittite area.

In contrast to Assyria and Babylonia, where dating practices were well established, the texts from the Hittite-dominated areas do not have any standardized method of dating. This fact, and the general unsecured absolute datings of this area and period, have resulted in several problems in dating the archives and libraries. Dates are, therefore, normally not expressed in exact absolute years, but in approximate years, often related to the reigns of named kings.

In addition to the archives and libraries discussed below, individual clay tablets or small remains of archives have been found at a number of other sites in the same area.[27]

27. For Ras Ibn Hani, cf. A. Bounni and J. Lagarce, "Ras Ibn Hani," *OEANE* 4 (1997), 411–413, with further bibliography; and W. H. van Soldt, *SAU*, 225; for Qadeš (modern Tell Nebi Mendo), cf. P. J. Parr, "Nebi Mend, Tell," *OEANE* 4 (1997), 114–115, with further bibliography; for Kumidi (modern Kamid el-Loz), cf. L. Badre, "Kamid el-Loz," *OEANE* 3 (1997), 265–266, with further bibliography; for Ta'nak (Ta'anach), cf. 2.1.6; and for Tarsus, cf. H. Goldman, ed., *Excavations at Gözlü Kule, Tarsus* 1–3 (1950–1963); and A. Goetze, "Cuneiform Inscriptions from Tarsus," *JAOS* 59 (1939), 1–16, no. 1.

2.2.1 *Ḫattuša (Boğazköy)*

Ḫattuša (modern Boğazköy) is situated about 150 kilometers east of Ankara. For a long period the city served as the capital of the Hittites. After a few older test diggings, German scholars have been conducting long-time, large-scale excavations. H. Winckler and T. Makridi excavated during 1906–1907 and 1911–1912; from 1907 together with O. Puchstein. K. Bittel directed excavations from 1931 to World War II, beginning again in 1952. The excavations continued under the leadership of P. Neve from 1978, and under J. Seeher since 1994.

The oldest habitation at the end of the third millennium B.C. was concentrated at Büyükkale, the later citadel, and the area immediately to the northwest. During the nineteenth and eighteenth centuries B.C., the city expanded further to the northwest. This pre-Hittite city with its Assyrian *kārum* was destroyed by fire ca. 1700 B.C., perhaps by the Hittite Anitta from Kuššara. Around 1600 B.C., Ḫattuša became the capital of the Hittite state. The city reached its largest extent during the final decades before the destruction ca. 1200 B.C. In the middle of the eighth century B.C., there was a Phrygian city there, during the Hellenistic and Roman times, a town; some Byzantine houses have also been unearthed. The excavations have been concentrated on the late Hittite capital, when the city had its largest extent, ca. 2200 × 1200 meters. The citadel Büyükkale was the main palace area, whereas the main temple was situated in the lower city, in the northwest. An administrative center has also been found in Nişantepe southwest of Büyükkale, and a number of temples have been unearthed in the southern, higher part of the city.[28]

28. General introductions to the excavations are K. Bittel, *Hattuscha: Hauptstadt der Hethiter*, 2nd ed. (1983); and for the latest excavations: P. Neve, *Ḫattuša – Stadt der Götter und Tempel*, Zaberns Bildbände zur Archäologie 8 (1993), both with basic bibliographies; cf. also H. G. Güterbock, "Boğazköy," *OEANE* 1 (1997), 333–335, with short bibliography. The main archaeological publications are O. Puchstein, *Boghasköi: Die Bauwerke*, WVDOG 19 (1912); K. Bittel, *Boğazköy: Die Kleinfunde der Grabungen 1906–1912 I: Funde hethitischer Zeit*, WVDOG 60 (1937); K. Bittel, et al., *Yazilikaya: Architektur, Felsbilder, Inschriften und Kleinfunde*, WVDOG 61 (1941); K. Bittel and R. Naumann, Boğazköy-Ḫattuša I, WVDOG 63 (1952); K. Bittel, et al., Boğazköy-Ḫattuša II, WVDOG 71 (1958); W. Orthmann, Boğazköy-Ḫattuša III, WVDOG 74 (1963); T. Beran, Boğazköy-Ḫattuša V, WVDOG 76 (1967); W. Schirmer, Boğazköy-Ḫattuša VI, WVDOG 81 (1969); R. M. Boehmer, Boğazköy-Ḫattuša VII, WVDOG 87 (1972); U. Seidl, Boğazköy-Ḫattuša VIII, WVDOG 88 (1972); R. M. Boehmer, Boğazköy-Ḫattuša X (1979); A. von den Driesch and J. Boessneck, Boğazköy-Ḫattuša XI (1981); P. Neve, Boğazköy-Ḫattuša XII (1982); R. M. Boehmer, Boğazköy-Ḫattuša XIII (1983); R. M. Boehmer and H. G. Güterbock, Boğazköy-Ḫattuša XIV (1987); H. Parzinger and R. Sanz, Boğazköy-Ḫattuša XV (1992); K. Bittel, *Boğazköy* [1], in APAW 1935, Phil.-hist. Klasse 1, K. Bittel and R. Naumann, *Boğazköy* II, APAW 1938, Phil.-hist. Klasse 1, K. Bittel, et al., *Boğazköy* III, ADOG 2 (1957); K. Bittel, et al., *Boğazköy* IV, ADOG 14 (1969); K. Bittel, et al., *Boğazköy* V, ADOG 18 (1975); and K. Bittel, et al., *Boğazköy* VI (1984). Preliminary reports can be found in *MDOG* and *Archäologischer Anzeiger* (=*AA*).

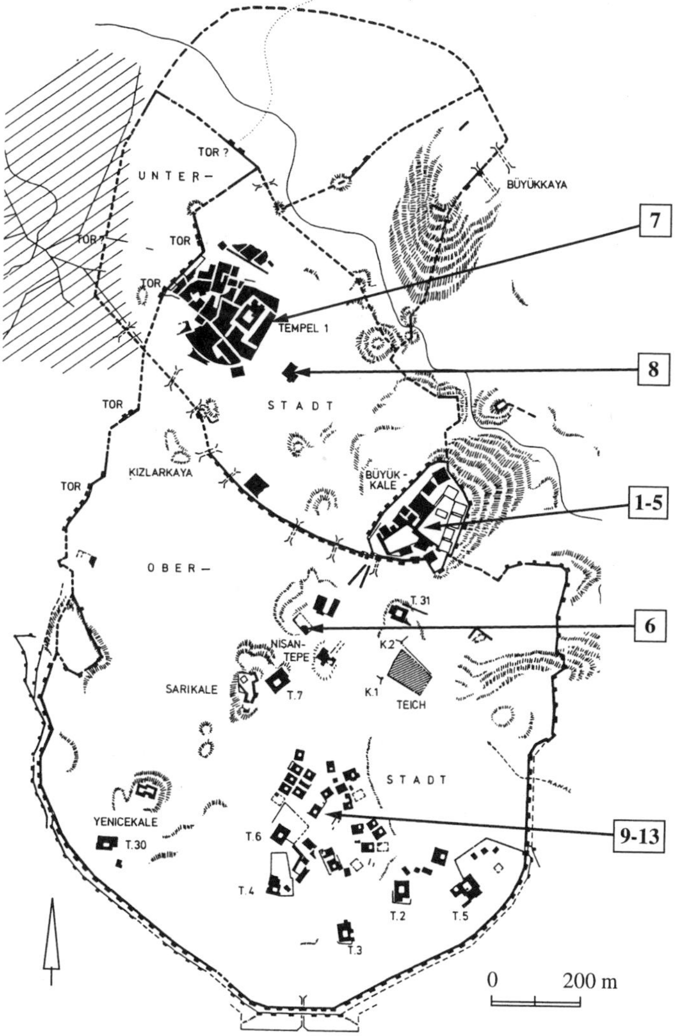

Plan 18. Ḫattuša.
General plan with archives and libraries **Ḫattuša 1-13**.
From P. Neve, *Ḫattuša – Stadt der Götter und Tempel* (1993), 16 fig. 27.

The following survey of archive and libraries is essentially based on the excavations from 1931 onwards. During the early excavations, 1906–1912, the recording procedures were unfortunately quite poor, and the provenances for the large number of clay tablets excavated during these years have been lost. For the ca. 10,000 clay tablets and fragments from the early excavations, it is, therefore, possible to reconstruct only three main areas with clay tablets, the Palace E with the nearby west slope of the citadel, the East Magazines of the main temple in the lower city, and the Building in the Slope, "Haus am Hang," in the slope between the other two areas. Later reexaminations of these areas have produced additional clay tablets and fragments, which sometimes can be combined with the earlier finds, thereby providing a limited means of reconstruction of these three findgroups; nonetheless, they remain quite uncertain. The total numbers of clay tablets in the different archives and libraries in Ḫattuša are more uncertain than for most of the other cities discussed. Future studies will probably lead to a refinement and to a substantial reduction in the number of tablets, due to joins between fragments. The excavators unearthed archives and libraries with a large number of clay tablets written in cuneiform script in Hittite, the Middle Babylonian dialect of Akkadian, Hurrian, Luwian, Palaic, and Hattic. Monumental inscriptions were sometimes written with a hieroglyphic script in Luwian. Only a limited number of private houses were excavated between the main temple and the northwestern town wall; no archives were found in the Hittite levels of these houses.[29]

2.2.1.1 Archives and Libraries in Palaces on the Citadel

Among the buildings on the citadel Büyükkale are Palaces E and D northwest of the Upper and Middle Courtyard, and Palace A southwest of the Middle Courtyard. Palace K is southeast of Palace A. Other buildings were situated northwest of and around the Lower Courtyard. The main entrance to the citadel was in the southwest.

2.2.1.1.1 Library and Archive in Palace A

Palace A is situated on the southwest side of the Middle Courtyard. An upper floor was on the level of the courtyard; a lower floor, attested in Rooms 1–6 in the south part of the building, existed because of the sloping terrain on the level of the

29. Most cuneiform texts are published in one of the series *Keilschrifttexte aus Boğazköy* (1916–) (=*KBo*) and *Keilschrifturkunden aus Boğazköi* (1921–) (=*KUB*). Editions of the texts may be found in, e.g., the series Boghazköi-Studien (=BoSt), Studien zu den Boğazköy-Texten (=StBoT), and Texte der Hethiter (=THeth). E. Laroche, *Catalogue des textes hittites* (1971) (=*CTH*) classified and listed all texts published at that time.

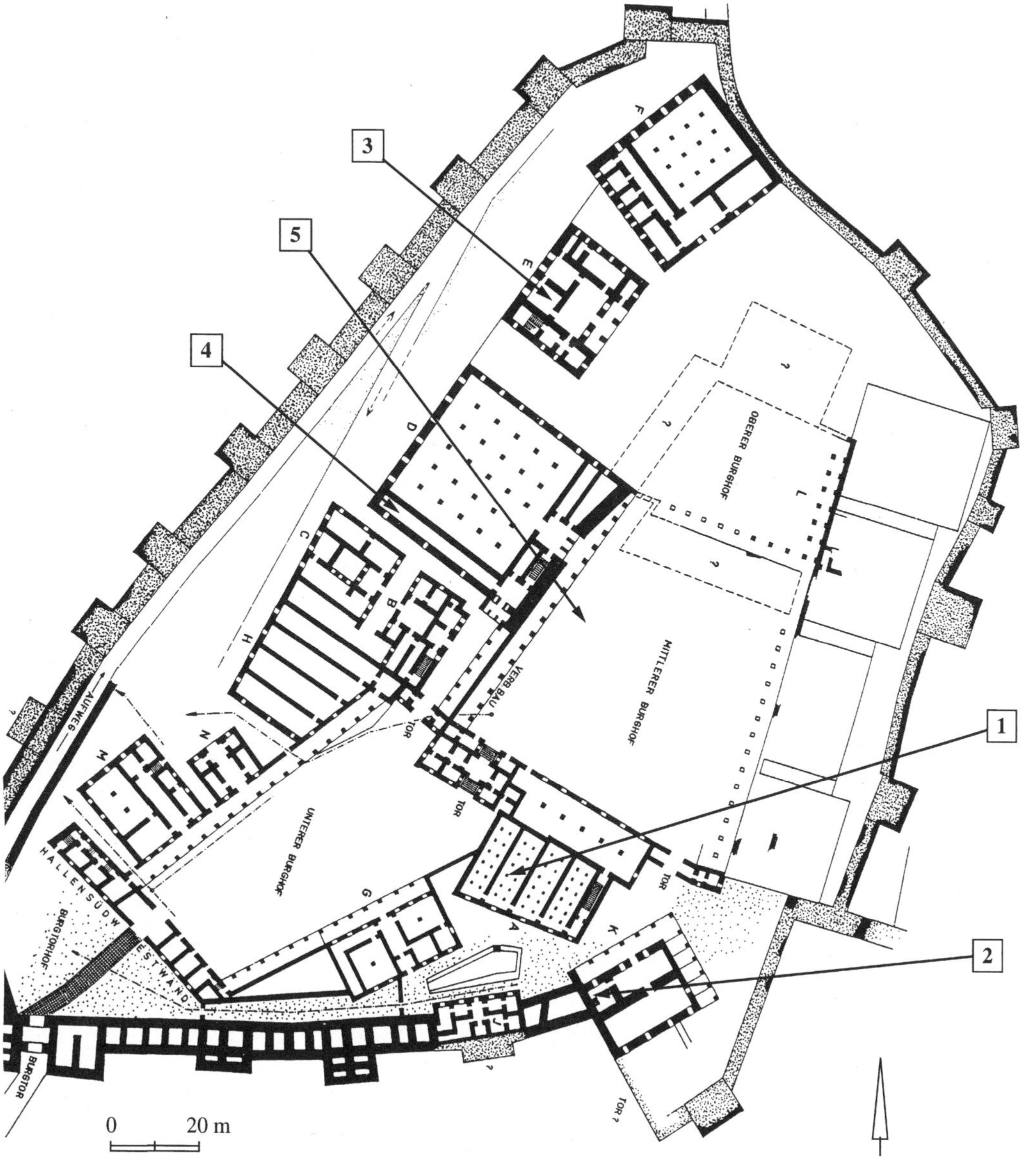

Plan 19. Ḫattuša.
Plan of the citadel Büyükkale with archives and libraries **Ḫattuša 1-5**.
From P. Neve, *Büyükkale: Die Bauwerke,* Boğazköy-Ḫattuša XII (1982), folding 45.

Lower Courtyard. These rooms may have served as magazines. About 4000 clay tablet fragments (joins will reduce the number of original clay tablets considerably, perhaps to ca. 2000 or less) were excavated in Rooms 1–6, most and best preserved in Room 5. A large number of additional fragments from this collection were found in secondary positions in and around Palace A, even at rather large distances from it within other buildings on the citadel. The tablets are the remains of a library with archive (**Ḫattuša 1**) that may have resided either on the upper or the lower floor of the palace. Most of the texts, ca. two-thirds of the total number of tablets in the library, are rituals or descriptions of religious festivals. There are also a number of incantations, omens, oracles, and other religious texts, including myths, hymns, and prayers. Also a selection of medical texts, annals and other historical texts, treaties, laws, horse texts, and a few lexical lists are attested. To keep order in the library, a number of tablets were catalogues of important titles. The archival part of the tablet collection was smaller, with some international letters and legal judgments. Most of the texts were written in Hittite, but a considerable number of tablets, especially concerning rituals or festivals, were composed in Hurrian or Luwian—some even in Hattic or Palaic. On the other hand, texts such as international letters, treaties, omens, and lexical lists were often composed in Akkadian or Akkadian-Sumerian. Together with the Hittite texts from the late empire, there are several that date to the Old or Middle Hittite period.[30]

2.2.1.1.2 Small Library in Palace K

Palace K in the southeast slope of the citadel is part of the late Hittite Level BK IIIa, built on the remains of a similar building from the previous Level BK IIIb/2. The Palace has been reconstructed with an entrance to the upper level, porticoes on the northwest and possibly also northeast sides, and three rooms, among them a large hall in the southeast part. Below was another floor with three similar rooms. In Room 3 of this lower floor, according to the excavators, 225 clay tablets or fragments were unearthed. This number will assuredly be reduced by joins between fragments. This is the remains of a small library (**Ḫattuša 2**) with a selection of literary texts often

30. For a preliminary survey, see S. Košak, "The Palace Library 'Building A' on Büyükkale," *FS Houwink ten Cate* (1995), 173–179. Texts have been published in *KBo* 8, 10, 14–21, 23–25, 27–30, 33, 34, 36, and *KUB* 29–35. Cf. K. Bittel and R. Naumann, Boğazköy-Ḫattuša I, WVDOG 63 (1952), 48–57; P. Neve, *Büyükkale: Die Bauwerke: Grabungen 1954–1966*, Boğazköy-Ḫattuša XII (1982), 104–107; K. Bittel, "B. Die Bauwerke," *MDOG* 72 (1933), (4–)12–17; H. G. Güterbock, "D. Die Texte," *MDOG* 72 (1933), 37–53; and H. G. Güterbock, "Bemerkungen über die im Gebäude A auf Büyükkale gefundenen Tontafeln," *AfO* 38–39 (1991–1992), 132–137.

attested in one or several copies also in the larger libraries. More than half of the texts are rituals and other texts concerning festivals. There are also a number of incantations and incantation rituals. In addition, there are individual texts of the following types: oracle, prayer, omens, first tablet of the Gilgamesh epic, royal annals, treaty, acts, instructions, a list of women, and a library catalogue. Almost all texts are written in Hittite, but two are in Akkadian (duplicates to a Hittite text in the library) and a few in Hurrian.[31]

2.2.1.1.3 Library and Archive in Palace E

Palace E is situated northwest of the Upper Courtyard in the northwest slope of the citadel. The building has been reconstructed with an entrance to an upper level on the southeast side. Below the excavators unearthed another floor with rooms in its northwestern part in the slope. During Winckler's excavations, a large number of clay tablets (2500 tablets and fragments during the first year of excavation) were found in Room 4 and some in Room 5; subsequently, a few tablets were found in other rooms of the building. The original place for the tablets may have been on the lower floor in Room 4, or in a room above. The poor handling of the tablets after the excavation makes it impossible to identify most of the tablets found there. However, almost 200 published tablets or fragments, mostly from later excavations but partly also from the earlier ones, can be shown to have been unearthed in the building or in the area sloping down in a northwestern direction. On the assumption that this is a representative selection of the complete collection, we may call it a library with archive (**Ḫattuša 3**), comprised of both literary texts and state documents. Letters, documents, and religious texts are attested, all dating to the late empire.[32]

2.2.1.1.4 Remains of an Archive with Bullae in Palace D

Palace D, west of the Middle Courtyard, is the largest building on the citadel. It is located on the northwest slope and has been reconstructed with an upper floor possibly consisting of a large columned hall with entrance from the courtyard, and a lower

31. For texts, see *KBo* 10, 11, 14:21-40, and 39. Cf. P. Neve, *Büyükkale: Die Bauwerke: Grabungen 1954–1966*, Boğazköy-Ḫattuša XII (1982), 107–111; K. Bittel, "Untersuchungen auf Büyükkale, a. Das Archiv im Gebäude K," *MDOG* 91 (1958), 57–61; H. Otten, "Keilschrifttexte," *MDOG* 91 (1958), 73–83.

32. For a survey, see S. Alaura, forthcoming. O. Puchstein, *Boghasköi: Die Bauwerke*, WVDOG 19 (1912), 25–32; P. Neve, *Büyükkale: Die Bauwerke: Grabungen 1954–1966*, Boğazköy-Ḫattuša XII (1982), 92–95; and H. Winckler, *MDOG* 35 (1907), 12–59; cf. also K. Bittel and R. Naumann, Boğazköy-Ḫattuša I, WVDOG 63 (1952), 55.

floor with magazines. The remains of an archive (**Ḫattuša 4**) consisting of 280 sealed clay bullae have been unearthed in Room 1 of the lower floor and in the slope outside it. The bullae may originally have been placed on the upper floor in the room beside the large hall. Most of them may have been fastened by string to wooden writing boards, a medium of writing often mentioned in clay tablets from the site, but not found there due to their perishable material. The larger finding of similar clay bullae at Nişantepe, discussed below, has led to the assumption that royal grants of lands were written on these writing boards.[33]

2.2.1.1.5 Remains of an Administrative Archive in the Middle Courtyard of the Palace Area

In secondary positions in area p-q/10–11 in the Middle Courtyard, just outside the main entrance to Palace D, the excavators unearthed 100 clay tablets, often fragmentary. Eighty-six of these texts are Hittite letters, but there are also Hittite oracle reports, inventories, and other types of texts. The letters, concerning administrative and military matters, are often addressed to the king, another member of the royal family, or a high official. The tablets seem to be the remains of an administrative archive (**Ḫattuša 5**) originally preserved in one of the buildings around the courtyard, but as a group removed and, perhaps, discarded. It is possible, but far from certain, that they had been previously stored as part of the archive in Palace A.[34]

2.2.1.2 Archive in the West Building of Nişantepe

Nişantepe is situated in the center of Ḫattuša, southwest of the citadel Büyükkale. A viaduct facilitated the communication between the two mounds. The excavators found an archive (**Ḫattuša 6**) with 3,268 sealed clay bullae in Rooms 1, 2, and 3 of the West Building of Nişantepe, as well as in the destruction fill in a ravine below these rooms. In addition, they unearthed 28 sealed clay tablets in Room 3 and in the destruction fill below. Both the bullae and the clay tablets found together with them were sealed and had a hole in the clay for a string. It has been suggested that the

33. P. Neve, *Büyükkale: Die Bauwerke: Grabungen 1954–1966*, Boğazköy-Ḫattuša XII (1982), 97–102; K. Bittel and R. Naumann, Boğazköy-Ḫattuša I, WVDOG 63 (1952), 61–63; K. Bittel, "C. Das Magazin in l–q/12–16 und der große Siegelfund," *MDOG* 75 (1937), 27–31; H. G. Güterbock, "3. Schrifturkunden, A. Die Siegel," *MDOG* 75 (1937), 52–60; H. G. Güterbock, *Siegel aus Boğazköy* I, AfO Beih. 5 (1940); H. G. Güterbock, *Siegel aus Boğazköy* II, AfO Beih. 7 (1942); and K. Bittel, "Bullen zum Teil Anhängsel an Holztafeln?" *JKlF* 1 (1950), 164ff.; cf. also the references below to the similar finding at Nişantepe.

34. For the texts, see *KBo* 18 and 25.

strings were fastened to wooden writing boards, a medium of writing often mentioned in clay tablets from the site, but not excavated there due to their perishable material. The clay tablets were royal grants of lands bearing the king's seal, and date from Ḫantili II to Muwatalli I, ca. 1500–1400 B.C. The bullae bear the seal of the king, sometimes the queen or an official, and date from Suppiluliuma I to Suppiluliuma II, ca. 1345–1200 B.C., with a strong concentration in the reigns of Mursili III, Ḫattusili III, and Tutḫaliya IV. The text on the assumed writing boards attached to the clay tablets probably was royal grants, continuing the documentation on the clay tablets. The majority of writing boards that were attached to the bullae were probably also royal grants, but of a later date. It cannot be excluded that some of the writing boards did not contain royal grants, but rather other documents of the king or officials.[35]

2.2.1.3 Archives and Libraries in Temples and Related Buildings

Temple 1, the main temple, was situated in the lower city, northwest of the citadel. Approximately thirty buildings, unearthed in the upper city in the south, have been identified by the excavators as temples.

2.2.1.3.1 Administrative Archive and Library in Temple 1 in the Lower City

Temple 1 in area K19 had two cellas northeast of an inner courtyard. The temple stood in a narrow courtyard or surrounded by streets, on all sides opposite buildings identified as magazines. In Rooms 10, 11, and 12 of the east magazine in area K19, an archive (**Ḫattuša 7**) with a large number of clay tablets was unearthed during the early, poorly recorded excavations. Possibly the archive was stored on an upper floor in a room above Room 11, but the information from the excavation is contradictory. During the later excavations some additional tablets were found in these rooms; around the temple area; in the dump from the early excavations; and in other rooms of the magazines. These may either be stray finds from the same main tablet collection or, in some cases, perhaps remains of small separate archives. On the assumption that they originally belonged to the main collection and are representative of the texts in that collection, we can form a preliminary reconstruction of the large library and state archive in the temple by examining the ca. 780 published clay tablets or fragments that were unearthed during the later excavations. The library section among

35. P. Neve, "Die Ausgrabungen in Boğazköy-Ḫattuša 1990," *AA* 1991, 299–348, especially the section 'Zu dem Tonbullenfund (von I. Bayburtluoğlu & P. Neve),' 325–335; and P. Neve, "Die Ausgrabungen in Boğazköy-Ḫattuša 1991," *AA* 1992, 307–338, especially 307–316. Cf. also P. Neve, "Šuppiluliuma I. oder II.," *FS Alp* (1992), 401–408.

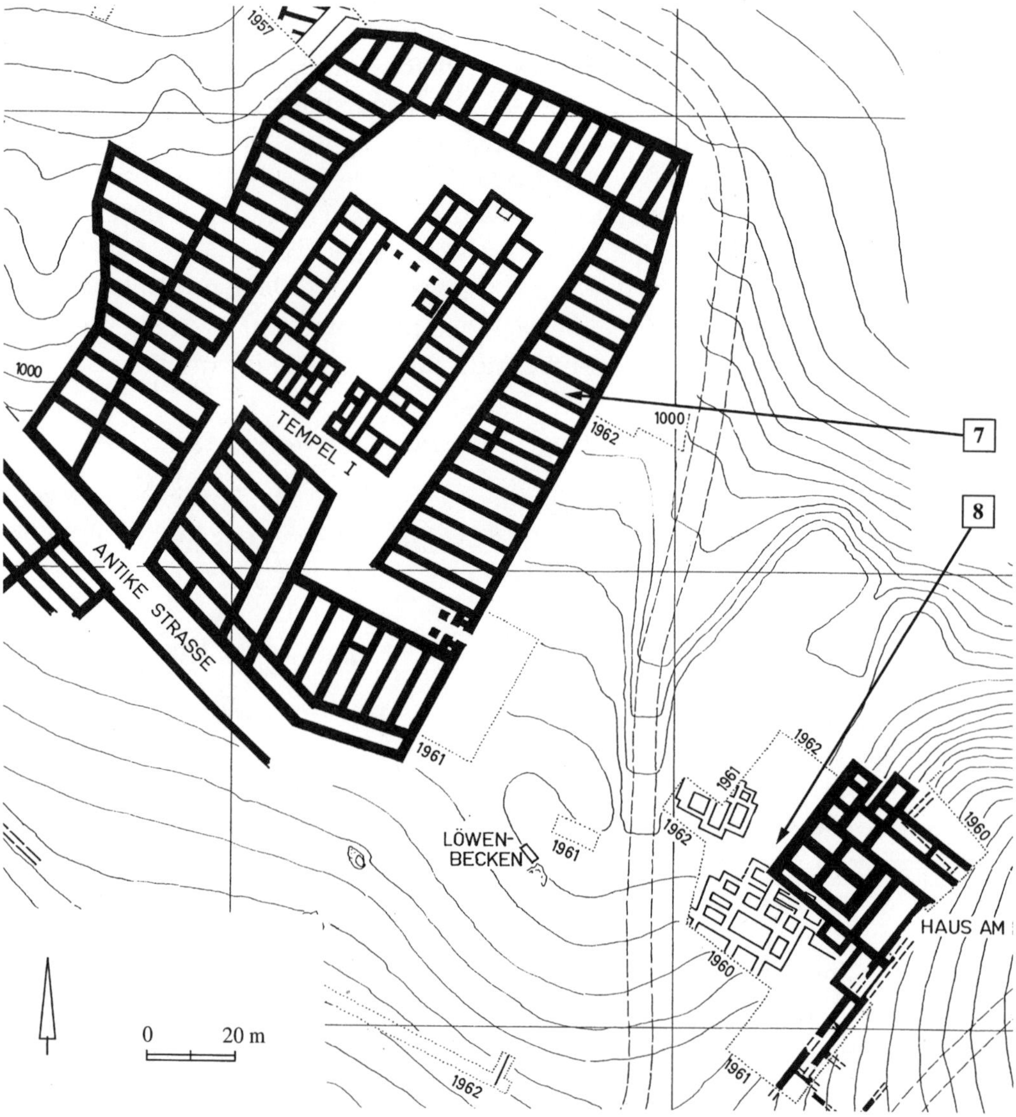

Plan 20. Ḫattuša.
Plan of the area with Temple 1 with archives and libraries **Ḫattuša 7-8**.
From W. Schirmer, *Die Bebauung am unteren Büyükkale-Nordwesthang in Boğazköy*, Boğazköy-Ḫattuša VI (1969), folding 2.

the later texts includes 160 rituals, descriptions of festivals, and cultic inventories; 147 epics, myths, and prayers; 59 incantations; five oracles; and two liver models. There are also 70 treaties and other historical documents; 11 laws; and 54 lexical lists. The archive section consists of 34 letters, often international; 18 lists of fields; and 13 inventories. Most texts were written in the Hittite language, but several, especially the international letters and treaties, were in Akkadian. Among the literary texts several were composed in Hurrian, Luwian, Palaic, and Hattic. It is probable that the texts unearthed from the main rooms of the archive and library during the early excavations were, to a large extent, of the same general types. Some joins with fragments from the early excavations have been reported, but a detailed reconstruction of this main library and archive will never be possible.[36]

2.2.1.3.2 Large Library in the House on the Slope

The building called House on the Slope ("Haus am Hang") by the excavators was situated in area L18, approximately 85 meters southeast of the east magazines of Temple 1. The function of the building has not been clearly demonstrated, but a connection with Temple 1 cannot be excluded. A library (**Ḫattuša 8**), the last of the three major collections of clay tablets from the early excavations, was unearthed in this building. Unfortunately, there is no record identifying the tablets belonging to this early excavated group. But during the better-recorded later excavations more than 500 now published clay tablets or fragments were unearthed, some in this building but mostly in the area immediately northwest of it; some of the later fragments even join fragments from the early excavation. The following description of the later findings may therefore give some idea of the tablet collection stored here. The largest groups consisted of more than 150 incantations or incantation rituals, and approximately 50 omens or oracles. Several other tablets contained rituals or other descriptions of festivals, myths, and epics. More than 50 tablets were historical texts, for example, annals and treaties from various periods of Hittite history. There were a limited number of lexical lists, laws, as well as a catalogue. Most of the texts are in the Hittite language, but some of the texts are in Akkadian, Hurrian, Luwian, or Palaic. The originally much larger number of tablets from the library probably consisted of these and possibly also of some other types.[37]

36. Cf. O. Puchstein, *Boghasköi: Die Bauwerke*, WVDOG 19 (1912), 93–135, esp. 123–126; *MDOG* 86 (1953), 56–57; and K. Bittel, et al., *Boğazköy IV: Funde aus den Grabungen 1967 und 1968*, ADOG 14 (1969), 12–13. The texts from the later excavations are in *KBo* 7, 17–22, 24–30, 33, 34, 36, and a few in *KUB* 29, 37, and 39.

37. W. Schirmer, *Die Bebauung am unteren Büyükkale-Nordwesthang in Boğazköy*, Boğazköy-Ḫattuša VI,

2.2.1.3.3 Archives or Libraries in Temples 8, 12, 15, 16, and Possibly 26

In several of the approximately 30 temples in the upper southern part of the city, clay tablets or clay bullae have been unearthed. In Temples 8, 12, 15, 16, and possibly 26—all situated in the central part of the upper city, Level Oberstadt 3—there are enough clay tablets or bullae to consider the assemblages to be archives or libraries. Some of the temples in the upper city were destroyed by fire; all the temples considered here belong to that group. The temples have basements under approximately one-third of their building area; it is here most of the interesting finds were made.

In Temple 8, in the northeast part of the central temple area, the excavators unearthed the remains of an archive (**Ḫattuša 9**) in the south part of the basement. There are 18 clay tablets or fragments, among them three Middle Hittite historical texts, a letter, and about ten Old and Middle Hittite royal land grants. In addition, there are 90 clay bullae with impressions made by Middle Hittite and sometimes Late Hittite royal seals; these may have been fastened to writing boards, possibly containing royal land grants, continuing the documentation on the clay tablets.[38] In Temple 26 were the remains of an archive (**Ḫattuša 10**) consisting of 85 clay bullae in secondary use. Nearby, more bullae of similar type were discovered in fill of a room in the basement; that room may originally have been the storage place for all the bullae. The seals are not royal. Among them, the seals of the scribe Tarḫu(n)tami are often represented. Therefore, if these bullae had been originally fastened to writing boards, the contents could not have been royal grants. Only two or three clay tablets were found in the building.[39]

Temples 12, 15, and 16 are situated next to each other in the northwestern part of the central temple area. They contained remains of small libraries, as well as a small number of clay bullae. In the basement of Temple 12, there were 40 clay tablets or fragments (**Ḫattuša 11**), mostly rituals. In Temple 15, in Room 6 of the basement and to the north, the excavators found a small number of clay tablet fragments (**Ḫattuša 12**), including four rituals and a few tablets of an important bilingual Hurrian-Hittite composition. The remains of a library (**Ḫattuša 13**) in Temple 16, mostly in the west room of the basement, probably preserved in the jar found nearby, consist of many clay tablet fragments from at least six tablets of the same Hurrian-Hittite composition

WVDOG 81 (1969), especially the plan on Beilage 10. The texts from the later excavations are in *KBo* 12, 13, 15, 16, 18, 25–30, 33, 34, 36, and *KUB* 37 and 39.

38. Cf. P. Neve, "Die Ausgrabungen in Boğazköy-Ḫattuša 1984," *AA* 1985, 330–335, and *KBo* 32.

39. Cf. P. Neve, "Die Ausgrabungen in Boğazköy-Ḫattuša 1985," *AA* 1986, 365–387, especially 384, and *KBo* 32.

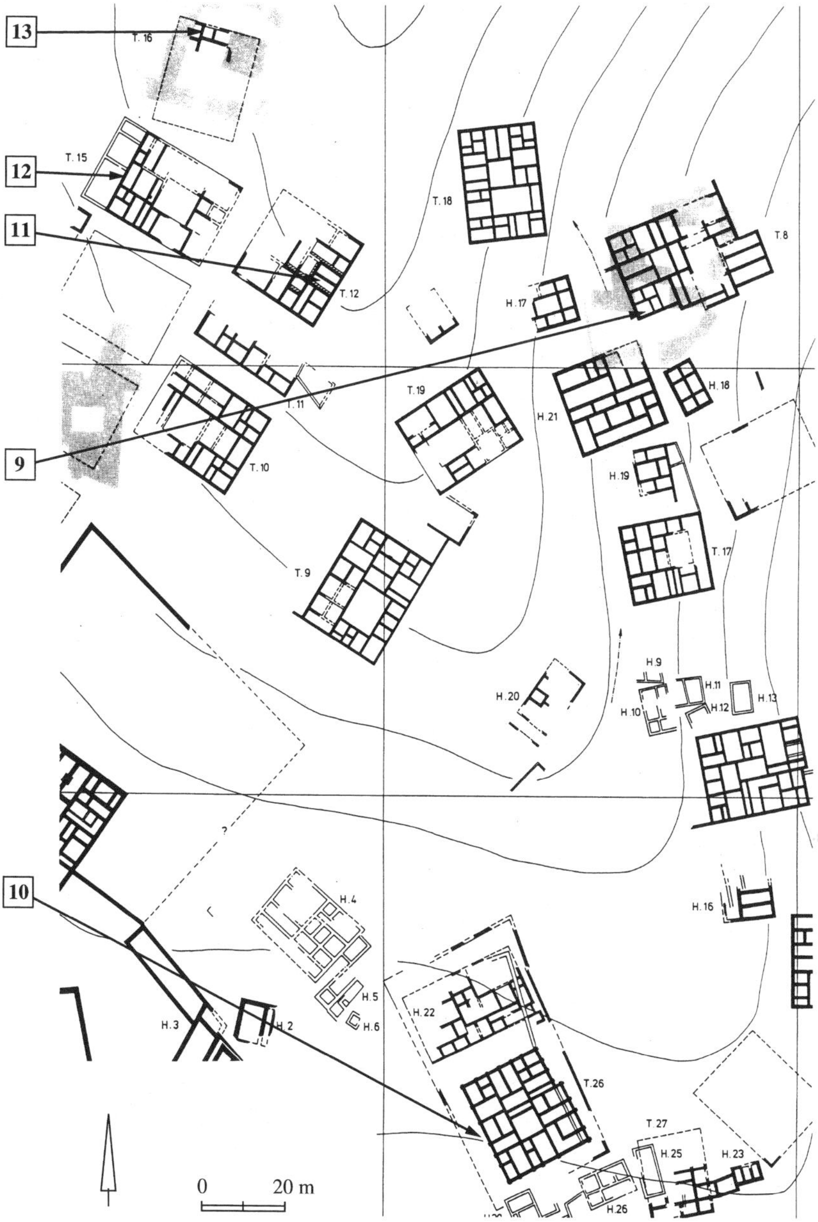

Plan 21. Ḫattuša.
Plan of the temple area in the upper southern part of the city with archives and libraries **Ḫattuša 9-13**.
From P. Neve, *Ḫattuša – Stadt der Götter und Tempel* (1993), 20 fig. 37.

(ca. 1400 B.C.) as in Temple 15. In addition, there are a few more tablets, among them a few tablets of an older version of the Akkadian Gilgamesh epic, as well as rituals or festival texts.[40]

2.2.2 *Šapinuwa (Ortaköy)*

Šapinuwa (modern Ortaköy) is situated about 60 kilometers northeast of Ḫattuša, approximately 50 kilometers southeast of Çorum, and 2.5 kilometers southwest of Ortaköy next to the village Tepelerarası. The site is situated on a large plateau south of a steep mountain. In 1990, A. Süel started excavations due to the occasional finding of clay tablets on the surface. Part of a large building was unearthed. The building, eventually destroyed by fire, probably dates to the thirteenth century B.C.

2.2.2.1 *Library and Administrative Archive in the Palace*

The large building, possibly a palace or another type of administrative building, consisted of a basement of stone walls and an upper floor with walls of mud brick. More than 3,000 clay tablets and fragments have been unearthed. Most of the tablets were found in fill from the upper floor, above Rooms 1 and 5 of the basement, where one or perhaps two archives combined with libraries (**Šapinuwa 1**) may have been stored. According to the quite preliminary reports, the unpublished texts were writ-

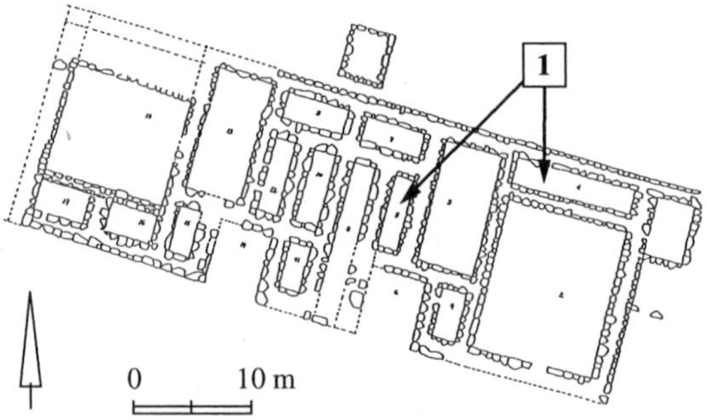

Plan 22. Šapinuwa.
Plan of southern part of palace with archive **Šapinuwa 1**.
From A. Süel, *FS Alp* (1992), 492 pl. 1.

40. Cf. P. Neve, "Die Ausgrabungen in Boğazköy-Ḫattuša 1983," *AA* 1984, 329–372, with H. Otten, "Die Tontafelfunde aus Haus 16," *AA* 1984, 372–375. Some of the texts are published in *KBo* 32.

ten in the Hittite and Hurrian languages. Religious texts and letters are the best-attested text groups, but there are also cult and temple inventories. The letters often have a military content. A number of the letters are from the king, other letters were sent to the king; some of these are from the queen. It cannot be determined from the published information whether the clay tablets found in Room 14 form a separate archive, or whether these texts were part of the aforementioned collection.[41]

2.2.3 Tapigga (Maşat Höyük)

Tapigga (modern Maşat Höyük) is situated 116 kilometers east of Ḫattuša, 20 kilometers south of Zile, west of the modern village of Yalınyazı previously called Maşat. The mountainous landscape is very fertile in this area. From 1973 until 1984, T. Özgüç has been excavating the city, which measured ca. 450 × 225 meters. It consisted of a citadel surrounded by a lower city that extended especially in the southeastern direction. Occupation is attested ca. 2500–350 B.C., with the most important periods being during Hittite Levels I-V, from ca. 1900 B.C., to the destruction ca. 1200 B.C. In the eighth century B.C., there was a Phrygian city here. The excavations have been concentrated on the citadel with a large palace, but a few private houses in the lower city have also been unearthed.[42]

2.2.3.1 Administrative Archive in the Palace

The main palace with a large columned courtyard is from Hittite Level III, which was destroyed by fire ca. 1400 B.C. It had one or two floors above a basement. Among the 117 clay tablets from this site approximately 100 clay tablets and several bullae were unearthed east of the courtyard in Rooms 8 and 9 of the basement and in the columned section of the courtyard, just west of these rooms. The tablets were found among burned debris from the collapsed first floor together with remains of burned wood. The excavator, therefore, concluded that the tablets originally were placed on wooden shelves on the first floor. The tablets written in the Hittite language are the

41. Cf. the preliminary reports by A. Süel, "Ortaköy: Eine hethitische Stadt mit hethitischen und hurritischen Tontafelentdeckungen," *FS Alp* (1992), 487–492; A. Süel, "Ortaköy'ün hitit çağındaki adi," *Belleten* 59 (1995), 271–283; A. Süel, "1994 yılı Çorum-Ortaköy kazı çalışmaları," *Kazı Sonuçları Toplantısı* 17. I (1996), 263–282; and M.-H. Gates, "Archaeology in Turkey," *AJA* 101 (1997), 259–260.

42. As an introduction to the site, cf. T. Özgüç, 'Maşathöyük, B, Archäologisch', *RLA* 7 (1987–1990), 444–446. The archaeological material has been published in T. Özgüç, *Maşat Höyük kazıları ve çevresindeki araştirmalar* (Excavations at Maşat Höyük and Investigations in Its Vicinity), TTKY V 38 (1978); and T. Özgüç, *Maşat Höyük II: Bağazköy'ün kuzeydoğusunda bir hitit merkezi* (Maşat Höyük II: A Hittite Center northeast of Boğazköy), TTKY V 38a (1982).

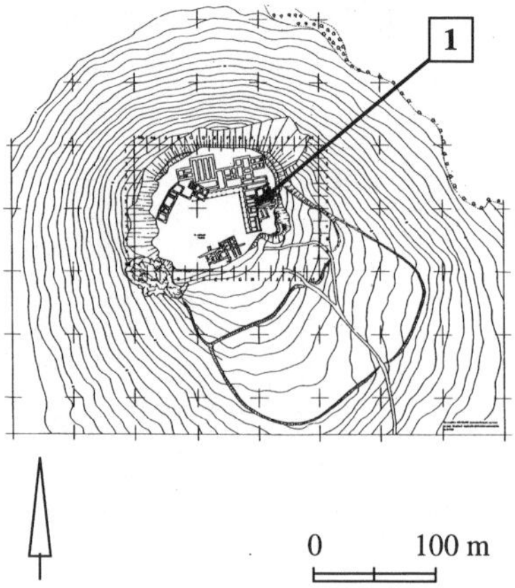

Plan 23. Tapigga.
General plan with archive **Tapigga 1**.
From T. Özgüç, *Maşat Höyük* II (1982), plan 4.

remains of an administrative archive (**Tapigga 1**). Kaššû, UGULA NIMGIR.ÉRIN.MEŠ, "military commander," and some other men were responsible for the administrative unit there. Most of the tablets have been dated to the reign of Tutḫaliya II, ca. 1400 B.C. The largest group of texts consists of 88 letters, 43 of which were sent from the king to Kaššû and some other men, often with instructions concerning military matters. The remaining texts are administrative lists of persons or materials.[43] In the later Hittite Level I, only one clay tablet has been found: an incantation from the thirteenth century B.C.[44]

43. T. Özgüç, *Maşat Höyük* I (1978), 57, pl. 2; however, the numbering of the rooms given here is not according to this publication, but follows the new numbering in *Maşat Höyük* II (1982) and all later publications. In *Maşat Höyük* I the later rooms 8 and 9 were rooms 7 and 8 (p. 57 incorrectly refers to room 9 and not room 7, but this is not the new numbering). S. Alp, *Maşat Höyük'te bulunan çivi yazılı hitit tabletleri* (Hethitische Keilschrifttafeln aus Maşat Höyük), TTKY VI 34 (1991); S. Alp, *Hethitische Briefe aus Maşat Höyük*, TTKY VI 35 (1991). Cf. also the study S. Alp, "Die hethitischen Tontafelentdeckungen auf dem Maşat-Höyük, Vorläufiger Bericht," *Belleten* XLIV no. 173 (1980), 25–59; and S. Alp, 'Maşathöyük, A, Philologisch, *RLA* 7 (1987–1990), 442–444.

44. T. Özgüç, *Maşat Höyük* II (1982), 152.

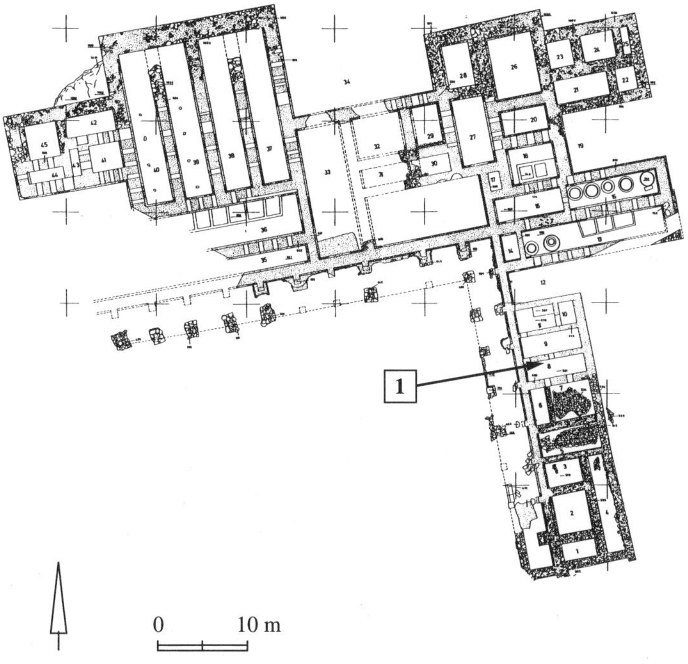

Plan 24. Tapigga.
Plan of palace with archive **Tapigga 1**.
From T. Özgüç, *Maşat Höyük* II (1982), plan 2.

2.2.4 *Šariššа (Kuşaklı)*

Šariššа (modern Kuşaklı) is situated about 210 kilometers southeast of Ḫattuša, approximately 50 kilometers south of Sivas in the eastern part of central Anatolia, next to the village Başören-Altınyayla. Since 1992 A. Müller-Karpe has directed excavations on the site, which measures about 500 × 600 meters. Buildings have been found dating to the Old Hittite period, but most of the excavations have concentrated on the period of the Late Hittite empire, from which the excavators unearthed a temple on the north terrace, private houses on the western slope, and a palace or administrative building on the acropolis.[45]

45. See provisionally A. Müller-Karpe, "Untersuchungen in Kuşaklı 1992–94," *MDOG* 127 (1995), 5–36.

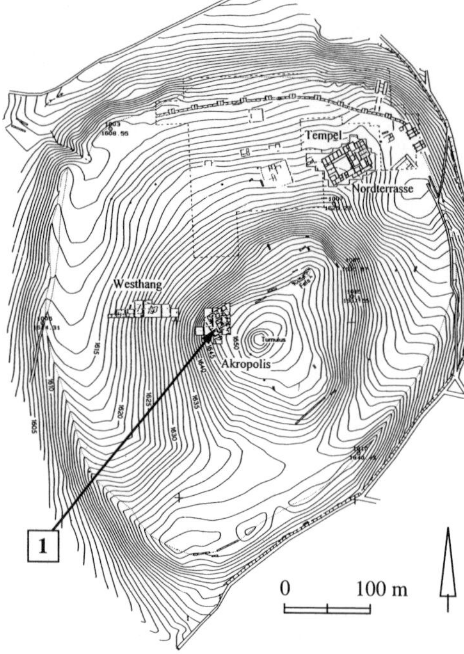

Plan 25. Šariššа.
General plan with archive **Šariššа 1**.
From A. Müller-Karpe, *MDOG* 127 (1995), 7 fig 2.

2.2.4.1 *Library in Palace*

In the room in the southern corner of the building on the acropolis, 42 fragmentary clay tablets were unearthed together with a clay etiquette. The tablets date to the second half of the thirteenth century B.C. and appear to be the remains of a library (**Šariššа 1**) with rituals, oracles, and cultic inventories. In Room 9 of the temple basement, 63 clay bullae were found. They have not been identified as the remains of an archive.[46]

46. G. Wilhelm, *Kuşaklı-Sarissa 1: Keilschrifttexte aus Gebäude A* (1997). Cf. the preliminary report by G. Wilhelm, "Die Tontafelfunde der 2. Ausgrabungskampagne 1994 in Kuşaklı," *MDOG* 127 (1995), 37–42; and A. Müller-Karpe, "Ausgrabungen in Kusaklı 1994," *Orient Express* 1995/1, 3–4.

2.2.5 Emar (Meskene)

Emar (modern Meskene, classical Barbalissos, classical Arabic Balis) is situated west of the Euphrates. The site is about 900 × 600 meters. The French excavation directed by J.-C. Margueron during 1972–1976 was concentrated on the late Bronze Age Level in the western half of the city. Earlier levels could not be found, and it has been suggested that the Emar known from older texts was situated somewhere nearby and has not yet been found. The excavated city seems to have been built at the beginning of Hittite rule and to have come to an end with that rule. In the eastern part of the tell, the Greek-Roman city Barbalissos and Arabic Balis were situated just above the Late Bronze Age city. Of special importance among the areas excavated are: a palace with the *ḫilānu* building in Area A in the northwest of the tell; the Ba'al and Astarte temples in Area E in the southwest; the temples M1 and M2 in Area M in the southern part of the central city east of Area E; and the private houses in Area D, just southwest of Area M. Emar was part of the Hittite empire, granted a local king under the authority of the Hittite viceroy in Karkemish. The cuneiform texts, most of which are written in Akkadian, but some also in Hurrian or Hittite, date to the period between ca. 1320 and the destruction of the city in ca. 1187 B.C.[47]

2.2.5.1 Large Library and Archive in Temple M1 and Archive in Temple M2

Two temples were situated in area M in the southern part of the central city. Temple M1 is situated in the northeast part of this area, and situated in the western part is the most monumental of all four excavated temples in Emar, temple M2.

Temple M1, also called "Temple of the Diviner" because of the contents of the clay tablets unearthed there, is the least monumental of the temples excavated in Emar. It consists of a cella with three rooms on its southeast side. The walls are not much heavier than those of normal private houses. Some scholars have suggested

47. As short introductions to the site, cf. J.-C. Margueron and M. Sigrist, "Emar," *OEANE* 2 (1997), 236–239; and J. Huehnergard, "Emar texts," *OEANE* 2 (1997), 239–240, both with further bibliographies. Cf. provisionally also D. Beyer, ed., *A l'occasion d'une exposition, Meskéné - Emar: Dix ans de travaux 1972–1982* (1982); J. Huehnergard and J.-C. Margueron, "Meskene (Imar/Emar)," *RLA* 8 (1993), 83–93, and J.-C. Margueron, "Emar, Capital of Aštaṭa in the Fourteenth Century BCE," *BA* 58 (1995), 126–138. The final publications will appear in the series *Emar*, Recherches au pays d'Aštata. The archaeological material will be published in *Emar* I–III, the seal impressions in *Emar* IV, the Hittite texts in *Emar* V, and the Hurrian texts in *Emar* VII. The Akkadian and Sumerian texts have received an unusually prompt publication by D. Arnaud, *Emar* VI: *Textes sumériens et accadiens* 1–4 (1985–1987). For a survey of the archives and libraries, based on the Akkadian and Sumerian texts published by D. Arnaud, *Emar* VI, cf. M. Dietrich, "Die akkadischen Texte der Archive und Bibliotheken von Emar," *UF* 22 (1990), 25–48. For a bibliography, cf. K. van der Toorn, "Gods and Ancestors in Emar and Nuzi," *ZA* 84 (1994), 39–41 n. 4.

that the building may not have been a temple at all, but the private house of the diviner. Among the considerable number of clay tablets in the temple or nearby forming a library and archive (**Emar 1**), there were about 1,000 (in the publication 659, because the duplicates were not counted there) Akkadian and Sumerian texts and a large number of Hurrian and Hittite texts; the Hurrian and Hittite texts remain so far unpublished. A family of *bārû* (lúḪAL), "diviners," has an important function in many of the texts. It is possible that many of the texts were stored on an upper floor of the building. Ba'al-malik and his father Ba'al-qarrad are the most frequently attested members of the family, either in documents or in colophons of literary texts.

Based upon findspots within the building there appear to be two groups of texts in areas M I and M III. In Area M I of the temple excavations, essentially in Room 3, which has a door-opening on the southeast side of the cella, the excavators found 225 clay tablets. Among these, 125 tablets constitute an archive of legal documents, and the remaining 100 tablets are a handbook library of liturgies and a selection of some other literary texts.

The largest groups within the archive of 125 clay tablets are the 41 purchase documents and 24 wills; several of the other documents are concerned with the acquisition of property. Twenty-six documents deal directly with the family of diviners, and six documents concern Iṣṣur-Dagan, son of the king. Among the purchase documents, 12 have the same seller, namely, the god Ninurta and the elders of Emar. The king and his relatives often serve as witnesses or have other important functions in these documents, giving them a more official character. In addition to the legal documents, there are 20 documents concerned with the administration of the cults of several gods in the city.

The handbook library consists of 100 clay tablets, of which 27 deal with the enthronement of the *entu*- and *muš'artu*-priestesses, and with the *zukru*- and *kissu*-festivals. Most of the liturgies recited throughout the year or for a month can be found here. In addition, there are: a selection of other rituals; some lexical lists; and a few texts concerned with subjects such as hemerology and omens.

In Area M III, namely, in the western part of the cella and nearby, 740 Akkadian and Sumerian clay tablets and a large number of Hurrian and Hittite tablets were excavated. The largest portion of these, 640 Akkadian and Sumerian tablets and the Hurrian and Hittite ones, constitutes a library with literary texts. The remaining 100 Akkadian tablets constitute an administrative archive. Half of the Akkadian(/Sumerian) tablets in the library are lexical lists, especially the series *urra* = *ḫubullu*, which is present in a large number of duplicates. There are about 120 rituals, including a few lists of offerings; 27 of the rituals are of Mesopotamian and 20 of Anatolian type. The 76 tablets with omens include liver and astrological types; the 60 hemerological texts

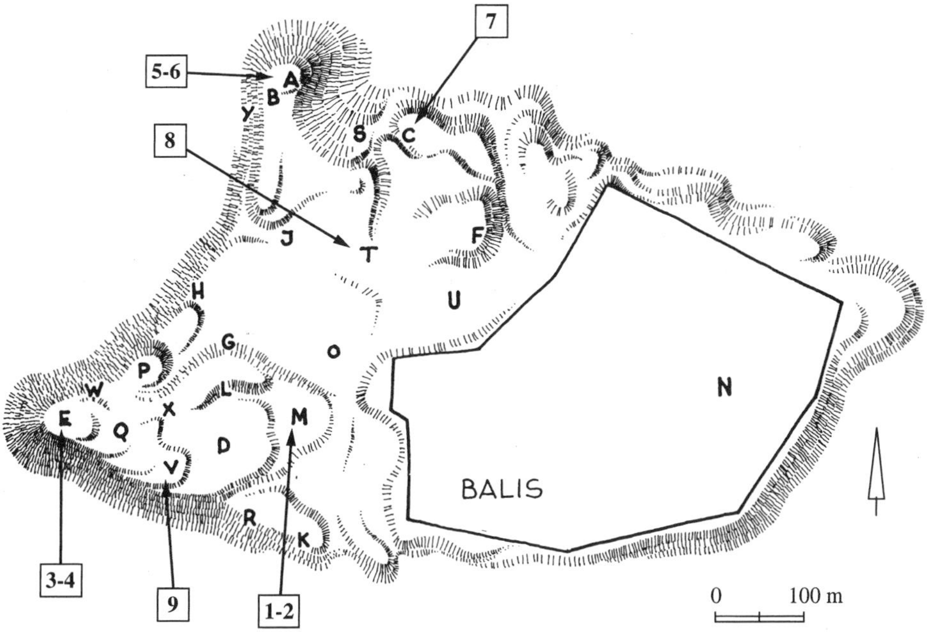

Plan 26. Emar.
General plan with archives **Emar 1-9**.
From J. Margueron, *AAAS* 32 (1982), 244 fig. 1.

include also some of the almanac types. Ten incantations are attested. There is also a selection of 19 Akkadian or Sumerian-Akkadian literary texts, including parts of the Epic of Gilgamesh and some fables. The numerous unpublished Hurrian texts are said to include liver and similar omens, as well as medical prognostications and a god-list; among the Hittite texts, there is a partly published omen report.

The administrative archive of almost 100 tablets consists of more than 80 administrative lists of different types, including inventories, lists of materials and objects, and lists of persons. In the same archive are almost all the 16 Akkadian letters; these deal not only with diviners but also with priests and other persons related to the temple service. At least one letter is written in Hittite with an order from the Hittite king concerning the diviner Zu-Bala, probably the father of Ba'al-qarrad.[48]

48. The Akkadian and Sumerian texts have been published by D. Arnaud, *Emar* VI.3 (1986), nos. 137–535, and D. Arnaud, *Emar* VI.4 (1987), nos. 537–793, 451 bis-ter. Cf. also E. Laroche, "Documents hittites et hourrites," in D. Beyer, ed., *A l'occasion d'une exposition, Meskéné - Emar: Dix ans de travaux 1972–1982*

The above division of texts in areas M I and M III may reflect storage in two totally separate locations, in Room 3 and in the cella. However, the division may also be the result, for example, of different shelves of an upper-story library and archive room collapsing in different directions.

The much more monumental Temple M2 was situated in the western part of area M, 20 meters southwest of Temple M1. In the temple six clay tablets and an inscribed pearl of agate were discovered. The tablets may be the remains of an archive (**Emar 2**) and includes two wills and some administrative lists.[49]

2.2.5.2 *Archives in the Ba'al and Astarte Temples*

The temples of Ba'al (^{d}IM or ^{d}U) and Astarte (^{d}INANNA) were situated in area E in the southwestern corner of the city, with a street between them, their cellas having the

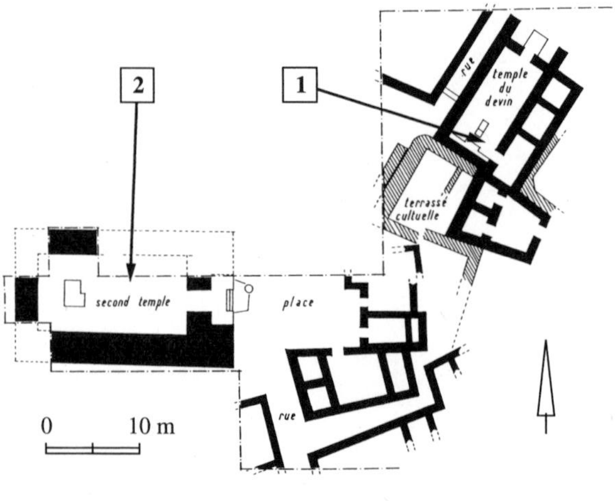

Plan 27. Emar.
Plan of area M with archives **Emar 1-2**.
From J. Margueron, *A l'occasion d'une exposition, Meskéné - Emar* (1982), 31, fig. 7.

(1982), 53–60. For a survey of the library, cf. D. Arnaud, "La bibliothèque d'un devin syrien à Meskéné-Emar (Syrie)," *Académie des inscriptions & belles-lettres, Comptes rendus* (1980), 375–388. Temple M1 has been treated as a private house by, e.g., P. Werner, *Die Entwicklung der Sakralarchitektur in Nordsyrien und Südostkleinasien: vom Neolitikum bis in das 1. Jt. v. Chr.*, Münchener Vorderasiatische Studien 15 (1994), 70–71.

49. D. Arnaud, *Emar* VI.3 (1986), nos. 68–74. The god mentioned in the dedication on the pearl may be the god of the temple. The name was read ^{d}KÚR.NUN by Arnaud, and ^{d}PAP.SUKKAL = Gaddu by M. Dietrich, *UF* 22 (1990), 36.

main door in the east. In the more southerly temple, the Ba'al temple, the excavators unearthed an archive (**Emar 3**) of 19 clay tablets and two labels of boxes. Most of the tablets are lists of objects or materials, often gold, silver, or bronze, sometimes specified as having been given to named persons. Three of the texts are notes of precious metals intended for the manufacture of objects. Most of the materials or objects were said to be owned by the god Ba'al, but one is by Astarte. In the Astarte temple there was a small archive (**Emar 4**) consisting of five clay tablets: lists of persons or materials for persons.[50]

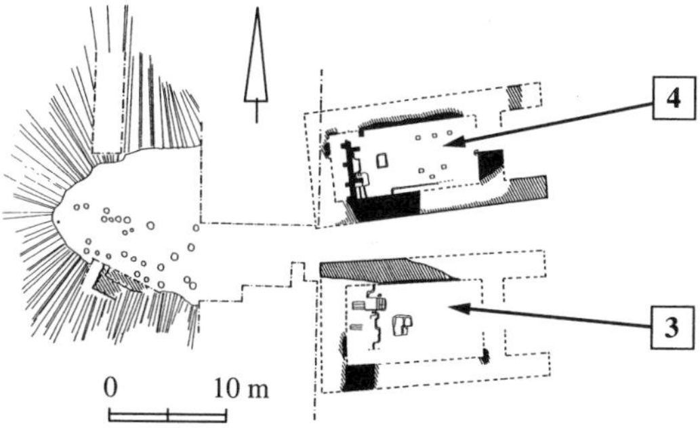

Plan 28. Emar.
Plan of area E with archives **Emar 3-4**.
From J. Margueron, *AAAS* 32 (1982), 247 fig. 4.

2.2.5.3 *Archives in the Palace Area and House A V*

A group of buildings in the northern part of Area A has been interpreted by the excavators as a palace with a *ḫilānu* entrance. One clay pot, found enclosed in a niche in the wall between Room 7 and Room 5 in Area A I NO, contained 13 (or 14) clay tablets. The tablets concern Ir'am-Dagan and his son, as well as Ḫinnu-Dagan, his son and grandson; whether these two groups of persons belong to the same family cannot be proved. Nine texts concern the purchase of houses, vineyards, or fields. There are also two exchange documents concerning houses, a document regarding the renting of slaves, and a will. This may have been a family archive (**Emar 5**), but if so, there are a few unusual traits: all the purchase documents have the same sellers, namely, the god Ninurta and the elders of Emar, and the king as well as royal relatives are often

50. D. Arnaud, *Emar* VI.3 (1986), nos. 42–62 (Ba'al temple), nos. 63–67 (Astarte temple).

witnesses or have other important functions in the documents, thus giving them a more official character. Three other clay pots from the building complex contained a few clay tablets. The excavators found a clay pot with three clay tablets in Room 3 in Area A I SO-SE. Another pot with three clay tablets was unearthed in Room 15 in Area A IV SO, and possibly in the same room, but in Area A II NO, a pot with just one clay tablet was found. No apparent owner of the texts from these pots can be determined. Most of the texts are various types of legal documents, sometimes with the king as witness. Two of the texts from Room 3 are statements by the king of Karkemish and by the son of the Hittite king concerning the latter's slave.[51]

In the southern part of Area A, in Room 18 (Area A V) of a house consisting of Rooms 18, 19, and 20, the excavators found an archive (**Emar 6**) of seven clay tablets; sometimes they are said to have been originally placed in a clay pot. Three of the tablets concern Tattašše (Raindu) and her husband Alazayu. Among the texts are two loan documents, two payments, a note about a caravan, an adoption document, and a letter. One of the loan documents is dated to the second year of the Kassite king Meli-Šipak, ca. 1187 B.C.—this is the only text in Emar dated according to the Babylonian fashion and is, therefore, important for the dating of the end of Emar.[52]

2.2.5.4 Archives in Private Houses in Area C, Area T, and Area V

In three other areas, the excavators unearthed groups of clay tablets in private houses. In Area C, situated about 150 meters east of Area A, nine clay tablets have been unearthed. It is not clear whether they were found together and, therefore, should be regarded as the remains of one archive (**Emar 7**), or whether they should be divided into several archives, or be treated as individual tablets. Among the tablets are four wills, two lists of persons, one lawsuit over an adoption, a receipt, and a short excerpt of a lexical list. An inscribed weight came from the same area.[53]

In a private house in Area T, about 150 meters south of Area C, the excavators unearthed 37 clay tablets. The tablets constitute the archive (**Emar 8**) of Dagan-kabar and Dagan-taliḫ, sons of Ḫima, and Dagan-kabar, son of Dagan-taliḫ, as well as a few other persons. Most identified texts are purchases of houses or slaves. There are also three loans, two wills, and a list of persons.[54]

51. D. Arnaud, *Emar* VI.3 (1986), nos. 1–22.

52. D. Arnaud, *Emar* VI.3 (1986), nos. 23–29. A tendency to date the end of Emar as early as possible has led to a dating of the end in the year 1187 B.C., even if there is nothing in the text itself to support it.

53. D. Arnaud, *Emar* VI.3 (1986), nos. 30–39.

54. D. Arnaud, *Emar* VI.3 (1986), nos. 75–108.

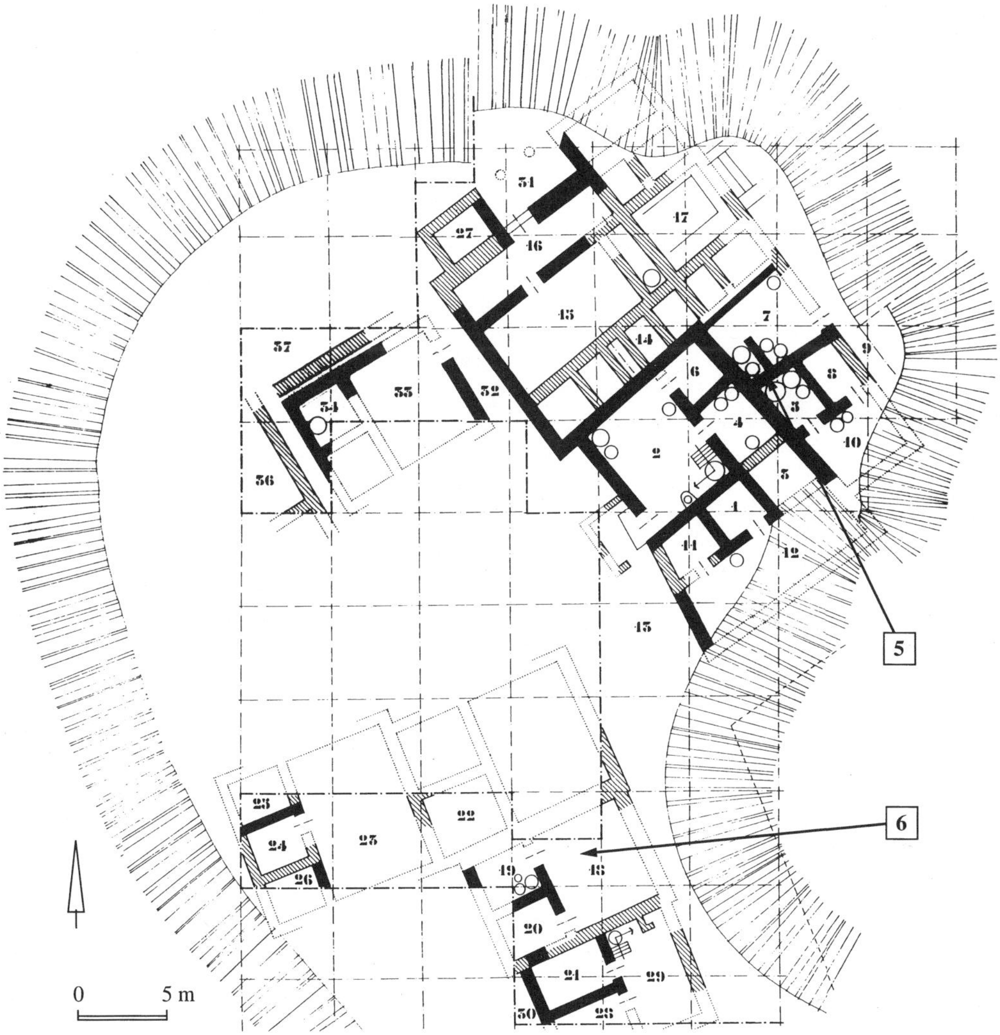

Plan 29. Emar.
Plan of area A with archives **Emar 5-6**.
From J. Margueron, *A l'occasion d'une exposition, Meskéné - Emar* (1982), 26, fig. 2.

In a private house in Area V (Square V I), on the southern edge of the city, approximately between areas E and M, 30 clay tablets were excavated. This archive (**Emar 9**) seems to have belonged to Aḫi-Dagan and his son Milki-Dagan; several other persons are also attested as possible owners of tablets. Most of the texts are purchase documents of houses, fields, or vineyards, but there are also some payments of debts, three wills, a marriage document, and a list of sheep.[55]

2.2.6 Ugarit (Ras Shamra)

Ugarit (modern Ras Shamra) is situated ca. 9 kilometers north of Lattaquié, ca. 800 meters from the shore of the Mediterranean Sea. French excavations were conducted by C. Schaeffer rather regularly beginning in 1929, and by M. Yon from 1978 on. Founded in the Pre-Pottery Neolithic period (ca. 6500 B.C.), the city was inhabited until the Late Bronze Age, when it was destroyed ca. 1175 B.C. in connection with the invasion of the so-called Sea Peoples, or perhaps by an earthquake. There was a settlement there in Hellenistic and Roman times, as well. The excavations have concentrated on the Late Bronze Age city, when the city covered the whole tell, ca. 600 × 600 meters in size. The palace of the local king was situated in the western part of the city, the temples of Ba'al and Dagan in the northeast. In the other areas of the city that have been excavated, there were private houses and some administrative buildings.[56]

The level where epigraphic materials have been found is Level I/3 or Ugarit Récent 3. It dates from the Hittite conquest by Suppiluliuma I, ca. 1365 B.C., until the destruction of the city. During this period, Ugarit was part of the Hittite state with a local king under the authority of the Hittite viceroy in Karkemish. Most texts date to the final half of the period, ca. 1230–1175 B.C., during the reigns of the Ugaritic kings Ammiṯtamru II, Ibiramu, Niqmaddu III, and Ammurapi. The scribes did not use any standardized system for dating documents; however, the reference to the name of the king in some texts helps in determining the period. Cuneiform script of the normal Mesopotamian syllabic-logographic type, sometimes with local sign-forms, was used to write Akkadian, Hurrian, and Hittite. Another cuneiform script, locally

55. D. Arnaud, *Emar* VI.3 (1986), nos. 109–136.

56. As brief introductions to the site, cf. M. Yon, "Ugarit," *OEANE* 5 (1997), 255–262; D. Pardee, "Ugaritic Inscriptions," *OEANE* 5 (1997), 264–266; and M. Yon, D. Pardee, and P. Bordreuil, "Ugarit," *The Anchor Bible Dictionary* VI (1992), 695–721, all with further bibliographies. More detailed introductions to Ugarit can be found in M. Yon, *The City of Ugarit at Tell Ras Shamra* (forthcoming 1998), and J.-C. Courtois, et al.,"Ras Shamra," *Supplément au Dictionnaire de la bible* 10 (1979), 1124–1466. Publications of the archaeological material can often be found in the series *Ugaritica* I (1939)–VII (1978); *Ras Shamra-Ougarit I* (1983)–IX (1992); and in the preliminary reports in *Syria* and *AAAS*.

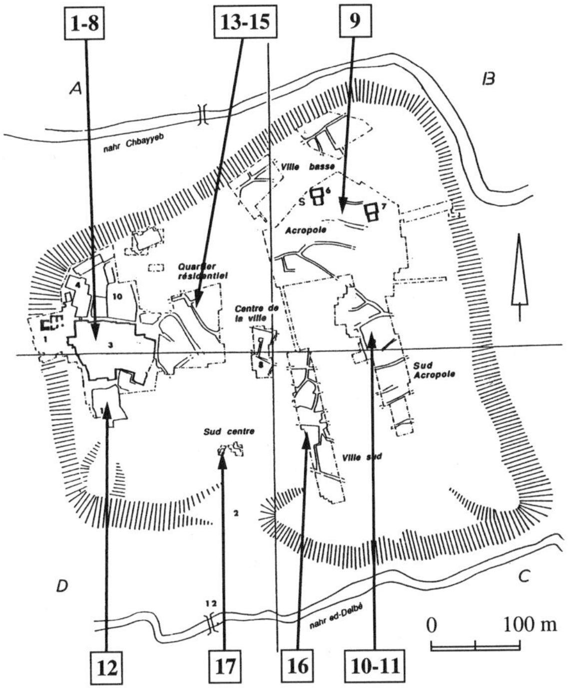

Plan 30. Ugarit.
General plan with archives
Ugarit 1-17.
From H. de Contenson,
Ras Shamra-Ougarit VIII (1992), 6.

developed and based on an alphabetic principle, was used for Ugaritic and Hurrian. Also a few texts in Cypro-Minoan script have been found there, as well as a number of objects with Egyptian hieroglyphics, mostly on stone. There was a tendency to use Akkadian for international matters and Ugaritic for local ones.[57]

57. The basic catalogues for a reconstruction of the archives and libraries are P. Bordreuil and D. Pardee, *La trouvaille épigraphique de l'Ougarit*, 1. *Concordance*, Ras Shamra-Ougarit V, 1 (1989); and J.-L. Cunchillos, *La trouvaille épigraphique de l'Ougarit*, 2. *Bibliographie*, Ras Shamra-Ougarit V, 2 (1990). A year by year bibliography can be found in M. Dietrich, et al., *Ugarit-Bibliographie* 1 (1973)–5 (1986). A reconstruction using this material can be found in Part I and Appendices A and B of W. H. van Soldt, *Studies in the Akkadian of Ugarit: Dating and Grammar* (=*SAU*), AOAT 40 (1986), 1–231, 525–746; information about the number of texts in the archives and libraries stems from this work, but I have tried to correct a few miscalculations, thereby sometimes giving other numbers. The alphabetic texts have received special interest and are now available in a modern edition (unfortunately without translations): M. Dietrich, O. Loretz, and J. Sanmartín, *The Cuneiform Alphabetic Texts from Ugarit, Ras Ibn Hani and Other Places* (KTU: second, enlarged edition), ALASPM 8 (1995).

2.2.6.1 *Archives, Sometimes with Library Section, in the Palace*

The royal palace covered ca. 110 × 75 meters in the western part of the city. The palace complex consisted of six courtyards surrounded by rooms. The excavators unearthed more than 1,000 clay tablets from the main archives and minor collections in the palace. The five main palace archives have been called the Western, the Eastern, the Central, the Southern, and the Southwestern archives.[58]

The Western archive (**Ugarit 1**) was found next to the main entrance in the northwest corner of the palace. The excavators unearthed 73 clay tablets in Rooms 4 and 5, as well as in some of the surrounding rooms. There is a possibility that this archive was stored on an upper floor. The largest group of texts are the 55, mostly Ugaritic, administrative lists, often of peoples and cities. There are also nine, mainly Akkadian, letters, including messages to the royal family and the governor (*sākinu*), an Ugaritic translation of an old treaty, two religious texts, and three Ugaritic school texts, including two alphabets. Two of the texts were written in Hurrian.[59]

The Eastern Archive (**Ugarit 2**) was stored at the northeast corner of the palace, where there was a side entrance in Room 53. This archive consists of 197 clay tablets. Most of the tablets were found in Rooms 56 and 53, with additional tablets in Rooms 52 and 54. The largest group of texts are the 125, mainly Ugaritic, administrative lists, but other quite important groups are the, mainly Akkadian, 50 letters and 16 legal documents. There are also three literary texts, including a Hurrian text, and an alphabet. Some of the tablets, especially the international letters, may have been preserved on an upper floor.[60]

The largest archive in the palace was the Central Archive (**Ugarit 3**) with 254 clay tablets, excavated in rooms around Courtyard IV, as well as probably in secondary position also in that courtyard, and in Courtyard VI and two of the rooms adjoining it. To judge from the distribution of tablets with different contents, there seems to be some differentiation of text types between the 177 texts in the Northern Wing, the 38 texts in the Eastern Wing, and the 39 texts in the Southern Wing of the archive.

58. Publications of many of the texts from the palace archives can be found in C. Virolleaud, *Le palais royal d'Ugarit* II: Textes en cunéiformes alphabétiques des archives est, ouest et centrales (1957); J. Nougayrol, *Le palais royal d'Ugarit* III: Textes accadiens et hourrites des archives est, ouest et centrales (1955); J. Nougayrol, *Le palais royal d'Ugarit* IV: Textes accadiens des archives sud (Archives internationales) (1956); C. Virolleaud, *Le palais royal d'Ugarit* V: Textes en cunéiformes alphabétiques des archives sud, sud-ouest et du petit palais (1965); and J. Nougayrol, *Le palais royal d'Ugarit* VI: Textes en cunéiformes babyloniens des archives du grand palais et du palais sud d'Ugarit (1970).

59. Cf. W. H. van Soldt, *SAU* (1986), 49–60 § 3.

60. Cf. W. H. van Soldt, *SAU* (1986), 60–73 § 4.

The most important group of the tablets in the Northern Wing are the 152 legal documents, almost all written in Akkadian. Most of them deal with domestic matters, especially the transfer of land, which was being carried out by, or in the presence of, the king. Among the remaining, mostly Ugaritic, texts there are seven letters and 14 administrative lists, which include lists of persons receiving fields or rations, or paying silver as taxes. The Eastern and Southern Wings contained fewer tablets, both in Ugaritic and Akkadian. The Eastern Wing consisted of some 17 administrative lists, eight letters, and seven legal documents. Among the letters are the Karkemish correspondence and letters to the queen. In the Southern Wing the largest group consists of the 24, mostly Ugaritic, administrative lists. Most of the remaining texts are Akkadian, of which ten are legal documents, often land transfer documents similar to those in the Northern Wing, but concerned with queen Ṯaryelli.[61]

The Southern Archive (**Ugarit 4**) consists of 133 clay tablets unearthed in Rooms 68 and 69 south of Courtyard V, as well as in secondary position in that courtyard. Almost all texts concerning Ugarit's relations with foreign powers, most prominently the Hittite king, the sovereign of Syria, and his viceroy, the king of Karkemish, derive from this archive. The most important text group consists of the 68 tablets with treaties and international legal documents. All these, like 17 other legal texts dealing with land transfer, and four letters, were written in Akkadian, with the exception of one Hittite letter. The remaining 26 tablets are essentially administrative lists, most written in Ugaritic.[62]

The 162 clay tablets of the Southwestern Archive, including a library section, (**Ugarit 5**) were unearthed in Rooms 81 and 80 west of Courtyard V, as well as in the western part of that courtyard. The 121, mostly Ugaritic, administrative lists form the largest group within the archive. There is a group of about 14 tablets, some Akkadian and some Ugaritic, with letters and legal texts, as well as a treaty. The small library section consisted of 25 religious or literary texts, 20 of them being Hurrian cultic texts, the remaining Ugaritic ones. Two alphabets can be found there, one with the pronunciation indicated.[63]

An oven for baking clay tablets was excavated in courtyard V. It was filled with 156 clay tablets written in Ugaritic (**Ugarit 6**) ready for baking just before the palace was destroyed. The largest group consisted of 144 administrative lists of types similar to those in the Southwest Archive. There are also 12 letters, one of them from a Hittite

61. Cf. W. H. van Soldt, *SAU* (1986), 74–96 § 5.

62. Cf. W. H. van Soldt, *SAU* (1986), 97–109 § 6.

63. Cf. W. H. van Soldt, *SAU* (1986), 114–124 § 8.

Plan 31. Ugarit.
Plan of palace with archives **Ugarit 1-8**.
From P. Bordreuil and D. Pardee, *Ras Shamra-Ougarit V*, 1 (1989), 77 fig. 23.

king to the last king of Ugarit, Ammurapi; this was probably an Ugaritic translation from an Akkadian one. There is also a Hurrian cultic text.[64]

Clay tablets were unearthed also in some other rooms of the palace. In Room 73 in the southwestern part of the palace, about 20 clay tablets (**Ugarit 7**) were found, most of which are in Ugaritic. The largest group consists of 16 administrative lists. Another group of 14 clay tablets (**Ugarit 8**), essentially administrative lists and legal documents, both Akkadian and Ugaritic, came from Room 90 in the southeastern

64. Cf. W. H. van Soldt, *SAU* (1986), 110–114 § 7.

extension of the palace. In the open place between the palace and the Southern Palace, 24 clay tablets were unearthed. The tablets probably come from the Southern Archive and the Southwestern Archive, or partly from the Southern Palace.[65]

2.2.6.2 Libraries with Archive Sections in Private Houses

In two or three of the private houses in the eastern part of the city, rather important libraries have been excavated. In addition, some smaller collections of literary texts will be discussed below, together with the archives.

2.2.6.2.1 The Library and Archive in the House of the High Priest

The house of the high priest was situated in the area between the Ba‘al and Dagan temples. South of the house ran the "Rue de la bibliothèque," north of it the "Rue du dieu Dagon." Unfortunately the other limits of the house have not been well established. An inner courtyard consisted of Rooms 3, 4, and 5. In Room 2 was a staircase, indicating that the house probably had an upper floor. Under the door connecting Rooms 3 and 6 was a depot of 74 bronzes, five of them with inscriptions mentioning the high priest (*rb khnm*).

A library with archive (**Ugarit 9**), consisting of 135 clay tablets, was found in or nearby the rooms of this house. In addition, some, or all, of a group of 24 similar texts

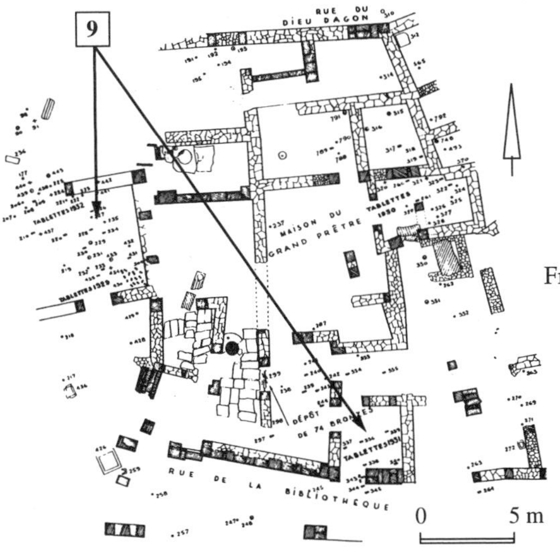

Plan 32. Ugarit.
Plan of private house with library
Ugarit 9.
From C. Schaeffer, *Ugaritica III* (1956), 252 fig. 216.

65. Cf. W. H. van Soldt, *SAU* (1986), 125–133 § 9, 143–148 § 11a.

found in the area of Tomb IV, about 50 meters further east along the continuation of "Rue de la bibliothèque," on the other side of the Dagan temple, may also have belonged to this library; they are here treated together with the main group of texts, but differentiated within parentheses.

Most of the clay tablets were unearthed northwest of the courtyard in Room 1, which was the main archive with a library of cultic texts. Room 7, next to the southern outer wall, housed the library with most of the famous literary texts. Other tablets were unearthed nearby these rooms or in Rooms 10 and 11. According to the texts, this seems to have been the house of the high priest (*rb khnm*). Several persons are attested, most frequently Ili-malku (*ilmlk* and DINGIR-LUGAL), who was a student of the high priest Attenu at the time when he wrote most of the literary texts; we do not know if he, himself, ever attained the high priesthood.

The most famous texts from the library, namely, the 24 (3 of them from the tomb area) myths and epics of Ba'al (and 'Anat), Keret, Aqhat, and Rephaim were, when detailed provenances are known, unearthed in Room 7, with the exception of two texts from Room 1. In Room 1 the excavators unearthed most of the 40 (6 of them from the tomb area) lists of offerings, rituals, prayers, and similar texts of religious usage, most of the 13 letters, and most of the 23 (2 of them from the tomb area) administrative texts, essentially lists of persons and items. All three god-lists and some of the 16 lexical lists also come from Room 1. Only three lexical lists have been identified as coming from Rooms 10–11. Most of the texts were written in alphabetic Ugaritic. However, a few of the letters and religious texts, one god-list, and all lexical lists were composed in cuneiform Akkadian or Sumerian, and several religious texts, one god-list, and part of one lexical list, are written in alphabetic Hurrian.[66]

2.2.6.2.2 Two Libraries and Archives of the Diviner in the So-Called House of the "Hurrian Priest" and of the "Lamaštu Tablets"

In the area with private houses, 130 meters south of the house of the high priest, the excavators unearthed a large house with the entrance off a street to its west. A library (**Ugarit 10**) with essentially alphabetic Ugaritic and Hurrian texts was unearthed in the northern part of the house, and another library with mostly Akkadian texts comes from the southwestern corner of the house. In view of the contents of the tablets, the owner of the house was a diviner or, perhaps, a priest. In the northern extension of the house, in Room 10 and partly also in Room 11, a library with

66. Cf. W. H. van Soldt, *SAU* (1986), 212–220 § 15; J.-L. Cunchillos, "Le Temple de Ba'al à Ugarit et la Maison du Grand Prêtre," *Annuaire de l'École pratique des Hautes Études, V^e^ section*, 93 (1984–1985), 231–243.

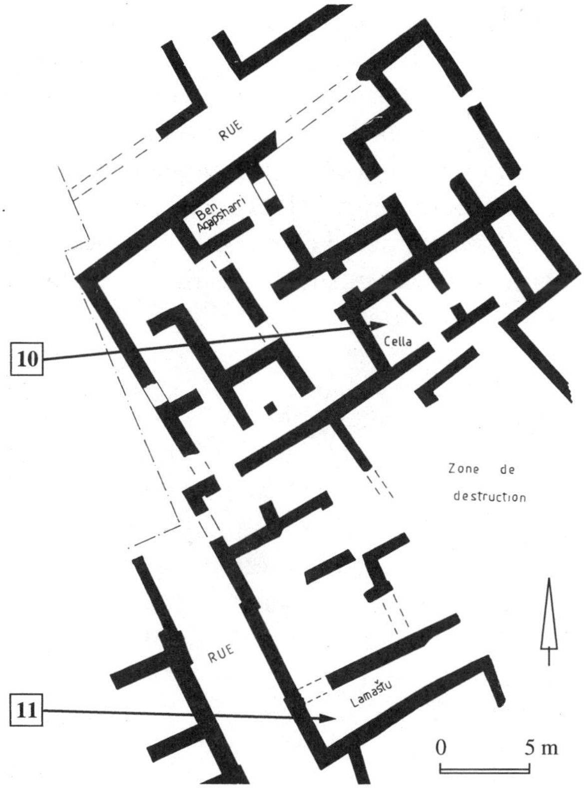

Plan 33. Ugarit.
Plan of private houses with libraries **Ugarit 10-11**.
From P. Bordreuil and D. Pardee, *Ras Shamra-Ougarit V*, 1 (1989), 298 fig. 39a.

archive was preserved with 64 clay tablets. Found together with the tablets were 21 clay liver models, six of which are inscribed in alphabetic Ugaritic, and one clay lung model inscribed in the same script. In addition to these models, the library consisted of 49 religious texts, one lexical list, and two alphabets. Among the religious texts were nine mythological texts of traditions other than those at the house of high priest; the remaining religious texts were rituals, lists of offerings, prayers, and a divinatory text, often rather similar to texts in the library of the high priest. There were also ten administrative lists, and two letters. The letters and one administrative list are written in Akkadian, the lexical list in Sumerian, the rest in alphabetic Ugaritic and alphabetic Hurrian.[67]

In the southwestern corner of the same house, in Room 7 and nearby, the excavators unearthed 76, mostly unpublished, clay tablets. In this second library with archive (**Ugarit 11**), all, except one, of the clay tablets were written in syllabic Akkadian or Sumerian (one also partly in Hittite). Almost half of the clay tablets, namely, 35 texts, are lexical lists of essentially Babylonian type, including, for example, *urra* = *ḫubullu*, god-lists, and grammatical lists. There are 21 religious and literary texts, among them omens, incantations (including the Lamaštu incantation, after which the library has been named), and wisdom texts. The archival portion consists of six letters, five legal documents, and nine administrative lists (the latter group includes the only Ugaritic text). Considering the extensive destruction in the central section of this house with two different libraries, perhaps the house had been divided into two separate family residences, each with one library.[68]

2.2.6.3 *Archives in Private Houses*

Several buildings with archives have been excavated in the area with private houses in the western and central parts of the city. The archives contained, in addition to private documents, a large number of lexical lists, as well as documents from the official administration.

2.2.6.3.1 *The "Palais sud" with the Archive of Yabninu*

The large house, in the publications called "Palais sud" or "Petit palais," is situated south of the main palace, with an open space between the buildings. About 100 clay tablets were unearthed in Rooms 203 and 204, including a few in some other rooms of the house or just north of it. The texts in the archive (**Ugarit 12**) were written in Akkadian, with the exception of 18 texts in alphabetic Ugaritic and two in Cypro-Minoan. Recent studies have identified the owner of the archive as Yabninu, probably identical with Yabni-Šapšu (DÙ-^{d}UTU), *šatammu rabû*, one of the most prominent

67. Cf. W. H. van Soldt, *SAU* (1986), 194–203 § 14a. Groups of texts have been published by E. Laroche, "III. Textes hourrites en cunéiformes alphabétiques," *Ugaritica* V (1968), 497–518; C. Virolleaud, "Les nouveaux textes mythologiques et liturgiques de Ras Shamra (XXIVe campagne, 1961)," *Ugaritica* V (1968), 545–606; A. Herdner, "Nouveaux textes alphabetiques de Ras Shamra - XXIVe campagne, 1961," *Ugaritica* VII (1978), 1–74; and D. Pardee, *Les textes para-mythologiques de la 24^{e} campagne* (1961), Ras Shamra-Ougarit IV (1988).

68. Cf. W. H. van Soldt, *SAU* (1986), 204–211 § 14b.

citizens besides the king himself. There are six letters and three legal texts. Most of the other texts are administrative lists of types similar to those found in the palace, and some record relations with foreign countries. This has been interpreted either as the administration of Yabninu's own business or Yabninu's keeping documents related to his official position at home.[69]

2.2.6.3.2 The House with the Archive of Rap'anu

In the residential quarters east of the royal palace on the northeast side of "Rue de Mineptah," the house of Rap'anu was situated. The large house, which was built with an upper floor, had in its northwestern part an inner courtyard. In Rooms 5, 6, and 7, which probably correspond to that courtyard and the two rooms southeast of it, almost all the 343 clay tablets from the archive (**Ugarit 13**) in this house were unearthed. The largest group of texts, two-thirds of all tablets here, is an impressive collection of 232 lexical lists, not only in Sumerian and Akkadian, but some in Hurrian and Ugaritic; three tablets had Ugaritic alphabets or similar texts, some with Akkadian grammatical forms. There were also 63, mostly Akkadian, letters. Among them, 25 letters concern the last kings of Ugarit or the royal family and concern relations, for example, with the Hittite overlord and with Alašia (Cyprus) and other states, just like the letters from the palace archives from where they may have been taken. A few letters concern Rap'anu and some other persons. More than half the 28 administrative lists and all the 14 legal documents are written in Akkadian. The archive contained also an Akkadian incantation, a Hurrian text, and a Cypro-Minoan clay tablet.[70]

2.2.6.3.3 The House with the Archive of Rašap'abu

In the residential quarters east of the royal palace on the northeast side of "Rue du Palais" was a house with seven rooms on the ground floor. An archive (**Ugarit 14**) consisting of 25 clay tablets was excavated in some of the rooms, as well as some being found scattered about in secondary positions outside the house. The house and the archive belonged to Rašap'abu, a man with the title *akil kāri* (literally "supervisor

69. J.-C. Courtois, "Yabninu et le palais sud d'Ougarit," *Syria* 67 (1990), 103–142. Cf. W. H. van Soldt, *SAU* (1986), 149–158 § 11b.

70. Cf. W. H. van Soldt, *SAU* (1986), 165–181 § 12c. Some of the texts have been published by J. Nougayrol, "III. Les archives 'de Rap'anu,'" *Ugaritica* V (1969), 41–259; and C. F. A. Schaeffer, "Commentaires sur les lettres et documents," *Ugaritica* V (1969), 638–768. The detailed archaeological publication of the house has not yet appeared.

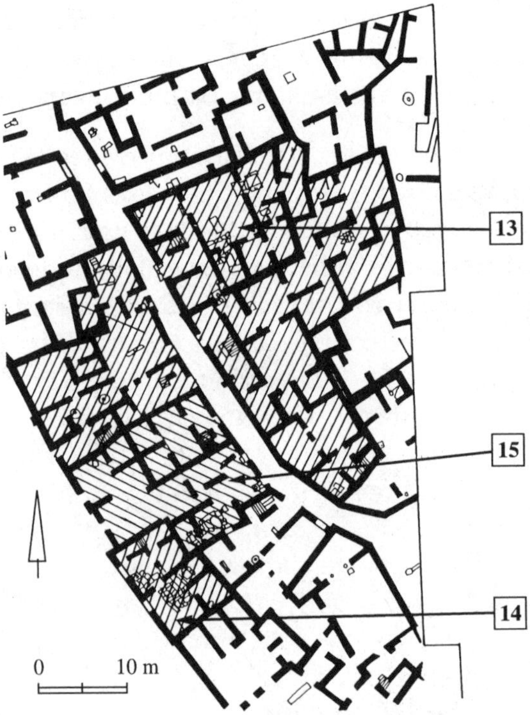

Plan 34. Ugarit.
Plan of private houses with archives **Ugarit 13-15**.
Due to lack of available detailed information, the rooms indicated as archives are only approximative. From P. Bordreuil and D. Pardee, *Ras Shamra-Ougarit* V, 1 (1989), 275 fig. 33a.

of the harbor"). Among the ten Akkadian legal documents of Rašap'abu, his father-in-law Izaldanu, and a few other persons, are purchase and adoption documents. There are five Akkadian and five Ugaritic administrative lists, an Ugaritic medical text concerning the treatment of horses, a few Sumero-Akkadian or Ugaritic school texts, and a Cypro-Minoan text.[71]

71. Cf. W. H. van Soldt, *SAU* (1986), 160–163 § 12a. Some of the texts have been published by J. Nougayrol, "I. Les archives de Rašapabu," *Ugaritica* V (1969), 1–21; and C. F. A. Schaeffer, "Commentaires sur les lettres et documents," *Ugaritica* V (1969), 607–629. The detailed archaeological publication of the house has not yet appeared.

2.2.6.3.4 *The House with the Archive of the "Lettré"*

The house with the remains of the small archive and library (**Ugarit 15**) of the "Lettré" is situated southwest of "Rue de Mineptah," and is the eastern neighbor of the house of Rašap'abu. Nineteen clay tablets are reported to have come from this house. However, at least one, perhaps several, of them is intrusive from the archive of Rašap'abu. Several of the ten lexical lists, including a god-list, are school texts. Two letters with identical contents, one in Sumerian and the other in Akkadian, are literary compositions. There are two incantations, three letters, among them the only Ugaritic text, and an administrative list.[72]

2.2.6.3.5 *Archive with Library in the "Maison aux Tablettes" in the "Ville Sud"*

In the area "Ville sud," south of a large open square, is the large house called "Maison aux tablettes." In the southern neighborhood of the house, gold and bronze smiths were to be found; seal cutters and a sculptor lived north of the square. Inside the door facing the square, in Rooms 1–5 of the north part of the house (and partly outside the house), 83 clay tablets were unearthed. The largest group among these mostly unpublished texts from the archive (**Ugarit 16**) are the 54 lexical lists, including *urra* = *ḫubullu* and other Mesopotamian lexical lists, grammatical lists, and god-lists; to these should be added an Ugaritic alphabet. Among the library texts, there are, in (Sumerian and) Akkadian, two wisdom texts, a Gilgamesh text, a flood story, and an omen text, as well as, in Ugaritic, a song, a possible ritual, and a horse text. The archival part of the tablet collection consists of 12 letters, three legal documents, all in Akkadian, as well as five Akkadian and five Ugaritic administrative lists.[73]

2.2.6.3.6 *Remains of an Archive in the "Sud center"*

In "Sud center," in a heap of rubble from the foundation pit of a concrete construction previously used by the Syrian army, archaeologists found 96 clay tablets and additional fragments. After removal of the construction, 61 additional, as yet unpublished, clay tablets were discovered in the western part of the pit and in some rooms excavated west of it. The tablets seem to be the remains of an archive (**Ugarit 17**) orig-

72. Cf. W. H. van Soldt, *SAU* (1986), 163–165 § 12b. Some of the texts have been published by J. Nougayrol, "II. La bibliothèque du lettré," *Ugaritica* V (1969), 23–40; and C. F. A. Schaeffer, "Commentaires sur les lettres et documents," *Ugaritica* V (1969), 629–638. The detailed archaeological publication of the house have not yet appeared.

73. Cf. W. H. van Soldt, *SAU* (1986), 182–193 § 13.

inating from the house, partly destroyed by the pit. Here only the first group of tablets can be described. The largest group of texts are the 43, mostly Akkadian, letters; among them are 18 international letters involving the king or the royal family. Some of the letters concern Uzzenu the governor (*sākinu*) of Ugarit; another group concerns Šipṭi-Ba'al and Urtenu, who did business with Emar. There are 15, both Ugaritic and Akkadian, administrative lists, as well as a treaty and a legal text in Akkadian. Furthermore, there are 30 lexical lists and three religious texts (two in Akkadian and one in Ugaritic).[74]

Small remains of libraries or archives were also excavated in other private houses. In "Centre ville," House A, the excavators unearthed the small remains of a possible library. Among the identified texts are four Akkadian or Sumerian religious texts, an Akkadian omen text, four lexical lists, and an international letter.[75] Thirteen Akkadian and Ugaritic tablets, mainly legal and administrative, found in a house on the "Terrasse est," east of the Dagan temple, may be the remains of an archive.[76]

2.3 Middle Assyrian Area

The archives and libraries with cuneiform texts from the Middle Assyrian area date to the Middle Assyrian period, ca. 1420–1050 B.C. Large excavations have been conducted in the ancient capital Assur (2.3.1), where a number of archives and libraries have been unearthed. Archives have also been found in the short-lived capital Kar-Tukulti-Ninurta (2.3.2), in Šibaniba (2.3.3) and Tell Rimah (2.3.4) in the Assyrian homeland, in Admannu (2.3.5) towards the Babylonian frontier, as well as in Dur-Katlimmu (2.3.6), Tell Fekhariya (2.3.7), Ḫarbe (2.3.8), Tell Sabi Abyad (2.3.9), and Tell Fray (2.3.10) in the Syrian provinces.

The texts are written in cuneiform script on clay tablets. There are references to wooden writing boards in the documents on clay tablets, but no writing board has yet been found from this period. Most texts are written in the Akkadian language, mostly in the Assyrian dialect using the Assyrian form of cuneiform, but some, especially literary, texts are in the Babylonian dialect and script or even in the Sumerian language.

74. P. Bordreuil, *Une bibliothèque au sud de la ville*, Ras Shamra-Ougarit VII (1991) with photos of several of the tablets in C. F. A. Schaeffer-Forrer, "Épaves d'une bibliothèque d'Ugarit," *Ugaritica* VII (1978), 399–405, pls. I–LXVIII. Cf. W. H. van Soldt, *SAU* (1986), 221–223 § 16.

75. Cf. W. H. van Soldt, *SAU* (1986), 224 § 17.

76. Cf. W. H. van Soldt, *SAU* (1986), 225 § 18.

The Assyrian scribes dated texts by means of eponyms. Unfortunately eponym lists are poorly preserved, and, therefore many of the texts can be dated only approximately to the reigns of specific kings.[77]

In addition to the archives and libraries discussed below, individual tablets or small remains of archives or libraries have been found at a number of other sites in approximately the same area.[78]

2.3.1 Assur (Qal'at Sherqaṭ)

Assur (modern Qal'at Sherqaṭ) is situated on the west bank of the Tigris, in the southwestern part of the central Assyrian area at the desert fringe. During the years 1903–1914, W. Andrae directed the large German excavations of the city. Later there were Iraqi excavations, and two short German ones directed by R. Dittmann (1988–1989) and B. Hrouda (1989–1990). Leaving a few possible early findings out of the discussion, the lowest level in Assur dates to the Early Dynastic III period, ca. 2500 B.C. The city was the Assyrian capital during the Old Assyrian period and most of the Middle Assyrian period, until the beginning of the Neo-Assyrian period. Even after the move of the Assyrian capital, Assur remained an important city with the main Assyrian sanctuary, the Aššur temple. The latest extensive buildings were destroyed ca. A.D. 250. The Middle Assyrian city consisted of an inner city (ca. 900 × 1000 meters), with an extension towards the south (ca. 500 × 300 meters). The temples, palaces, and most other administrative buildings were situated in the northern part of the inner city; private houses were excavated in the southern and western parts of

77. For the Middle Assyrian eponyms, cf. C. Saporetti, *Gli eponimi medio-assiri*, Bibliotheca Mesopotamica 9 (1979), with updatings and additions in H. Freydank, *Beiträge zur mittelassyrischen Chronologie und Geschichte*, SGKAO 21 (1991).

78. E.g., for Nineveh, cf. the Middle Assyrian references in W. G. Lambert and A. R. Millard, *Catalogue of the Cuneiform Tablets in the Kouyunjik Collection of the British Museum*, Second Supplement (1968), listed by C. Saporetti, *Onomastica Medio-Assira* II (1970), 328–329; for Tell Bazmusian, cf. J. Læssøe, "The Bazmusian Tablets," *Sumer* 15 (1959), 15–18, pls. 1–5; for Kulišḫinaš (Tell Amuda), cf. M.-J. Aynard and J.-M. Durand, "Documents d'Epoque Medio-Assyrienne," *Assur* 3/1 (1980); and P. Machinist, "Provincial Governance in Middle Assyria and Some New Texts from Yale," *Assur* 3/2 (1982); for Kaḫat (Tell Barri), cf. M. Salvini, "I testi cuneiformi della campagna 1989 a Tell Barri," *Consiglio Nazionale delle Ricerche Istituto per gli Studi Micenei ed Egeo-Anatolici*, Seminari anno 1990 (1991), 67–69; and for el-Qiṭar, cf. D. C. Snell, "The Cuneiform Tablet from el-Qiṭār," *Abr-Nahrain* 22 (1983–1984), 159–170; and W. Culican and T. L. McClellan, "El-Qitar: First Season of Excavations, 1982–83," *Abr-Nahrain* 22 (1983–1984), 29–63.

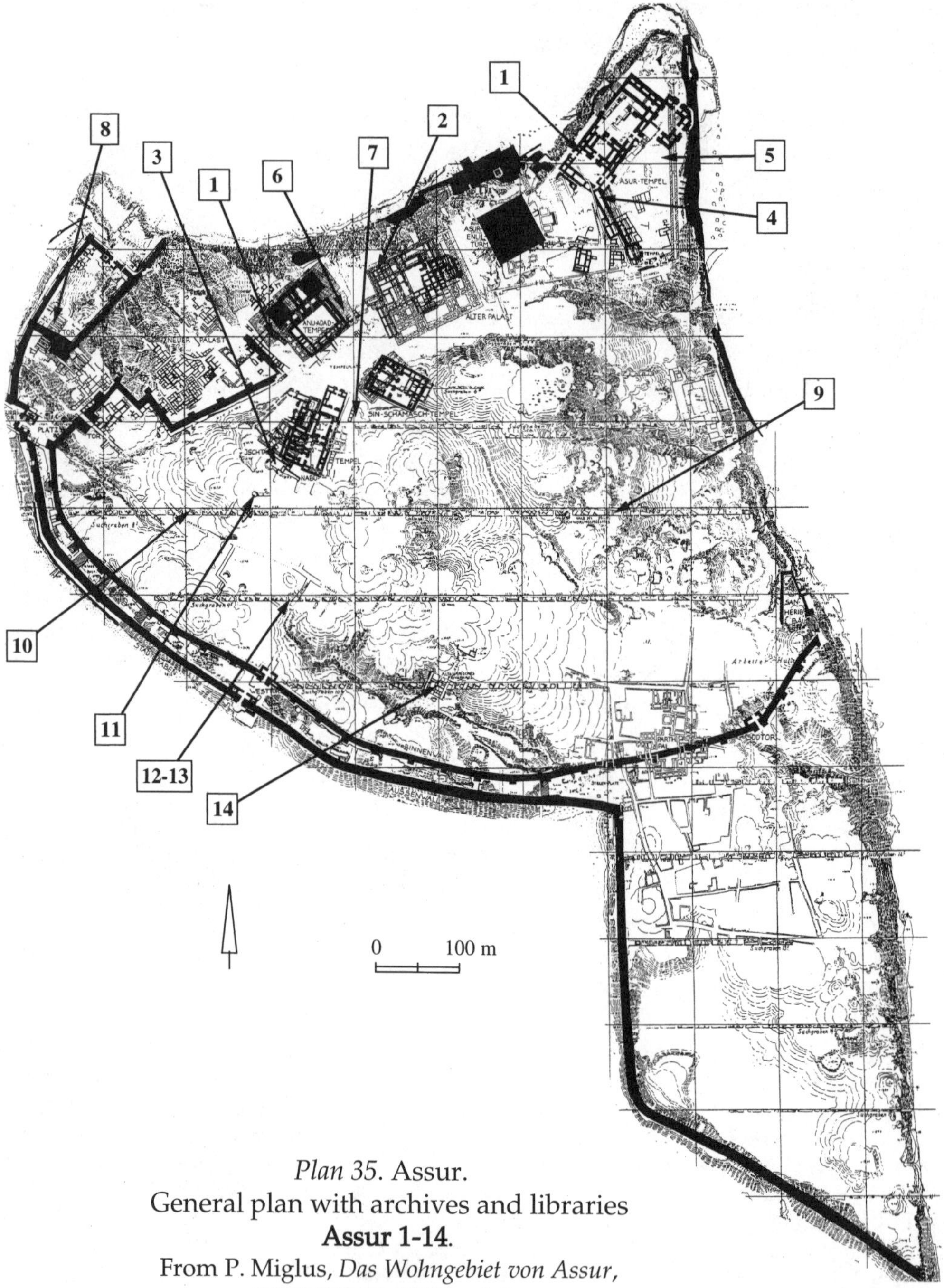

Plan 35. Assur.
General plan with archives and libraries
Assur 1-14.
From P. Miglus, *Das Wohngebiet von Assur*,
WVDOG 93 (1996), pl. 1.

the inner city, often by means of excavation trenches. The description of the later periods will follow in section 3.1.1.[79]

2.3.1.1 Libraries in Private Houses as well as in Official Buildings

The remains of what may have been a Middle Assyrian library M 2 (**Assur 1**) were unearthed in different findspots in the northern part of the city. One hundred clay tablets from the Neo-Assyrian tablet collection in the Aššur temple (cf. also 3.1.1.3) were Middle Assyrian (including eight Middle Babylonian) literary texts. The excavators found 60 clay tablets of similar date and content in a secondary, early Neo-Assyrian archaeological context southwest of the Anu-Adad temple, in approximately the area eA5V–6II, as well as partly scattered around in the 400 meter long area between this place and the Aššur temple. (Within the same area, southwest of the Anu-Adad temple, were also the remains of an archive of 100 unpublished Middle Assyrian documents; it is unclear whether they may have been part of the library or may have formed a separate collection.) The tablets include a large number of lexical lists as well as regulations on palace and harem life, laws, royal rituals, hymns, myths, incantations, medical prescriptions, and texts concerning the treatment of horses, the manufacture of perfumes, mathematics, astronomy, and astrology. Several of the tablets were written by the brothers Marduk-balassu-eriš and Bel-aḫa-iddina from a family of scribes (*ṭupšarru*), during the decades before the reign of Tiglath-Pileser I, around the middle of the twelfth century B.C. Some other scribes had

79. For an introduction to the archaeological material, see W. Andrae, *Das wiedererstandene Assur*, Sendschrift der Deutschen Orient-Gesellschaft 9 (1938), Neudruck (1977), with select bibliography; cf. also R. W. Lamprichs, "Aššur," *OEANE* 1 (1997), 225–228, with additional bibliography. For the archives and libraries, see O. Pedersén, *Archives and Libraries in the City of Assur: A Survey of the Material from the German Excavations*, part I and II (=*ALA* I and II), Acta Universitatis Upsaliensis, Studia Semitica Upsaliensia 6 and 8, (1985, 1986); cf. also O. Pedersén, "Die Assur-Texte in ihren archäologischen Zusammenhängen," *MDOG* 121 (1989), 153–167; and O. Pedersén, "The Libraries in the City of Assur," *Keilschriftliche Literaturen*, CRRAI 32 (1986), 143–147. The main publications of the archaeological material and many of the texts have appeared in the series Wissenschaftliche Veröffentlichung der Deutschen Orient-Gesellschaft (=WVDOG): Among the archaeological publications are W. Andrae, WVDOG 10 (1909); W. Andrae, WVDOG 23 (1913); W. Andrae, WVDOG 24 (1913); W. Andrae, WVDOG 39 (1922); W. Andrae, WVDOG 46 (1924); W. Andrae, WVDOG 53 (1931); W. Andrae and H. Lenzen, WVDOG 57 (1933); W. Andrae, WVDOG 58 (1935); C. Preusser, WVDOG 64 (1953); A. Haller, WVDOG 65 (1953); C. Preusser, WVDOG 66 (1955); A. Haller, WVDOG 67 (1955); and P. A. Miglus, WVDOG 93 (1996). Among the text publications are L. Messerschmidt, WVDOG 16 (1911); E. Ebeling, WVDOG 28 (1919); E. Ebeling, WVDOG 34 (1920); O. Schröder, WVDOG 35 (1920); O. Schröder, WVDOG 37 (1922); M. Lizbarski, WVDOG 38 (1921); E. Ebeling, WVDOG 50 (1927); H. Freydank, WVDOG 92 (1994); as well as L. Jakob-Rost and F. M. Fales, WVDOG 94 (1997). The preliminary reports can be found in *MDOG*.

also written tablets in the collection. It is not clear whether all the tablets diverted in Neo-Assyrian times had, during the Middle Assyrian period, belonged to one, single library or whether they may have been divided into a few separate libraries. Among the creators of the library may have been the aforementioned scribal family. The original storage location(s) of the tablets may have been in a private house southwest of the Anu-Adad temple, inside that temple, in the Old Palace, or in the Aššur temple.

Another collection of six clay tablets, library M 1 (**Assur 2**), was unearthed in a door opening between Rooms 42 and 43, in the western corner of the Old Palace in area fB5II. The texts are incantations from late Middle Assyrian or early Neo-Assyrian time, and may have been a handbook library for the exorcist of the king (*āšip šarri*).

In the tiny remains of what may have been a private house in area eA7III southwest of the Ištar-Temple, archaeologists unearthed a small collection M 3 (**Assur 3**) consisting of a four school texts.[80]

2.3.1.2 Archives in Official Buildings

In the official buildings in the northern half of the city there were five archives of essentially administrative texts (M 4–8).

The excavators unearthed archive M 4 (**Assur 4**), which consisted of 650 clay tablets from at least ten clay pots, three of which were inscribed, in Room 3′ in the building along the southwest side of the large forecourt of the Aššur temple in area hE4III. Ezbu-lešir, supervisor of the offerings (*rab ginā'e*), and servant of Tiglat-pileser I, was responsible for the creation of most of the texts preserved in the archive, but there are also several texts from his predecessors: Aba-la-ide, who bore the title *ša muḫḫi ginā'e*, and Sîn-uballiṭ and Sîn-nadin-apli, these two probably bearing the same title as Aba-la-ide or Ezbu-lešir. Frequently mentioned are officials with the titles *alaḫḫinu* (one who prepares some special bread and dishes) and brewers. The texts date from the end of the reign of Tukulti-Ninurta I (ca. 1207 B.C.) to the reign of Tiglat-pileser I (1114–1076 B.C.), with most texts dating to the latter period. The texts provide information about the *ginā'u* offerings in the Aššur temple, and are administrative documents, some in the form of tabular lists, as well as some letters. Best documented is the delivery from different provinces of corn, honey, sesame, and fruit to the

80. O. Pedersén, *ALA* I (1985), 29–42 M 1–3, with bibliographical references. For a dating of many of the Middle Assyrian literary tablets about 50 years before, and not during, the reign of Tiglath-Pileser I, see now H. Freydank, *Beiträge zur mittelassyrischen Chronologie und Geschichte*, SGKAO 21 (1991), especially 94–97. Therefore, the opinion expressed by E. Weidner, "Die Bibliothek Tiglatpilesers I.," *AfO* 16 (1952–1953), 197–215, that the library was created for Tiglath-Pileser I, cannot be upheld.

temple, but there may also be information about the use of offerings or, in some cases, about products loaned to various persons. The remains of another archive M 5 (**Assur 5**) were excavated in area iD3V in the northeast part of the large forecourt of the Aššur temple in a later secondary context. Only a few of the large number of texts (at least 65, but possibly many more) have been published. The known texts date to the thirteenth century B.C. and are administrative documents often in the form of lists, but other text types, such as letters, are also attested. The administrative documents concern corn and people, and refer to several important individuals of the time.

A broken clay pot containing archive M 6 (**Assur 6**) with 115 clay tablets was unearthed in a secondary position in area eE5IV northeast of the Anu-Adad temple and northwest of the gate between that temple and the Old Palace. The tablets date from one calendar year during the reign of Aššur-dan I (1178–1133 B.C.), when his son Ninurta-tukul-Aššur was responsible for the government. The texts are administrative, concerning the receipt, treatment, and use of sheep and cattle given to Ninurta-tukul-Aššur. Mutta, bearing the titles *zāriqu* and *ša kurissi'e*, "fattener," was responsible for this administration.

Part of an administrative building with a large courtyard surrounded by rooms was excavated between the Ištar temple and the Sîn-Šamaš temple. The excavators unearthed the remains of archive M 7 (**Assur 7**), consisting of at least 420 clay tablets

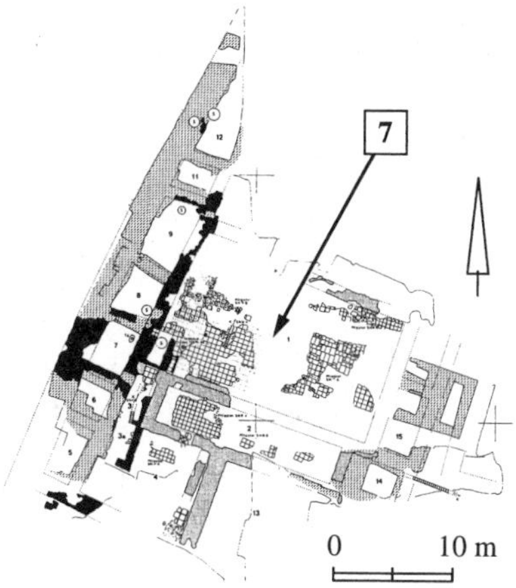

Plan 36. Assur.
Plan of official building, with archive **Assur 7**.
From P. Miglus, *Das Wohngebiet von Assur*, WVDOG 93 (1996), pl. 120.

in areas eE6V/7I and fA6V in the southern part of this courtyard. The tablets span a long period, 1273–1056 B.C., from the reign of Shalmaneser I to Aššur-bel-kala, with a concentration of tablets from the last third of this period. Almost all texts are administrative, often in the form of lists or tables. They deal with raw materials and finished goods belonging to the palace and placed under the responsibility of a series of men, such as Nabû-bela-uṣur, Saggi'u, Samnuḫa-ašared, and Apliya, all of whom bore the title *abarakku* (or *abarakku rabi'u*), "steward." Among the tablets were, in addition, at least one letter and 14 Old Assyrian tablets.

In the northwestern section of the city wall, a series of attack gates were discovered in area bB6I. Sixty clay tablets were found in a broken clay pot immediately southwest of these gates. Within the four southwesternmost gate openings, as well as inside the town wall in this area, at least 140 additional tablets and fragments were unearthed. Archive M 8 (**Assur 8**) consists of these two groups, the second much less known than the first. The tablets date to Shalmaneser I and Tukulti-Ninurta I (1273–1207 B.C.) and are mostly administrative notes or lists. In the pot there were also 17 letters dealing with administrative and legal matters. From the published texts, it appears that Ubru and several other men had important positions within the administrative unit. There may be a police or military function to this archive.[81]

2.3.1.3 *Archives in Private Houses*

In the area with private houses in the southern half of the main part of the city, which the excavation cut through with about four-meter-wide trenches each 100 meters of town area, six archives were unearthed (M 9–14). This should indicate that most of the archives in private houses from this period and area have not yet been unearthed.[82]

In a room of a private house in area iA8I the excavators unearthed archive M 9 (**Assur 9**) consisting of 140 clay tablets belonging to Kidin-Adad, his father Iddin-Kube, and, in some cases, his grandfather; also other persons are attested. Most of the texts cover the period ca. 1420–1300 B.C., a few are earlier, the oldest date ca. 1650 B.C. (possibly a few should be dated during the thirteenth century B.C.). Almost half the texts deal with loans; the loans may have, for example, fields as security. A number of other texts deal with the purchase of fields. There are also documents dealing with

81. O. Pedersén, *ALA* I (1985), 42–89 M 4–9, with bibliographical references; cf. H. Freydank, *Beiträge zur mittelassyrischen Chronologie und Geschichte*, SGKAO 21 (1991).

82. For archaeological details, see P. A. Miglus, *Das Wohngebiet von Assur: Stratigraphie und Architektur*, WVDOG 93 (1996).

adoption, inheritance, receipts, and other legal texts, including some royal documents, such as donations. Most of the texts document property, essentially fields acquired by the family.

In a house situated next to the main street, archive M 10 (**Assur 10**) of Urad-Šeru'a, his father Meli-Saḫ, and his grandfather Aššur-aḫa-iddina was unearthed in area dA8I. The 83 clay tablets and some fragments date from Adad-nirari I to Tukulti-Ninurta I (1305–1207 B.C.). Family members held important posts, such as governor (*bēl pāḫete*), in the state. Therefore, in addition to a large number of documents dealing with loans or obligations, a few purchase documents, and an interesting inventory of property stored in a storeroom (the objects listed include 25 boxes with clay tablets), there were several official administrative documents and lists from the public duties of Urad-Šeru'a in the northern provinces.

In a room in area dE7IV, above a grave adorned with more expensive grave goods than any other grave excavated in Assur, the excavators found more than 60 clay tablets from archive M 11 (**Assur 11**) belonging to Babu-aḫa-iddina, possibly the most influential man in Assyria aside from the king. The texts date from the reigns of Adad-nirari I to Tukulti-Ninurta I (1305–1207 B.C.). Most of the numerous letters and other documents concern the administration of, what seems to be, the private property of this man.

A small room to the right of the entrance to a house in area eA9I was found full of clay pots. In one of the pots, archive M 12 (**Assur 12**), consisting of about 60 clay tablets, was found. Most of the texts date to the reigns of Shalmaneser I and Tukulti-Ninurta I (1273–1207 B.C.), but there may exist earlier texts. The main person responsible was Uṣur-bel-šarra, with the titles *nāqidu*, "shepherd," and *bēl pāḫete*, "governor." He was in charge of cattle and sheep, and was responsible for the delivery of milk in skins or clay pots to the palace. There are several administrative notes and lists documenting his work. Riš-Aššur and a family that we are unable to relate to him or to Uṣur-bel-šarra are mentioned in several loan documents, as well as in a few purchase texts and other documents.

Archive M 13 (**Assur 13**), consisting of 56 clay tablets, was unearthed in a house in area eC9I. The texts date from the reigns of Shalmaneser I to Tukulti-Ninurta I (1273–1207 B.C.). The tablets are administrative notes, receipts, and accounts for Ṣilli-Aššur, who deals with metals, people, and horses, as well as for Atanaḫ-ili, an *alaḫḫinu*, who, according to the texts in the archive, prepares bread.

In a completely excavated house in fE10I, the excavators found archive M 14 (**Assur 14**), consisting of 35 clay tablets; in the same house were also three inscribed stone amulets. A majority of the tablets date to the reigns of Shalmaneser I and Tukulti-Ninurta I (1273–1207 B.C.). Several other tablets are from a much earlier period approximately the reigns of Eriba-Adad and Aššur-uballiṭ (1390–1363 B.C.). The texts from the earlier period document the acquisition of fields or record loans with fields as security. Many of the texts from the later period record the administration of sheep by Adad-zera-iqiša, as well as several loans of his.[83]

2.3.2 *Kar-Tukulti-Ninurta (Tulul al-'Aqar)*

During the reign of Tukulti-Ninurta I (1243–1207 B.C.), the capital was moved from Assur to a place he named Kar-Tukulti-Ninurta (modern Tulul al-'Aqar), situated slightly north of Assur, on the opposite bank of the Tigris. W. Bachmann directed excavations on the site 1913–1914, and R. Dittmann continued work 1986–1989. The main remains date to the reign of Tukulti-Ninurta I, but the site continued to be inhabited during later Middle Assyrian and Neo-Assyrian times. Important remains include the large palace complex in the northwestern part of the city, near the Tigris, two temples, and the city wall with its gates.[84]

2.3.2.1 *Administrative Archives in Official Buildings*

Although most of the clay tablets still remain unpublished, some general observations can be made about the four unearthed archives that date to the reign of Tukulti-Ninurta I. From the east corner of the large terrace in the southeast part of the palace complex, three large rooms, possibly magazines, extended in a southeastern direction. In one of the small rooms north of the magazines, the remains of an archive (**Kar-Tukulti-Ninurta 1**) with a number of large administrative documents, often lists, were excavated. Another archive (**Kar-Tukulti-Ninurta 2**) with similar types of texts was unearthed in Room 7 of the palace, situated in the area of rooms extending in a southeastern direction from the south corner of the terrace; this archive included also an inventory of a large number of precious objects. The Aššur temple, situated southeast of the palace, consisted of a low temple built with a zikkurrat on its southwestern side. A few meters southwest of the zikkurrat was a building with, according to the excavators, a staircase, possibly leading to the zikkurrat. In the room with this staircase, an archive (**Kar-Tukulti-Ninurta 3**) of at least 25, perhaps 50, clay tablets

83. O. Pedersén, *ALA* I (1985), 89–125 M 9–14, with bibliographical references.

84. As an introduction to the site, cf. R. Dittmann, "Kar-Tukulti-Ninurta," *OEANE* 3 (1997), 269–271. The archaeological publications are T. Eickhoff, *Kār Tukulti Ninurta: Eine mittelassyrische Kult- und Residenzstadt*, ADOG 21 (1985); and (preliminary) R. Dittmann, "Ausgrabungen der Freien Universität Berlin in Assur und Kār-Tukultī-Ninurta in den Jahren 1986–89," *MDOG* 122 (1990), 157–171; cf. also T. Eickhoff, "Kār-Tukulti-Ninurta. B. Archäologisch," *RLA* 5 (1976–1980), 456–459.

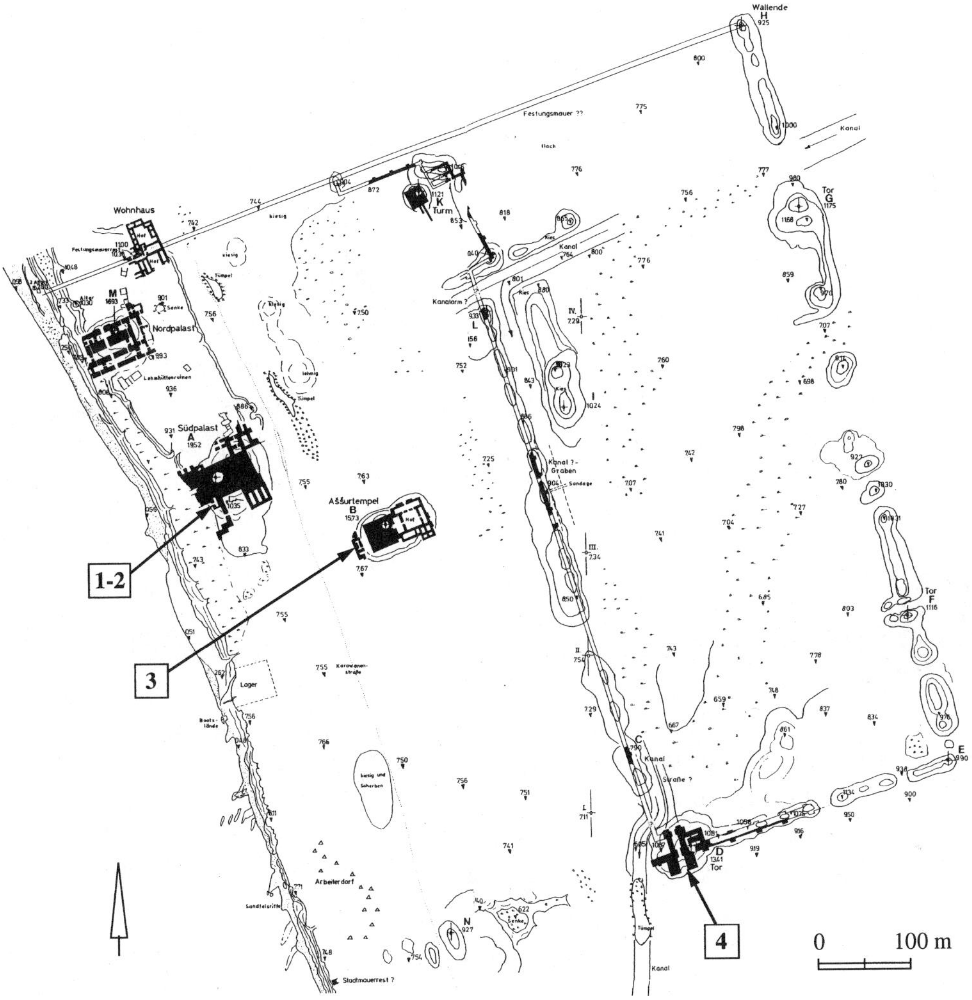

Plan 37. Kar-Tukulti-Ninurta.
General plan with archives **Kar-Tukulti-Ninurta 1-4**.
From T. Eickhoff, *Kār Tukulti Ninurta*, ADOG 21 (1985), pl. 1.

probably concerning administrative matters was unearthed. In Gate D of the city wall, which divided the inner city from the southern living quarters, six clay tablets, mainly administrative lists, constitute a small archive (**Kar-Tukulti-Ninurta 4**).[85]

2.3.3 Šibaniba (Tell Billa)

Šibaniba (modern Tell Billa) is situated in the central Assyrian area northeast of Nineveh, 12 kilometers southeast of Dur-Šarrukin. The tell had its largest extension along a west-to-east axis and measured ca. 600 × 500 meters. E. A. Speiser and C. Bache, who directed American excavations 1930–1934, unearthed only limited areas in the northeastern and southwestern parts of the site. In deep soundings, material dating to the Jemdet-Naṣr, Early Dynastic, and Old Akkadian-Ur III periods have been established, but the major excavations were concentrated at Mitannian Level 3, Middle Assyrian Level 2, and Neo-Assyrian Level 1. At the northern corner of the tell are remains of an even later occupation. (For the later periods, see 3.1.6.)[86]

2.3.3.1 An Archive, Possibly Administrative

In Level 2, the excavators unearthed 67 clay tablets dating to the reigns of Shalmaneser I (1273–1244 B.C.) and Tukulti-Ninurta I (1243–1207 B.C.). Most of them came from a building in area R-S 3-5, situated on the southern side of a large wadi, which had cut away the northern part of the building. Due to the incomplete publication of the archaeological material, the building cannot be reconstructed and the number of tablets found together cannot be determined. However, it is clear that most of the tablets belonged to an archive (**Šibaniba 1**) of Aššur-kašid and his son Sîn-apla-eriš, both bearing the title *ḫassiḫlu*, "district chief." Possibly the texts of Aššur-šuma-iddina, *rab alāni*, "mayor," belong here. The texts are documents, often concerning

85. Cf. T. Eickhoff, *Kār Tukulti Ninurta*, ADOG 21 (1985), 22, 31, 39, 61–94; and H. Freydank, "Kār-Tukulti-Ninurta. A. Philologisch," *RLA* 5 (1976–1980), 455–456; I thank R. Dittmann for sharing with me information about some details of the provenance of the archives. The texts are being prepared for publication by H. Freydank.

86. Only incomplete preliminary publications of the archaeological materials exist. Only a preliminary contour plan of the tell and a plan of Level I of the southwest area has been published. Cf. articles and letters by E. A. Speiser in *BASOR* 40 (1930), 11–14; 41 (1931), 19–24; 42 (1931), 12–13; 44 (1931), 2–5; 45 (1932), 32–34; 46 (1932), 1–9; 48 (1932), 35; C. Bache in *BASOR* 49 (1933), 12–14; 50 (1933), 3–7; 51 (1933), 20–22; and E. A. Speiser, "The Pottery of Tell Billa: A Preliminary Account," *Museum Journal* 23 (1932), 249–283, pls. XLVII–LXXII; and C. Bache, "The First Assyrian Level at Tell Billa," *Museum Journal* 24 (1935), 33–48, pl. XI.

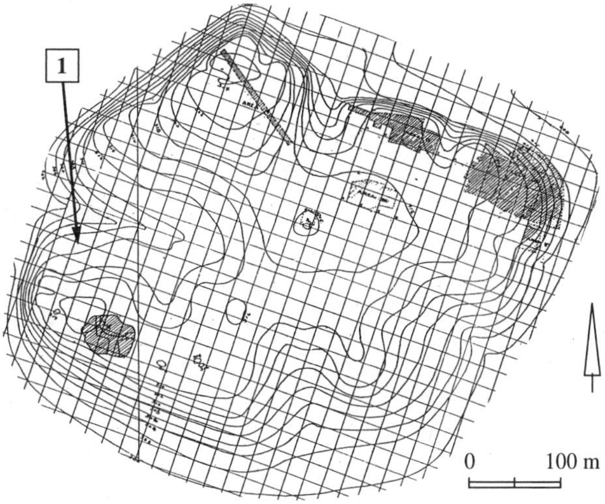

Plan 38. Šibaniba.
General plan with archive **Šibaniba 1**.
From C. Bache, *Museum Journal* 23 (1932), pl. XLVII.

loans given and received, receipts, administrative documents including different kinds of lists, some letters, and two lexical lists.[87]

2.3.4 Tell Rimah

Tell Rimah, ancient Qaṭara or possibly Karana, is situated west of the central Assyrian area 13 kilometers south of modern Tell ʻAfar and more than 60 kilometers west of Mosul. D. Oates and T. A. Carter conducted excavations from 1964–1968 on the site. The tell is about 700 × 600 meters, and dates from prehistoric times to the Neo-Assyrian period. A monumental temple could be followed in Area A through several periods of occupation. Archives have been unearthed dating to the Old Babylonian period. The excavated Middle Assyrian Level, of interest here, includes the temple area and private houses with a small shrine.[88]

87. J. J. Finkelstein, "Cuneiform Texts from Tell Billa," *JCS* 7 (1953), 114, 119–136, nos. 1–67; cf. E. A. Speiser, "Gleanings from the Billa Texts," *FS Koschaker* (1939), 141–150; E. A. Speiser, *BASOR* 46 (1932), 2–3, 6–8; and C. Bache, *BASOR* 51 (1933), 22.

88. As introductions to the site, cf. S. Dalley, "Karanā," *RLA* 5 1976–1980, as well as S. Dalley, "Rimah, Tell er-," *OEANE* 4 (1997), 428–430, which contains further bibliography. For a bibliography concerning the ancient name of the city, cf. J. Fincke, *RGTC* 10 (1993), 133.

2.3.4.1 Archives in the Temple Area

In the area of the temple, two (or possibly three) archives were excavated at Level Ib. They possibly originated from an upper story above or near the antechamber of the temple. Both archives are dated to the reigns of Shalmaneser I (1273–1244 B.C.) and Tukulti-Ninurta I (1243–1207 B.C.). Fragments of a jar were found with 25 clay tablets, the remains of the archive (**Tell Rimah 1**) of the three sons of Ili-naṣir.[89] Most of the documents are loans or payments of loans; of unusual interest is the division of inheritance among the three sons of Ili-naṣir.[90]

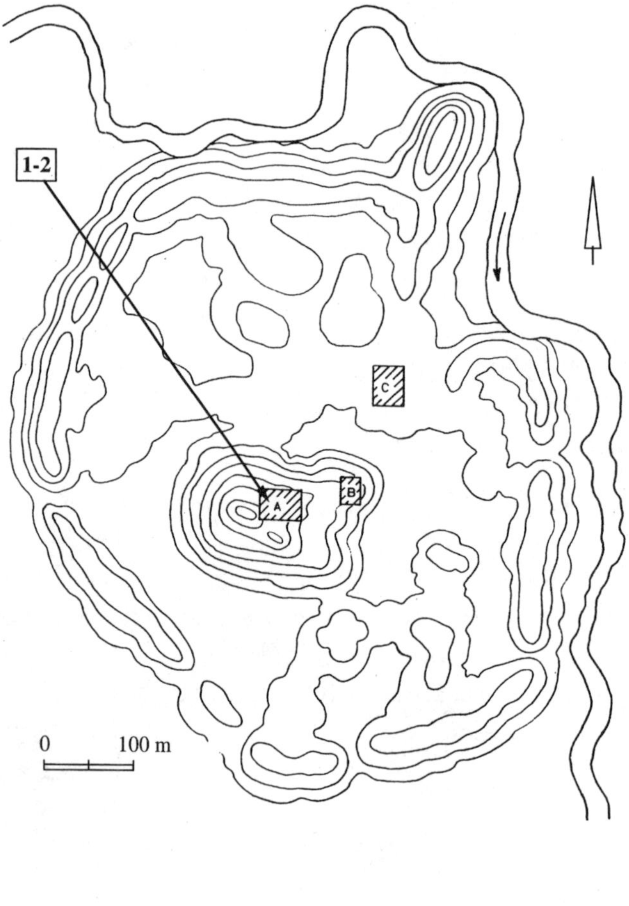

Plan 39. Tell Rimah. General plan with archives **Tell Rimah 1-2**. From D. Oates, *Iraq* 27 (1965), pl. XII.

89. D. Oates, *Iraq* 27 (1965), 75.

90. D. J. Wiseman, J. N. Postgate, and J. D. Hawkins, *Iraq* 30 (1968), 186–187, pls. LXVII–LXXIV.

In the temple courtyard fragments of another jar were associated with about 100 tablets forming an archive (**Tell Rimah 2**) of Abu-ṭab, his sons, and a few other members of his family. Nearby were about 40 tablets from the father and brother of Abu-ṭab, which may have originally either belonged to the same archive or constituted a separate one.[91] Most of the tablets in Abu-ṭab's archive are documents concerning loans, payments of loans, and receipts; but there are also some purchase documents and other legal documents, as well as some letters.[92]

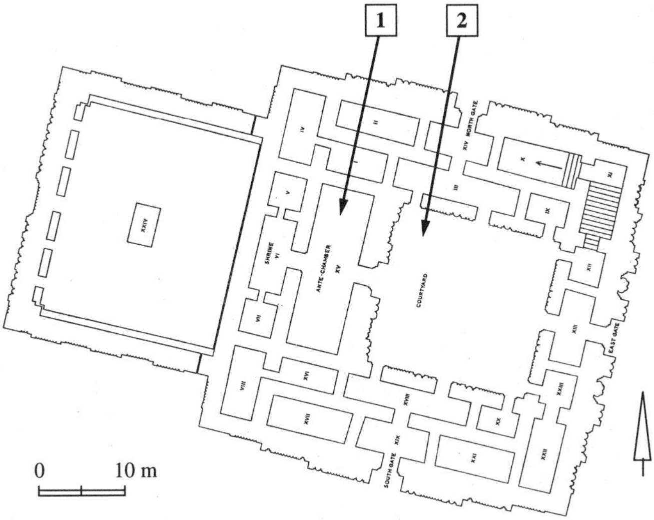

Plan 40. Tell Rimah.
Plan of temple with archives **Tell Rimah 1-2**.
From D. Oates, *Iraq* 29 (1967), pl. XXX.

91. D. Oates, *Iraq* 28 (1966), 130–131, and D. Oates, *Iraq* 29 (1967), 90–91.

92. H. W. F. Saggs, *Iraq* 30 (1968), 154–174, pls. XLIII–LXVI; and D. J. Wiseman, *Iraq* 30 (1968), 175–205. According to standard readings of cuneiform signs, there is an Abu-ṭab son of Šadâna-bel-nišešu and an Abu-ṭab son of Šadâna-ašared(SAG) as main persons in this archive. This cannot be completely excluded, but it would be much easier to understand the archive if we assume that the Middle Assyrian scribes either invented a pseudo-logogram SAG = *bel-nišešu*, or used both names for the same person.

2.3.5 Admannu (Tell 'Ali)

Admannu (modern Tell 'Ali) is situated on the southern side of the lower Zab river, 42 kilometers west of Kirkuk, not far from the earlier Kurruḫanni (cf. 2.1.2). There has so far not been any scientific excavations of the tell.

2.3.5.1 Remains of an Archive

In 1978 irregular excavations unearthed the remains of an archive (**Admannu 1**) consisting of 24 clay tablets, as yet unpublished. The majority of the tablets mention the shepherd Ekuza, who seems to be responsible for the archive. The tablets are Middle Assyrian administrative documents said to date to the reigns of Adad-nirari I, Shalmaneser I, and Tukulti-Ninurta I (1305–1207 B.C.). The documents basically are notes on the delivery or receipt of sheep, wool, or textiles.[93]

2.3.6 Dur-Katlimmu (Tall Šeḫ Ḥamad)

Dur-Katlimmu (modern Tall Šeḫ Ḥamad) is situated on the eastern side of the lower part of the Khabur river. H. Kühne has directed the German excavations since 1978. Occupation is attested from the Late Uruk period until Roman times, that is, from the end of the fourth millennium B.C. until ca. A.D. 650, with a limited Islamic settlement thereafter. The main findings have been from the Middle Assyrian and Neo-Assyrian periods. From about 2000 B.C. the city measured ca. 250 × 350 meters and consisted of the Citadel on the old tell and Lower Town I southeast of it. This was the size of the Middle Assyrian city of interest here, which was destroyed by fire. During the following Neo-Assyrian period, the city expanded greatly to the north-east (cf. section 3.1.7).[94]

93. Cf. B. K. Ismail, "Informationen über Tontafeln aus Tell-Ali," *Gesellschaft und Kultur im Alten Vorderasien*, SGKAO 15 (1982), 117–119.

94. As a short introduction to the site, cf. H. Kühne, "Sheikh Ḥamad, Tell," *OEANE* 5 (1997), 25–26. The results of the excavations will be published in the series Berichte der Ausgrabung Tall Šēḫ Ḥamad/ Dūr-Katlimmu (=BATSH). So far H. Kühne, ed., BATSH 1 (1991); P. Pfälzner, BATSH 3 (1995); and E. C. Cancik-Kirschbaum, BATSH 4 (1996), have been published; they contains further bibliographical references. Cf. the preliminary reports by H. Kühne, "Tall Šeḫ Ḥamad/Dūr-katlimmu 1981–1983," *AfO* 31 (1984), 166–170; H. Kühne, "Tall Šeḫ Ḥamad/Dūr-katlimmu 1984," *AfO* 31 (1984), 170–178; and H. Kühne, "Tall Šeḫ Ḥamad/Dūr-katlimmu 1988–1990," *AfO* 40–41 (1993–1994), 267–272.

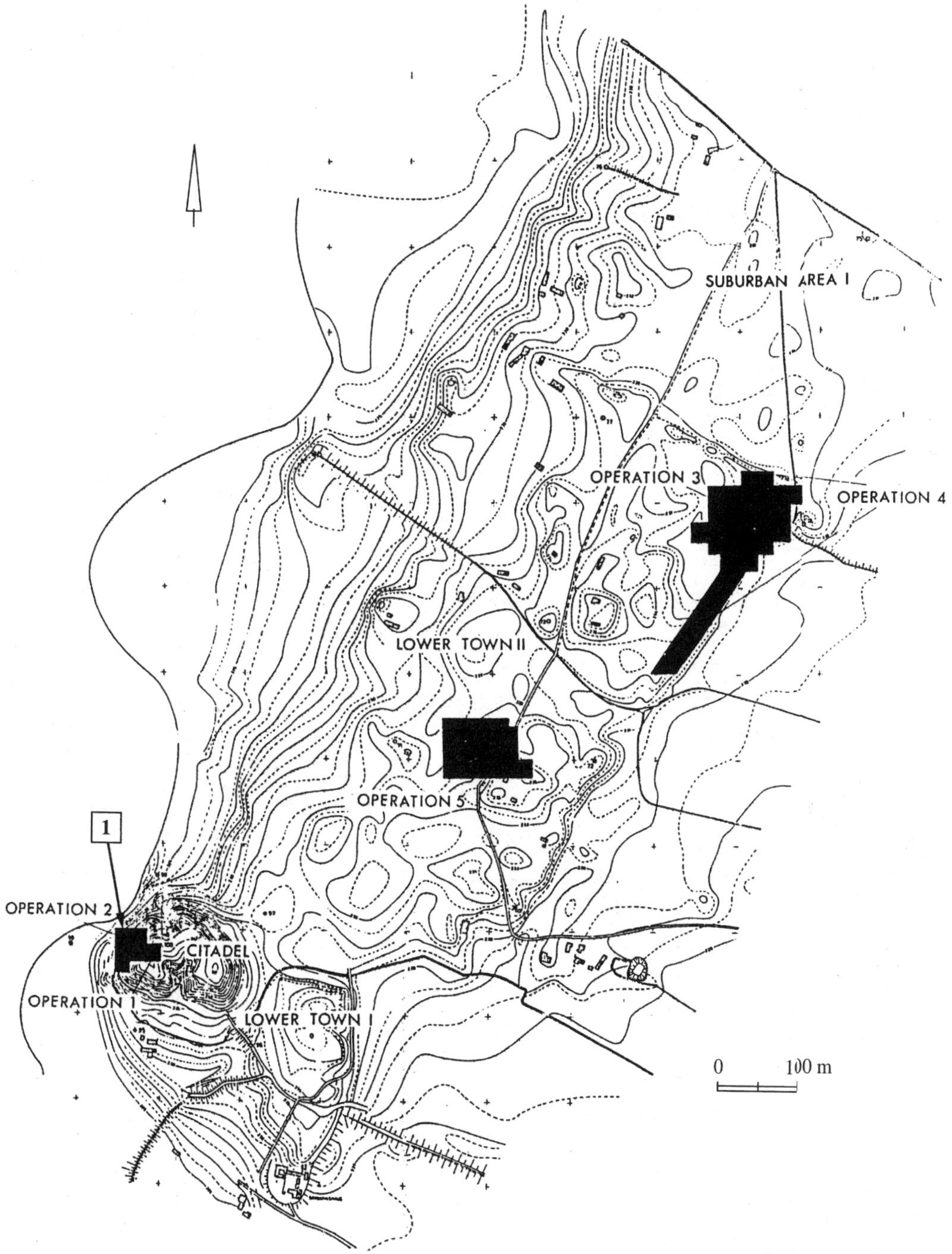

Plan 41. Dur-Katlimmu.
General plan with archive **Dur-Katlimmu 1**.
From H. Kühne, *SAAB* 7 (1993), 90.

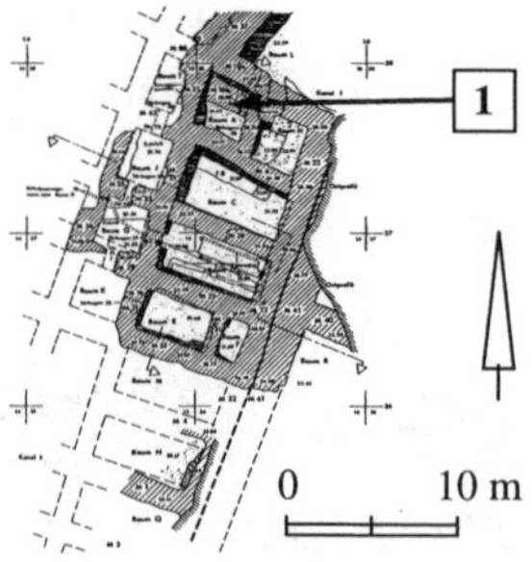

Plan 42. Dur-Katlimmu.
Plan of excavated section of Building P with archive **Dur-Katlimmu 1**.
From H. Kühne, *AAAS* 33 (1983), 246 fig. 6.

2.3.6.1 *Archive in a Possible Palace*

On the western slope of the tell, excavators unearthed sections of the large Building P, possibly the palace of the governor, with at least two floors. An archive (**Dur-Katlimmu 1**) consisting of about 600 clay tablets together with jar sealings, bullae, and clay vessels had fallen down from the collapsed upper floor into Room A of the basement. The texts date to the reigns of Shalmaneser I (1273–1244 B.C.) and Tukulti-Ninurta I (1243–1207 B.C.), and come from the provincial palace administration of this area. The owner of the archive seems to be Aššur-iddin, a high official with the title *sukkallu*, later on even called *sukkallu rabi'u*. There are long lists of grain for various individuals, lists of cattle given to shepherds, documents concerning loans of grain made from the palace by officials, receipts of materials given for *iškaru*-work, and an itinerary. There is also a series of 31 letters (with additional fragments of envelopes) dealing with administrative matters, one of them from the Assyrian king.[95]

2.3.7 *Tell Fekhariya*

Tell Fekhariya is situated on the east side of the upper part of the Khabur river. The tell covers approximately 800 × 900 meters. An American expedition directed by

95. The letters have been published together with a general introduction by E. C. Cancik-Kirschbaum, *Die Mittelassyrischen Briefe aus Tall Šēḫ Ḥamad*, BATSH 4, Texte 1 (1996). Cf. also W. Röllig, "Ein Itinerar aus Dūr-Katlimmu," *DaM* 1 (1983), 279–284; and A. Tsukimoto, "Aus einer japanischen Privatsammlung: Drei Verwaltungstexte und ein Brief aus mittelassyrischer Zeit," *WO* 23 (1992), 21–38.

C. W. McEwan could conduct only a few soundings in 1940 before it had to leave the tell on short notice. Older levels therefore were not reached, but in the eastern part of the city they unearthed parts of a Middle Assyrian house in Sounding VI, and some rooms of a Palace in Sounding IX, with further occupation in Roman or Byzantine times. In 1955 and 1956, A. Moortgat with a German expedition made a few soundings and established an occupation during the Mitannian period. In Neo-Assyrian times the city was called Sikani, and it seems probable that it was the Mitannian capital Waššukkanni, in Middle Assyrian texts called Uššukkanni or Aššukani.[96]

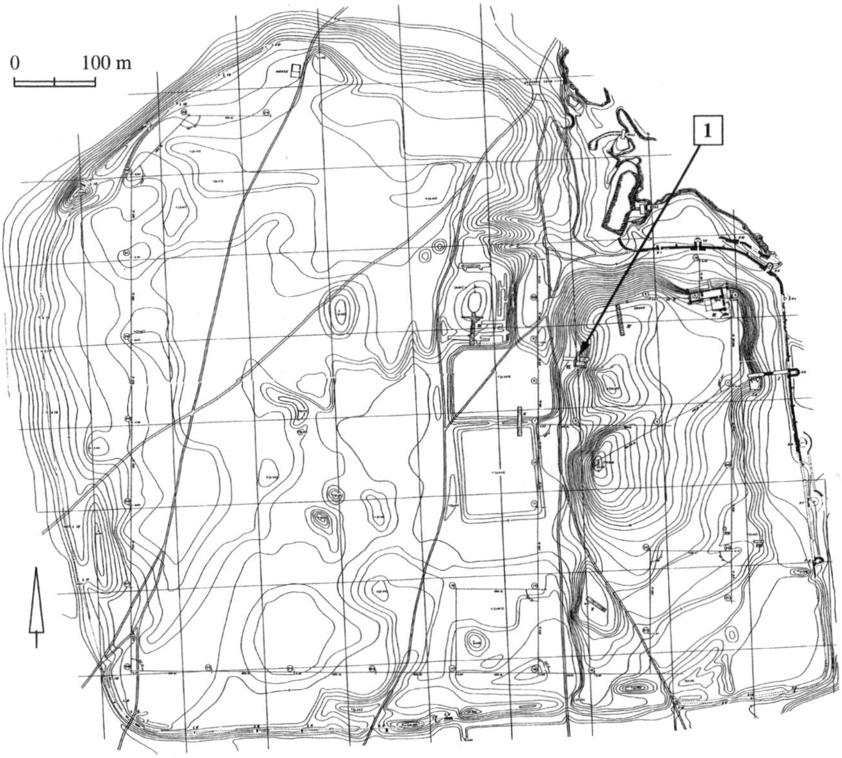

Plan 43. Tell Fekhariya.
General plan with archive **Tell Fekhariya 1**.
From C. W. McEwan et al., *Soundings at Tell Fakhariyah* (1958), pl. 87.

96. For a short introduction to the site, cf. A. Abou Assaf, "Fakhariyah, Tell," *OEANE* 2 (1997), 300–301. The main archaeological publications are C. W. McEwan, et al., *Soundings at Tell Fakhariyah*, OIP 79 (1958); A. Moortgat, *Archäologische Forschungen der Max Freiherr von Oppenheim-Stiftung im nördlichen*

2.3.7.1 Remains of an Archive

The partly excavated house in Sounding VI, Floor 2 was probably a private residence, although it has been suggested that, on the basis of contents, it may have been a temple. Here the excavators found ten clay tablets and a number of clay bullae. Perhaps all of the tablets are the remains of an archive (**Tell Fekhariya 1**) dating to the reigns of Shalmaneser I (1273–1244 B.C.) and Tukulti-Ninurta I (1243–1207 B.C.). There are letters, loans, two documents dated the same day about a division of property, and two lists.[97]

2.3.8 Ḫarbe (Tell Chuera)

Ḫarbe or Ḫurbe (modern Tell Chuera) is situated in northernmost Syria between the Khabur and Balikh rivers on the eastern side of Wadi Chuera, 6 kilometers south of the Syrian-Turkish border. A. Moortgat directed German excavations in 1958–1976, U. Moortgat-Correns in 1982–1985, and W. Orthmann since 1986. The large tell, 1 × 1 kilometers with a higher mound about 600 × 600 meters in the center, was a main city in the Early Dynastic period, ca. 2800–2300 B.C. But the city was inhabited also during the Mitanni and Middle Assyrian periods, about 1600–1100 B.C., although limited to the northeastern part of the central tell.[98]

2.3.8.1 Archive in the Governor's Palace

A section of the large house or palace of the governor has been unearthed in the Middle Assyrian settlement. From the monumental Entrance 1 in the southeastern

Mesopotamien 1955, Arbeitsgemeinschaft für Forschung des Landes Nordrhein-Westfalen, Abhandlung 62 (1957); and A. Moortgat, *Archäologische Forschungen der Max Freiherr von Oppenheim-Stiftung im nördlichen Mesopotamien 1956*, Wissenschaftliche Abhandlungen der Arbeitsgemeinschaft für Forschung des Landes Nordrhein-Westfalen 7 (1957). The famous Neo-Assyrian/Aramaic statue found in 1979 has been published by A. Abou-Assaf, P. Bordreuil, and A. R. Millard, *La Statue de Tell Fekherye* (1982). For the identification of the ancient name, cf., e.g., K. Nashef, *RGTC* 5 (1982), 277–278, with more references.

97. H. G. Güterbock, "The Cuneiform Tablets," in C. W. McEwan, et al., *Soundings*, 86–90; cf. the plan of the house on pl. 6A.

98. As a short introduction to the site, cf. W. Orthmann, "Chuera, Tell," *OEANE* 1 (1997), 491–492, with some bibliographical references. The preliminary archaeological results are published in the series *Tell Chuēra in Nordost-Syrien*, eds. A. Moortgat, U. Moortgat-Correns, W. Orthmann, et al. (1960–); and especially W. Orthmann, et al., *Ausgrabungen in Tell Chuēra in Nordost-Syrien I: Vorbericht über die Grabungskampagnen 1986 bis 1992*, Vorderasiatische Forschungen der Max Freiherr von Oppenheim-Stiftung 2 (1995). Cf. also the preliminary survey by U. Moortgat-Correns, "Ḫuēra, Tell (Tell Chuēra)," *RLA* 4 (1972–1975), 480–487, and the short reports by W. Orthmann, *Tell Chuera, Ausgrabungen der Max Freiherr von Oppenheim-Stiftung in Nordost-Syrien* (1990); and W. Orthmann, *AJA* 98 (1994), 120–122.

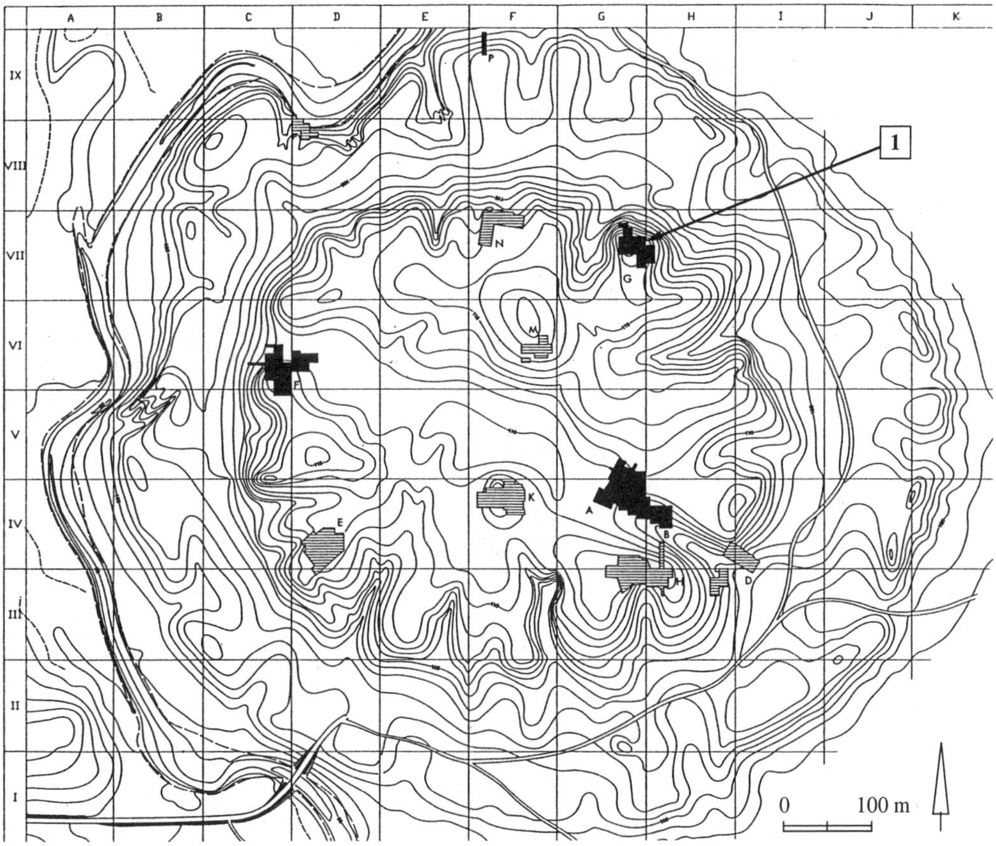

Plan 44. Ḫarbe.
General plan with archive **Ḫarbe 1**.
From W. Orthmann et al., *Ausgrabungen in Tell Chuēra in Nordost-Syrien* I (1995), folding 2.

outer wall, a Passage 7 opens onto a central Courtyard 8 surrounded by rooms. Southwest of Passage 7, inside a small Room 2, the excavators during the summer of 1992 unearthed in Room 3 (area Gi.VII6) at Level 3b an archive (**Ḫarbe 1**) of about 60 clay tablets. The findspots of the tablets suggest that the tablets were originally placed on wooden shelves in a niche in the northeastern wall of the room between two doors. This was the administrative archive of the governor, who, at least for a period, had the name Suti'u. The unpublished texts date to the time of Tukulti-Ninurta I (1243–1207 B.C.) and consist of 20 letters and 40 administrative documents, mostly lists of rations or lists of persons, but also some notes on delivery. Together

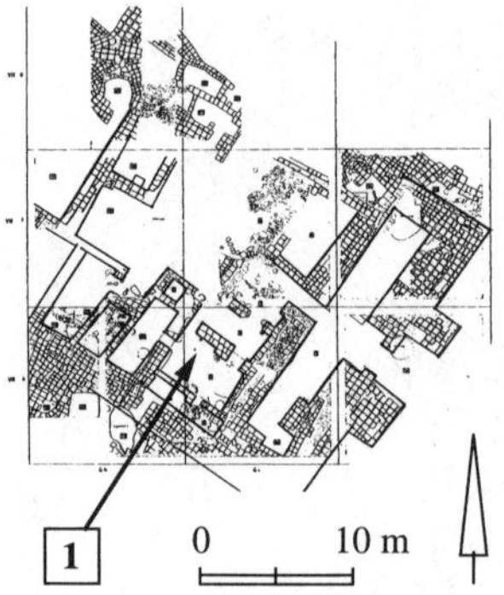

Plan 45. Ḫarbe.
Plan of Governor's Palace with archive **Ḫarbe 1**.
From W. Orthmann et al., *Ausgrabungen in Tell Chuēra in Nordost-Syrien* I (1995), folding 18.

with the texts were a few fragments of seal impressions on clay. In a lower level of the palace, remains of an earlier archive have been attested.[99]

2.3.9 Tell Sabi Abyad

Tell Sabi Abyad is situated on the eastern side of the Balikh river, 65 kilometers north of Raqqa in northern Syria. The tell covers some 200 × 250 meters. Recent excavations directed by P. M. M. G. Akkermans have documented an extensive settlement in the sixth millennium B.C. and a smaller settlement in the Middle Assyrian period. From the Middle Assyrian period, during the reigns of Shalmaneser I (1273–1244 B.C.) and Tukulti-Ninurta I (1243–1207 B.C.), is a walled settlement, ca. 60 × 65 meters, with a central fortress, a partly palace-like administration building west of it, and several other buildings filling out the area inside the surrounding walls.[100]

99. A preliminary report of the texts can be found in C. Kühne, "Ein mittelassyrisches Verwaltungsarchiv und andere Keilschrifttexte," in W. Orthmann, et al., *Ausgrabungen in Tell Chuēra in Nordost-Syrien* I (1995), 203–225. Cf. also the report of the excavation of the building by H. Klein, "Die Grabung in der mittelassyrischen Siedlung," in W. Orthmann, et al., *Ausgrabungen* I (1995), 185–201, Beilage 2 and 18.

100. Cf. P. M. M. G. Akkermans, "Sabi Abyad," *AJA* 98 (1994), 114–116, and the presentation by P. M. M. G. Akkermans at the RAI 1994 in Berlin. The excavation of the Middle Assyrian settlement before the finding of the archive has been summarized in P. M. M. G. Akkermans, J. Limpens, and R. H. Spoor, "On the Frontier of Assyria: Excavations at Tell Sabi Abyad, 1991," *Akkadica* 84–85 (1993), 1–52.

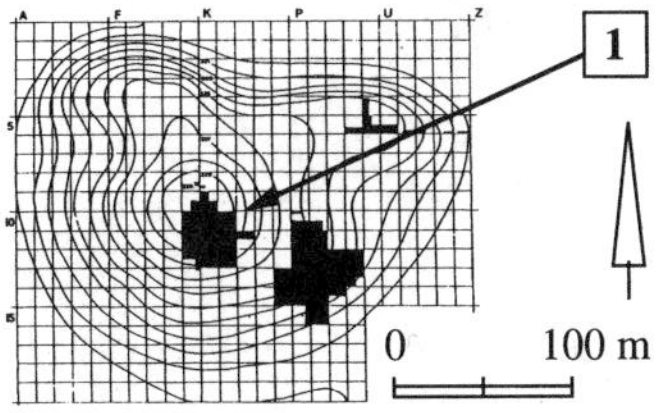

Plan 46. Tell Sabi Abyad.
General plan with archive **Tell Sabi Abyad 1**.
P. M. M. G. Akkermans et al., *Akkadica* 84-85 (1993), 4 fig. 2a.

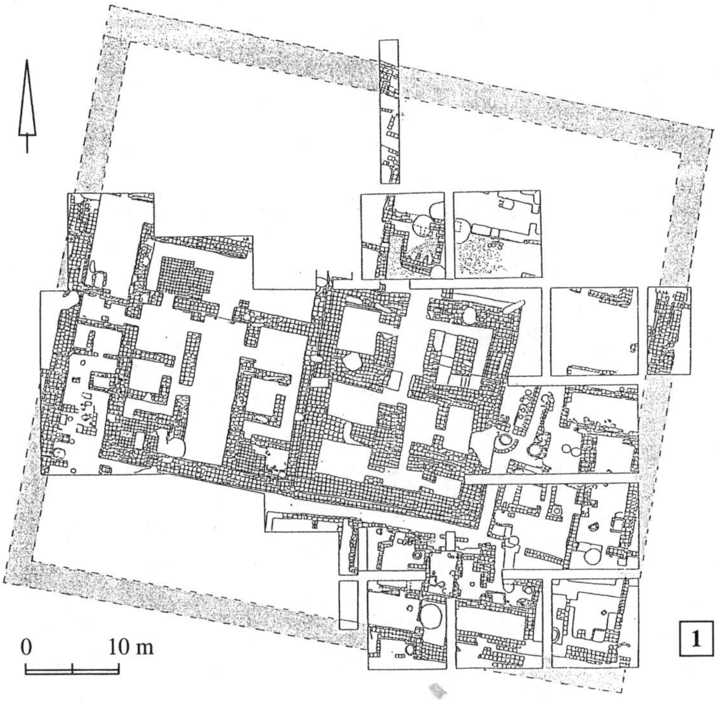

Plan 47. Tell Sabi Abyad.
Plan of fortress with surrounding buildings. Remains of archive **Tell Sabi Abyad 1** were spread around in these houses around the fortress.
Courtesy P. M. M. G. Akkermans.

2.3.9.1 *Archive of the Governor*

In some of the rooms of the building southeast of the fortress, the excavators unearthed 50 clay tablets. These still unpublished tablets are reported to be the archive (**Tell Sabi Abyad 1**) of Tamite, the Assyrian governor. Among the tablets, 12 letters and 14 administrative texts have been identified. Some tablets report relations with Ili-ipadda, the Assyrian prince, who served as viceroy of Ḫanigalbat.[101]

2.3.10 *Tell Fray*

Tell Fray was situated on the northern bank of the Euphrates, 20 kilometers west of the Tabqa dam, next to the village Safrah, in an area now covered by the water of the dam. In 1972 and 1973 excavations were conducted by Syrian, Syro-Italian, and Syro-American expeditions. The tell measures 300 × 270 meters. Five main levels date from the Early Bronze Age to the Islamic period. During the time of Level IV, which was destroyed ca. 1270 B.C., possibly by the Assyrians, the town had its largest extent. From this level, the excavators have unearthed in the northern area a temple, and in the central area of the mound another temple, a "small palace" (or a large private house), and a road along a north-south axis surrounded by private houses.

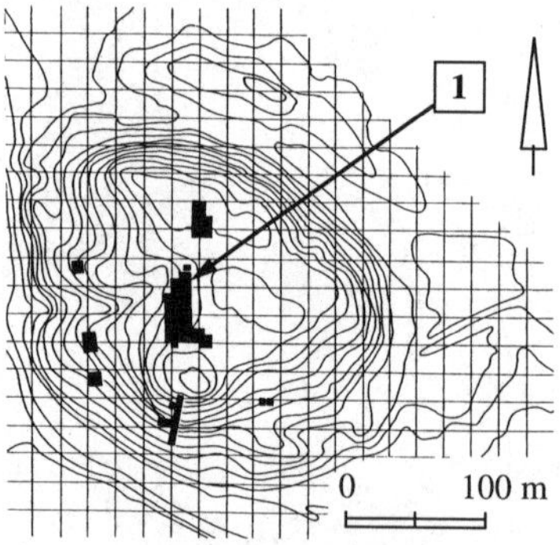

Plan 48. Tell Fray.
General plan with archive **Tell Fray 1**.
From A. Bounni and P. Matthiae, *Archéologia* 140 (1980), 32.

101. Cf. the presentation by F. Wiggerman at the RAI 1994 in Berlin. Only two tablets from a nearby house have been published by R. Jas, "Two Middle-Assyrian Lists of Personal Names from Sabi Abyad," *Akkadica* 67 (1990), 33–39.

2.3.10.1 *Archive in Private House*

The north house on the western side of the north-south road in the central area of Level IV of the tell is reported to have had a complex plan. Here the excavators unearthed an archive (**Tell Fray 1**) consisting of 11 clay tablets in two rooms inside an inner courtyard. The unpublished texts have often been referred to as Middle Assyrian. They have been described as three letters and some legal documents said to be dated to the fourteenth and thirteenth centuries B.C. The supposed Middle Assyrian character of the texts is the reason for inclusion in the Middle Assyrian area here. On the other hand, there were also relations with the Hittite area as shown by, for example, a bulla with the impression of the seal of Ḫattušili III in the small palace more to the south in the same excavation area.[102]

2.4 *Middle Babylonian Area*

The archives and libraries with cuneiform texts from the Middle Babylonian area date to the second half of the Kassite period, ca. 1350–1150 B.C., with a few tablets either somewhat earlier or later.

The limited excavations of sites and levels from this period have resulted in rather few archives or libraries found. This is the situation in the Kassite capital Dur-Kurigalzu (2.4.1) and in the old capital Babylon (2.4.2), as well as in Ur (2.4.4) and Tell Imlihiye (2.4.5). In Nippur (2.4.3) several large archives, especially from the old, less well-documented, excavations have been unearthed. Many more important archives and libraries surely existed, but the appropriate levels are covered by later ones and have therefore not been examined.

The preserved texts are written with cuneiform script on clay tablets. Most texts are in the Babylonian dialect of the Akkadian language, but Sumerian was also used. The Babylonian scribes dated texts by the year of the king's reign. With a margin of error of only a few years, the chronology is fixed for this period and had the excavations and publications been of better quality our knowledge of this period would be far more advanced.

102. Cf. A. Bounni and P. Matthiae, "Tell Fray, ville frontière entre hittites et assyriens au XIIIe siècle av. J-C," *Archéologia* 140 (1980), 30–39; P. Matthiae, "Ittiti ed Assiri a Tell Fray: Lo scavo di una città medio-siriana sull'Eufrate," *SMEA* 22 (1980), 35–51; A. Bounni, "Tell Fray," in O. Rouault and M. Masetti-Rouault, eds., *L'Eufrate e il tempo: Le civiltà del medio Eufrate e della Gezira siriana (1993)*, 199–202; and A. Bounni, P. Matthiae, and C. Shaath, "Tell Fray 1973," in A. Bounni, *Antiquités de l'Euphrate: Exposition des découvertes de la campagne internationale de sauvegarde des antiquités de l'Euphrate* (1974), 33–41. The texts have recently been assigned to G. Wilhelm for publication.

In addition to the archives and libraries discussed below, individual tablets or small remains of archives have been found at several other sites in the same area.[103]

2.4.1 Dur-Kurigalzu ('Aqr Quf)

Dur-Kurigalzu (modern 'Aqr Quf) is situated about 30 kilometers west of Baghdad. From 1942–1945, T. Baqir, assisted by S. Lloyd, directed Iraqi excavations on the site. The city covered 600 meters by more than two kilometers in a northwestern to southeastern direction. It was founded and used as the capital in the Kassite period, and there are only minor remains of later periods. In the northwest (Tell al-'Abyad), the large palace complex is situated. About a kilometer to its southeast is the Enlil temple with the zikkurrat, as well as some associated temples.[104]

2.4.1.1 Administrative Archives in Palace

The large palace complex consisted of several palaces built around inner courtyards. If all buildings that the archaeologists unearthed in this area belonged to the palace complex, it covered more than 300 × 300 meters. The walls of most rooms were traced near the present surface and only a few rooms were excavated to the floor. This is probably the reason why so few archives have been unearthed in this large palace area. Palace A seems to have been the main building, with the throne hall northeast of the courtyard. The rooms inside the eastern corner of this courtyard were used for keeping valuable objects, as shown by many broken fragments of gold and other valuable materials in Room 5 of Level IV and Room 15 of Level III. In these rooms a few tablets were unearthed. An archive (**Dur-Kurigalzu 1**) of 64 clay tablets and fragments was found in the small recessed "chamber" in the wall of Room 4 from Level II. This room is situated between the two rooms with the valuable objects. Most

103. A catalogue of dated texs from the Kassite period can be found in J. A. Brinkman, *Materials and Studies for Kassite History I: A Catalogue of Cuneiform Sources Pertaining to Specific Monarchs of the Kassite Dynasty* (1976). For Mê-Turran (Tell Sib/Tell Ḥaddad/Tell Baradan) and Tell Zubeidi in the Hamrin area, cf. K. Kessler, "Zu den Tontafeln," and "Die Tontafeln," in R. M. Boehmer and H.-W. Dämmer, *Tell Imlihiye, Tell Zubeidi, Tell Abbas*, BaF 7 (1985), 18 and 74–79, as well as K. Kessler, "Drei Keilschrifttexte aus Tell Baradān," *FS Boehmer* (1995), 281–283.

104. For a short introduction to the site, cf. H. Kühne, "'Aqar Quf," *OEANE* 1 (1997), 156–157. T. Baqir, "Iraq Government Excavations at 'Aqar Qūf, First Interim Report 1942–1943," *Iraq Supplement* (1944); T. Baqir, "Iraq Government Excavations at 'Aqar Qūf, Second Interim Report 1943–1944," *Iraq Supplement* (1945); and T. Baqir, "Iraq Government Excavations at 'Aqar Qūf, Third Interim Report 1944–1945," *Iraq* 8 (1946), 73–93.

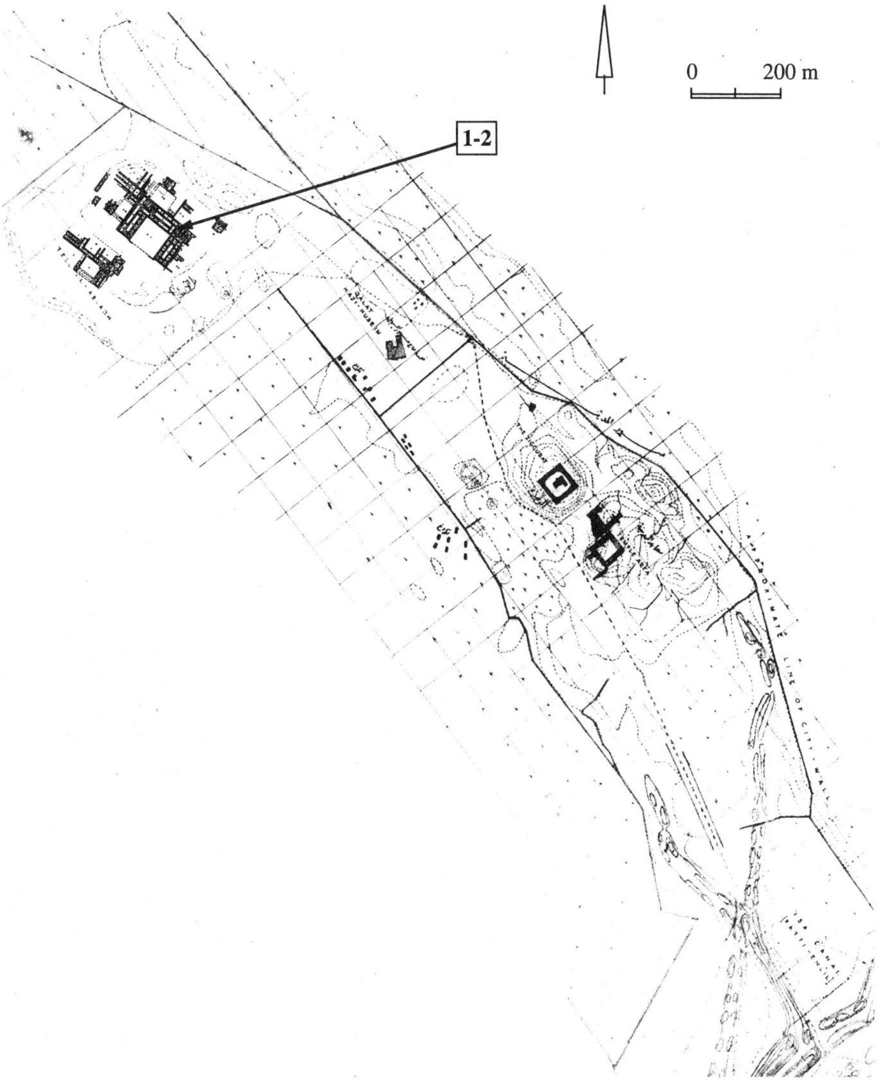

Plan 49. Dur-Kurigalzu. General plan with archives **Dur-Kurigalzu 1-2**.
From T. Baqir, *Iraq Supplement* (1944), pl. 1.

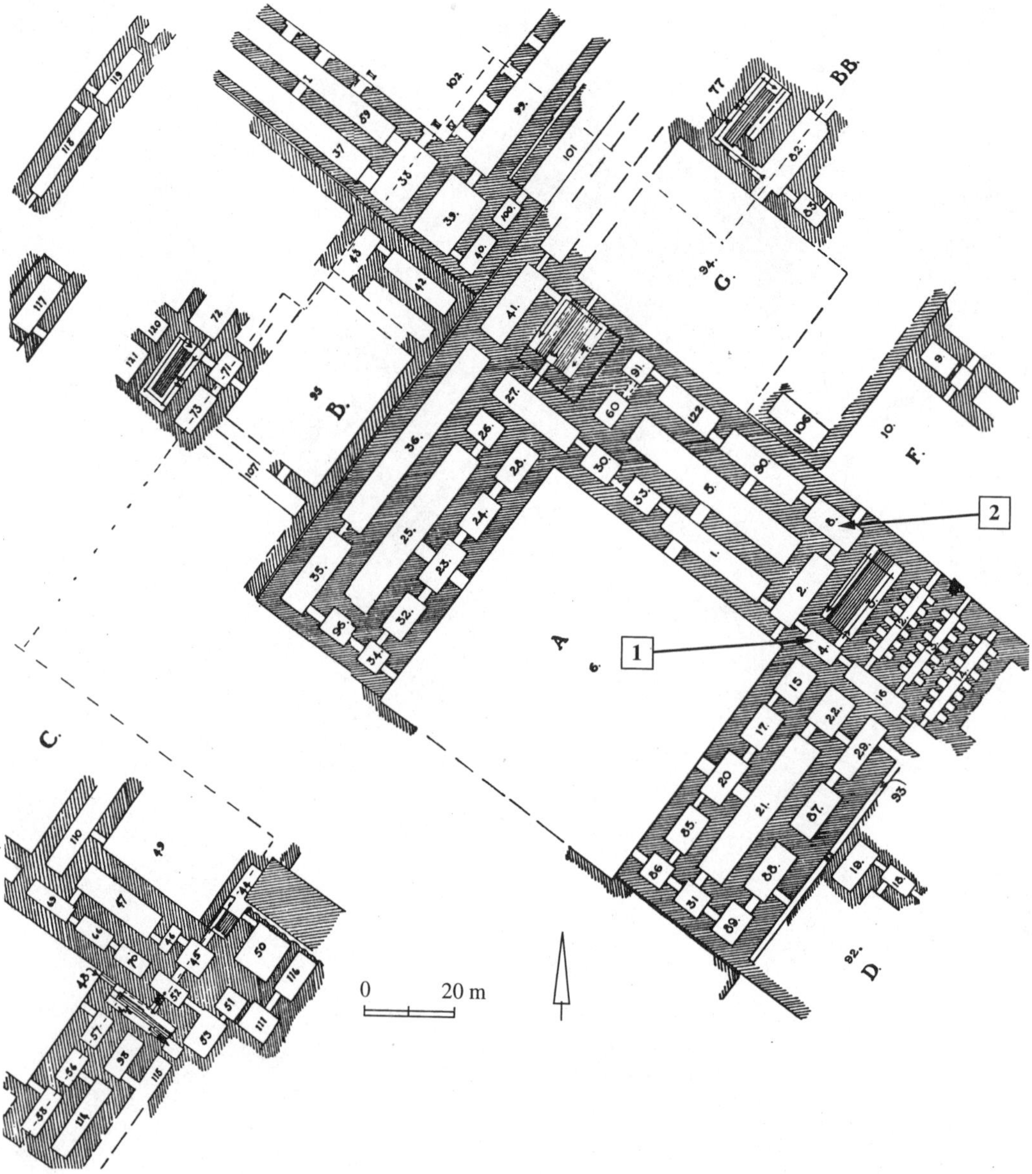

Plan 50. Dur-Kurigalzu.
Plan of palace with archives **Dur-Kurigalzu 1-2**.
From T. Baqir, *Iraq* 8 (1946), 73-93, pl. IX.

of the tablets date to the reign of Kaštiliašu (1232–1225 B.C.), but one or two date to Kudur-Enlil (1254–1246 B.C.). Almost all texts are administrative records concerning gold and other precious materials given to goldsmiths, for, among other things, the adornment of two palaces.

A rebuilding, especially of Room 15, occurred, creating a series of three rooms with vaulted side-chambers for storage. The remains of a small archive (**Dur-Kurigalzu 2**) of eight clay tablets were unearthed just north of this storage unit in Rooms 8 and 2 from Level IA. They are dated to the reign of Merodach-Baladan I (1171–1159 B.C.) and most are administrative lists of various garments received or distributed. Shortly afterwards the palace and city were destroyed by fire.[105]

2.4.2 Babylon

Babylon is situated on the eastern, and partly also the western side of the Euphrates, south of modern Baghdad. Babylon was the capital during the Old Babylonian period. During the Kassite, Middle Babylonian, and Neo-Assyrian periods, it was a leading cultural center, sometimes capital for the Babylonians. Later, during the Neo-Babylonian period, it served as the capital of the Babylonian empire. After early explorations by others, R. Koldewey conducted large scale German excavations in 1899–1917. In recent years, there have been additional excavations by Iraqi and Italian expeditions, and restoration work has been performed by Iraqi archaeologists. The modern high level of the ground water has prevented most systematic examinations of the earlier levels of the city, and excavations are thus concentrated on the Neo-Babylonian and Persian Levels. Kassite and Middle Babylonian Levels, which are of interest here, were, like the Old Babylonian Levels, only excavated in some limited trenches in the Merkes area of the central city. Therefore, we do not know how much of this quite large Neo-Babylonian city was inhabited during the Kassite and Middle Babylonian periods.

After its destruction by fire at the end of the Old Babylonian period, there was a more or less continuous occupation until the destruction of the city during the reign

105. T. Baqir, "Iraq Government Excavations at 'Aqar Qūf, Second Interim Report 1943–1944," *Iraq Supplement* 1945, 4–15; O. R. Gurney, "Texts from Dur-Kurigalzu," *Iraq* 11 (1949), 131–149; and O. R. Gurney, "Further Texts from Dur-Kurigalzu," *Sumer* 9 (1953), 21–34 and 11 plates. Cf. J. A. Brinkman, *Materials and Studies for Kassite History I* (1976), 43.

The description above follows the report by T. Baqir. The provenances given by O. R. Gurney would indicate that part of the documents from the reign of Kaštiliašu concerning delivery of gold to goldsmiths stem from Room 4 Level II and another part from Room 15 Level IV. If this is correct, the stratigraphy has to be changed, or we have to consider a more complicated situation with more than one story.

of the Neo-Assyrian king Sennacherib. Because most of the archives and libraries from the Kassite and Middle Babylonian periods remain unpublished and unstudied, the description below about Babylon can give only some of the main lines about the largest archives and libraries. The description of the later periods will follow in section 3.2.1.[106]

2.4.2.1 Archives in Private Houses

A private house at a street corner in the old Kassite level was cut by excavation trenches. In a room southeast of the central courtyard in the southeastern part of trench Merkes 24/25q2, a clay pot was standing by a wall of a small room. In this pot, seven clay tablets were packed in straw. All the tablets of this private archive (**Babylon 1**) remain unpublished. The tablets are legal documents that date to the reigns of the kings Kurigalzu (II?), Kadašman-Turgu, and Kudur-Enlil (ca. 1332–1246 B.C.), during the early years of the Kassite period.[107]

Merkes 27p1 is part of an area without preserved buildings in the old Kassite level. The area may have served as an open space for the manufacture and storage of clay pots, since a number of pots were found there. Together with the pots was an archive (**Babylon 2**) of 38 clay tablets. All the tablets of this private archive remain unpublished. Most of the tablets are loan documents that date to the reigns of the kings Kurigalzu (II?), Kadašman-Turgu, and Kudur-Enlil (ca. 1332–1246 B.C.), during the early years of the Kassite period.[108]

The remains of a floor in Merkes 25p2 is all that is preserved of a house from the late Kassite Level. The excavators found under the floor 31 clay tablets, which are the remains of a private archive (**Babylon 3**). All the tablets remain unpublished, but they seem to be short administrative documents, dated to the reigns of the kings Enlil-

106. An introduction to the site can be found in R. Koldewey, *Das wieder erstehende Babylon*, 5th ed. revised and expanded by B. Hrouda (1990), with bibliography; cf. also E. Klengel-Brandt, "Babylon," *OEANE* 1 (1997), 251–226, with short bibliography. Most of the final publications have appeared in the series Wissenschaftliche Veröffentlichung der Deutschen Orient-Gesellschaft (=WVDOG): R. Koldewey, WVDOG 1 (1900); R. Koldewey, WVDOG 2 (1901); F. H. Weissbach, WVDOG 4 (1903); R. Koldewey, WVDOG 15 (1911); R. Koldewey, WVDOG 32 (1918); O. Reuther, WVDOG 47 (1926); F. Wetzel, WVDOG 48 (1930); R. Koldewey and F. Wetzel, WVDOG 54 (1931); R. Koldewey and F. Wetzel, WVDOG 55 (1932); F. Wetzel and F. H. Weissbach, WVDOG 59 (1938); F. Wetzel, E. Schmidt, and A. Mallwitz, WVDOG 62 (1954). The preliminary reports were published in *MDOG*.

107. O. Reuther, *Die Innenstadt von Babylon (Merkes)*, WVDOG 47 (1926), 13–14, 54–55, fig. 6, pls. 5, 11, 12, Bab 39233ff.

108. O. Reuther, *Die Innenstadt von Babylon (Merkes)*, WVDOG 47 (1926), 13–14, 56–57, pls. 4, 11, Bab 34287ff.

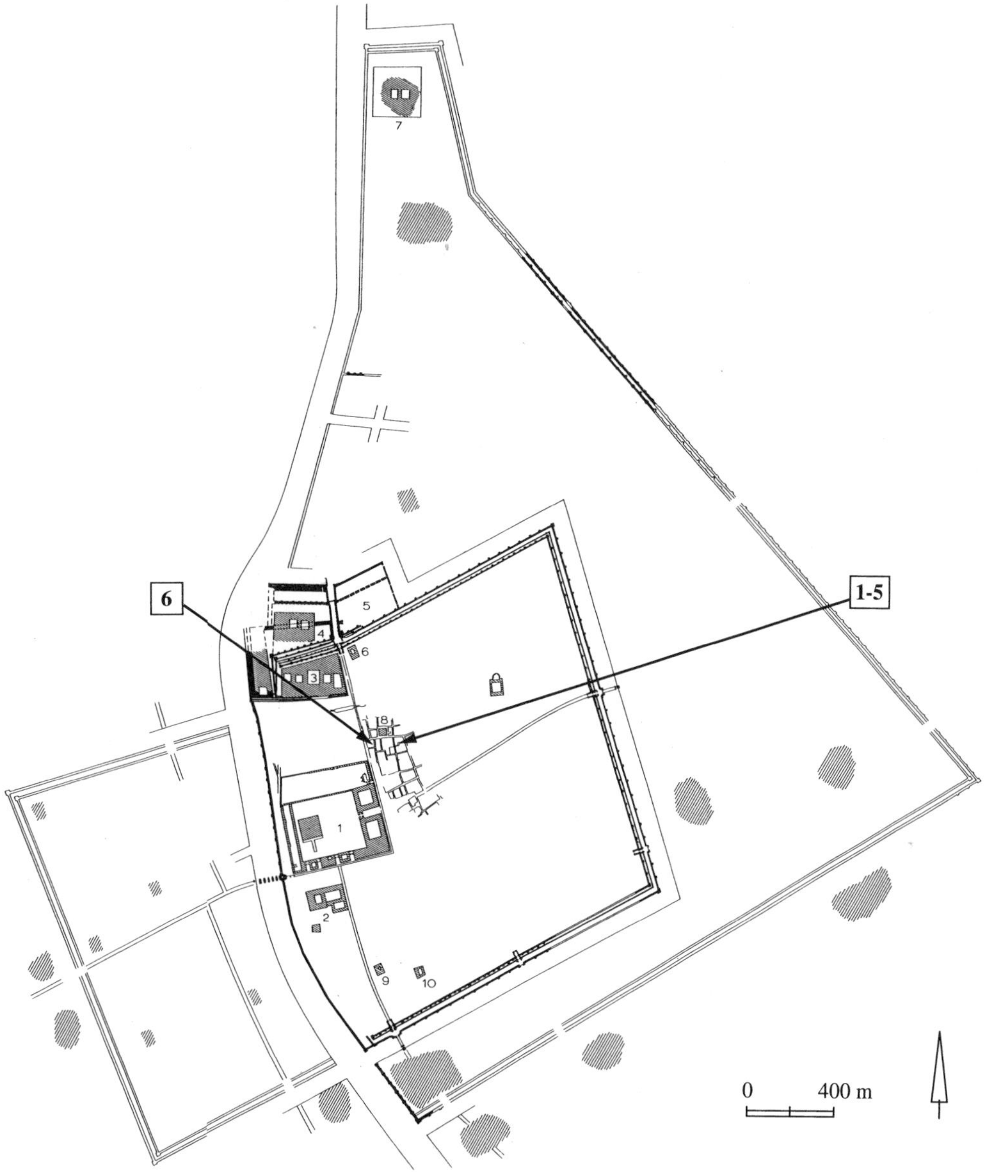

Plan 51. Babylon.
General plan with archives **Babylon 1-6**.
From E. Heinrich, *Die Tempel und Heiligtümer im alten Mesopotamien* (1982), fig. 382.

nadin-šumi, Meli-Šipak, and Merodach-Baladan I (ca. 1224–1159 B.C.), during the late part of the Kassite period.[109]

2.4.2.2 Libraries in Private Houses

East of the somewhat north-to-south street in Merkes 25m1 to 28m1, a private house in the late Kassite Level was cut by excavation trenches Merkes 26 and 27. In Merkes 26n2 in the northern part of this building, the excavators uncovered a room with two floors; the upper floor was covered with asphalt. Fifty-six clay tablets were carefully placed in the sand level between the two floors. These are the remains of a

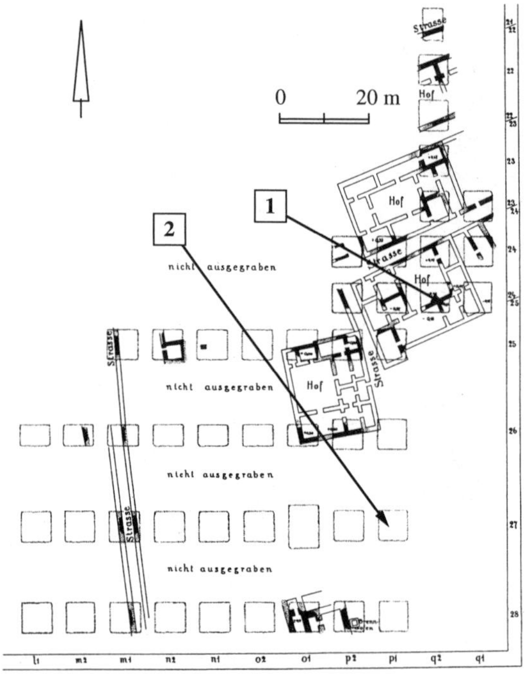

Plan 52. Babylon.
Plan of area with old Kassite period houses in Merkes, with archives **Babylon 1-2**.
From O. Reuther, *Die Innenstadt von Babylon* (1926), pl 11.

109. O. Reuther, *Die Innenstadt von Babylon (Merkes)*, WVDOG 47 (1926), 13, 58, pls. 3, 13, 14, Bab 34553ff.

library (**Babylon 4**) of some diviners, *bārû*; so far, the names of two, Ilima-aḫi and Ṭab-ṣilli-[x], have been published. Among these tablets are some quite large texts. Most of the tablets contain omens from the inspection of animal offerings. The reverse side of some of the tablets contains drawings of intestines with explanatory text. There are also tablets with the omen series *šumma izbu* and *iqqur īpuš*, as well as the god-list *An=Anum* and *Astrolab B.*[110]

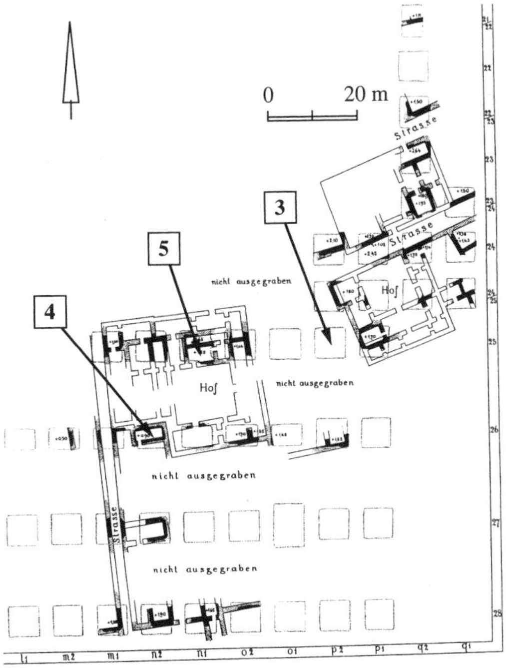

Plan 53. Babylon.
Plan of area with late Kassite period houses in Merkes,
with libraries and archive **Babylon 3-5**.
From O. Reuther, *Die Innenstadt von Babylon* (1926), pl 13.

110. O. Reuther, *Die Innenstadt von Babylon (Merkes)*, WVDOG 47 (1926), 18, 59, pls. 3, 13, 14, Bab 36383ff.; R. Koldewey, *MDOG* 38 (1908), 15; E. Weidner, *MVAG* 21 (1916), 191ff.; F. Böhl, *Analecta Orientalia* 12 (1935), 6ff.; and E. Weidner, *AfO* 16 (1952–1953), 73. Cf. J. van Dijk, *Literarische Texte aus Babylon*, VS 24 (1987), p. 18.

East of the somewhat north-to-south street in Merkes 25m1 to 28m1, a large private house in the late Kassite Level was cut by excavation trenches Merkes 25 and 26. The excavators unearthed 136 unbaked clay tablets (**Babylon 5**) in a 30 cm high clay level on the floor of two rooms in Merkes 25n1. Because the clay level was of the same type of clay as the tablets and because many of the tablets had been intentionally destroyed, the excavators deduced that old clay tablets were being recycled in these rooms into new clay tablets. The tablets are essentially school texts, and most remain unpublished. The two published ones are literary texts dated to the Old Babylonian period. Should the datings of these two be representative of the collection, it may have been an Old Babylonian library in the process of being reused for contemporary writings.[111]

In Merkes 26g2, 100 meters west of the aforementioned house, there was in the late Kassite Level a rather well-constructed house, which seems to have belonged to a stone cutter. In addition to a *kudurru*, there were a lot of stone pearls, as well as flakes of the same stone, and undecorated cylinder seals. In one spot, the excavators found 96 clay tablets, some of which contained drawings of animals. Its designation as a library (**Babylon 6**) is uncertain, since the contents of most of the tablets are not available.[112]

2.4.3 Nippur

Nippur (modern Nuffar or Niffer) was situated southeast of Babylon along an eastern branch of the Euphrates. Early American excavations were conducted between 1889–1900 by H. V. Hilprecht, J. P. Peters, and J. H. Haynes. Excavations were resumed by D. E. McCown and R. C. Haines beginning in 1948, and since 1972 have been continued by McGuire Gibson. The city measures ca. 1.7 × 0.9 kilometers in a northeast to southwest direction. A northwest to southeast canal cuts the city into the two main parts: the West City or West Mound in the southwest, and the East City or East Mound in the northeast. In the East City, the Enlil temple (Ekur) and the Inanna temple and the North (possibly Ninurta) temple were situated. The southern part of the East City with private houses is called the Tablet Hill (TA, TB and TC). In the West City a palace (WB) and the Gula temple (WA), as well as private houses, have been excavated.

111. O. Reuther, *Die Innenstadt von Babylon (Merkes)*, WVDOG 47 (1926), 58–59, pls. 3, 13, 14, Bab 36574ff.; and J. van Dijk, *Literarische Texte*, VS 24 (1987) 41 and 93.

112. O. Reuther, *Die Innenstadt von Babylon (Merkes)*, WVDOG 47 (1926), 16–17, 59–60; cf. pl. 3, Bab 39028ff.

Archaeology has shown settlement as early as the early Ubaid period and as late as ca. A.D. 800. During the third millennium B.C. the city, with the temple of the god Enlil, had been the leading Sumerian cultic center. In the Old Babylonian period, it was a center of scholarly activity, especially at Tablet Hill. After about three hundred years, during which the city was largely abandoned, Nippur regained its position during Kassite rule in the fourteenth and thirteenth centuries B.C. Nippur of the Kassite period has yielded about 12,000 clay tablets and fragments. Due to insufficient recording procedures during the early excavations—when most of the tablets were unearthed—only three administrative and two private archives can be described here and, unfortunately, at a rather preliminary level. Other smaller administrative archives, as well as private archives and private libraries, may also have been unearthed, but available documentation is too meager to enable any meaningful analysis. (cf. 3.2.5. for the later periods).[113]

2.4.3.1 *Archives in Official Buildings*

In area WB, part of a Kassite palace was unearthed. The area had been previously cut by trenches in the early excavations. The excavated area consists of a large central courtyard and three ranges of rooms southwest of it. Comparison with the contemporary palace in Dur-Kurigalzu makes it probable that the palace included large areas on all sides of WB, including the area southwest of WB where about 10,000 Kassite clay tablets were reported to have been excavated during the early excavations. In the unfortunately unsatisfactory reports from the early excavations, one

113. As an introduction to the site, cf. R. L. Zettler, "Nippur," *OEANE* 4 (1997), 148–152, with further bibliography. A bibliography of Nippur publications is published as L. B. Bregstein and T. J. Schneider, "Nippur Bibliography," *Nippur at the Centennial*, CRRAI 35 (1992). Main archaeological publications are H. V. Hilprecht, *Explorations in Bible Lands during the 19th Century* (1903), 289–568; C. S. Fisher, *Excavations at Nippur: Plans, Details and Photographs of the Buildings, with Numerous Objects Found in Them during the Excavations of 1889, 1890, 1893–1896, 1899–1900* (1905); D. E. McCown, et al., *Nippur* I: *Temple of Enlil, Scribal Quarter, and Soundings*, OIP 78 (1967); D. E. McCown, et al., *Nippur* II: *The North Temple and Sounding E*, OIP 97 (1978); R. L. Zettler, *Nippur* III: *Kassite Buildings in Area WC-1*, OIP 111 (1993); McGuire Gibson, et al., *Excavations at Nippur: Eleventh Season*, OIC 22 (1975); and McGuire Gibson, *Excavations at Nippur: Twelfth Season*, OIC 23 (1978). Cf. also the preliminary reports: McGuire Gibson, "Nippur 1975, A Summary Report," *Sumer* 34 (1978), 114–121; McGuire Gibson, et al., "The Southern Corner of Nippur, Excavations during the 14th and 15th Seasons," *Sumer* 39 (1983), 170–190; and McGuire Gibson, "16th Season at Nippur, 1985," *Sumer* 43 (1984), 252–254. Most of the published clay tablets from the early excavations have appeared in one of the two series: The Babylonian Expedition of the University of Pennsylvania (=BE) and Publications of the Babylonian Section, University of Pennsylvania, The University Museum (=PBS); cf. also H. P. H. Petschow, *Mittelbabylonische Rechts- und Wirtschaftsurkunden der Hilprecht-Sammlung Jena: Mit Beiträgen zum mittelbabylonischen Recht*, ASAW 64, 4 (1974).

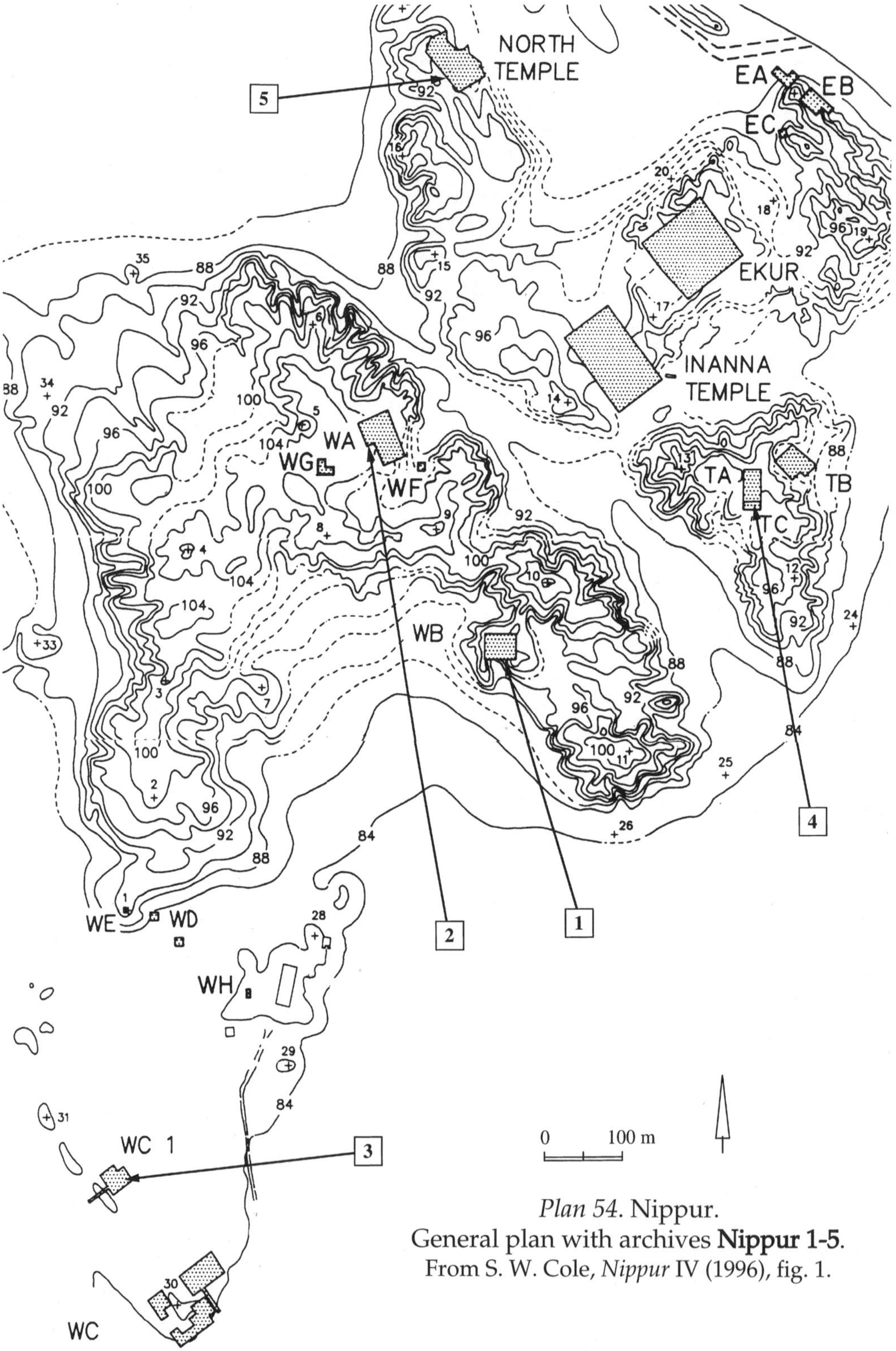

Plan 54. Nippur.
General plan with archives **Nippur 1-5**.
From S. W. Cole, *Nippur* IV (1996), fig. 1.

room is reported to have contained clay tablets still standing side-by-side, as if having fallen from a collapsed shelf. In some of the rooms of WB the excavator found the remains of an archive (**Nippur 1**) consisting of administrative texts. Some of the texts contain date formulae between the fourth year of Burna-Buriaš (1356 B.C.) and the reign of Kadašman-Ḫarbe II (1223 B.C.). Most of the texts date to the later decades of this period. The large number of unpublished tablets from the early excavations are administrative texts of the same types as those from WB. Unfortunately, it cannot be determined whether all the tablets from this area of the city come from one archive in this palace, from several palace archives, or even from houses nearby. The archive, or one of the larger archives if there were more than one, may have belonged to the governor (*šandabakku*) of Nippur. The administrative texts, often lists, concern, for example, the receipt and delivery of agriculture products. Also a collection of letters may come from this archive.[114]

In area WA, the north part of the temple of the goddess Gula has been unearthed. A Seleucid and Parthian building was later built over part of the temple area. Southwest of this building an administrative archive (**Nippur 2**) of 300 clay tablets was found during the early excavations. Whether this is a section of the Gula temple not yet touched by the modern excavators or is a separate building nearby may be clarified by new excavations. The texts date from the 25th year of Burnaburiaš II to the accession year of Šagarakti-Šuriaš, 1335–1246 B.C. Innannu, Martukkû, and some other persons seem to have been responsible for the administration. Almost all texts record the delivery or receipt of barley, and the recipients are often specified as bakers or brewers. The barley is sometimes specified for *iškaru*-work.[115]

In area WC-1, in the southern corner of the West Mound, part of a building was exposed in Level II. In some of the small rooms northwest of the central courtyard the remains of an archive (**Nippur 3**) of several clay tablets were found. More than 50 additional tablets were unearthed in secondary context in Level I, but probably orig-

114. McGuire Gibson, "Nippur 1975, A Summary Report," *Sumer* 34 (1978), 117–118, fig. 14; J. A. Brinkman, *Materials and Studies for Kassite History I (1976)*, 41–42. A selection of texts from this archive has been prepared for publication by L. Sassmannshausen, who gave a preliminary report on them during the RAI 1994 in Berlin. H. Radau, *Letters to Cassite Kings from the Temple Archives of Nippur*, BE 17, 1 (1908), may, at least partly, contain letters from this archive.

115. For a summary, cf. L. Sassmannshausen, *Beiträge zur Verwaltung und Gesellschaft Babyloniens in der Kassitenzeit* (diss. Tübingen 1995), to be published in BaF. Many of the tablets in the following publications are said to be from the archive in this house: A. T. Clay, *Documents from the Temple Archives of Nippur Dated in the Reigns of Cassite Rulers (Complete Dates)*, BE 14 (1906); A. T. Clay, *Documents from the Temple Archives of Nippur Dated in the Reigns of Cassite Rulers (Incomplete Dates)*, BE 15 (1906); and A. T. Clay, *Documents from the Temple Archives of Nippur Dated in the Reigns of Cassite Rulers*, PBS II/2 (1912).

inating in Level II of the same house. Most of the texts, still unedited, are receipts or accounts of grain; others are accounts of goats, sheep, hides, and oil. There are a few legal texts, for example, a repayment of a loan and a legal settlement. Among the few lexical texts is a list of gods. The texts are dated to the reigns of Nazi-Maruttaš, Kudur-Enlil, Šagarakti-Šuriaš, Kaštiliaš IV, and Kadašman-Ḫarbe II (1307–1223 B.C.).[116]

2.4.3.2 Archives in Private Houses

In the area with private houses in Tablet Hill, an archive (**Nippur 4**) of 24 clay tablets was unearthed in Room (Locus) 90 on the final floor of House 107 in Area TA from the redated Level VI* (previously TA Levels IV and V). The unpublished mostly fragmentary tablets are reported to be business documents dated to the reigns of Kadašman-Enlil II (1263–1255 B.C.), Kudur-Enlil (1254–1246 B.C.), and an earlier king.[117]

The so-called North Temple (perhaps a Ninurta Temple) was situated in the northern part of the East City. A small part of what possibly was a private house was excavated next to the southwest side of the temple's platform (SE Level V). A clay pot containing eight clay tablets and two more clay tablets nearby were found in Room (Locus) 3 of this house on the elevation of a floor 2. Because the actual floor is missing, the relation between the tablets and the house is somewhat uncertain. This archive (**Nippur 5**) is said to consist of Middle Babylonian business documents dating to the reigns of Kadašman-Enlil II (1263–1255 B.C.), Kudur-Enlil (1254–1246 B.C.), and the first year of Šagarakti-Šuriaš (1245 B.C.).[118]

2.4.4 Ur (Muqayyar)

Ur (modern Muqayyar) is situated by an arm of the Euphrates southeast of Uruk. During 1918–1919, H. R. Hall commenced British excavations on the site. These were followed by the important British-American expeditions 1922–1934 directed by L. Woolley. Occupation is attested from the Ubaid period to the Neo-Babylonian period. Ur was an important Sumerian city and the center of the empire of the Third Dynasty

116. R. L. Zettler, et al., *Nippur* III: *Kassite Buildings in Area WC-1*, OIP 111 (1993), 20–25, 41–53, 93–111 (by J. A. Brinkman), pls. 18–20.

117. J. A. Armstrong, *The Archaeology of Nippur from the Decline of the Kassite Kingdom until the Rise of the Neo-Babylonian Empire*, diss. University of Chicago (1989), 128–131, 163, fig. 52.

118. D. E. McCown, et al., *Nippur* II: *The North Temple and Sounding E*, OIP 97 (1978), 37–38, 47–48, pls. 36, 43; and J. A. Armstrong, *The Archaeology of Nippur*, 186–187.

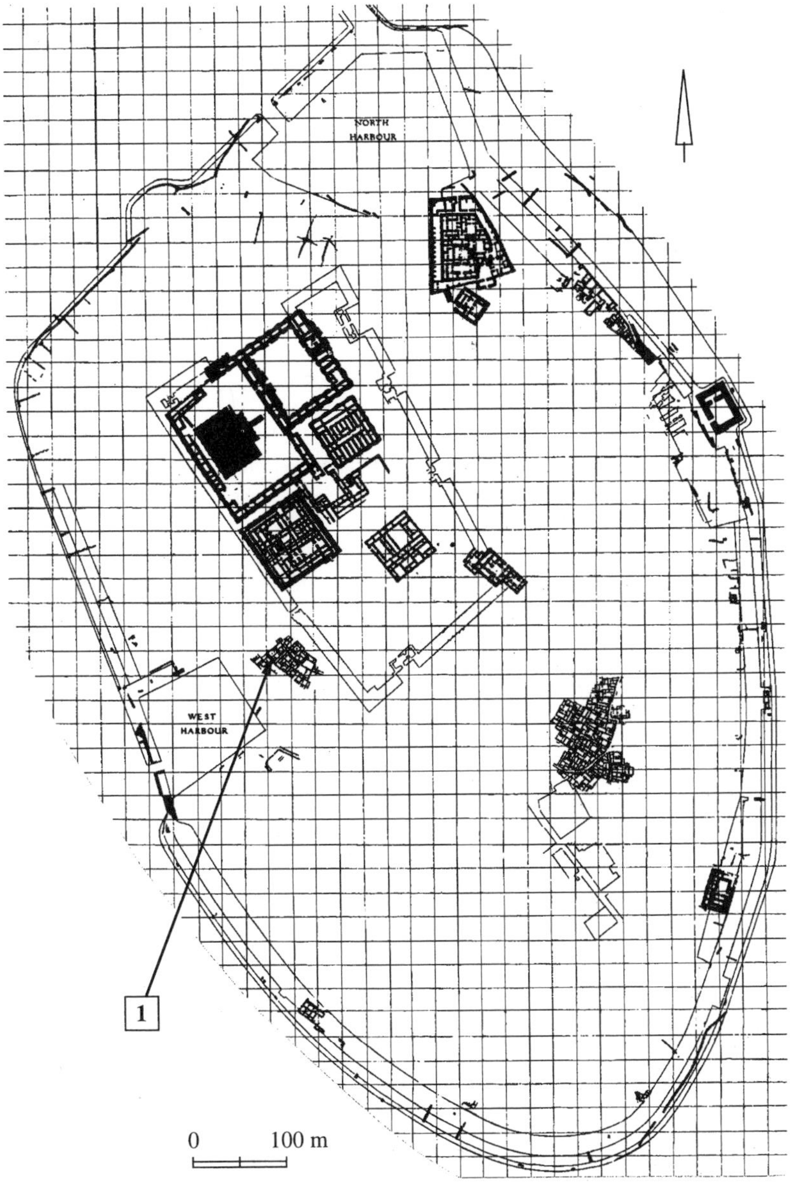

Plan 55. Ur.
General plan with archive **Ur 1**.
From L. Woolley, *Ur Excavations* VII (1976), pl. 116.

of Ur. During the Old Babylonian period, it remained a large city and in the second half of the second millennium B.C., that is, the period of interest here, Ur was still an important city within the Kassite culture. The archaeologists exposed a city wall encircling an oval-shaped urban area with axes measuring ca. 1200 × 700 meters. The excavations were concentrated in areas with monumental buildings, especially at the Sîn temple, but areas with private houses were also explored; two areas with private dwellings dating to the Old Babylonian period reached into the Kassite period. The description of the later periods will follow in section 3.2.6.[119]

2.4.4.1 Archive in Private House

In the EM area with private houses about 200 meters south of the zikkurrat, the excavators unearthed the remains of quite ruined private houses of the Kassite period immediately above the rather well-preserved private houses of the Old Babylonian period. An archive (**Ur 1**) of 72 clay tablets was found in these ruined houses for which no plans could be determined due to the severity of their destruction. The tablets date from the fifteenth year of Kadašman-Turgu (1267 B.C.) to the fifth year of Merodach-Baladan I (1166 B.C.). One text bears a much later date, the third year of Marduk-šapik-zeri (1079 B.C.)—it is unclear whether it is a later intrusive tablet. The texts are the archive of the family of Dayyanatu and some other brewers (*sirāšû*) of the temple of Sîn. Well-attested members of the family are Šamaš-eṭir, Abu-ṭab, and Sîn-bununi. The archive consists of a number of legal settlements and other legal documents, several purchase documents, but only a few loans. There are also a number of lists and other documents concerning the family's administration. Many of the documents concern cattle, but some deal with grain, slaves, or other matters. A few of the texts can be directly related to the professional work of the brewers.[120]

119. For an introduction to the site, cf. S. Pollock, "Ur," *OEANE* 5 (1997), 288–291, with bibliography; cf. also as a general overview L. Woolley, *Ur of the Chaldees: The Final Account, Excavations at Ur,* revised and updated by P. R. S. Moorey (1982). The final archaeological publications have appeared in the series *Ur Excavations,* and publications of texts can be found in the series *Ur Excavation Texts.* The archaeological material of the period under discussion can be found in L. Woolley and M. Mallowan, *Ur Excavations* VII: *The Old Babylonian Period* (1976); and L. Woolley, *Ur Excavations* VIII: *The Kassite Period and the Period of the Assyrian Kings* (1965).

120. O. R. Gurney, *The Middle Babylonian Legal and Economic Texts from Ur* (1983), nos. 1–47, 49–73, with the copies in O. R. Gurney, *Ur Excavation Texts* VII: *Middle Babylonian Legal Documents and Other Texts* (1974).

2.4.5 *Tell Imlihiye*

Tell Imlihiye was a small settlement situated six kilometers west of the city Mê-Turran (modern Tell Sib/Tell Ḫaddad/Tell Baradan), ca. four kilometers north of the Diyala river in the lowest part of the Hamrin basin. After the finding of clay tablets by local farmers, German excavations in 1978 and 1979 showed that the site was a natural hill with a small Kassite occupation consisting of only a few houses on the east side of the hill.[121]

2.4.5.1 *Archive Found next to a Private House*

East of the remains of Kassite houses, in area D/18, the local farmers had, the year before the excavations began, discovered a clay pot containing at least 45 clay tablets. They constitute the archive (**Tell Imlihiye 1**) of Apil-Nergal and Buna-Nergal, sons of Ili-šemi. The texts date between the reign of Kadašman-Enlil II (1263–1255 B.C.) and the sixth year of Kaštiliašu IV (1227 B.C.), most texts coming from the later years of that period. The texts seem to have belonged to an agricultural unit. They consist of business documents often in the form of lists dealing with animals, wool, and textiles,

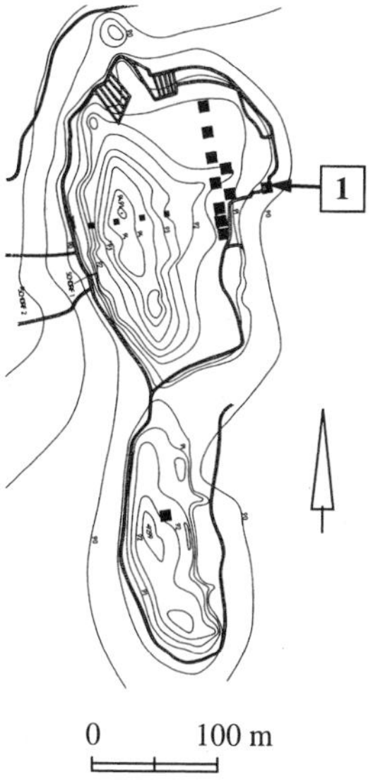

Plan 56. Tell Imlihiye.
General plan with archive **Tell Imlihiye 1**.
From R. M. Boehmer and H.-W. Dämmer, *Tell Imlihiye* (1985), pl. 2.

121. R. M. Boehmer and H.-W. Dämmer, *Tell Imlihiye, Tell Zubeidi, Tell Abbas*, BaF 7 (1985), 1–19, pls. 1–57.

notes on delivery of corn, loans of corn (mostly received), as well as a few payments, a purchase document, and a letter.[122]

2.5 Elamite Area

The archives and library with cuneiform texts from the Elamite area date to the Middle Elamite period during the fourteenth and twelfth to eleventh centuries B.C.

In Kabnak (2.5.1) the excavators unearthed three archives, one of them combined with a library, and in Anshan (2.5.2) two archives have been found. Surprisingly, to date, archives or libraries have not been found from this period in the main capital, Susa. Due to the few sites and often rather small areas excavated, more archives and libraries may be expected from this area.

Year datings cannot be found in the published texts. Therefore, the datings of the archives are only approximations. The preserved texts are written with cuneiform script on clay tablets either in the Akkadian language or in the Elamite language. In addition to the archives and libraries discussed below, individual tablets have been found in the same area.[123]

2.5.1 Kabnak (Haft Tepe)

Kabnak, modern Haft Tepe, is situated in the southwestern province of Khuzistan in Iran, 16 kilometers southeast of Susa. Iranian excavations, initiated due to the construction of a sugar cane plant on the site, were conducted by E. O. Negahban during 1966–1980. The site, which consists of several mounds, covered ca. 1,500 × 800 meters. The main habitation level dates to perhaps 100 or 150 years during the Middle Elamite period (1450–1100 B.C.), when the site was the capital and burial place of Tepti-ahar, ca. 1375 B.C. The excavations were concentrated to the western part of the site, where a temple with graves and some administrative buildings, associated with what may be the remains of two terraces or zikkurrats, were unearthed. Excavations were also conducted on Mound B in the southeastern part of the site, south of the modern railway station.[124]

122. K. Kessler, "Kassitische Tontafeln vom Tell Imliḫiye," *BaM* 13 (1982), 51–116, and cf. also K. Kessler, "Die Tontafeln," in R. M. Boehmer and H.-W. Dämmer, *Tell Imlihiye*, BaF 7 (1985), 18–19.

123. For a bibliography of Elamite texts from the period, cf. M.-J. Steve, *Syllabaire Elamite, histoire et paleographie*, CPOP 1 (1992), 19–21.

124. For an introduction to the site, cf. E. O. Negahban, "Haft Tepe," *OEANE* 2 (1997), 454–457, with bibliography. The archaeological material has been published in E. O. Negahban, *Excavations at Haft Tepe, Iran*, University Museum Monograph 70 (1991).

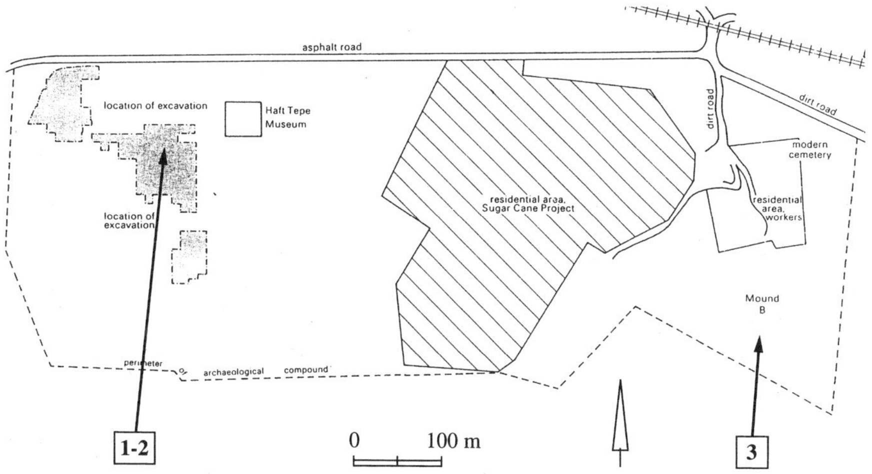

Plan 57. Kabnak.
General plan with archives and library **Kabnak 1-3**.
From E. O. Negahban, *Excavations at Haft Tepe, Iran* (1991), plan 1.

2.5.1.1 Administrative Archives and a Library

The excavators unearthed several thousand, mostly fragmentary, clay tablets. Only a few selections of the texts have been published, and the distribution of these texts on the individual findspots has not been available. Therefore, the following short description is very preliminary. Three main archives are reported to have been discovered. As far as is known, the tablets from the archives were Akkadian administrative texts and letters, dated to the fourteenth century B.C. Two of the archives were found in rooms just north of Terrace I. One of these archives (**Kabnak 1**) was unearthed in a small room in trench H XXXI—this may be the room west of the northern part of Hall 5. In the eastern part of the so-called "Corridor" north of the Northwestern Courtyard, 40 meters southwest of the room with the archive, were a number of clay bullae with seal impressions. Another archive (**Kabnak 2**) together with a library was found in the Eastern Courtyard in front of the so-called "Artist's Workshop" in the eastern part of Terrace Complex I. Many tablets were school texts, often written on round tablets. A number of omen texts may also be from this collection. In the same courtyard clay bullae bearing seal impressions were uncovered. In a build-

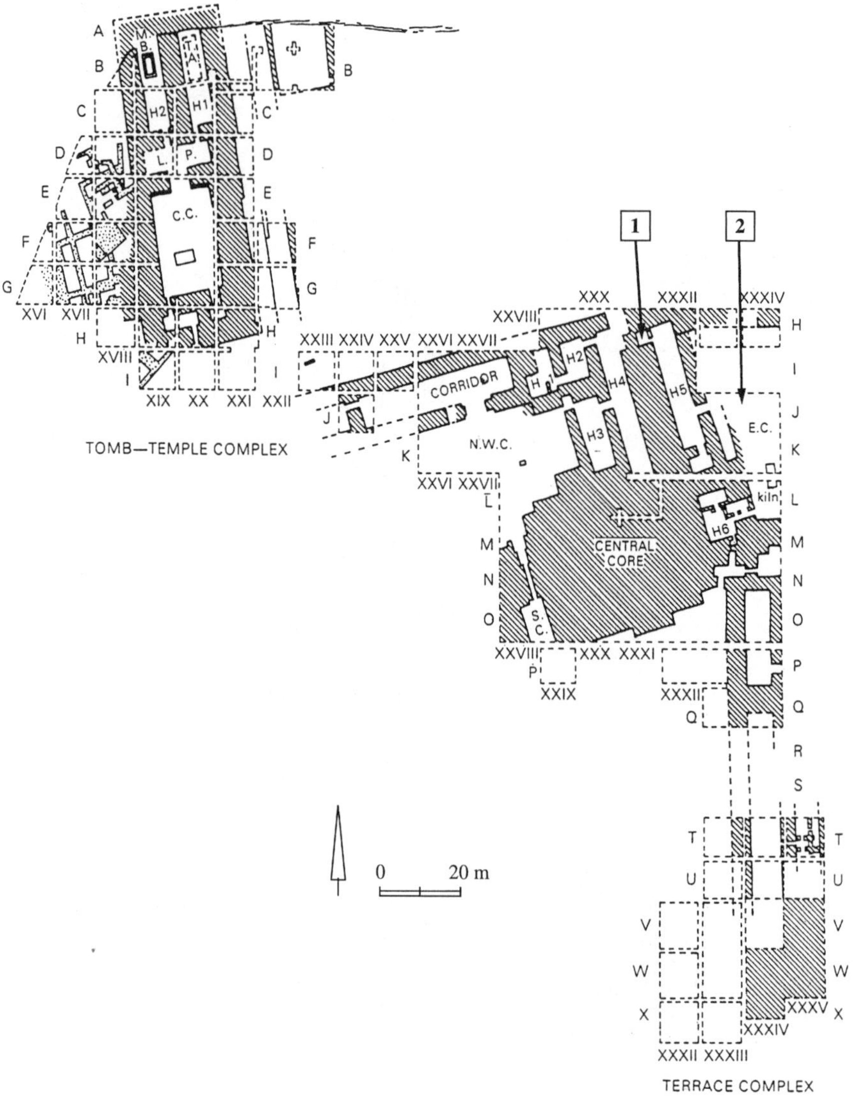

Plan 58. Kabnak.
Plan of main excavated buildings with archives and library **Kabnak 1-2**.
From E. O. Negahban, *Excavations at Haft Tepe, Iran* (1991), plan 2.

ing in Mound B the third main archive (**Kabnak 3**) was unearthed, possibly also consisting of administrative texts.[125]

2.5.2 *Anshan (Tall-e Malyan)*

Anshan (modern Tall-e Malyan) is situated near the western edge of a large intermontane valley system drained by the Kur river in the Fars province of southwestern Iran, 43 kilometers west of Persepolis and 46 kilometers north of Shiraz. An American expedition directed by W. M. Sumner excavated some selected areas, called operations, between 1971 and 1978. Anshan is the largest known pre-Achaemenid site in Fars, measuring 1.5 × 1.6 kilometers. Main building levels have been unearthed dating from 3400–900 B.C., with a possible hiatus in the occupation. Earlier and later evidence is scantier. Archives with Proto-Elamite, Sumerian, and Middle Elamite clay tablets have been found. Two archives from the Middle Elamite period will be discussed here.[126]

2.5.2.1 *Administrative Archives in a Possible Palace*

A large building was partly unearthed in Area (or Operation) EDD, Level IV, in the northwestern part of the tell, near its highest point. The building, which may have been a palace or perhaps a temple, was destroyed by fire. The unearthed section is the southwest end of the building, consisting of a courtyard surrounded by rooms. East of the courtyard, about 200 clay tablets were unearthed. The largest group (81 published texts) stem from Room 76 southeast of the courtyard; the smaller group (30 published texts) are from the eastern corner of the Corridor 95/60, east of the courtyard. Together, the tablets represent an archive (**Anshan 1**) divided into two subdivisions or dossiers. All texts are written in Middle Elamite, and derive probably from the end of the Middle Elamite kingdom, possibly during the eleventh century B.C.

125. Cf. J.-J. Glassner, "Les textes de Haft Tépé, la Susiane et l'Elam au 2ème millénaire," *Mesopotamie et Elam*, CRRAI 36 (1991), 109–126. Publications of the texts can be found in E. O. Negahban, *Excavations at Haft Tepe, Iran*, University Museum Monograph 70 (1991), which includes a reprint of P. Herrero, "Tablettes administratives de Haft-Tépé," *CDAFI* 6 (1976), 93–116, as well as in the series of articles by P. Herrero and J.-J. Glassner, "Haft-Tepe: Choix de textes I–IV," in *Iranica Antiqua* 25 (1990), 1–45; *Iranica Antiqua* 26 (1991), 39–80; *Iranica Antiqua* 28 (1993), 97–135; and *Iranica Antiqua* 31 (1996), 51–82; a division of the texts into archives and a library is not possible on the basis of the published material.

126. As introductions to the site, cf. W. M. Sumner, "Maljān, Tall-e (Anšan)," *RLA* 7 (1987–1990), 306–320, and W. M. Sumner, "Malyan," *OEANE* 3 (1997), 406–409, both with bibliographies. E. Carter, *Malyan Excavations* II: *Excavations at Anshan (Tal-e Malyan), The Middle Elamite Period*, University Museum Monograph 82 (1996), was not available to me.

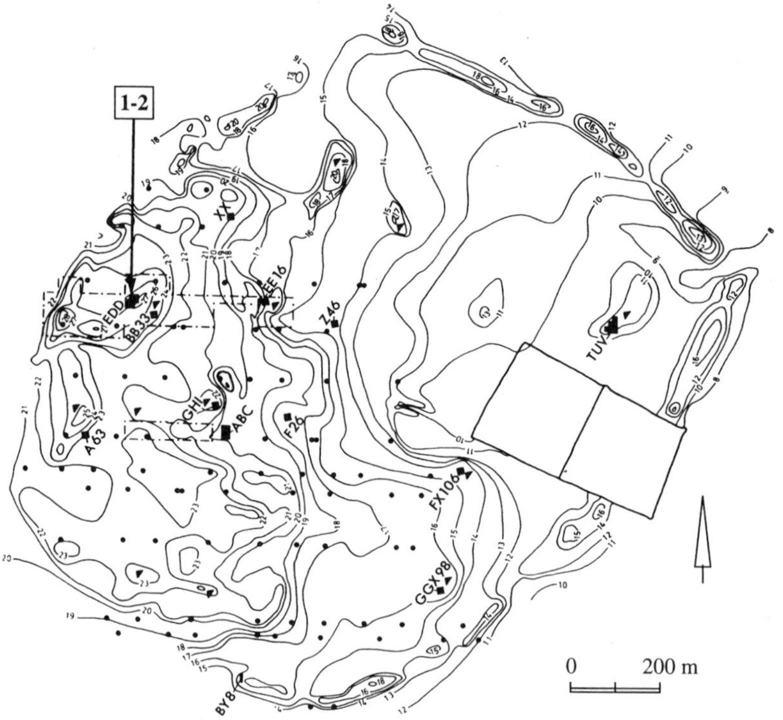

Plan 59. Anshan.
General plan with archives **Anshan 1-2**.
From W. M. Sumner, "Maljān, Tall-e (Anšan)," *RLA* 7 (1987-1990), 307 fig. 1.

They are dated with the month and day, but not the year, possibly indicating that they were needed for only a short time, after which they were discharged somewhere else. Most of the texts are administrative records from an administrative unit in the large building. They deal with the disbursal and control of metals to be used for the manufacture of objects or for business (KASKAL). The two subdivisions involve the same individuals and use essentially the same administrative procedures. The main difference is that most of the texts in Room 76 deal with copper and tin, whereas most of the texts in Corridor 95/60 deal with gold and silver.

Another archive (**Anshan 2**) from the same level of the large building was unearthed in Room 152 in the northeasternmost part of the excavated area. About forty texts in poor condition remain unpublished. They are Middle Elamite administrative documents, concerning the administration of animals, hides, and foodstuffs.[127]

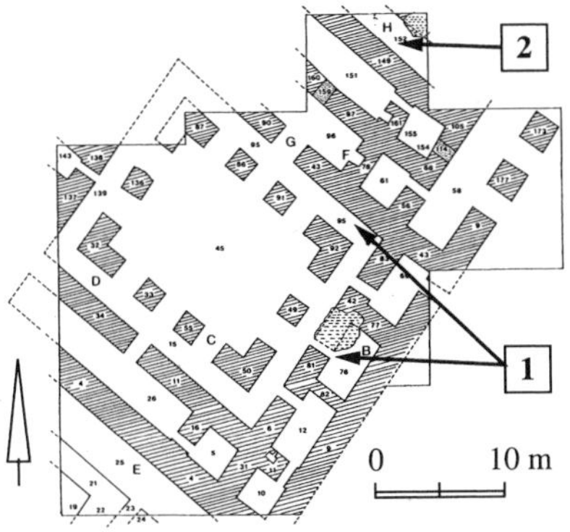

Plan 60. Anshan.
Plan of large building with archives **Anshan 1-2**.
From M. W. Stolper, *Texts from Tall-i Malyan* I (1984), 4 fig. 3.

127. M. W. Stolper, *Texts from Tall-i Malyan I: Elamite Administrative Texts (1972–1974)*, Occasional Publications of the Babylonian Fund 6 (1992). Cf. W. M. Sumner, "Maljān, Tall-e (Anšan)," *RLA* 7 (1987–1990), 311, 318. The date of the texts follows the publication of the texts; a somewhat later date has been suggested by M.-J. Steve, *Syllabaire Elamite, histoire et paleographie*, CPOP 1 (1992), 21.

1000–300 B.C.

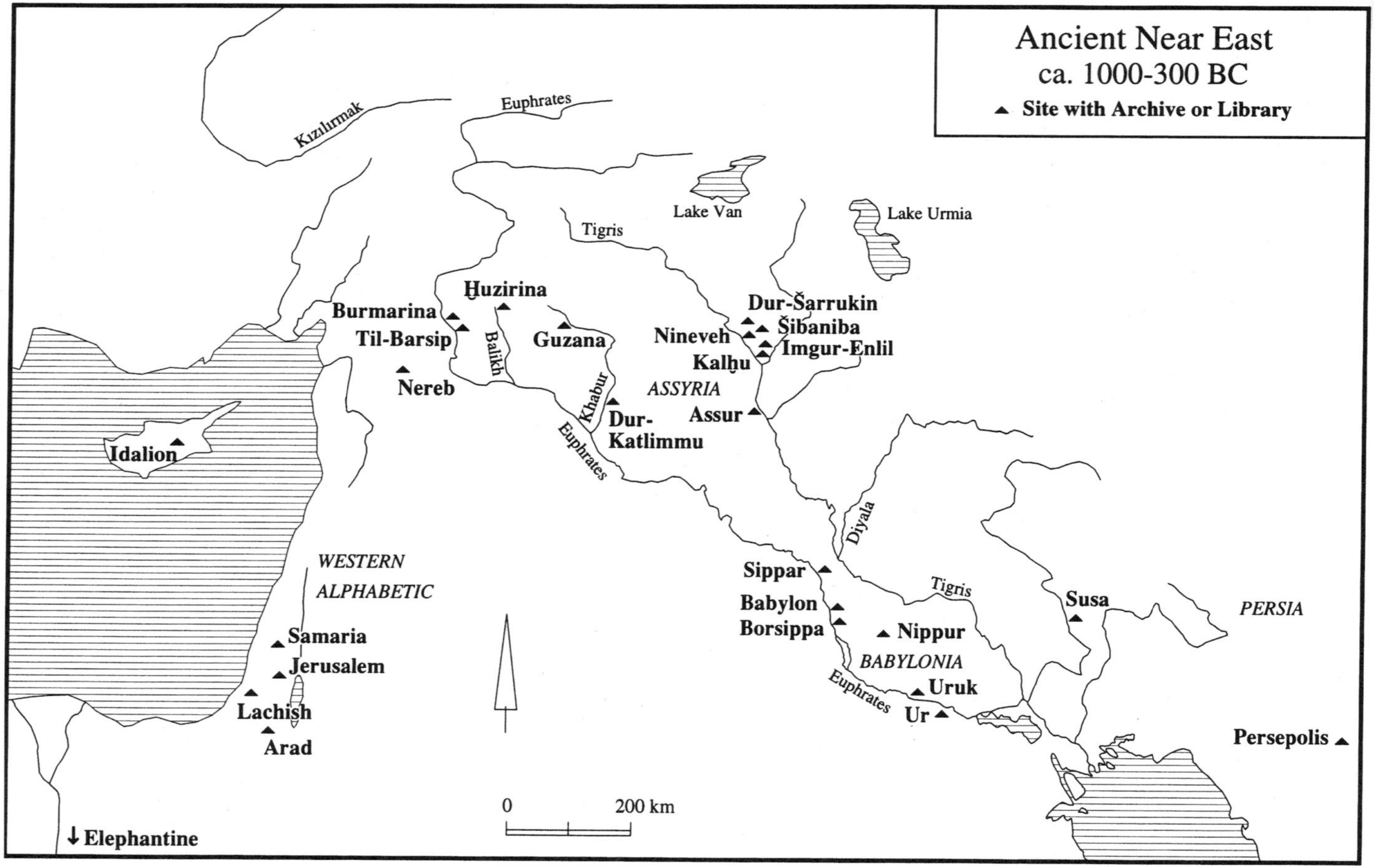

Plan 61.
Ancient Near East. Map showing cities with archives and libraries ca. 1000–300 B.C.

Chapter 3

Archives and Libraries in the Near East 1000–300 B.C.

The period 1000–300 B.C. was dominated by the Neo-Assyrian, Neo-Babylonian, and Persian Achaemenid empires. In the west, in the Levant, there were several smaller alphabetic-using states or city-states that were more or less dominated by the great powers. This period has also been called the Iron Age for various parts of the Near East. The presentation of the cities where archives or libraries have been found is, on the basis of cultural and political criteria, divided into four sections: the Neo-Assyrian area, the Neo-Babylonian area, the Persian area, and the Western Alphabetic area.

In the Neo-Assyrian area, after a period of weakness, the Assyrian kings established during the ninth century B.C. a large state, and a series of powerful kings maintained the large Neo-Assyrian Empire from approximately 744 B.C. until its end in 612 B.C. The Neo-Babylonian area, sometimes independent during the Neo-Assyrian period but often incorporated into Assyria, dominated during the time of the Neo-Babylonian Empire 612–539 B.C., approximately over the same area as the Assyrians had governed. The Persian Achaemenids, during this time, strengthened their position eastward and northward until they, from 539 B.C., could include Babylonia in their empire. The Achaemenid Empire lasted until the Hellenistic period, which started with the conquest of Alexander around 330 B.C. The Persian area in the present work covers the main Iranian part of the empire. Because there was a rather high degree of continuity in Babylonia—not only between the Neo-Babylonian and Achaemenid empires, but also into the following Hellenistic period—the archives and libraries in the Neo-Babylonian area that continued the older cuneiform tradition have been followed to their end, not only into the Achaemenid period but also into the Hellenistic period, some centuries after the lower general time limit otherwise used in this work. For the smaller countries in the Western Alphabetic area, the interest is here on their local alphabetic cultures, which have been followed from their previous periods of independence into the Achaemenid period.[1]

The great majority of the preserved written documentation from this period is found in archives or libraries consisting of clay tablets with cuneiform script used for different languages or dialects. The alphabetic script was increasingly used during this period, first in the Western Alphabetic area, but soon after also in all other areas. During the final centuries discussed here, it became as frequent as the cuneiform and finally replaced it. The alphabetic texts were essentially written on perishable writing material, and are therefore underrepresented in the excavated material in comparison with the cuneiform texts. Hieroglyphic Luwian script has only occasionally been found in archives.

3.1 Neo-Assyrian Area

The archives and libraries with cuneiform texts from the Neo-Assyrian area date from 900 B.C. to the end of the Assyrian Empire, ca. 612 B.C., including one archive (Dur-Katlimmu 3) that continued Neo-Assyrian traditions for several more years.

Several archives and libraries have been unearthed in the old capital, Assur (3.1.1), and in Kalḫu (3.1.2), which served as capital from the time of Assurnasirpal II. The short-lived capital, Dur-Šarrukin (3.1.3), has yielded only a few remains of the archives and libraries once there. The last main Assyrian capital, Nineveh (3.1.4), has produced a large number of clay tablets, essentially from old excavations, which makes a reconstruction of the archives and libraries rather difficult. Archives have been found in the central Assyrian area at Imgur-Enlil (3.1.5) and Šibaniba (3.1.6). In the western provinces, in Syria, archives have been found at Dur-Katlimmu (3.1.7), Guzana (3.1.8), Til-Barsip (3.1.9), Burmarina (3.1.10), and Ma'allanat (3.1.12), as well as a library in Ḫuzirina (3.1.11).

So too, in other areas, during parts of this period under Assyrian rule, archives have been found. From the Neo-Babylonian area, archives have been unearthed in Babylon (3.2.1), Nippur (3.2.5), and Uruk (3.2.7). Contemporary archives in areas outside Assyrian control will be discussed for Susa (3.3.1) in the Persian area, and Samaria (3.4.2) in the Western Alphabetic area.

Almost all preserved texts are written in cuneiform script on clay tablets. Writing boards were also used for writing cuneiform, as is known from text references; some writing boards have actually been found in Kalḫu and Assur. The language used is

1. For general historical information, cf. Chapter 1, n. 5.

normally Akkadian in the Assyrian dialect, but for literary texts the Babylonian dialect, and sometimes the Sumerian language, were used. Alphabetic texts, essentially in the Aramaic language, were frequently used on perishable writing material, as can be seen from the sealed dockets, often with cuneiform or alphabetic inscriptions, which were attached to, for example, scrolls of perishable materials; some ostraca have also been discovered. A few hieroglyphic Luwian texts on rolled lead strips have been unearthed.[2]

The Assyrian scribes used eponyms for dating texts. Several lists of eponyms are quite well preserved. Therefore, many of the texts can be assigned a rather secure dating. Problems with the dating due to the lack of preserved lists of eponyms are limited to the beginning and the end of the period—in particular, a well-established list of eponyms for the period 650–612 B.C. is not yet available.[3]

In addition to the archives and libraries discussed below, individual tablets or small remains of archives or libraries have been found at a number of other sites in the same area.[4]

2. In addition to the rolled lead strips treated in section 3.1.1.3.2 (archiv Assur 28), a few strips have been found in Kululu, 50 kilometers northeast of Kültepe in Anatolia, cf. T. Özgüç, *Kültepe and Its Vicinity in the Iron Age*, TTKY V 25 (1971), 32–64, 94–116, figs. 106–107, pls. L–LII; and J. D. Hawkins, "The Kululu Lead Strips: Economic Documents in Hieroglyphic Luwian," *AnSt* 37 (1987), 135–162, with further references.

3. For Neo-Assyrian eponyms, cf. A. Millard, *The Eponyms of the Assyrian Empire*, SAAS 2 (1994).

4. For general references to sites, cf., K. Radner, *Die neuassyrischen Privatrechtsurkunden als Quelle für Mensch und Umwelt*, SAAS 6 (1997), 4-18. Among the references are, for Tarbiṣu (Sherif Khan), cf. A. Sulaiman, "Discovery of the Assyrian City of Tarbīṣu," *Adab al-Rafidain* 2 (1971), 15–49, especially 24–28 (in Arabic); for Tell Baqaq, cf. K. T. Yusif, "Excavations at Tulul Al-Baqaq, Baqaq 2," *Researches on the Antiquities of Saddam Dam Basin Salvage and other Researches* (1987), 40–49 (Arabic section); R. Killick and M. Roaf, "Excavations in Iraq, 1981–82," *Iraq* 45 (1983), 208; and B. K. Ismail, "Two Neo-Assyrian Tablets," *SAAB* 3 (1989), 61–64; for Mê-Turnat (Tall Ḥaddad), cf. A. K. Muhamed, *Old Babylonian Cuneiform Texts from the Hamrin Basin: Tell Haddad*, Edubba 1 (1992), 23; for Tell Rimah, cf. J. N. Postgate, *Iraq* 32 (1970), 31–35; for Nabula/Nabur (modern Girnawaz), cf. V. Donbaz, "Some Neo-Assyrian Contracts from Girnavaz and Vicinity," *SAAB* 2 (1988), 1–30; for Karkemish, cf. R. C. Thompson, "The Cuneiform Tablet from House D," in C. L. Woolley, *Carchemish, Report on the Excavations at Jerablus on behalf of the British Museum II: The Town Defences* (1921), 135f., fig. 54, pls. 19, 26; for Tarsus, cf. A. Goetze, "Cuneiform Inscriptions from Tarsus," *JAOS* 59 (1939), 1–16, nos. 2–9; for Hama, cf. H. Ingholt, Rapport préliminaire sur sept campagnes de fouilles à Hama en Syrie (1932–1938), *Det Kgl. Danske Videnskabernes Selskab, Archæologisk-kunsthistoriske Meddelelser* 3/1 (1940), 115; S. Parpola, "A Letter from Marduk-apla-usur of Anah to Rudamu/Urtamis, King of Hamath," in P. J. Riis and M.-L. Buhl, *Hama, Fouilles et recherches de la fondation Carlsberg 1931–1938* II 2: Les objects de la période dite Syro-Hittite, Nationalmuseets Skrifter, Større Beretninger 12 (1990), 257–265.

3.1.1 Assur (Qal'at Sherqaṭ)

Assur was the capital of Assyria during most of the Middle Assyrian period (cf. 2.3.1) and the beginning of the Neo-Assyrian period. Even after Assurnasirpal II (883–859 B.C.) had moved the Assyrian capital to Kalḫu, Assur remained an important city with the main Assyrian sanctuary, the Aššur temple. This Neo-Assyrian city consisted of an inner city (ca. 900 × 1000 meters) with an extension towards the south (ca. 500 × 300 meters). The temples, palaces, and most other administrative buildings were situated in the northern part of the inner city; more private houses were excavated in the southern and western parts of the inner city than in any other city discussed in this book. Most of the archives and libraries were unearthed in these private houses.[5]

3.1.1.1 Archives and Libraries in the Aššur Temple and the Palaces

Archives and libraries in temples or palaces from Neo-Assyrian times are rather few. The most important, consisting of at least 300 clay tablets and perhaps several hundreds more, were unearthed in the southwestern courtyard of the Aššur temple and in the rooms around the courtyard, that is, areas hC/hD3V/4II. The tablets constitute N 1, a library combined with an archive (**Assur 15**). It is not clear whether the tablets originally were placed in some of the rooms in the precinct around the courtyard or, as sometimes has been suggested, on its upper floor; some tablets may have been placed in other rooms on the southwestern side of the outer courtyard. In addition to many texts from Neo-Assyrian times, the library contained about 60 literary texts selected from an earlier Middle Assyrian library (cf. 2.3.1.1). The texts contain regulations of palace and harem life, laws, royal rituals, hymns, myths, incantations, lexical lists, and some hemerological, mathematical, astronomical, and astrological texts. The library was combined with an archive—whether in the same rooms or not is unknown—which included lists of royal officials and royal decrees concerning offerings in the Aššur temple, dating to the ninth century B.C. Among the texts from the late seventh century B.C. were some letters.[6]

5. For literature about Assur, see the references to section 2.3.1. For the archives and libraries, see especially O. Pedersén, *Archives and Libraries in the City of Assur: A Survey of the Material from the German Excavations*, parts I and II (=*ALA* I and II) (1985, 1986).

6. O. Pedersén, *ALA* II (1986), 12–28 N 1; for a dating of many of the Middle Assyrian tablets to about 50 years earlier, and not during the reign of Tiglath-Pileser I, see now H. Freydank, *Beiträge zur mittelassyrischen Chronologie und Geschichte*, SGKAO 21 (1991).

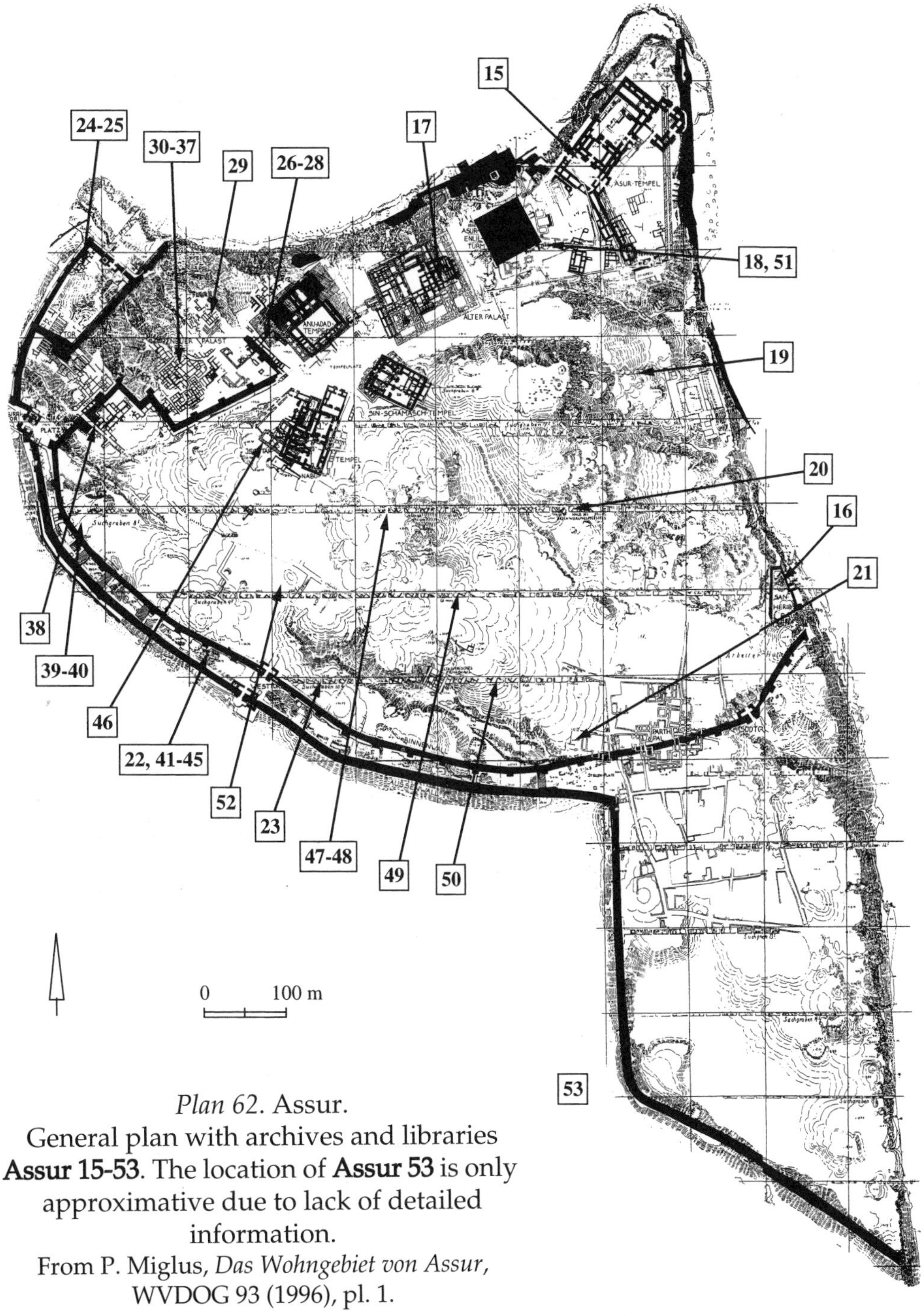

Plan 62. Assur.
General plan with archives and libraries **Assur 15-53**. The location of **Assur 53** is only approximative due to lack of detailed information.
From P. Miglus, *Das Wohngebiet von Assur*, WVDOG 93 (1996), pl. 1.

One library N 5 (**Assur 16**) including an archive, with at least 90 cuneiform clay tablets, was found in the Prince's Palace in the southeastern part of the inner city in area lA9II. Found with the cuneiform tablets was one Aramaic docket, possibly once fastened to an Aramaic scroll of papyri or similar material. At present, it is possible to find only a few of the texts excavated in the palace, so the picture is not coherent. So far, this library with archive can only be said to have contained common exorcistic literature and administrative texts. Ten clay tablets, which represent the remains of another administrative archive (**Assur 17**), were found in the Old Palace; lists of charioteers were frequently attested here.[7]

3.1.1.2 Libraries, Sometimes with Archive Sections, in Private Houses

Houses with libraries were found mainly in the eastern part of the city, not far from the Tigris. This was possibly the quietest part of the town, since the main traffic arrived at the western part of Assur, presumably where the business people lived. In the east, three larger libraries were found in three separate private houses.[8]

In a house in area hB4V near the main zikkurrat, a family of scribes (*ṭupšarru*) had a library N 2 (**Assur 18**). Among the scribes were Nabû-aḫa-iddina and his son Šumma-balaṭ. The library, dating primarily to the seventh century B.C., contained ca. 65 clay tablets (many of which are still unidentified): a large number of lexical lists, but also astronomical, astrological and similar texts, including omens of the *šumma ālu* type. All these texts were typical of the *ṭupšarru*-profession. In addition there are a few incantations and two purchase documents.[9]

The eastern slope of the highest mound (modern "Gräberhügel") towards the Tigris contained in area iC6III, and possibly also iB6III, a house with a library N 3 (**Assur 19**) of more than 130 clay tablets for *nargallu* ("chief singers" or "musicians"), one of whom was named Aššur-šuma-iškun. The texts date to the eighth century B.C. and later, with many hymns and similar texts for the use of singers and musicians. Some of these and other literary texts found here tended towards theological elaboration with some concentration on Ištar and related gods. There is also a collection of

7. O. Pedersén, *ALA* II (1986), 76–81 N 5 and *ALA* I (1985), 30 n. 7.

8. For archaeological details, see P. A. Miglus, *Das Wohngebiet von Assur: Stratigraphie und Architektur*, WVDOG 93 (1996).

9. O. Pedersén, *ALA* II (1986), 29–34 N 2, excluding N 2M, for which see below. For a discussion of the types of texts typical of different Neo-Assyrian scholarly professions, based not on extant libraries but on references in texts, see S. Parpola, *Letters from Assyrian Scholars to the Kings Esarhaddon and Assurbanipal*, part IIA (1971), 12ff., summarized in part II (1983), XIV.

lexical lists, some in the form of school tablets. An archive section consisted of at least 13 documents of different types.[10]

The largest library N 4 (**Assur 20**) excavated in Assur was found in area hD8I in a house of a family of exorcists (*āšipu*), who stored about 800 clay tablets dating mostly to the seventh century B.C. in Room 10, which served as a library and was supplied with a door opening onto inner Courtyard 7. A writing board of ivory was found in secondary position west of the house; it may have belonged to the library. The two best-attested persons in the colophons of the texts are Kiṣir-Aššur and his nephew Kiṣir-Nabû. The career of these and other persons can be followed in the texts, e.g., Kiṣir-Aššur is called "student" (*šamallû*) in the earliest texts of the library. Under the floors of several of the rooms of their house, including the library, were apotropaic figurines used to keep evil away. The majority of the texts in the library were incantations and prescriptions to counteract various sicknesses and evils. There were also prayers, lists of stones and plants for medical use, as well as lexical and hemerological texts. Most of these texts were intended for the exorcists' professional use and were often enumerated in the text called the "Exorcist's Manual" and in catalogues of text groups found in the library. The library included other texts that were less specific to the profession. Some, for example, concern the ruler's attitude toward the cult, especially in Babylon, others with the destruction and rebuilding of Babylon. There were also copies of the "Topography of Assur" and a group of royal rituals that were

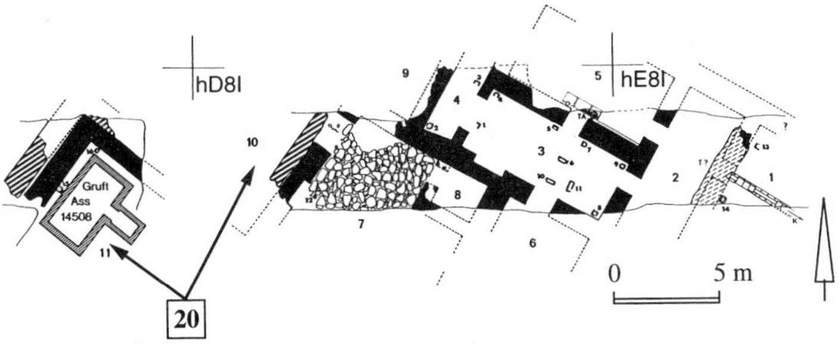

Plan 63. Assur.
Plan of excavation trench 8I with exorcists' house, with library **Assur 20**.
From P. Miglus, *Das Wohngebiet von Assur*, WVDOG 93 (1996), pl. 132d.

10. O. Pedersén, *ALA* II (1986), 34–41 N 3. Future research may be able to show that what has been treated as a single library was in fact a series of libraries in different archaeological levels. Since the types of texts in different levels are so similar, they may have belonged to different generations of persons with the same profession, presumably within the same family.

performed usually in connection with the Aššur temple. There was an archive section in the separate Room 11 above a grave chamber in area hC8I in the western part of the same house, containing 36 documents, including lists enumerating rations of bread for a number of women and a few men; about 20 documents were found in the library room.[11]

The excavators found three smaller libraries in private houses in the southern area of the city. In the remains of a private house in area hC10IV, the excavators unearthed a library N 6 (**Assur 21**) of about 20 clay tablets. Most of the texts are incantations, omens, and lexical lists, but there are also a few other types, including a list of persons, and one or two documents dating to the final years of the empire. Library N 7 (**Assur 22**), consisting of about 25 clay tablets, was unearthed in area cD9II. Among the texts are epics, omens, and a list of persons, possibly also a king-list. The small library N 8 (**Assur 23**), numbering only eight clay tablets, was found in a private house in area eD10I. Most are school texts; in addition, there was one purchase document.[12]

3.1.1.3 Archives in Private Houses

In addition to libraries, which sometimes contained archival texts, the excavation unearthed 30 archives in private houses in the southern and western parts of Assur, namely, N 9–35, N 2M, and two recently excavated ones (**Assur 24–53**). In the southern half of the city, the area with private houses was only cut by about four-meters-wide excavation trenches each 100 meters of town area. It is, therefore, reasonable to assume that the majority of the private archives or libraries in this area have, as yet, not been excavated.[13]

The rooms of a typical private house in this part of the city were arranged around one or more inner courtyards. The family graves were often placed under the floor of the innermost room of the house. The family archive was, in many cases, kept in that same room. This room often had a door opening onto a courtyard, was often rather large and may have served a number of different purposes for the family. Houses with archives are one-sixth to one-fourth of all private houses in areas where the houses were rather well preserved and excavated completely. A few of the archives were found in clay pots, but most of them were uncovered on the floor or in the fill of

11. O. Pedersén, *ALA* II (1986), 41–76 N 4; Iraqi excavations of parts of the house left unexplored by the Germans have unearthed a large number of additional tablets of the same types as already recorded there.

12. Cf. O. Pedersén, *ALA* II (1986), 81–85 N 6–8.

13. For archaeological details, see P. A. Miglus, *Das Wohngebiet von Assur*, WVDOG 93 (1996).

a room. The archives date to the final decades or last century of the Assyrian Empire and were written in the Neo-Assyrian dialect on clay tablets when not otherwise specified below as alphabetic Aramaic or hieroglyphic Luwian.[14]

3.1.1.3.1 Archives in Houses in the Northwest Area

In the northwest area of the town wall, Houses 66 and 67–68 were inhabited by related families with the title *ḫunduraya*. In House 66, the excavators unearthed archive N 9 (**Assur 24**), which consisted of 86 cuneiform clay tablets; one of which is a docket possibly once fastened to an Aramaic scroll of papyri or similar material. Among these tablets, 64 were found in the archive Room k next to the inner courtyard, the others in the courtyard and the rooms southwest of it. The archive belonged to Mudammiq-Aššur, his father Dada-aḫḫe, as well as his son Šar-ili and some of his brothers. Among the documents dated from 681 B.C. to the end of the empire are many concerning loans and investments, several purchase documents, work contracts, receipts, legal settlements, divisions of inheritance, as well as an administrative list. Archive N 10 (**Assur 25**), consisting of 48 clay tablets or fragments, belonged to Aššur-eriba and his family. The documents consist of loans, investments, work contracts, purchase documents, and a legal settlement.[15]

3.1.1.3.2 Archives in Houses Southwest of the Anu-Adad Temple

In houses southwest of the Anu-Adad temple, three small archives were discovered. Archives N 11 and N 12 (**Assur 26–27**) consisted essentially of small collections of loan documents on clay tablets. Archive N 13 (**Assur 28**), from a house in area eB5V next to the temple, consisted of six letters in hieroglyphic Luwian written on lead strips. The archive probably belonged to Takasla and is dated, on archaeological grounds, to the final years of the empire.[16]

14. In addition to the detailed treatment in O. Pedersén, *ALA* II (1986), 85–136 N 9–35, cf. also O. Pedersén, "Private Archives in Assur Compared with Some Other Sites," *SAAB* 1 (1987), 43–52.

15. O. Pedersén, *ALA* II (1986), N 9–10. The presentation of N 9 above is a correction of the findspots given in *ALA*; groups B and C were not found in Room d and the courtyard of House 65 but in Room k and the courtyard of House 66 according to excavation notes, which I had previously not seen. Many of the texts from N 9–10 have now been published by F. M. Fales and L. Jakob-Rost, "Neo-Assyrian Texts from Assur: Private Archives in the Vorderasiatisches Museum of Berlin, part 1," *SAAB* 5 (1991); and L. Jakob-Rost, F. M. Fales, and E. Klengel-Brandt, *Keilschrifttexte aus neuassyrischer Zeit 1: Neuassyrische Rechtsurkunden* 1, WVDOG 94 (1996).

16. O. Pedersén, *ALA* II (1986), N 11–13; several of the texts from N 11 have been published by K. Deller, F. M. Fales, and L. Jakob-Rost, with contributions by V. Donbaz, "Neo-Assyrian Texts from

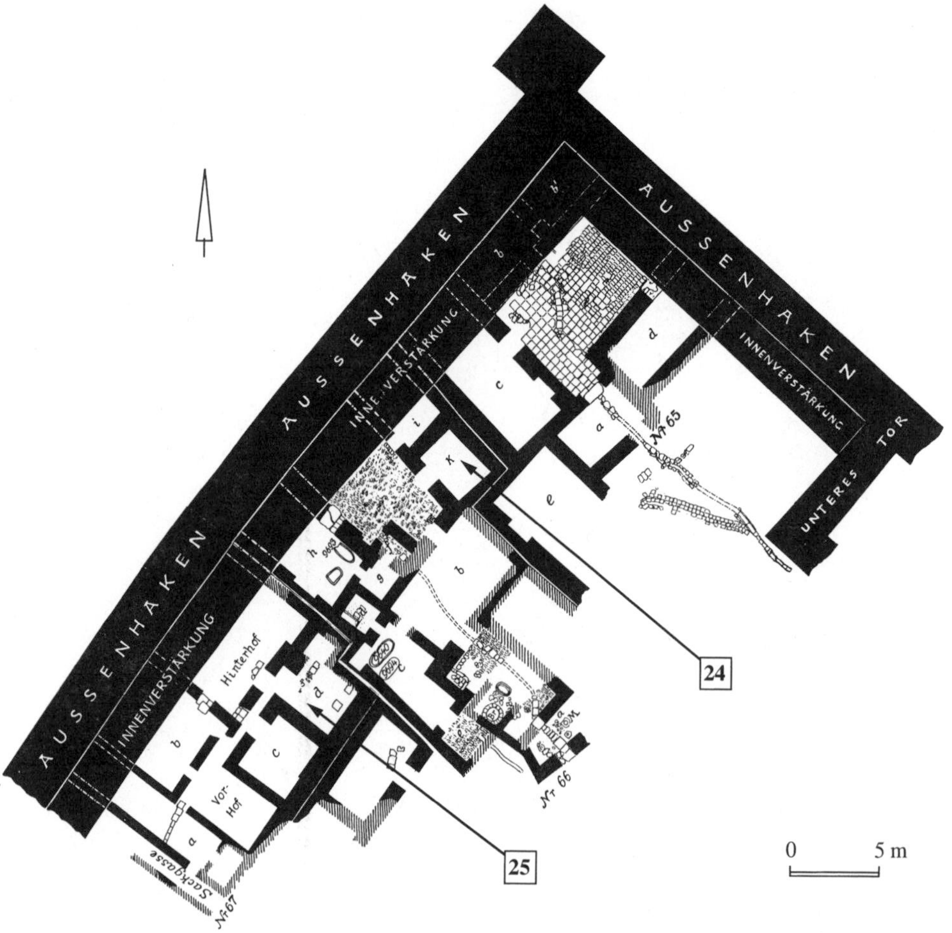

Plan 64. Assur.
Plan of area with private houses, with archives **Assur 24-25**.
From C. Preusser, *Die Wohnhäuser in Assur*, WVDOG 64 (1954), pl. 24.

3.1.1.3.3 Archives in Houses above the Ruined New Palace

In the northwestern area, above the Middle Assyrian New Palace that was ruined and abandoned during the Neo-Assyrian period, the excavators unearthed large areas of blocks of private houses surrounded by roads and lanes. In House 33 in area dB5IV, the small archive N 14 (**Assur 29**), consisting of eight clay tablets, was unearthed in the innermost room above a grave chamber as well as in some other places. The archive consists of a letter of complaint, purchase documents, a division of inheritance, a receipt, and a list. Archive N 15 (**Assur 30**), consisting of about 20 clay tablets, was unearthed in one of the private houses in area cD6I. The documents concern purchases or loans. In an inner room of House 5, situated next to the place where "Winkelgasse" joined "Krumme Gasse," archive N 16 (**Assur 31**) with 15 clay tablets was unearthed. As far as known, the tablets are various documents. The houses with archives N 17 and N 18 were situated next to each other but with entrances from different lanes. Archive N 17 (**Assur 32**) was found in the innermost room above the graves of House 9 at a small lane ("Gasse") in area dA6IV. It consists of 14 clay tablets, of which 11 are written in cuneiform. Three tablets are written in Aramaic; one of them is a regular clay tablet, the other two are clay dockets, probably once fastened to Aramaic scrolls of papyri or similar material with a rather identical text. Most of the texts detail loans of silver made by Kakkullanu and some other man; one text concerns a joint business venture. Two of the texts are lists of amounts of silver associated with different persons, possibly for internal record keeping. In the neighboring House 12, situated at "Winkelgasse" in area dA6IV, archive N 18 (**Assur 33**), which contained at least 17 clay tablets, was also placed in the innermost room above the graves. Two of the clay tablets are Aramaic dockets. The archive belonged to Nagahi and some other men. Most of the texts are loan documents, but there are also a few receipts, purchase documents, and legal settlements. Archive N 19 (**Assur 34**) found nearby consists of only four tablets. Archive N 20 (**Assur 35**) found in inner rooms of House 15–15a in area eE6IV consists of more than 40 clay tablets, forming the archive of Šarru-iqbi. Among the documents are several dealing with loans, as well as a purchase document, adoption document, and a list. Archive N 21 (**Assur 36**), which lay in House 20 in area cE6III partly above the family grave and partly in it as a result of destruction of the grave, consists of 14 clay tablets with cuneiform writing. It belonged to Mutaqqin-Aššur and some other men with the title *atû*, "door-keeper" (possibly in the Aššur temple). At least eight of the texts are documents concerning loans of silver or corn that were made by Mutaqqin-Aššur or his colleagues. At least two of the loans were made to groups of persons, including the creditor himself, to invest in joint business ventures. Two other documents concern the purchase of a slave and a legal settlement. In area c6 a small archive N 22 (**Assur 37**) of five documents belonging to Nanunu was found; it contains loan documents and a purchase agreement.[17]

Assur: Private Archives in the Vorderasiatisches Museum of Berlin, part 2," *SAAB* 9 (1995, printed 1997). For another group of a few lead strips from Kululu in Anatolia, cf. references in Chapter 3 n. 2.

17. O. Pedersén, *ALA* II (1986), N 14–22. For Nanunu's archive, cf. O Pedersén, "One More Text from

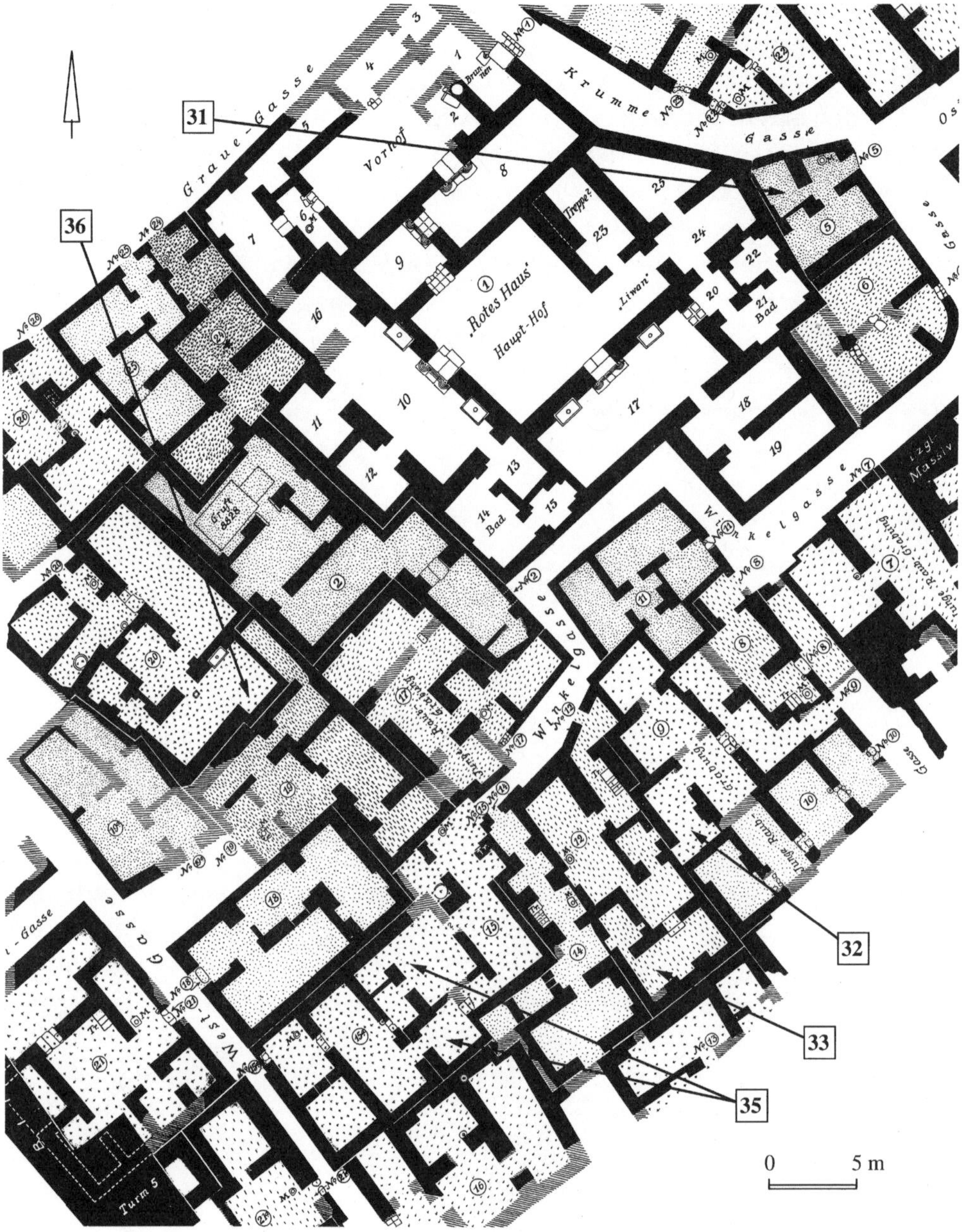

Plan 65. Assur.
Plan of area with private houses, with archives **Assur 31-36**.
From C. Preusser, *Die Wohnhäuser in Assur*, WVDOG 64 (1954), pl. 9.

3.1.1.3.4 *Archive in House Southwest of the Ruined New Palace*

The remains of archive N 23 (**Assur 38**), consisting of 11 clay tablets, was discovered in the main street from the Tabira gate into the city in area bE7I; it may originally have been kept in one of the houses nearby. The tablets are documents, some dealing with purchases and loan. In an inner room of House 81, next to the town wall north of the Tabira gate in area bA6IV, the excavators unearthed the fragments of a large ostracon with an Aramaic letter from Babylonia.[18]

3.1.1.3.5 *Archives in Houses inside the Southwest Town Wall*

The inner town wall was abandoned during the latter part of the Neo-Assyrian period. Later on, private houses were built on both sides of the wall, as well as above it. In an inner room above a grave chamber in a private house, situated in area bE8I some distance from the wall, the excavators unearthed archive N 24 (**Assur 39**), consisting of 29 clay tablets. This is the archive of Nabû-šar-aḫḫešu, Sagib-Aššur, and some other persons. Most of the identified tablets are purchase and loan documents. Just inside the ruins of the inner town wall in area bD8II, 87 clay tablets forming archive N 25 (**Assur 40**) were discovered in a partly collapsed grave chamber. When the house was destroyed and the grave chamber collapsed, it seems that the archive fell down into it. The fragmentary tablets are documents concerned with purchases and other matters. Archive N 26 (**Assur 41**) from area cC9I is quite small, with just a few documents. In an inner room of a private house built against the outside of the then-ruined inner town wall in area cD9II, the excavators unearthed archive N 27 (**Assur 42**), consisting of 22 clay tablets, three of them in Aramaic. Eight of the tablets are formed as dockets fastened to what may have been documents written in Aramaic. The archive belonged to Aššur-šallim-aḫḫe. Most of the texts concern loans or purchases; there also seems to be a letter. Thirty-eight clay tablets found above a grave in a house next to the outer side of the ruined inner town wall in area dA9III formed archive N 28 (**Assur 43**). This archive belonged to Nabû-šuma-iddina and consists of purchase documents, loan documents, legal settlements, and some other types of documents; there is also an examination text preserved. A clay pot found in area dD9IV contained 11 clay tablets. They form archive N 29 (**Assur 44**), which

Nanūnu's Archive (*ALA* II, N 22)," *SAAB* 3 (1989), 69–74. Several of the texts from N 14–15, N 17–22, and N 24 have now been published by K. Deller, F. M. Fales, and L. Jakob-Rost, with contributions by V. Donbaz, "Neo-Assyrian Texts from Assur: Private Archives in the Vorderasiatisches Museum of Berlin, part 2," *SAAB* 9 (1995, printed 1997).

18. O. Pedersén, *ALA* II (1986), N 23 and p. 114 n. 1.

belonged to Samidu—all known texts are purchase documents. Archive N 30 (**Assur 45**), consisting of 15 clay tablets, was unearthed in a private house above the ruined gate to the inner town wall in area dE9V. Most texts are documents dealing with loans, but there is also a purchase document and a letter.[19]

3.1.1.3.6 Archives in Houses in the Inner and Eastern Parts of the City

In a private house on the southeastern side of the main road in area eA7II, the excavators unearthed 43 clay tablets forming archive N 31 (**Assur 46**). Another group of 44 clay tablets, which according to their content seem to belong to the same archive, were found about 350 meters to the southeast in area gE9I. The owners of the archive were Urad-Aššur and Kiṣir-Aššur. Egyptians had an important role in the texts. The largest text group is comprised of loan documents, but there are also some purchase documents, marriage documents, a division of inheritance, and a letter. In the middle of the city, two adjoining houses contained archives that differed greatly in terms of number of texts and text type. Archive N 32 (**Assur 47**) in area fC8I contains only seven clay tablets. It was a small family archive, reflecting transactions of a few generations of a family of tanners (*ṣāripu*) during the seventh century B.C. There are purchase documents concerning a slave, a slave girl, and a building plot, as well as a document of a legal settlement and two documents concerning divisions of inheritance. By contrast, archive N 33 (**Assur 48**) in area fD8I includes about 80 clay tablets that date from the middle and later parts of the seventh century B.C. It belonged to Nabû-zera-iddina and some other gold- and silversmiths (*ṣarrāpu*, *kutimmu*), who apparently were rather wealthy. At least five of the texts are letters. There are several documents about loans that were made, three purchase documents, and two documents of legal settlements. There are a number of lists relating to internal administration, the largest group of which records weights of silver for various individuals. Archives N 34 and N 35 (**Assur 49–50**) consist of just a few documents. In one of the private houses next to the zikkurrat in area hB4V, a clay pot was unearthed with 13 clay tablets. They have turned out to be from a house other than that of the rest of N 2, and constitute a separate archive N 2M (**Assur 51**), belonging to Aššur-bissu-epuš and others. There are various types of documents, including purchase documents.[20]

19. O. Pedersén, *ALA* II (1986), N 24–30.

20. O. Pedersén, *ALA* II (1986), N 31–35 and N 2M.

The excavation directed by B. Hrouda unearthed 57 clay tablets in fill from a private house in area eA8V. The tablets constitute the archive (**Assur 52**) of Dur-Aššur. The texts consist of letters, purchase documents, divisions of inheritance, and other legal documents, as well as administrative lists.[21]

In the New City, that is, the extension of the city towards the south, an archive (**Assur 53**) was unearthed by Iraqi archaeologists in the area of the southwestern corner of the town wall, possibly in a private house. The 52 tablets, which date to the post-canonical period with a few older texts, were the archive of Aššur-mata-taqqin and some related men. Among the texts are 15 loan documents, 13 purchase documents, a few lawsuits, a letter, an adoption document, division of inheritance, and a list of expenses.[22]

3.1.2 Kalḫu (Nimrud)

Assurnasirpal II (883–859 B.C.) moved the Assyrian capital northward to Kalḫu, situated on the east bank of the Tigris. Kalḫu lay more in the middle of the Assyrian homeland, about halfway between Assur and Nineveh. Excavations were conducted by early British archaeologists in 1845–1879. M. E. L. Mallowan then mounted the well-known excavation in 1949–1963, which David Oates continued. Polish (1974–1976), Italian (1987–1989), and Iraqi scholars (especially since 1969) made further investigations. The area within the city wall covered ca. 2.3 × 2 kilometers. The citadel (modern Nimrud), ca. 400 × 600 meters, was situated in the southwestern part of the city. Buildings inside the city wall enclosing the citadel were the Northwest Palace in the west, the Governor's Palace in the east, the temples of Ninurta, Šarrat-nipḫi, and Kidmuri next to the zikkurrat in the northwest, and the Burnt Palace and the Nabû temple in the southeast; in the northeast there were also a few private houses for some high-ranking persons. In a separate tell (modern Tell 'Azar) in the southeastern corner of Kalḫu, a large building complex measuring ca. 200 × 300 meters, called Fort Shalmaneser by the excavators, was almost completely excavated. Clay tablets were found in most of the houses excavated in Kalḫu. Large areas with private houses were probably situated in the extended area of the lower city that has not been excavated. It is likely, therefore, that many more private archives and libraries existed

21. Cf. K. Hecker, "Zu den Keilschrifttexten der Grabung Frühjahr 1990 in Assur," *MDOG* 123 (1991), 111–114; and B. Hrouda, "Vorläufiger Bericht über die neuen Ausgrabungen in Assur Frühjahr 1990," *MDOG* 123 (1991), 95–109, especially 99–100.

22. A. Y. Ahmad, "The Archive of Aššur-mātu-taqqin Found in the New Town of Aššur and Dated Mainly by Post-Canonical Eponyms," *Al-Rāfidān* 17 (1996), 207–288.

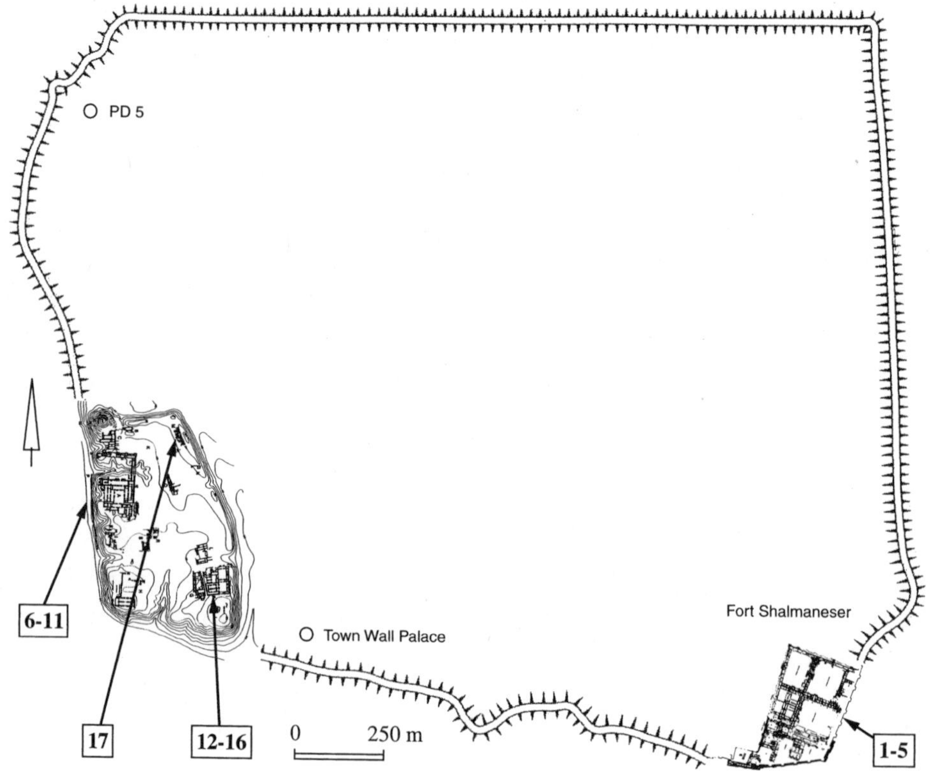

Plan 66. Kalḫu.
General plan with archives and libraries **Kalḫu 1-17**.
Combined from M. E. L. Mallowan, *NR* (1966), foldings I and VIII, and U. Finkbeiner et al., *Tübinger Atlas des Vorderen Orients* B IV 20: Beispiele altorientalischer Städte, Residenzen des Assyrischen Reiches 2.1 Kalḫu (Nimrūd) (1993).

than the single private archive so far excavated. As can be seen from the following survey, many of the texts in the archives date from the period just before the move of the capital to Dur-Šarrukin, during the last years of the reign of Sargon II (721–705 B.C.). Another concentration of tablets originates from a higher level dating to the seventh century B.C., just before the destruction of the city, during the collapse of the Assyrian Empire.[23]

23. For an introduction, see J. N. Postgate and J. E. Reade, "Kalḫu" *RLA* 5 (1976–1980), 303–323, with bibliography; cf. also J. Curtis, "Nimrud," *OEANE* 4 (1997), 141–144, with short bibliography. The final

3.1.2.1 Archives in Fort Shalmaneser

The building complex Fort Shalmaneser, in the texts called *ekal māšarti*, the "Review Palace," consisted of two large northern courtyards surrounded by rooms for administration, and a central courtyard, whose southern doors opened onto the throne room in the southern part of the building complex. The latter area also contained rooms for the royal family. Two main levels yielded cuneiform tablets, one from the eighth, the other from the late seventh century B.C.

The text groups from the eighth century B.C. come primarily from the archive (**Kalḫu 1**) in Rooms NE 47–50 at the northern side of the northeast courtyard; a few were found in other rooms nearby. The clay tablets may have fallen down from an upper story. The main archive consists of about 80 unsealed administrative texts. Among them are 22 horse lists, reflecting musters of the cavalry and chariotry; some of these lists enumerate personnel from different areas. There are also 48 wine lists, documenting the use of specified amounts of wine. It seems that both the wine lists and the horse lists can be assigned to musters and feastings during the month before and the month after the new year, a period of several years. The remains of an archive (**Kalḫu 2**) consisting of 11 clay tablets were discovered in Room SW 6, which served as a wine store. Two of the tablets are notes about delivery of wine from the province; most of the rest are lists of wine recording the use of wine.

Three archives date to the late seventh century B.C. The remains of the archive (**Kalḫu 3**) of the *rab ekalli*, "palace manager," found in the northern corner of the south courtyard, most in Rooms SE 1 and SE 10, include 27 clay tablets. There are letters and documents connected with the *rab ekalli*'s work as manager of the Review Palace. Most of the tablets are sealed. In addition, there are several sealed clay bullae that apparently were once applied to wooden objects with a flat surface and secured with a string. These objects could either have been wooden boxes or wooden writing boards, called *lē'u* in contemporaneous texts, possibly inscribed with lists of soldiers. In Rooms SE 14–15 another archive (**Kalḫu 4**) consisted of 19 clay tablets. The reasons for placing this archive in the palace is not clear; possibly the persons concerned were palace employees. Most of the texts are purchase documents, but there are also some loan documents, a release document, a legal settlement, and a letter; one of the loans is written in Neo-Babylonian. The remains of the archive (**Kalḫu 5**) of the queen's household and of her *šakintu*, "woman manager," were excavated in Room S 10 in the inner southern part of the palace and consist of 18, mostly sealed, clay tablets. The

archaeological publications are M. E. L. Mallowan, *Nimrud and Its Remains* (=*NR*) I, II, and foldings (1966), and in the series Ivories from Nimrud. The final text editions are in the series Cuneiform Texts from Nimrud (=CTN) I– (1972–). Preliminary publications of archaeological matters and texts are in *Iraq*.

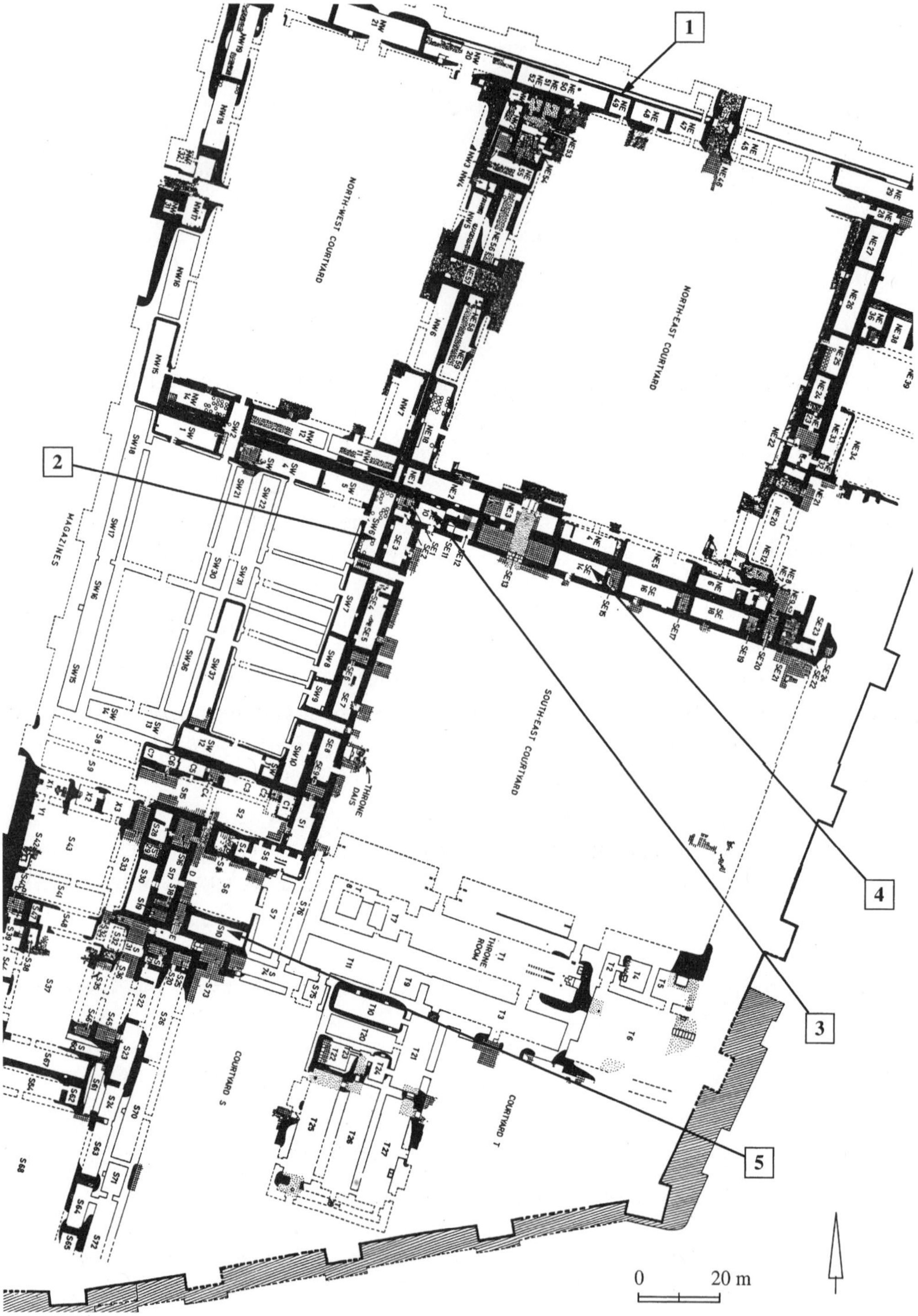
1
2
3
4
5
NORTH-WEST COURTYARD
NORTH-EAST COURTYARD
SOUTH-EAST COURTYARD
MAGAZINES
THRONE DAIS
THRONE ROOM
COURTYARD S
COURTYARD T
0
20 m

main text categories are purchase documents, loans, and lawsuits, all generally in favor of the *šakintu* or the queen.[24] An Aramaic ostracon with a list of persons was found in another room and testifies to the use of an alphabetic writing system in the palace. Some ivories also have short notes in Aramaic or Hebrew on the backside.[25]

3.1.2.2 Archives and Remains of Library in the Northwest Palace

The citadel must be entered through a gate in the eastern wall surrounding it. A street opens inside the gate, with the Governor's Palace on the northern side and the Nabû Temple and "Burnt Palace" on the southern side. The Northwest Palace was situated northwest of the Governor's Palace with several buildings between them.

Assurnasirpal II (883–859 B.C.) built the large Northwest Palace. In the north, the palace had a large courtyard surrounded by rooms for administration. On the southern side of this courtyard, doors led to the throne room and the rest of the palace, which consisted of other courtyards surrounded by a large number of rooms. The southern part of the palace served, at least during some periods, as living quarters for the royal family, until Sargon II moved the capital during the second half of his reign. Many of the texts from this palace date to the years just before the move to Dur-Šarrukin; these groups of texts will be treated first, followed by a discussion of the later texts.

Room ZT 4, measuring 9.5 × 4.2 meters, on the northern side of the northern courtyard, yielded approximately 400 clay tablets in the fill. Most of the eastern half of the room was occupied by two benches made of burnt bricks. Between the benches were two rows of brick boxes open at the top, seven of them in the northern and six in the southern row. It has been suggested that the boxes may have been used for storing clay tablets. The tablets are the remains of the royal archive (**Kalḫu 6**) of Sargon II and some of his predecessors. The texts include letters to the king, some

24. J. V. Kinnier-Wilson, *The Nimrud Wine Lists*, CTN I (1972); and S. Dalley and J. N. Postgate, *The Tablets from Fort Shalmaneser*, CTN III (1984); cf. also my review of the last-mentioned book in *AfO* 35 (1988), 169–173.

25. J. B. Segal, *Iraq* 19 (1957), 139–145, and A. R. Millard, *Iraq* 24 (1962), 41–51.

← *Plan 67*. Kalḫu.
Plan of Fort Shalmaneser with archives **Kalḫu 1-5**.
From M. E. L. Mallowan, *NR* (1966), folding VIII.

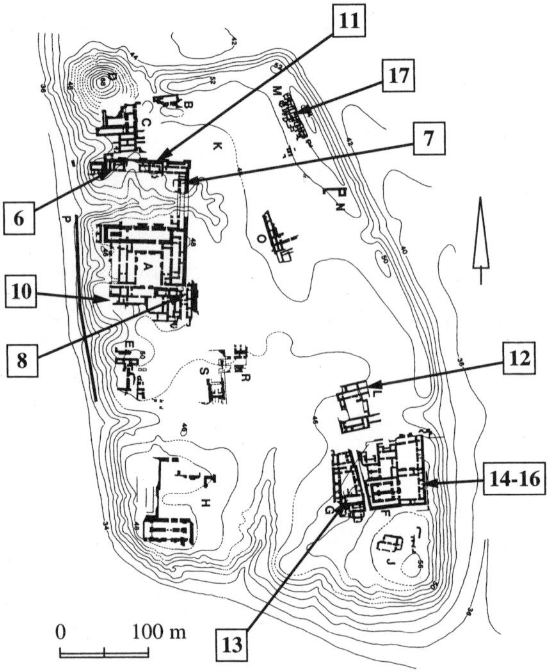

Plan 68. Kalḫu.
Plan of citadel with archives **Kalḫu 6-17**.
From J. Meuszynski, *Die Rekonstruktion der Reliefdarstellungen und ihrer Anordnung im Nordwestpalast von Kalḫu (Nimrūd)* [I], BaF 2 (1981), plan 1.

copies of letters sent by the king, a number of administrative texts, long lists or short notes concerning people and objects, occasional records of payments from conquered areas, and one literary text.[26]

26. Cf. M. E. L. Mallowan, *NR* I (1966), 172, fig. 106. B. Parker, *Iraq* 23 (1961), 15–67, pls. XI–XXX. The letters are partially published by H. W. F. Saggs in *Iraq* 17 (1955), 21–50, pls. I-IX; *Iraq* 17 (1955), 126–154, pls. XXX–XXXV; *Iraq* 18 (1956), 40–56, pls. IX–XII; *Iraq* 20 (1958), 182–212, pls. XXXVII–XLI; *Iraq* 21 (1959), 158–179, pls. XLIII–XLIX; *Iraq* 25 (1963), 70–80, pls. XI–XIV; *Iraq* 27 (1965), 17–32, pls. II–VII; *Iraq* 28 (1966), 177–191, pls. LIII–LVI; and *Iraq* 36 (1974), 199–221. These letters are now in the process of being republished in the State Archives of Assyria (=SAA) series; a few can already be found in S. Parpola, *The Correspondence of Sargon II*, part I, Letters from Assyria and the West, SAA 1 (1987) and G. B. Lanfranchi and S. Parpola, *The Correspondence of Sargon II*, part II, Letters from the Northern and Northeastern Privinces, SAA 5 (1990).

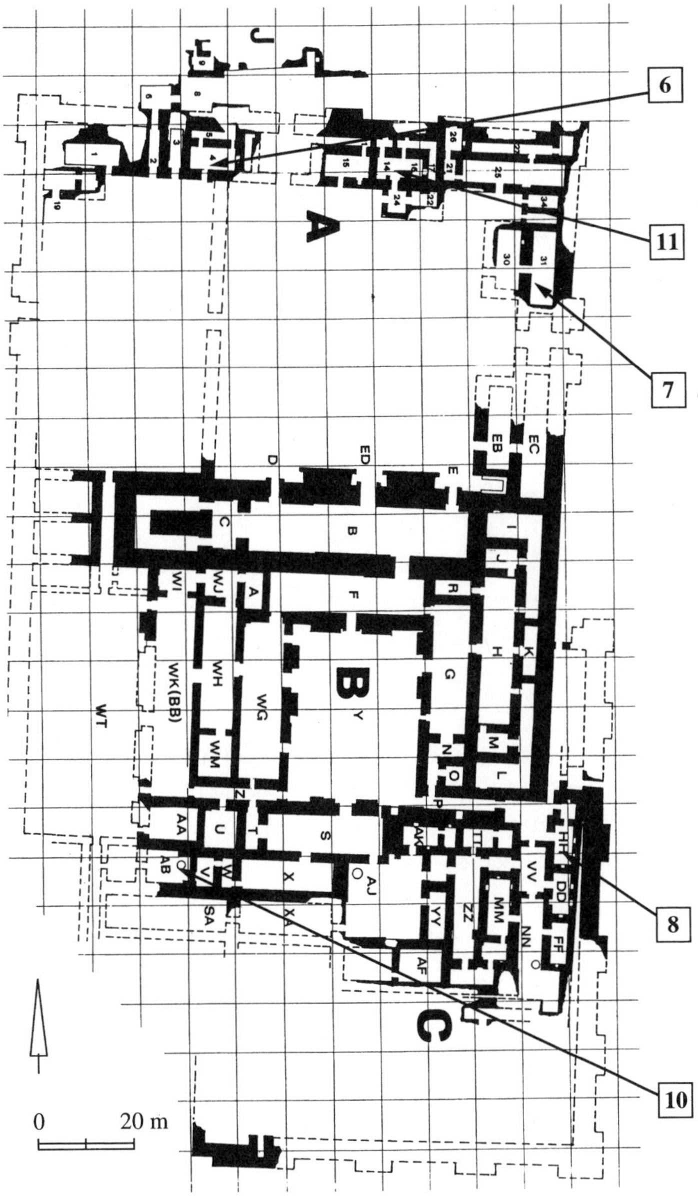

Plan 69. Kalḫu.
Plan of Northwest Palace with archives **Kalḫu 6-11**.
From S. M. Paley and R. P. Sobolewski, *The Reconstruction of the Relief Representations and their Positions in the Northwest-Palace at Kalḫu (Nimrūd)* II, BaF 10 (1987), plan 1.

Rooms ZT 30 and 31, on the eastern side of the northern courtyard, contained a few tablets (**Kalḫu 7**) and a number of large jars. Among the administrative texts are lists of quantities of stored oil, which probably was kept in the very jars excavated in the rooms.[27]

In the southeastern part of the palace, Room HH contained 14 small clay tablets and clay sealings, some of which had the remains of jar necks on their backs. They date to 719–715 B.C. and represent a small fraction of the documentation of the palace administration (**Kalḫu 8**).[28]

An archive (**Kalḫu 9**) of about 180 clay tablets has recently been unearthed in Room 57. Only 20 of the texts have been made accessible in a preliminary publication. These texts date to 800–736 B.C. and consist of purchase documents, as well as a list of oxen. An older group among these texts consists of the documents of Nabû-tuklatuya, a palace scribe (*ṭupšar ekalli*), and concern the purchase of slaves and houses; a younger group deals with the acquisition of fields by other men, some of them servants of the queen.[29]

In two wells in the southern part of the Northwest Palace, hidden valuables, especially ones made of ivory, were unearthed. While excavating inside the well in Room AB to a depth of 20 meters, below the water level, excavators found the remains of a library (**Kalḫu 10**) planned for Dur-Šarrukin. Sixteen leaves of ivory writing boards and the remains of at least the same number of leaves of wooden writing boards were unearthed. Remains of the wax that had originally covered the boards could be seen; traces of cuneiform writing in the wax show that an astrological series had been written on the boards. According to the cuneiform script on the outer cover of the ivory boards, the series was destined to be placed in Sargon's palace at Dur-Šarrukin. This is the largest and best-preserved discovery of writing boards in Mesopotamia. According to contemporaneous texts, such writing boards (*lēʾu*) appear to have been used frequently for longer literary texts, as well as for administrative purposes.[30]

So far, all the texts discussed from the Northwest Palace have dated to the period prior to the move of the capital to Dur-Šarrukin. An archive (**Kalḫu 11**) from a higher

27. D. J. Wiseman, *Iraq* 15 (1953), 137, 139, and 148.

28. J. N. Postgate, *The Governor's Palace Archive*, CTN II (1973), nos. 250–263.

29. K. Deller and A. Fadhil, "Neue Nimrud-Urkunden des 8. Jahrhunderts v. Chr.," *BaM* 24 (1993), 243–270, pls. 55–114. No plan of the appropriate part of the palace excavated by the Department of Antiquities and Heritage, Baghdad, in 1989 has so far been published.

30. D. J. Wiseman, "Assyrian Writing-Boards," *Iraq* 17 (1955), 3–13, M. Howard, "Technical Description of the Ivory Writing-Boards from Nimrud," *Iraq* 17 (1955), 14–20, and M. E. L. Mallowan, *NR* I (1966), 149–163.

level in Rooms ZT 13–17 in the northern part of the northern courtyard postdates the move; about 60 clay tablets date between 687 B.C. and the end of the Assyrian period. There are loan documents, purchase documents involving slaves and land, court judgments, marriage documents, and a few administrative lists.[31]

3.1.2.3 Archives in the Governor's Palace and the Burnt Palace

The Governor's Palace, or "Governor's House," as it was called in contemporaneous texts, had a central courtyard around which rooms were grouped. North of the courtyard was a large Audience Room M, whose western wall had a door to the small Room K and whose eastern wall had a door to Room S; in these three rooms an archive (**Kalḫu 12**) of 217 clay tablets was unearthed. The tablets in Rooms K and M are generally of the same types and may originally have been preserved in Room K, which may have served as an archive room for legal documents. Room S, on the other side of the audience room, contained letters (most of which were addressed to the governors) and most of the administrative texts in the combined collection. The texts date from 835 until 710 B.C. and are the remains of five successive governors (*šaknu* and *bēl pāḫete*) of Kalḫu, namely Mušezib-Ninurta, Bel-tarṣi-iluma, Bel-dan, Marduk-remani, and Šarru-duri. The archives concern their official duties and are not their private archives, which may have been maintained elsewhere. A literary text and a recipe for the preparation of perfumes belongs to this same collection.[32]

On the southern side of the central courtyard of the Burnt Palace, situated just west of the Nabû temple, was a throne room (Room 8). In this room, or in adjoining ones, the excavators unearthed letters to Sargon II (**Kalḫu 13**). They also found some inscribed clay jar sealings.[33]

3.1.2.4 Library and Archives in the Nabû Temple

The Ezida, the temple of Nabû, the god of the art of writing, was situated south of the main entrance to the citadel and opened onto two main courtyards, one behind the other. On the western side of the inner courtyard the cellas of Nabû and his consort Tašmetu were situated. The remains of a library (**Kalḫu 14**) were found in disturbed archaeological contexts in and around Room NT12, on the eastern side of the inner courtyard. The excavators unearthed most of the clay tablets in secondary

31. B. Parker, *Iraq* 16 (1954), 29–53, pls. V–IX; *Iraq* 23 (1961), 15–21, pls. IXf.

32. J. N. Postgate, *The Governor's Palace Archive*, CTN II (1973), nos. 1–217.

33. J. N. Postgate, *The Governor's Palace Archive*, CTN II (1973), nos. 231–246.

position in Room NT12 and in the courtyard nearby, but some tablets were also uncovered in Rooms NT13 and NT14. Seven fragments of badly preserved wooden and ivory writing boards were also found in Room NT13. The library contains about 280 clay tablets of diverse types: the largest group consists of 79 tablets with different types of omens, especially astrological ones, 75 with incantations and medical texts, as well as 37 lexical lists; but there are also some prayers and hymns, hemerological texts, epics, and rituals. There are several royal inscriptions—on clay prisms and cylinders—in the collection. A number of administrative documents found together with these texts remains unpublished. Just a few texts in the library have information about those writing them; best attested are members of a family of scribes (*ṭupšarru*), as well as exorcists (*āšipu*). Evidence may point to the existence of the library from around 800 B.C. to the end of the Assyrian Empire.[34]

West of the first courtyard of the Nabû temple complex lay another courtyard at the northern side of which was a throne room. In this room the excavators unearthed the remains of an archive (**Kalḫu 15**) of fragments of at least eight or nine large clay tablets with treaties in which Esarhaddon made different Median rulers swear under oath to obey Assurbanipal, his son, after his death. The tablets were written 672 B.C., all of them within a time period of a few days. Some scholars have speculated that when the Medes later conquered the Assyrian Empire and Kalḫu, they smashed these treaty tablets in the throne room where the oaths had once been sworn.[35]

In Room NT16, on the southern side of the inner courtyard, the excavators unearthed an archive (**Kalḫu 16**) with 21 cuneiform clay dockets that may once have been tied to Aramaic scrolls of papyri or other perishable material. They may be in a secondary position. The dockets date between 699 and 652 B.C. and concern loans of corn with the quite unusual formulation that the loans were made by the god Nabû.[36]

3.1.2.5 Archive in Private House

In a private house among the TW53 houses next to the citadel wall, in the north-eastern part of the citadel, the inner Room 19 contained 47 cuneiform clay tablets, two

34. D. J. Wiseman and J. A. Black, *Literary Texts from the Temple of Nabû*, CTN IV (1996), with further references; cf. also the preliminary report by D. J. Wiseman, "The Nabu Temple Texts from Nimrud," *JNES* 27 (1968), 248–250.

35. D. J. Wiseman, "The Vassal-Treaties of Esarhaddon," *Iraq* 20 (1958), 1–99, pls. 1–53, I–XII (also published as separate book); K. Watanabe, *Die adê-Vereidigung anlässlich der Thronfolgeregelung Asarhaddons*, BaM Beih. 3 (1987); and S. Parpola and K. Watanabe, *Neo-Assyrian Treaties and Loyalty Oaths*, SAA II (1988), Text 6.

36. B. Parker, *Iraq* 19 (1957), 125–138, pls. XXVII-XXXIII.

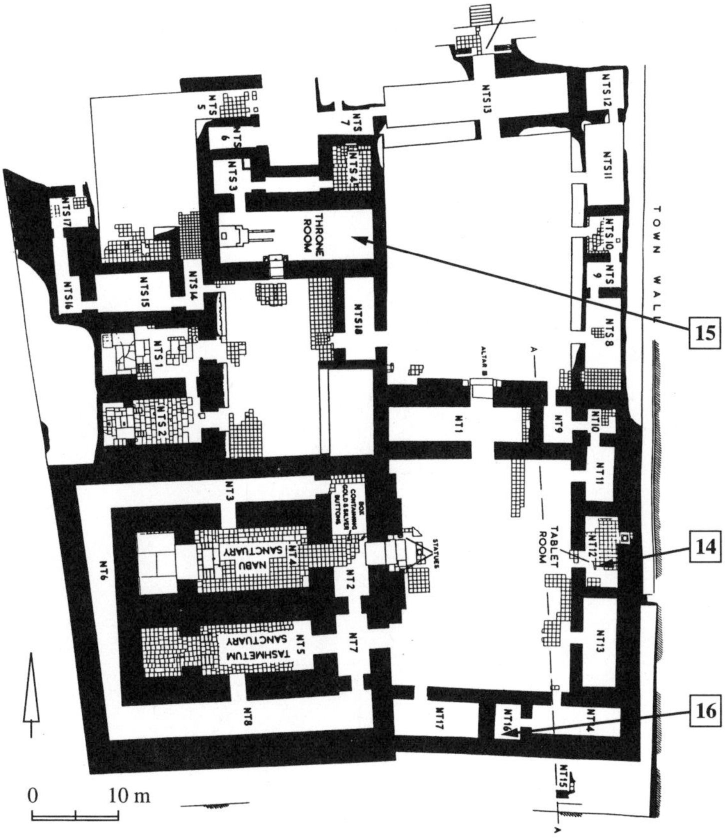

Plan 70. Kalḫu.
Plan of Nabû Temple with archives **Kalḫu 14-16**.
From D. J. Wiseman and J. A. Black, *Literary Texts from the Temple of Nabû* (1996), pl. facing p. 1.

of which are dockets possibly once fastened to Aramaic scrolls of papyri or other material. The texts date to the seventh century B.C., before the end of the Assyrian Empire, and represent the private archive (**Kalḫu 17**) of the eunuch (*ša rēši*) Šamaš-šarru-uṣur and some other men. Most of the texts are documents concerning loans of silver, corn, or birds, that were made by the owners of the archive. There are eleven documents detailing the purchases of female and male slaves and of a house. Among the few other documents is a list of silver and birds that pertained to different persons, possibly an account.[37]

37. D. J. Wiseman, *Iraq* 15 (1953), 135–160.

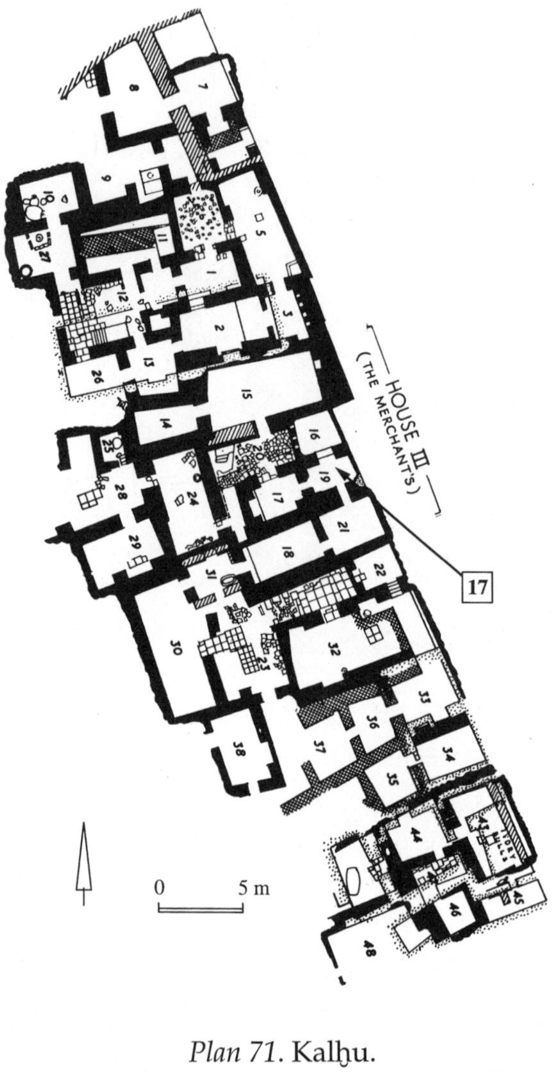

Plan 71. Kalḫu.
Plan of private houses with archive **Kalḫu 17**.
From M. E. L. Mallowan, *NR* I (1966), 185.

3.1.3 Dur-Šarrukin (Khorsabad)

Sargon II (721–705 B.C.) moved to a new capital, Dur-Šarrukin (modern Khorsabad), situated about 20 kilometers north of Nineveh in the northern part of the central Assyrian area. P. E. Botta and V. Place conducted early French excavations at the site (1843–1855), and during the years 1928–1935 H. Frankfort lead an American expedition. The area inside the city wall was ca. 1800 × 1900 meters. The excavations were concentrated in the citadel, ca. 700 × 400 meters, with the royal palace and a temple complex situated on a higher level and the Nabû temple and houses for high-ranking persons on a somewhat lower level. Only small areas outside the citadel were excavated, essentially in the southwestern fortification. The city served as capital only a short time and the extent to which it was inhabited in the large lower city is unknown due to the limited extent of the excavated area. The number of cuneiform tablets found to date in Dur-Šarrukin seems to be rather limited. For writing boards destined to be placed in a library at the palace in Dur-Sharrukin, compare the above discussed remains of a library from Kalḫu (Kalḫu 10).[38]

3.1.3.1 Remains of Archives and Libraries in the Nabû Temple

In the Nabû temple in the southwestern part of the lower citadel area, scanty remains of archives and libraries were unearthed. Most texts were preserved in two gaterooms southwest and south of Forecourt I that led to inner parts of the temple; in one (Room H 13) were a few lexical lists, god-lists, prayers, and omens, and in the other (Room H 29) a few incantations and some documents. In Room H 12, on the southeastern side, a clay tablet with the Assyrian king-list was found. The most interesting room was Room H 5 (**Dur-Šarrukin 1**) on the northwestern side of Forecourt I; in its northeastern part were three tiers of niches in the wall, each measuring 25–30 cm square and being 40–50 cm deep, separated from one another by 10 cm partitions. In the archaeological publications, a few fragments of clay tablets and inscribed prisms found within the niches were said to be indicative of, but not firm proof for the existence of, a temple library. Room H 15 (**Dur-Šarrukin 2**), on the northwestern side of central Courtyard II, opposite the main cella of Nabû, had two similar tiers of niches on one side. No objects of any sort were found in these niches, but their similar construction of the niches makes an identical function very probable. The discovery

38. As an introduction to the site, cf. G. Frame, "Khorsabad," *OEANE* 3 (1997), 295–298, with short bibliography. Main archaeological publications are G. Loud, *Khorsabad I: Excavations in the Palace and at a City Gate*, OIP 38 (1936); and G. Loud and C. B. Altman, *Khorsabad II: The Citadel and the Town*, OIP 40 (1938), both with further references.

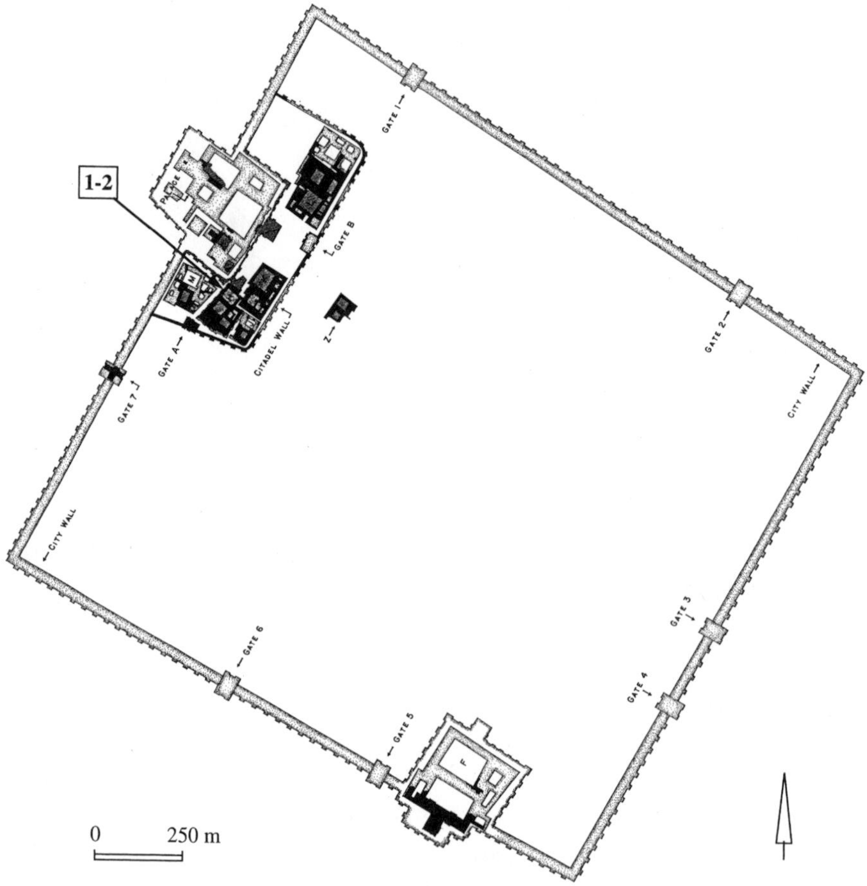

Plan 72. Dur-Šarrukin.
General plan with archives and libraries **Dur-Šarrukin 1-2**.
From G. Loud and C. B. Altman, *Khorsabad* II (1938), pl. 69.

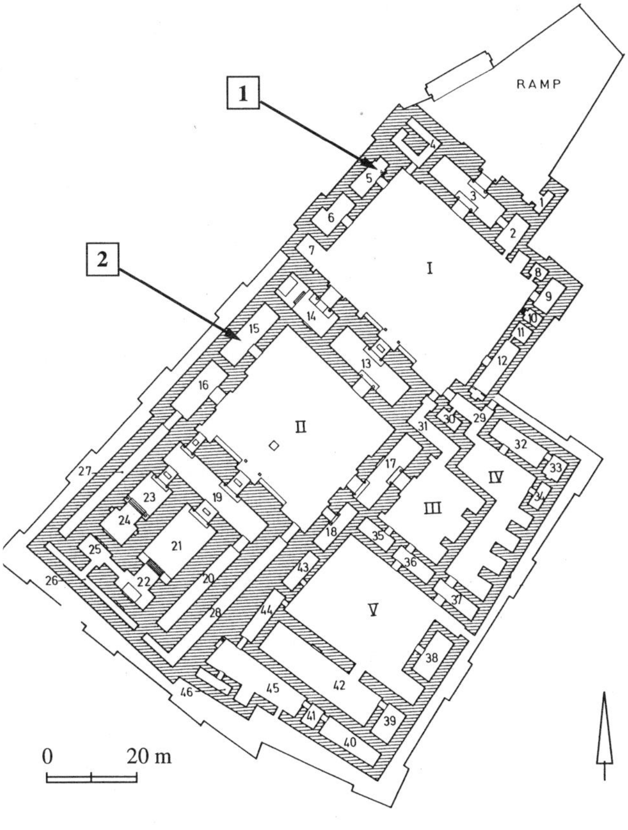

Plan 73. Dur-Šarrukin.
Plan of Nabû Temple with archives and libraries **Dur-Šarrukin 1-2**.
From E. Heinrich, *Die Tempel und Heiligtümer im Alten Mesopotamien* (1982), pl. 355.

of the temple library in Sippar (3.2.4.2) filled with numerous clay tablets with literary contents, to be discussed below, makes the interpretation of the rooms in the Nabû temple of Dur-Šarrukin as temple libraries much more probable now than when it was first suggested during the excavations. The empty niches or shelves may either be due to the possible transfer of the main parts of the archives and libraries to Nineveh when Sennacherib moved the capital to that city, or perhaps, at least partly, to the use of perishable writing materials, such as writing boards, papyri, and leather.[39]

3.1.4 Nineveh (Kuyunjik)

After the death of Sargon, Sennacherib (704–681 B.C.) moved the capital to Nineveh on the eastern bank of the Tigris, just opposite modern Mosul. P. E. Botta and V. Place conducted French excavations at the site as early as 1842–1855. During 1845–1932 several British expeditions headed by A. H. Layard, H. Rassam, R. C. Thompson, and others excavated several of the monumental buildings; during the period 1951–1987 several Iraqi expeditions directed by T. Madhloom and others continued work at the site. An American excavation headed by D. Stronach started new excavations in 1987–1990. The large number of cuneiform clay tablets found in the monumental buildings in Nineveh during the early excavations ("Assurbanipal's Library") contributed greatly to the rise of the discipline of Assyriology at the end of the nineteenth century. The large area enclosed by the city walls was ca. 5 × 2 kilometers. There were two citadels in the western part of the city at the bank of the Tigris: the largest citadel (modern Kuyunjik), ca. 900 × 500 meters, with Sennacherib's Southwest Palace and Assurbanipal's North Palace, as well as the Nabû and Ištar temples between the palaces, was situated on a tell whose earliest layers established in an excavation trench contained findings from the Hassuna, Uruk, and Nineveh 5 periods. Most of the smaller citadel (modern Nebi Yunus) has not been excavated because of modern buildings on the site, but there seems to have been other monumental buildings, among them at least one palace. The very large area in the lower city is essentially unexcavated, and many private houses, as well as some official buildings, were probably situated there. Most of the excavated houses contained large quantities of clay tablets; unfortunately, the poor recording procedures during the early excavations make a reconstruction of individual archives and libraries very uncertain. Since so few private houses have been excavated, the majority of

39. Cf. G. Loud and C. B. Altman, *Khorsabad II* (1938), 46, 56–64, 104–105.

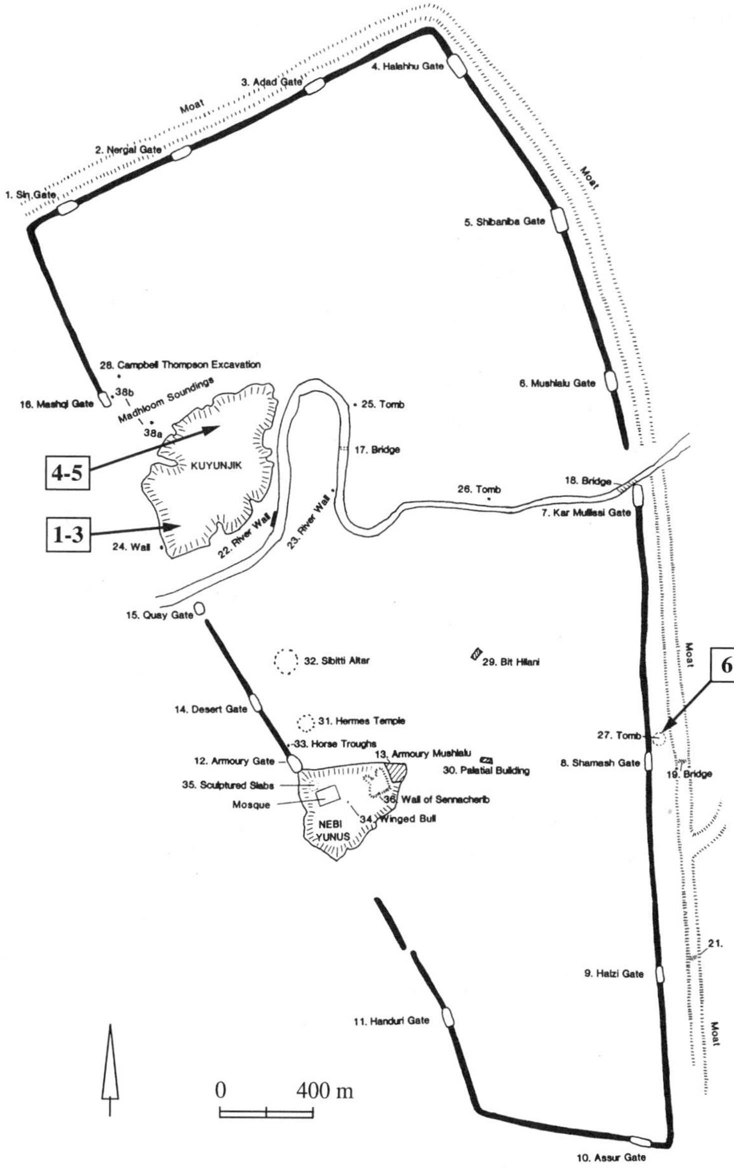

Plan 74. Nineveh.
General plan with archives and libraries **Nineveh 1-6**.
From M. L. Scott and J. Macginnis, *Iraq* 52 (1990), 73 fig. 4.

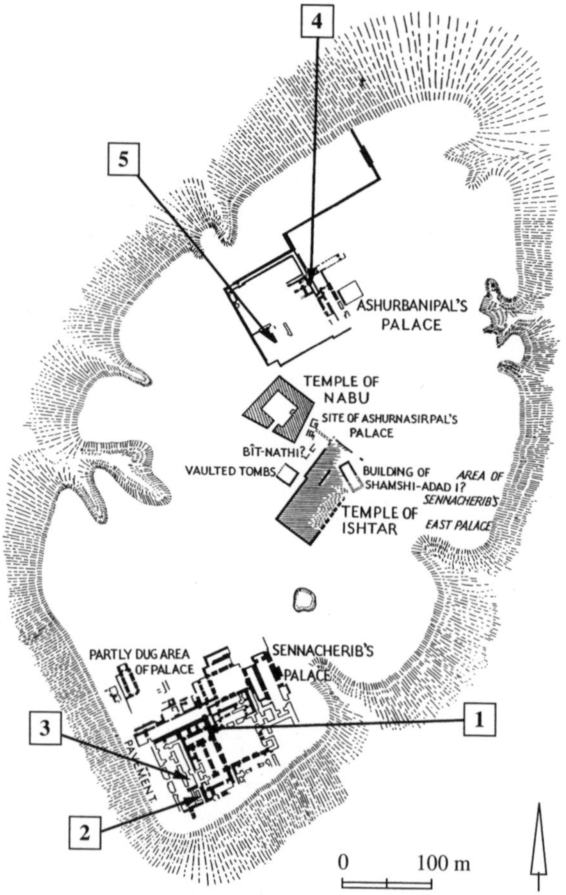

Plan 75. Nineveh.
General plan of Kuyunjik with archives and libraries **Nineveh 1-5**.
From R. Campbell Thompson, *Iraq* 1 (1934), 97 fig. 1.

private archives and libraries, which certainly existed in large numbers in Nineveh, have not been uncovered.[40]

40. As an introduction to the site, cf. D. Stronach and K. Codella, "Nineveh," *OEANE* 4 (1997), 144–148, with bibliography. For a list of directors of expeditions to Nineveh with summaries of excavations outside Kuyunjik, cf. M. L. Scott and J. Macginnis, "Notes on Nineveh," *Iraq* 52 (1990), 63–73, with further bibliography.

Due to the great difficulties in reconstructing correct provenances for many of the texts from Nineveh, the main areas, where the remains of archives or libraries were found, will first be described.[41]

3.1.4.1 Archives and Libraries in the Royal Palaces

Clay tablets were widely distributed in different parts of the palaces; in a few places, however, the early excavators reported large concentrations of textual remains that should possibly be classified as archives and libraries, even if almost all detailed information about the individual texts from these collections is presently unavailable.

3.1.4.1.1 Archive and Library Rooms in the Southwest Palace

The Southwest Palace is described in historical texts as the palace of Sennacherib (704–681 B.C.). It was the main royal palace in Nineveh. Rooms XL and XLI were situated in the central part of the Southwest Palace, which had stone reliefs on the walls. Room XLI was accessible from a large hall, whereas Room XL was accessible only from Room XLI. In these two rooms, and in some of the adjoining rooms, the excavators unearthed a library (**Nineveh 1**) containing a large number, perhaps most, of the clay tablets containing literary texts that have been found in Nineveh. During the time of Assurbanipal (668–627 B.C.) these tablets were probably part of his library. Some archival texts also seem to come from these rooms—what types of documents and how many is unclear. It is also unclear whether these rooms served as the original location of a library combined with an archive; the library may also have been placed on an upper floor, above these rooms.

Room LXI, located towards the southern end of what is preserved of the palace, may have served as a ramp to an upper floor. About 450 clay bullae were unearthed in this ramp. The bullae had seal impressions on one side, and on the back were indi-

41. The description here essentially follows what is presently known about the provenances as presented by J. Reade, "Archaeology and the Kuyunjik Archives," *Cuneiform Archives and Libraries*, CRRAI 30 (1986), 213–222, who refers to additional, older literature. In the same volume, S. Parpola, "The Royal Archives in Nineveh," *Cuneiform Archives and Libraries*, CRRAI 30 (1986), 223–236, offers another reconstruction, based more on the contents of the texts; on several points he disagrees with Reade. Unfortunately, Reade and Parpola, the two leading scholars who have dealt with the archaeological background and contents of the Nineveh archives, respectively, were not given the opportunity to read each other's contributions to the cited volume. As a result, conflicting opinions are expressed, which makes it difficult for others to use the important information given. The seal impressions on the clay tablets, as well as the clay bullae, have been studied by S. Herbordt, *Neuassyrische Glyptik des 8.–7. Jh. v. Chr.*, SAAS 1 (1992).

cations that they had been fastened with ropes to other objects. The traditional interpretation from the time of the excavation has been that these objects were scrolls of papyri or other material. Because most of the bullae were not fastened directly to another object, but hung by means of attached ropes like dockets, it is not possible to

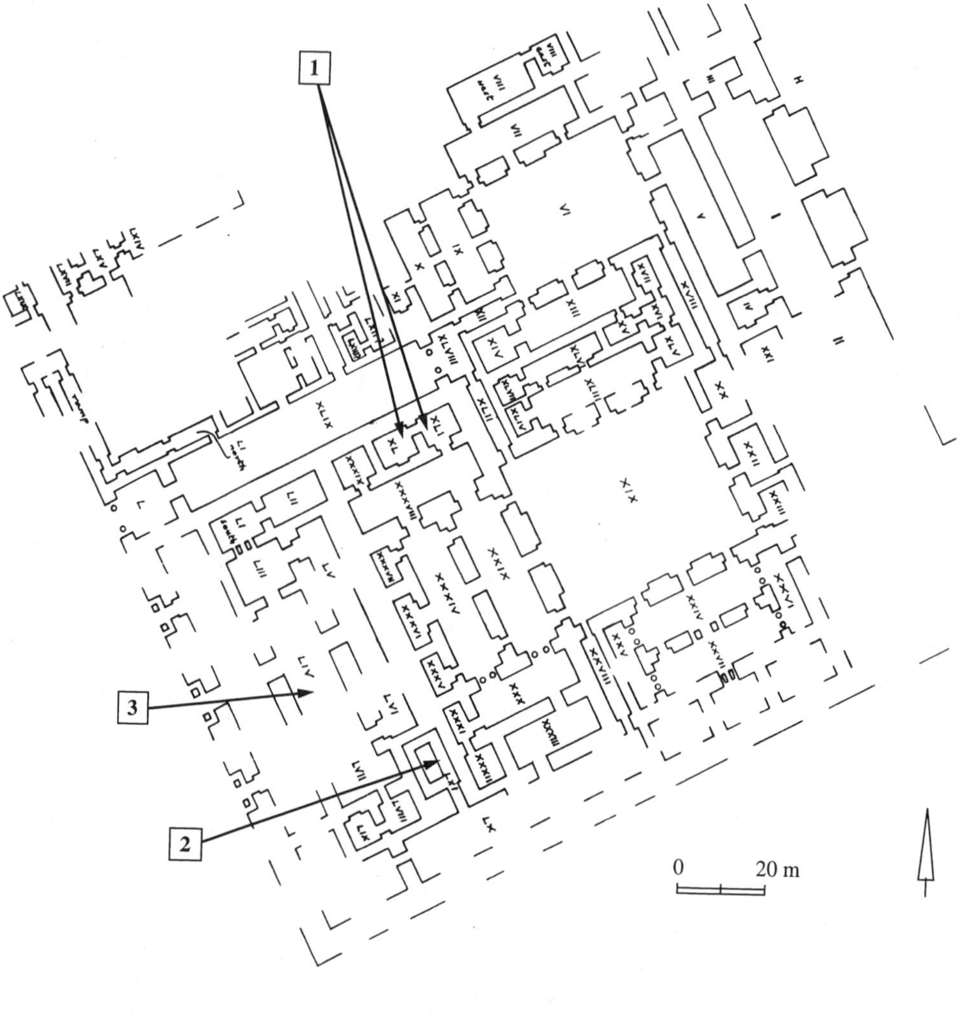

Plan 76. Nineveh.
Plan of Southwest Palace with archives and libraries **Nineveh 1-3**.
From J. E. Reade, *BaM* 10 (1979), 87 fig. 9.

say whether the objects consisted of papyri, leather, or writing boards; they may have been objects without writing. These bullae are the only remains of a possible archive (**Nineveh 2**) of documents and, perhaps, letters on papyri written in Aramaic. Also in the southern part of the palace, in the area of Room LIV, west of the room with the bullae, were the remains of an archive (**Nineveh 3**) with a number of cuneiform documents on clay tablets. On some of these tablets were, in addition to the cuneiform, short summary notes in Aramaic.

Minor groups of clay tablets were unearthed in several other rooms of the palace. Some of these may have been minor archives, while others may have been a few tablets set aside for use just before the destruction of the palace. A few tablets in or next to the throne room, in the northeastern part of what has been excavated of the palace, may represent the latter phenomenon. As far as is known, all the tablets are letters from Uruk.

3.1.4.1.2 Archive and Library Rooms in the North Palace

The North Palace is described in the building inscriptions as the Crown-Prince Palace (*bīt ridûti*). Room C, in the reception part of the building, contained a large number of clay tablets. The few tablets that can be identified indicate that this was the remains of an archive (**Nineveh 4**) that included documents for military officers (*rab kiṣri*) and others. It has sometimes been suggested that this archive may have been stored on an upper floor. Whether, in addition to archival documents, literary texts were found in this room depends on the interpretation of the published notes.

A library (**Nineveh 5**) with a large number of literary texts seems to have been found in the southern corner of the North Palace. This was part of what has been referred to as "Assurbanipal's Library"; some of the literary texts with longer colophons come from this library. However, since the texts were recovered just next to the Nabû temple, mixing with a possible library there cannot be excluded.

3.1.4.2 Possible Library in the Nabû Temple

The Nabû temple was situated immediately south of the North Palace. According to the colophons on a limited number of clay tablets, they come from a library in the Nabû temple. However, only two tablets are known to have been found in that vicinity, but a mixing with tablets said to originate from the southern corner of the North Palace cannot be excluded. These alternatives make it impossible to determine whether the Nabû temple housed a small library or one of the major ones.

3.1.4.3 General Notes on Texts from Archives and Libraries in Palaces and Temples

The essentially old excavations make reconstructions of which texts belonged to which archive or library, in most cases, impossible. Due to the importance of the findings in this city, short notes will be given on the total number of texts from Nineveh, even if this information falls outside the theme of the work. About 30,000 clay tablets or fragments of clay tablets are said to come from this city. Many of the fragments can be joined with certainty, so the number of original tablets can be reduced to about a third. This more realistic number will now be divided into libraries and archives.

The number of literary texts excavated from the libraries has been roughly estimated to be 5,000. Many of the texts have colophons with the name of Assurbanipal; these are texts copied for his library. Other texts have colophons with different names; these are tablets originally destined for other libraries, but incorporated into the library of Assurbanipal. According to references in various texts, the libraries contained, in addition to clay tablets, numerous writing boards, which have not been preserved. The main categories of texts in the libraries were omens, incantations, medical texts, and lexical lists, but all types of traditional Mesopotamian literature can be found, including, for example, epics, prayers, myths, historical texts, and wisdom texts. Most of the preserved texts are in the Standard Babylonian dialect, but some are in Sumerian and older dialects of Akkadian.

The archives excavated in Nineveh contain about 6,000 clay tablets. Most of the letters, reports, and queries belonged to the royal archives. Most of the ca. 3,000 letters to the king, or copies of letters sent by the king, are written in the Neo-Assyrian language, but 1,000 of them, dealing with matters in Babylonia, are written in Neo-Babylonian. The letters date to the times of Sargon II, Esarhaddon, and Assurbanipal (721–627 B.C.), and deal often with what was considered to be of major interest to the king and the state. The 500 or so astrological reports and the 350 queries to the sun-god, from the time of Esarhaddon and Assurbanipal (680–627 B.C.), also deal with matters of importance for the king and the state. The presence of only about 500 administrative texts, often in the form of lists, may indicate that much of the administration was done without writing on clay tablets. Most of the 804 documents, for example, loan documents and purchase documents, date between 702 and the end of the Assyrian Empire, that is, during the reigns of Sennacherib, Esarhaddon, Assurbanipal, and their successors, but a limited number are from the earlier period 747–704 B.C. The documents were often written for officials of the king, for example, military officers, or the woman manager (*šakintu*) of the harem. A division of these different types of texts into the main archives excavated, as described above, and possibly also into other minor archives, unfortunately cannot be made. In addition to the usual

Neo-Assyrian and Neo-Babylonian cuneiform texts, documentation in Aramaic and, possibly, a group of Elamite texts are attested.[42]

3.1.4.4 Archive Possibly from a Private House

During the excavation of tunnels with Parthian graves north of the Šamaš Gate, Iraqi archaeologists found a clay pot with about 30 clay tablets in a secondary context. The pot with the tablets may come from a Neo-Assyrian house nearby. The tablets are the archive (**Nineveh 6**) of Ninurta-šarru-uṣur, *mār ekalli*, "son of the palace," and related persons, including some Egyptians. The texts, dating between 669 B.C. and the end of the Assyrian Empire, are loans, purchases, and legal settlements, as well as some additional documents, including a letter.[43]

3.1.5 Imgur-Enlil (Balawat)

Imgur-Enlil (modern Balawat) is situated in central Assyria, northeast of Kalḫu, about 28 kilometers southeast of Mosul. Due to the presence of modern graves, Brit-

42. Cf., e.g., A. L. Oppenheim, *Ancient Mesopotamia*, 2nd ed., revised by E. Reiner (1977), especially 15–18; S. Parpola, "Assyrian Library Records," *JNES* 42 (1983), 1–30; and S. Parpola, "The Royal Archives in Nineveh," *Cuneiform Archives and Libraries*, CRRAI 30 (1986), 223–236. For texts in the libraries, cf. E. Leichty, *A Bibliography of the Cuneiform Tablets of the Kuyunjik Collection in the British Museum* (1964). The texts from the archives are in the process of being republished in the series State Archives of Assyria (=SAA); so far, see especially S. Parpola, *The Correspondence of Sargon II*, part I, Letters from Assyria and the West, SAA 1 (1987); S. Parpola and K. Watanabe, *Neo-Assyrian Treaties and the Loyalty Oaths*, SAA 2 (1988); I. Starr, *Queries to the Sungod*, SAA 4 (1990); G. B. Lanfranchi and S. Parpola, *The Correspondence of Sargon II*, part II, Letters from the Northern and Northeastern Privinces, SAA 5 (1990); T. Kwasman and S. Parpola, *Legal Transactions of the Royal Court of Nineveh*, part I, Tiglath-Pileser III through Esarhaddon, SAA 6 (1991); F. M. Fales and J. N. Postgate, *Imperial Administrative Records*, part I, Palace and Temple Administration, SAA 7 (1992); H. Hunger, *Astrological Reports to Assyrian Kings*, SAA 8 (1992); S. Parpola, *Letters from Assyrian and Babylonian Scholars*, SAA 10 (1993); F. M. Fales and J. N. Postgate, *Imperial Administrative Records*, part II, *Provincial and Military Administration*, SAA 11 (1995); and L. Kataja and R. Whiting, *Grants, Decrees, and Gifts of the Neo-Assyrian Period*, SAA 12 (1995). Other recent publications of texts are S. Parpola, *Letters from Assyrian Scholars to the Kings Esarhaddon and Assurbanipal*, parts I and II, AOAT 5/1 and 2 (1971, 1983); T. Kwasman, *Neo-Assyrian Legal Documents in the Kouyunjik Collection of the British Museum*, Studia Pohl: Series Maior 14 (1988); and F. M. Fales, *Aramaic Epigraphs on Clay Tablets of the Assyrian Period*, Studi Semitici, Nuova Serie 2 (1986). For the Elamite texts, cf. F. H. Weissbach, "Susische Thontäfelchen," *Beiträge zur Assyriologie und semitische Sprachwissenschaft* 4 (1902), 168–202; and J. Reade, "Archaeology and the Kuyunjik Archives," *Cuneiform Archives and Libraries*, CRRAI 30 (1986), 213–222, who maintains that Nineveh was the place of excavation despite objections by F. H. Weissbach and others.

43. N. Postgate and B. K. Ismail, *Texts from Nineveh*, Texts in the Iraq Museum 11 (1993), nos. 3–30e; T. Madhloom, "Nineveh, The 1967–1968 Campaign," *Sumer* 24 (1968), 45–52; cf. O. Pedersén and L. Troy, "Egyptians in Nineveh," *N.A.B.U.* 1993/48.

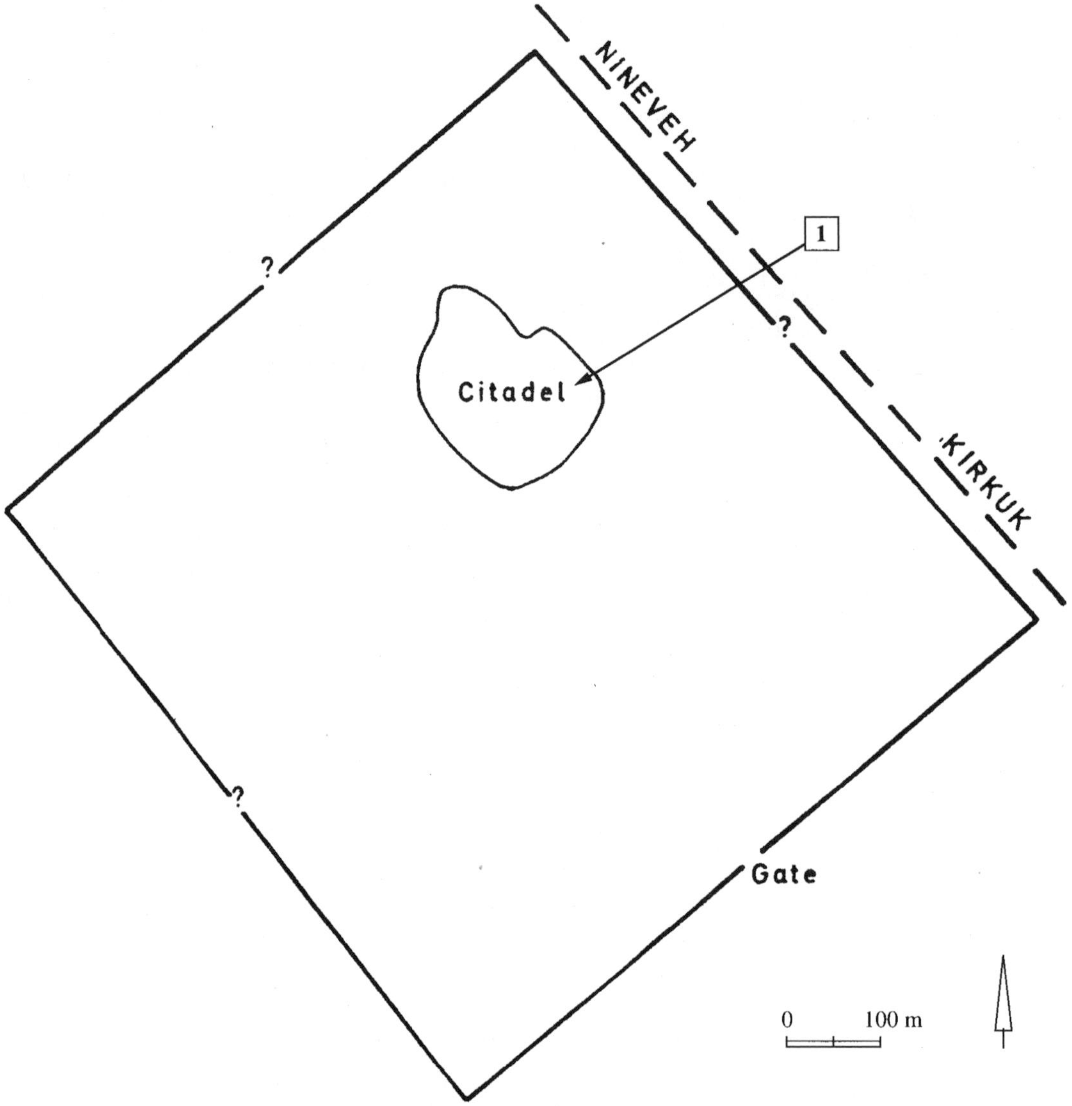

Plan 77. Imgur-Enlil.
General plan with archive **Imgur-Enlil 1**.
From D. Oates, Iraq 36 (1974), pl. XXIV.

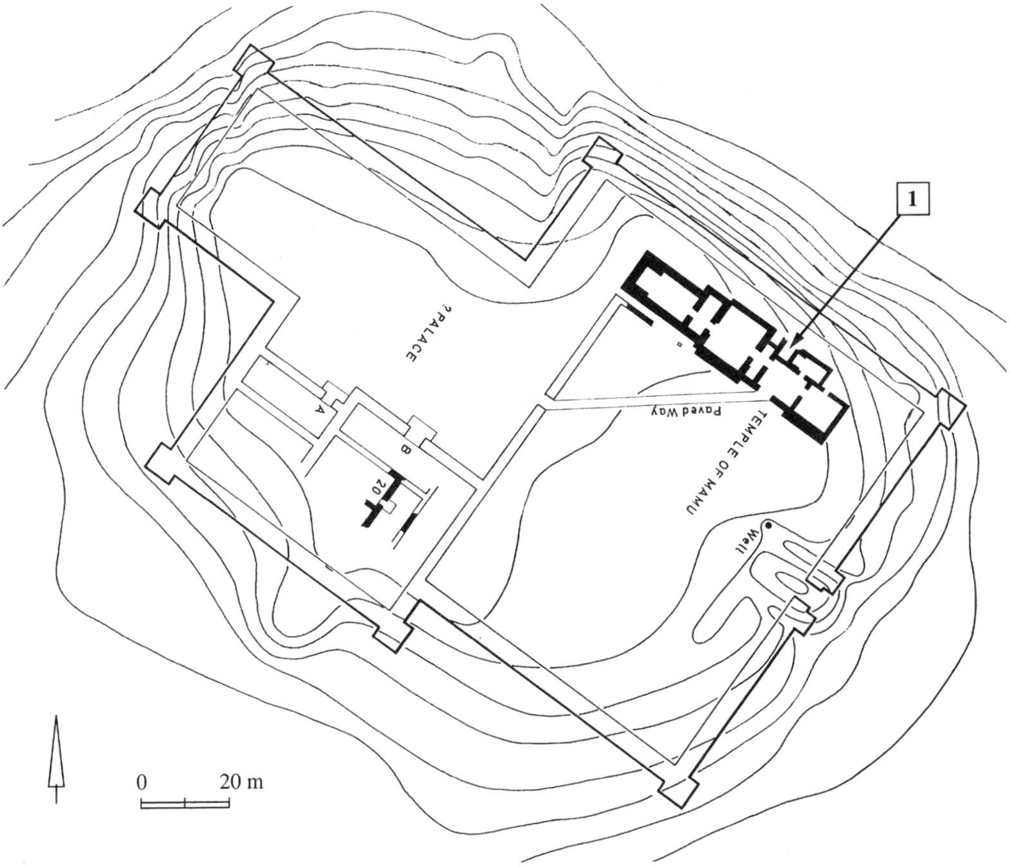

Plan 78. Imgur-Enlil.
Plan of temple with archive **Imgur-Enlil 1**.
From D. Oates, *Iraq* 36 (1974), pl. XXVI.

ish excavations, conducted first in 1878 and later on directed by M. E. L. Mallowan in 1956–1957, were able to unearth only parts of the citadel. The citadel, ca. 230 × 160 meters, stands towards the northern corner of the lower city, a square enclosed by a city wall ca. 800 × 800 meters. When entering the citadel from the southeast, one first encounters a large courtyard with the Mamu temple on the northeastern side; the palace area was situated in the northwestern part of the citadel.[44]

44. J. N. Postgate, "Imgur-Enlil," *RLA* 5 (1976–1980), 66–67; and D. Oates, "Balawat (Imgur Enlil): The Site and Its Buildings," *Iraq* 36 (1974), 173–178.

3.1.5.1 Archive in the Mamu Temple

The Mamu temple also had a small secondary cella; behind it was the small Room 8 with an archive (**Imgur-Enlil 1**) of 40 clay tablets. Almost all texts date to 697–671 B.C., but three are from the previous century, 734–710 B.C. The main persons responsible for the archive seem to be Šumma-ilu, possibly a *šangû*-priest, and Mamu-iqbi. There are several debt-notes concerning loans, some leases, one purchase agreement, and some other legal documents.[45]

3.1.6 Šibaniba (Tell Billa)

Šibaniba (modern Tell Billa), situated in central Assyria, northeast of Nineveh, measured ca. 600 × 500 meters (cf. 2.3.3). The American excavations (1930–1934) were able to unearth only limited areas in the northeastern and southwestern parts of the site. Beside the Middle Assyrian archive, an archive from the Neo-Assyrian period has been unearthed.[46]

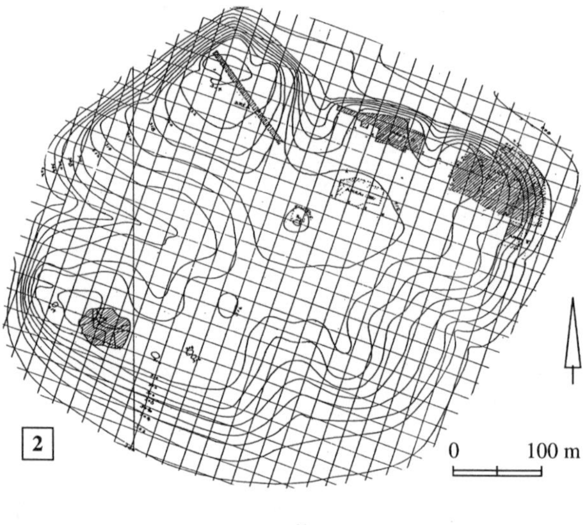

Plan 79. Šibaniba.
General plan with archive **Šibaniba 2**. The location is only approximative due to lack of detailed information.
From C. Bache, *Museum Journal* 23 (1932), pl. XLVII.

45. B. Parker, *Iraq* 25 (1963), 86–103, pls. XIX–XXVI.

46. For the very incomplete preliminary publications of the archaeological materials, see the references to section 2.3.3.

3.1.6.1 Archive in the Southwest Area

In the southwestern area of the tell, the excavators unearthed at least 15 clay tablets that may be the remains of an administrative archive (**Šibaniba 2**). The texts are essentially lists of different kinds, most enumerating soldiers or workers. One loan document may also come from the same archive, but this is not clear. Most of the texts date to 853–826 B.C., during the reign of Shalmaneser III; there are, perhaps, also a few older, dating to the reign of Assurnasirpal II.[47]

3.1.7 Dur-Katlimmu (Tall Šeḫ Ḥamad)

Dur-Katlimmu (modern Tall Šeḫ Ḥamad), on the eastern side of the lower part of the Khabur River, was, during the Middle Assyrian period, an important provincial capital (cf. 2.3.6). However, it was during the Neo-Assyrian period that it achieved its largest extent, consisting of both the Citadel with Lower Town I and, in a northeastern direction, the large Lower Town II, covering ca. 1000 × 400 meters, with additional suburbs outside.[48]

3.1.7.1 Archives in Lower-City Buildings

In the northeastern corner of the lower town, a large building complex (Building F and W) probably constituted the local palace. In the innermost Room B of Building F, the excavators unearthed a small archive (**Dur-Katlimmu 2**). It consists of 19 Aramaic dockets that probably were fastened to documents of perishable material written in Aramaic, one Aramaic tablet, and six Neo-Assyrian tablets. South of these tablets, in a somewhat more disturbed context, was a Neo-Babylonian letter. Several of the texts are probably loan documents. A few more texts, including another Neo-Babylonian one, were discovered in rooms just to the west. Further cuneiform tablets and a fragment of another Aramaic clay docket were excavated in Room K 3 of Building W of the same building complex, somewhat more to the west of the findspot of the archive in Building F. The texts date between 676 B.C. and the end period of the empire.

In the central part of the lower town there were Neo-Assyrian houses that were also partly used or reconstructed in the early Neo-Babylonian period. The large so-

47. J. J. Finkelstein, "Cuneiform Texts from Tell Billa," *JCS* 7 (1953), 111–176, nos. 68–90; details about the findspots have not been published. Cf. also E. A. Speiser, "Gleanings from the Billa Texts," *FS Koschaker* (1939), 141–150.

48. For the publications of the archaeological materials, see the references to section 2.3.6.

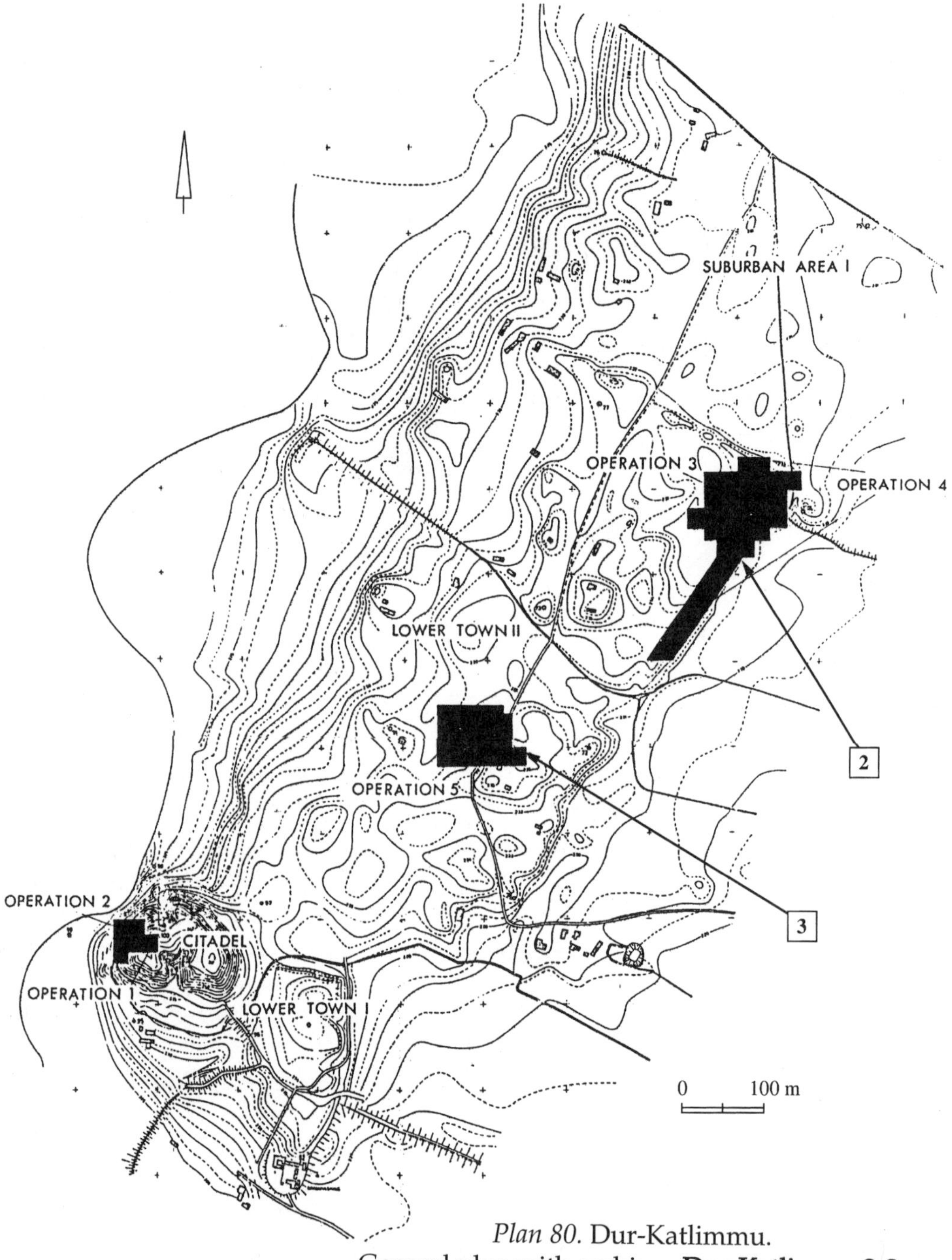

Plan 80. Dur-Katlimmu.
General plan with archives **Dur-Katlimmu 2-3**.
From H. Kühne, *SAAB* 7 (1993), 90.

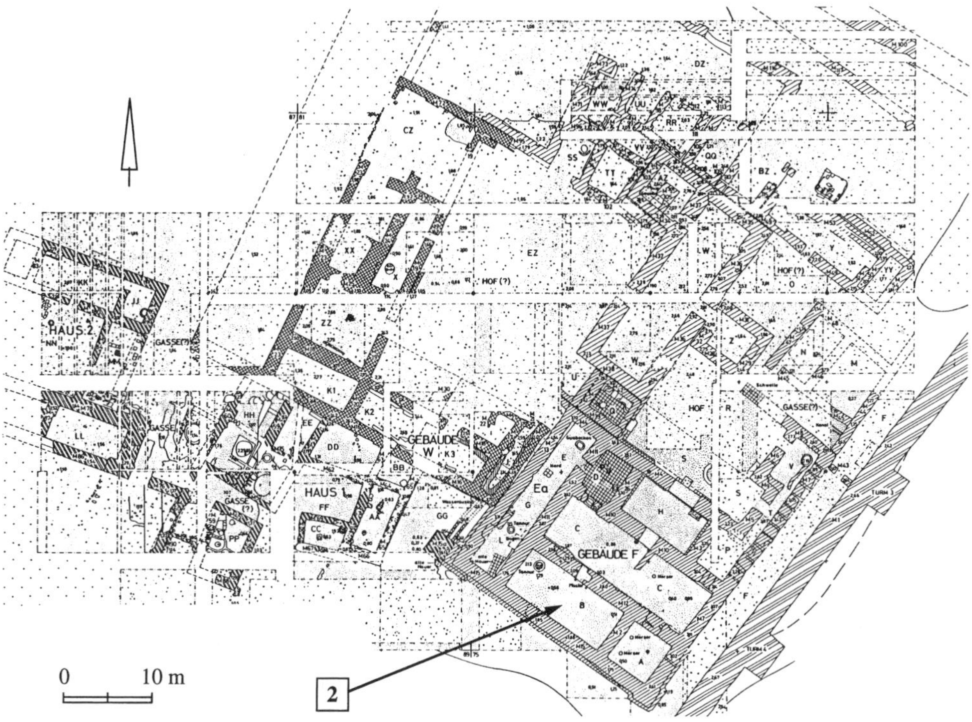

Plan 81. Dur-Katlimmu.
Plan of Building F with archive **Dur-Katlimmu 2**.
From H. Kühne, *AfO* 36-37 (1989–1990), fig. 118 between pp. 308 and 309.

called Red House was destroyed by fire, causing the collapse of an upper floor. In the southeast section of the house in Room JW, the excavators found in the fill from an upper floor the remains of an archive (**Dur-Katlimmu 3**) of 31 Aramaic dockets that probably were tied to Aramaic documents written on perishable material; together with them were hundreds of clay bullae and potsherds. There were additional Aramaic dockets and bullae in the adjoining corridor LW. The unpublished Aramaic documents are from the last years of the Assyrian Empire. In Room XX in the northern corner of the same house, the excavators found four Neo-Babylonian tablets, written in Neo-Assyrian dialect and script with Aramaic notes. These texts record purchases of fields by Adad-aplu-iddina and another man during 603–600 B.C., that is, the early years of Nebuchadnezzar II. From the available information, it cannot be determined whether the latter texts may represent the chronological continuation of the same archive or whether they should be treated as a separate archive.[49]

3.1.8 Guzana (Tell Ḥalaf)

In the upper Khabur area, the city Guzana (modern Tell Ḥalaf) was situated on the southern bank of the Khabur River in the northernmost part of modern Syria. German excavations were directed by M. v. Oppenheim in 1899, 1911–1913, and 1927–1929. The main levels of occupation date to the so-called Ḥalaf period (sixth millennium B.C.), which could be reached only in deep test pits, and to the first millennium B.C., which was more extensively excavated; there were also limited later remains. The citadel measured ca. 200 × 300 meters. It was situated along the river in the northern part of the lower city, a square enclosed by a city wall measuring ca. 600 × 1000 meters. In the west the citadel had a temple-palace and in the northeast a palace. A few areas were also excavated in the lower city, including a temple and remains of private houses. Guzana was the capital of an Aramaic state from the beginning of the first millennium B.C. until 894 B.C., when it was incorporated into the Assyrian Empire and served as the seat of Assyrian provincial governors.[50]

3.1.8.1 Archive of a Governor next to a Palace

In the eastern room of a house on the southern side adjoining the terrace of the northeastern palace (here corrected to area C1/VI3 according to the citadel plan), 85 clay tablets were unearthed in a secondary context, probably as fill in a later rebuilding. Possibly the tablets had originally been placed inside the palace. These are the remains of the archive (**Guzana 1**) of Mannu-ki-Aššur, who served as Assyrian governor in Guzana during the first quarter of the eighth century B.C. The texts include letters, some giving orders from the king and other high officials to Mannu-ki-Aššur,

---

49. Cf. H. Kühne, "Preliminary Report of the Excavation at Tall Šēḫ Ḥamad / Dūr-katlimmu in 1986," *AAAS* 36–37 (1986–1987), 242–267; W. Röllig, "Aramaica Haburensia II: Zwei datierte aramäische Urkunden aus Tall Šēḫ Ḥamad," *AoF* 24 (1997), 366–374; H. Kühne, "Der Gott in der Mondsichel," *AoF* 24 (1997), 375–382; and H. Kühne, *Tall Šēḫ Ḥamad / Dūr-Katlimmu 1995*: Auszug aus DFG-Bericht (manuscript kindly made available by H. Kühne). The latter, four tablets were published by H. Kühne, J. N. Postgate, W. Röllig, J. A. Brinkman, and F. M. Fales in *SAAB* 7 (1993), 75–150. The final publications of both the archaeological and the epigraphic material will be published in the series BATSH.

50. As short introductions to the site, cf. R. H. Dornemann, "Ḥalaf, Tell," *OEANE* 2 (1997), 460–462; and B. Hrouda, "Ḥalaf, Tell," *RLA* 4 (1972–1975), 54, both with bibliographies. The archaeological material has been published in the series *Tell Halaf*; of interest here is especially M. v. Oppenheim and R. Naumann, *Tell Halaf* II: *Die Bauwerke* (1950).

as well as copies of letters from Mannu-ki-Aššur to other officials, and administrative lists of persons, animals, and various objects, often with notes concerning who was responsible for what.[51]

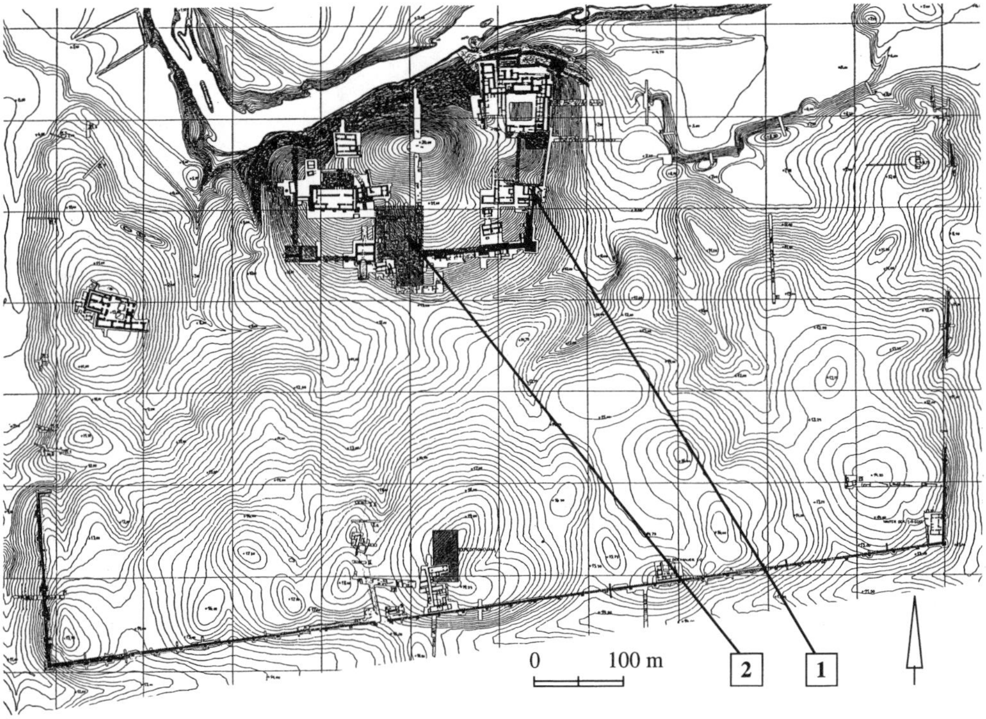

Plan 82. Guzana.
General plan with archives **Guzana 1-2**.
From M. v. Oppenheim and R. Naumann, *Tell Halaf* II (1950), pl. 1.

51. J. Friedrich, G. R. Meyer, A. Ungnad, and E. F. Weidner, *Die Inschriften vom Tell Halaf: Keilschrifttexte und aramäische Urkunden aus einer assyrischen Provinzhauptstadt*, AfO Beih. 6 (1940), Neudruck (1967), 8–46, with additions in M. Fales, "Studies on Neo-Assyrian Texts I: Joins and Collations to the Tell Halaf Documents," *ZA* 69 (1979), 192–216. The findspot is described in M. v. Oppenheim and R. Naumann, *Tell Halaf* II: *Die Bauwerke* (1950), 195–201, figs. 95–97, where the provenance is given as the house in B3-C1/VI3; cf. however, J. Friedrich, et al., *Die Inschriften vom Tell Halaf* (1967), 8, which gives B3/VII1.

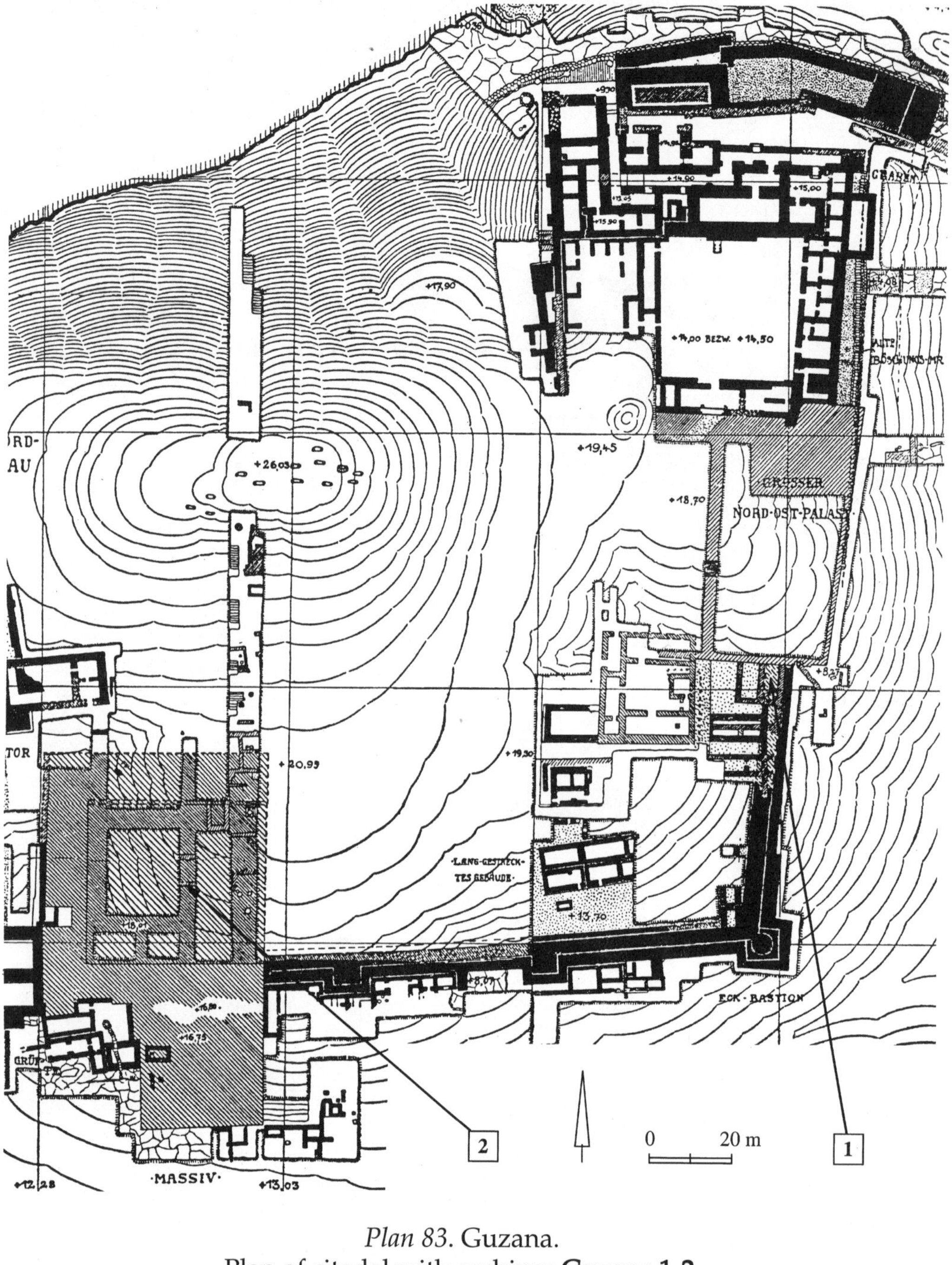

Plan 83. Guzana.
Plan of citadel with archives **Guzana 1-2**.
From M. v. Oppenheim and R. Naumann, *Tell Halaf* II (1950), pl. 2.

3.1.8.2 Private Archive

Among the few remains of private archives, reference should be made to the ten clay tablets found in a clay pot in an area with rather destroyed private houses above the ruins of the earlier "Massiv" east of the citadel gate (area B1/IV2 on the citadel plan). This is the archive (**Guzana 2**) of a man with the Aramaic name Il-manani, and dates to the last years of the Assyrian Empire. Five clay tablets are written in Assyrian cuneiform; they consist of three loan documents, one purchase document regarding a slave, and one legal settlement. The other five are Aramaic dockets concerning loans of corn, which probably were once tied to documents of perishable material written in Aramaic.[52]

3.1.9 Til-Barsip (Tell Aḫmar)

Til-Barsip (modern Tell Aḫmar) was situated along the northeastern shore of the Euphrates about 20 kilometers southeast of Karkemish. F. Thureau-Dangin conducted French excavations 1929–1931, and from 1988, G. Bunnens has been directing Australian excavations. The occupation dates to the Chalcolithic and Early Bronze Age as well as to the Iron Age, with some later remains. During the Iron Age, first as an independent Aramaic and possibly also Neo-Hittite city, and later on under Assyrian rule, the city consisted not only of the citadel, measuring 250 × 150 meters, but of a large, sometimes less densely populated lower city within town walls covering a half circle about 1200 meters in diameter.[53]

3.1.9.1 Remains of Archive in Private House

Area C of the Lower City consisted of private houses. The large House C1 consisted of two courtyards surrounded by rooms; northwest of this complex was House C2, which had been added somewhat later. In House C1 three main occupational phases have been noted. In the destruction level of the earliest phase, 35 clay tablets and fragments were found in and around the doorway between Rooms XI and

52. J. Friedrich, et al., *Die Inschriften vom Tell Halaf* (1967), 47–56. The findspot is given in M. v. Oppenheim and R. Naumann, *Tell Halaf* II: *Die Bauwerke* (1950), 151–152, pl. 6, as above B1/IV2; cf. however, J. Friedrich, et al., *Die Inschriften von Tell Halaf* (1967), 47, which gives A3/IV2. Three of the letters excavated at Guzana are Neo-Babylonian; this may be the remains of a settlement later than the Neo-Assyrian period.

53. As an introduction to the site, cf. R. H. Dornemann, "Til Barsip," *OEANE* 5 (1997), 209–210, with short bibliography. G. Bunnens, *Tell Ahmar: 1988 Season*, Publications of the Melbourne University Expedition to Tell Ahmar 1, Abr-Nahrain Supplement Series 2 (1990).

XII in a secondary position. These are the remains of an archive (**Til-Barsip 1**) belonging to a man called Ḫanni, but also including texts of Ištar-duri son of Samiraya. The tablets, at present unpublished, were written in Assyrian cuneiform, with the exception of two that are in Aramaic. The texts date to the period between 683 B.C. and the end of the Assyrian Empire, and are reported to consist of purchase and loan documents, and some other types of private documents, including a list.[54]

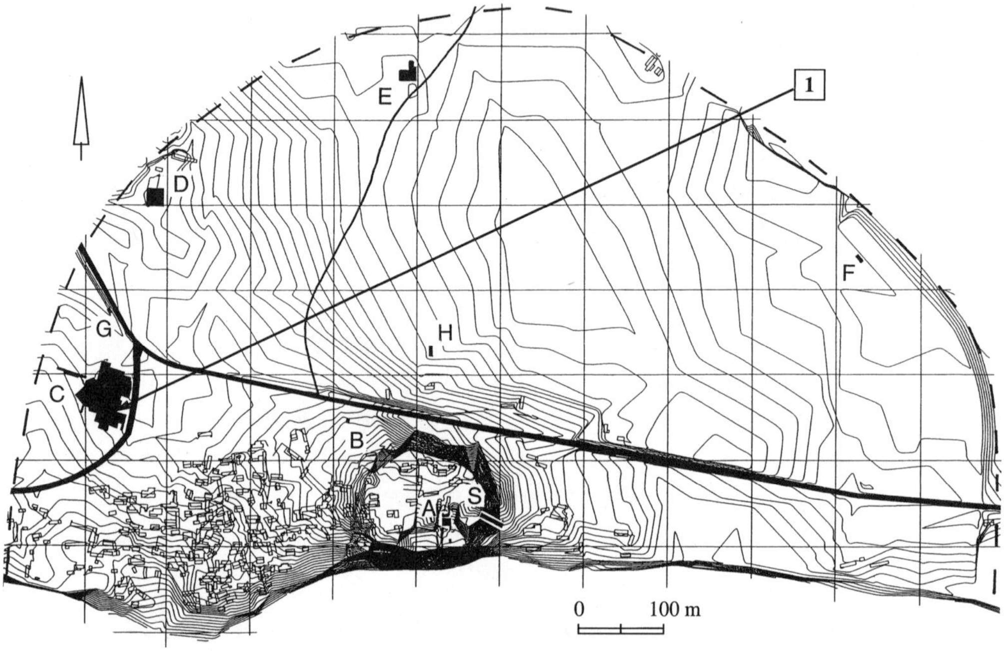

Plan 84. Til-Barsip.
General plan with archive **Til-Barsip 1**.
Courtesy G. Bunnens.

54. Cf. the preliminary report by G. Bunnens "Ahmar," in H. Weiss, "Archaeology in Syria," *AJA* 101 (1997), 101–104 with fig. 4. The Akkadian texts will be published by S. Dalley and the Aramaic by P. Bordreuil and F. Briquel-Chatonnet in a forthcoming volume of Abr-Nahrain. I thank G. Bunnens, S. Dalley, and J. M. Russell for their kindness in sharing with me additional information about the findings.

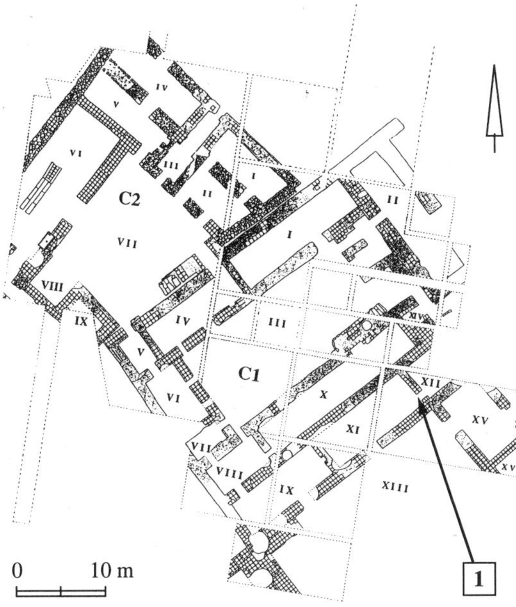

Plan 85. Til-Barsip.
Plan of Houses C1 and C2 with archive **Til-Barsip 1**.
Courtesy G. Bunnens.

3.1.10 *Burmarina (Tell Shioukh Fawqâni)*

Burmarina (modern Tell Shioukh Fawqâni) was a small town situated along the eastern shore of the Euphrates five kilometers southeast of Karkemish. Since 1994 there have been joint Syrian, Italian, and French excavations directed by L. Bachelot. The occupation of the quite small site dates from the Uruk period until the Byzantine period. During the Iron Age this was a town belonging to the area of the city Til-Barsip, which later came under Assyrian rule.[55]

3.1.10.1 *Archive in Private House*

In two rooms of what may have been a private house in Area F near the center of the tell during Iron Age II, the excavators unearthed an archive (**Burmarina 1**) consist-

55. Cf. the preliminary report by L. Bachelot, "Burmarina découverte d'une cité araméenne," *Archéologia* 323 (1996), 34–39; and L. Bachelot, et al., "La 4e campagne de fouilles à Tell Shioukh Faouqani (Syrie)," *Orient Express* 1997/3, 79–85.

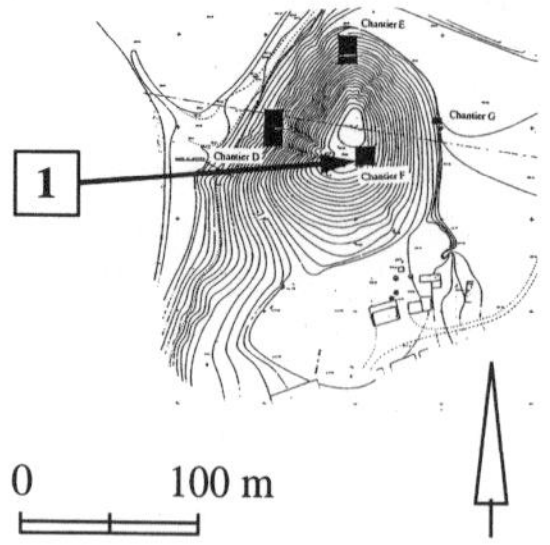

Plan 86. Burmarina.
General plan with archive **Burmarina 1**.
From L. Bachelot, *Orient Express* 1997/3, 79, fig. 1.

ing of about 130 clay tablets, some in the form of bullae. Most of the tablets were written in Assyrian cuneiform, but several were composed in Aramaic; some had short additional Aramaic notes written in ink. The unpublished texts, dating to the seventh century B.C., seem to be an archive for the family living in this house. Most of the cuneiform texts are loan or purchase documents; some are short notes; and there is also a list. The Aramaic texts concern loans or are short notes on bullae.[56]

3.1.11 Ḫuzirina (Sultantepe)

Ḫuzirina (modern Sultantepe) was situated along a northern extension of the Balikh River between modern Urfa (that is, the Syriac capital Edessa) and Harran in the southern part of modern Turkey. A British-Turkish expedition that mounted excavations in 1951–1952 unearthed only a few selected areas in some of the houses of the central part of the tell; no complete buildings were excavated. The small remains of an archive in a room of a larger building in the northwestern section of the tell consist of only four legal documents, dating from 684–674 B.C., and will not be separately discussed here.[57]

3.1.11.1 Library Found next to a Private House

In area F in the northeastern part of the tell, the expedition unearthed the corner of a private house with a central courtyard. About 400 clay tablets were uncovered in

56. Cf. F. M. Fales, et al., *Semitica* 46 (1997), 81–121; and L. Bachelot, et al., "La 4e campagne de fouilles à Tell Shioukh Faouqani (Syrie)," *Orient Express* 1997/3, 82-83.

57. S. Lloyd and N. Gökçe, "Sultantepe," *AnSt* 3 (1953), 27–51; and J. J. Finkelstein, "Assyrian Contracts from Sultantepe," *AnSt* 7 (1957), 137ff.

a secondary position outside this house, a few meters east of the entrance door, next to the outer wall of the house. Since a similar type of clay tablet was found in the central courtyard of the house, it is reasonable to assume that all the tablets originally were placed inside the house. The tablets are the remains of a library (**Ḫuzirina 1**), which according to the colophons, was created between 718 B.C. and the final period of the empire by a family of *šangû*-priests: Qurdi-Nergal, his son Mušallim-Baba, and other persons (in their younger days often with the title *šamallû*, "student"). There are a number of incantations and incantation rituals, medical texts, prayers, hymns, and lexical lists, including god-lists. There are also some epics, myths, wisdom literature, omens, and astrological texts. In short, many of the traditional literary categories of cuneiform literature are represented here, with some preference for exorcistic works, in spite of the fact that priests, not exorcists, seem to be the main creators of the library.[58]

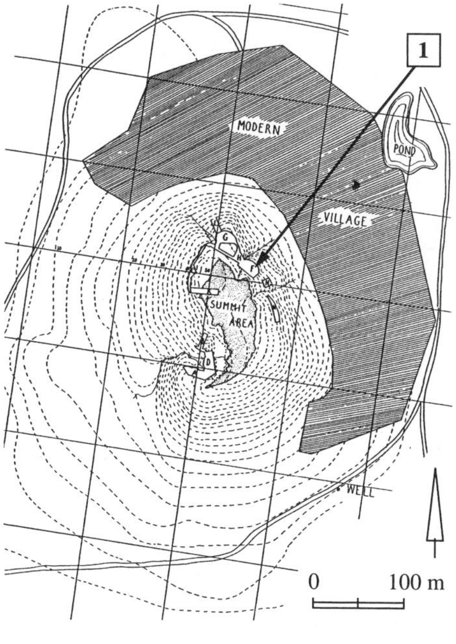

Plan 87. Ḫuzirina.
General plan with archive **Ḫuzirina 1**.
From S. Lloyd and N. Gökçe, *AnSt* 3 (1953), 29, fig. 1.

58. O. R. Gurney and J. J. Finkelstein, *The Sultantepe Tablets* I (1957), and O. R. Gurney and P. Hulin, *The Sultantepe Tablets* II (1964). For the family, cf. O. R. Gurney, "Scribes at Huzirina," *N.A.B.U.* 1997/17.

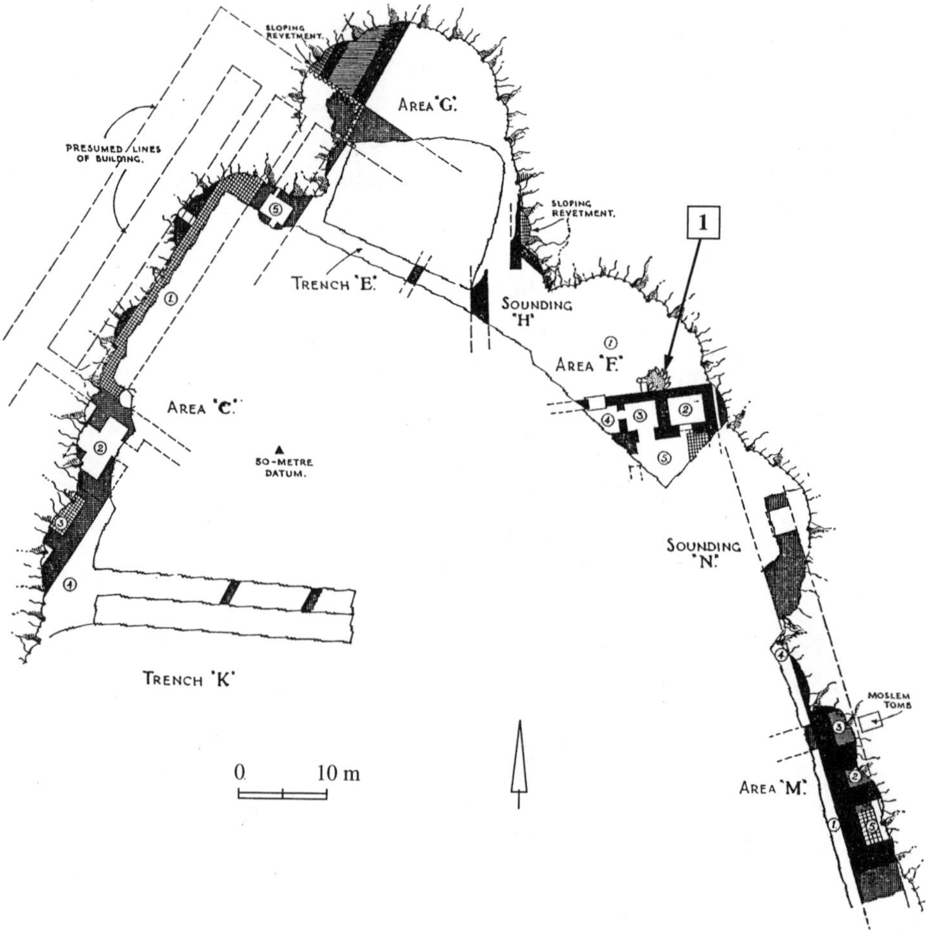

Plan 88. Ḫuzirina.
Plan of the north section of the central part of the tell with archive **Ḫuzirina 1**.
From S. Lloyd and N. Gökçe, *AnSt* 3 (1953), 30, fig. 2.

3.1.12 Ma'allanat

Ma'allanat (modern name unknown) was situated somewhere in the area between Harran and Guzana in southern Turkey or in the nearby part of northern Syria. The site has not been identified through scientific excavations, but an archive of clay tablets sold on the antiquities market originates, according to the texts, from this city.

3.1.12.1 Archive Possibly from a Private House

The archive (**Ma'allanat 1**) consists of 32 to 40 clay tablets with Neo-Assyrian and three with Neo-Babylonian cuneiform writing, as well as 24 written in Aramaic; the texts are unpublished. They belonged to the archive of Ḫandi, steward of the palace (*šaknu ša ekalli*), his son Ḫarranayu, as well as Śehr-nuri (perhaps identical to Sîn-namir, son of Ḫarranayu), and date (at least) to the period 686–622 B.C. In the archive there were loan documents, many of which concern silver and corn, as well as payments of loans, purchase documents concerning slaves and land, and some other documents.[59]

3.2 Neo-Babylonian Area

Most of the archives and libraries with cuneiform texts from the Neo-Babylonian area date to the Neo-Babylonian period and approximately the first half of the Persian period, ca. 625–404 B.C. The archives and libraries in Babylonia dated during the Persian period belong historically to the Persian area (3.3), but from a cultural point of view they are a continuation of the Babylonian area, and are, therefore, treated here. In Babylon, Nippur, and Uruk, there are also some older archives dating back to 754 B.C.; they belong historically to the Neo-Assyrian area (3.1), but culturally

59. Cf. E. Lipinski, "Les tablettes araméennes de Bruxelles," *Études Sémitiques*, ed. A. Caquot, Actes du XXIXe Congrès international des orientalistes (1975), 25–29; E. Lipinski, "Textes juridiques et économiques de l'époque sargonide," *Acta Antiqua Academiae Scientiarum Hungaricae* 22 (1974) (=*Wirtschaft und Gesellschaft im Alten Vorderasien*, 1976), 373–384; D. Homès-Fredericq, "Glyptique sur les tablettes araméennes des Musées royaux d'Art et d'Histoire," *RA* 70 (1976), 57–70; E. Lipinski, "Les temples néo-assyriens et les origines du monnayage," *State and Temple Economy in the Ancient Near East* II, ed. E. Lipinski, OLA 6 (1979); P. Garelli, "Les archives inédites d'un centre provincial de l'empire assyrien," *Cuneiform Archives and Libraries*, CRRAI 30 (1986), 241–246; D. Homès-Fredericq, "La glyptique des archives inedites d'un centre provincial de l'empire assyrien," *Cuneiform Archives and Libraries*, CRRAI 30 (1986), 247–259; E. Lipinski, "Aramaic Clay Tablets from the Gozan-Harran Area," *Ex oriente lux* 33 (1993–94), 143–150. A publication by P. Garelli, E. Lipinski, and D. Homès-Fredericq is in preparation.

to the Babylonian one, and are for that reason discussed here. In Babylon and Ur, archives with clay tablets date through the time of Alexander, ca. 317 B.C., and in Uruk, clay tablets in archives date even later, until 162 B.C. These quite late archives fall, strictly speaking, outside the limits of this study, but they are included here, because they represent the cultural continuity, and end, of the traditional Babylonian culture. The contemporary remains of Greek archives, for example in Seleucia at the Tigris, are not discussed here.[60]

Several archives and libraries have been found in the capital Babylon (3.2.1). In Nereb (3.2.3) in Syria an archive has been excavated. The archives from the old excavations in Borsippa (3.2.2) are problematic to reconstruct. In Nippur (3.2.5) several archives have been found, and during the excavations of Sippar (3.2.4), Ur (3.2.6), and Uruk (3.2.7) several archives and libraries have been unearthed.

In other cultural areas, remains of archives, dating to the Neo-Babylonian period, have been found in Dur-Katlimmu (3.1.7) in the Neo-Assyrian area, as well as Lachish (3.4.3), Arad (3.4.4), and Jerusalem (3.4.5) in the Western Alphabetic area. For archives and libraries dating to the Persian period, cf. the Persian area (3.3).

The Babylonian scribes dated texts by regnal year. Therefore, many of the texts can be assigned a secure dating.[61]

A possible library and one or more archives from Mound W at Kish, east of Babylon, and an archive from the Nergal temple in Mê-Turnat (Tell Ḥaddad) in the Hamrin Basin have not been possible to include here.[62] In addition to the archives and libraries discussed below, individual tablets or small remains of archives have been found at a number of other sites in the same area.[63]

60. For the ca. 25,000 clay bullae from Seleucia, cf., e.g., the preliminary summary by A. Invernizzi, "Ten Years Research in the Al-Mada'in Area Seleucia and Ctesiphon," *Sumer* 32 (1976), 167–175, esp. 169–170, with further references. Cf. also Chapter 1 n. 6.

61. For the chronology of the period, cf. R. A. Parker and W. H. Dubberstein, *Babylonian Chronology 626 B.C.-A.D. 75*, Brown University Studies 19 (1956).

62. For Kish, cf. P. R. S. Moorey, *Kish Excavations 1923–1933* (1978), 48–54; and S. H. Langdon and L. C. Watelin, *Excavations at Kish* I (1924), III (1930), and IV (1934); and for Mê-Turnat (Tall Ḥaddad), cf. A. K. Muhamed, *Old Babylonian Cuneiform Texts from the Ḥamrin Basin: Tell Haddad*, Edubba 1 (1992), 23.

63. Short surveys of Neo-Babylonian documents from a chronological point of view can be found in M. A. Dandamayev, "The Neo-Babylonian Archives," *Cuneiform Archives and Libraries*, CRRAI 30 (1986), 273–277; and M. A. Dandamaev, *Slavery in Babylonia: From Nabopolassar to Alexander the Great (626–331 BC)* (1984), 6–29. For the Hellenistic period, see J. Oelsner, *Materialien zur babylonischen Gesellschaft und Kultur in hellenistischer Zeit (=Materialien)*, Assyriologia 7 (1986). Cf. also, e.g., D. Arnaud, "Larsa. A. Philologisch"; J. Margueron and J. L. Hout, "Larsa. B. Archäologisch," *RLA* 6 (1980–1983), 496–506; and S. Dalley, "The Cuneiform Tablet," in C.-M. Bennett and P. Bienkowski, *Excavations at Tawilan in Southern Jordan*, British Academy Monographs in Archaeology 8 (1995), 67–68, figs. 3.29–30, 7.1–7.

3.2.1 Babylon

Babylon, situated on both sides of the Euphrates south of modern Baghdad, was the capital during the Old Babylonian period (cf. 2.4.2). During the Neo-Assyrian Empire it was also a leading cultural center for the Assyrians and periodically served as the political center of an independent Babylonia. During the reigns of Nabopolassar (625–605 B.C.) and Nebuchadnezzar II (604–562 B.C.), until that of Nabonidus (555–539 B.C.), Babylon was the capital of the Neo-Babylonian, or Chaldean, Empire. Under Persian rule, Babylon was the center of the richest Persian province, Babylonia, in which many of the old traditions continued to exist at least during the reign of the first rulers. In the course of ensuing Seleucid and Parthian rule, some old traditions continued but finally came to an end.

After early excavations by others, R. Koldewey excavated in 1899–1917 essentially the Neo-Babylonian and Persian Levels. The high level of the ground water prevented him from examining the earlier levels of the city systematically. The central part of Babylon, situated on the eastern bank of the Euphrates, was enclosed by a city wall measuring ca. 1.7 × 1.6 kilometers. A corresponding part of the city covering ca. 1.6 × 1.0 kilometers was situated on the western bank of the Euphrates. A triangular outer city wall (ca. 5 × 4 × 3.5 kilometers) enclosed the central part of the city and surrounding areas on the eastern bank. Koldewey concentrated his efforts on the central part of the city, which consisted of a number of mounds known by their modern names. Among these, reference will be made below to Kasr with the palaces in the north, Merkes with private houses in the center, as well as Amran and Ishin Aswad, with temples and private houses, to the southwest and southeast. In recent years Iraqi archaeologists have re-excavated and restored some of the buildings previously unearthed by Koldewey. New buildings have also been excavated. The provenances of the clay tablets found in the early excavations are essentially unknown, and only a few of the text groups from Koldewey's better-recorded excavations have been published or are otherwise available; this makes a reconstruction possible for only a few of the many archives and libraries that have been excavated.[64]

3.2.1.1 Archives and Libraries in Palaces and Temples

The south palace was situated on the shore of the Euphrates, in the Kasr area, in the northwestern part of the central city. This large building complex was organized around a number of inner courtyards with reception rooms in the center, living quarters in the west and administrative areas in the east of the palace. In the northeast

64. For publications, see the references to section 2.4.2.

were a number of exceptionally heavy foundations, which Koldewey thought could have been the foundations for what the later Greek tradition called the "hanging gardens." An archive (**Babylon 7**) of ca. 290 clay tablets was unearthed in a room with a staircase leading to the rooms inside these foundations in Kasr s21. The tablets, dating to 595–570 B.C. during Nebuchadnezzar's time, were administrative documents concerning the distribution of oil, corn, and dates to prominent prisoners of war. The best-known of the prisoners mentioned in these texts is king Jehoiachin of Judea, who was deported by Nebuchadnezzar II.[65]

The north palace, situated immediately north of the south palace and the city wall surrounding the central city, has not been completely excavated. An archive (**Babylon 8**) of about 950 clay tablets was unearthed in a Persian Level in Kasr n-r12–15. Many tablets date to the reigns of Artaxerxes I and Darius II, 465–404 B.C. From the small group of published texts, it may be concluded that the tablets were documents concerning obligations in connection with leases and loans, and documents concerning the purchase of plots or houses. In some of the texts, Belšunu, governor (*pīḫātu* (^{lú}NAM)) of Babylon, is the responsible person. On at least 21 of the tablets, there are, in addition to the main cuneiform text, short incised Aramaic notes summarizing the cuneiform contents. A few of the texts from the Persian period have Greek seal impressions, in addition to common Babylonian types. It has been suggested that a number of clay tablets from earlier, illicit excavations may also come from this archive.[66]

The Belet-ili (Ninmaḫ) temple was situated southeast of the Ištar gate in the northern part of the central city. The entrance to the temple was in the north, a courtyard lay in the center, surrounded by rooms, and a door to the cella was located in the southern portion of the courtyard. About 40 clay tablets were excavated in fill below the level of the middle pavement in Room W.2 west of the courtyard. When no longer of any use, this archive (**Babylon 9**) seems to have been used as fill under the replastered floor. According to published preliminary notes, the unpublished texts date to the time of Nebuchadnezzar II and his successor, Evil-Merodach (604–560 B.C.). The archive includes lists of workers and deliveries of bricks and straw, possibly in connection with a rebuilding of the temple. In Room A.2 inside the cella, a trench was

65. E. Weidner, "Jojachin, König von Juda, in babylonischen Keilschrifttexten," *FS Dussaud* 2 (1939), 923–935, Bab 28097ff.

66. L. Jakob-Rost and H. Freydank, "Spätbabylonische Rechtsurkunden aus Babylon mit aramäischen Beischriften," *FuB* 14 (1972), 7–35; E. Klengel-Brandt, "Siegelabrollungen aus dem Babylon der Spätzeit," *OrAnt* 8 (1969), 329–336, pls. LX–LXIII, M. W. Stolper, "Bēlšunu the Satrap," *FS Reiner* (1987), 389–402; and M. W. Stolper, "The Kasr Archive," *Achaemenid History* IV: Centre and Periphery, eds. H. Sancisi-Weerdenburg and E. Kuhrt, (1990), 195–205, Bab 49958ff.

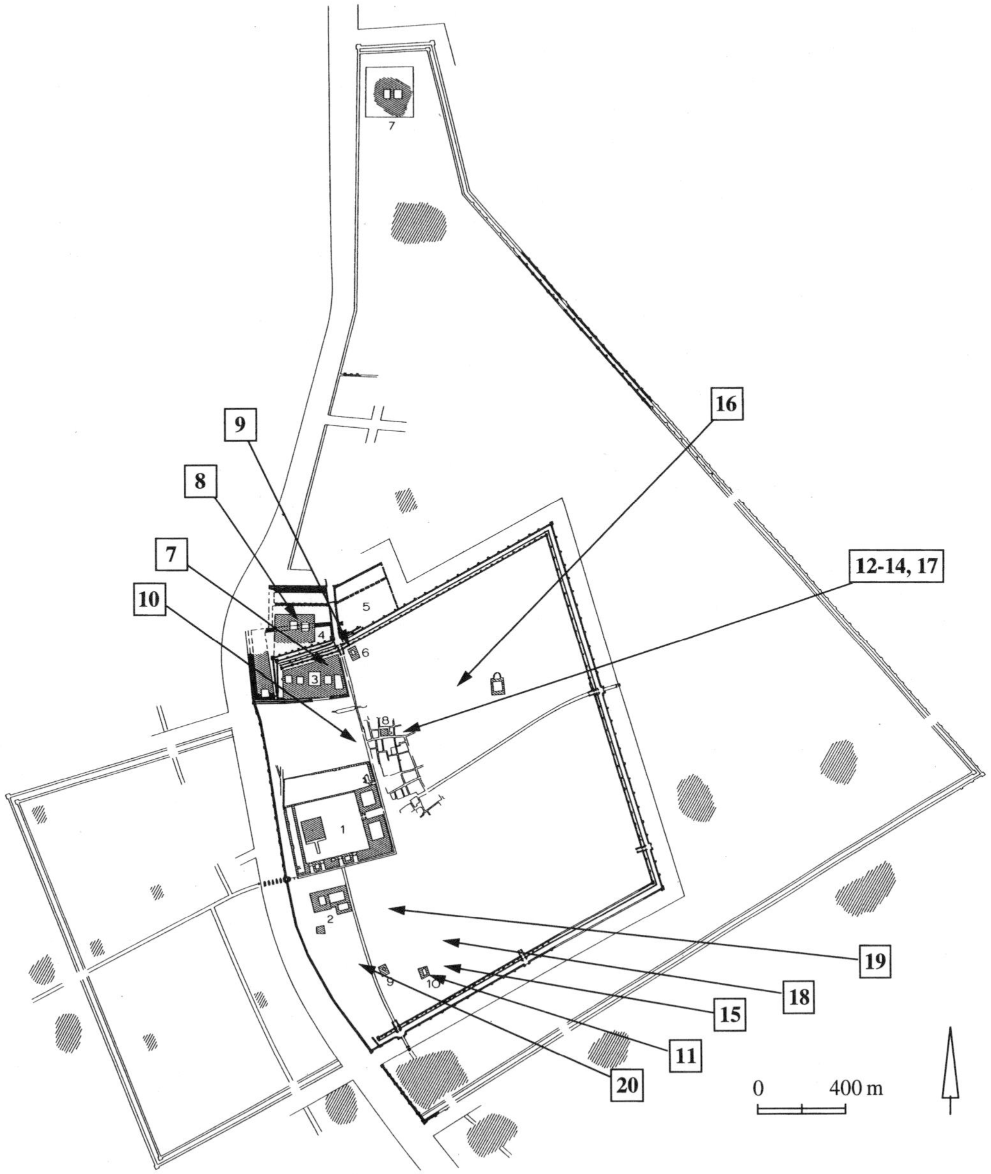

Plan 89. Babylon.
General plan with archives **Babylon 7-20**.
From E. Heinrich, *Die Tempel und Heiligtümer im Alten Mesopotamien* (1982), fig. 382.

made to the foundation of the walls, eight meters below the plaster. At the foundation level, the excavators found 16 clay tablets next to a cylinder with an inscription of Assurbanipal. The unpublished tablets are lists of workers; one of the texts is dated to year 5 of Nabuchadnezzar II (600 B.C.). It is not clear whether these remains of an archive from the time of a rebuilding of the temple may have been part of the other archive in this temple, or whether they form a separate one.[67]

In the recently excavated temple of Nabû *ša ḫarê*, between the Marduk temple and the south palace, more than 1,500 clay tablets (**Babylon 10**) were found. Most of the tablets were used as fill between the two main floor levels in two rooms at the northwestern corner of the temple. From the publication of selected texts, it seems that these were school tablets, probably written by students in this temple of the god of the scribes. The texts are often brief excerpts from well-known Mesopotamian literary texts.[68]

The Ninurta temple is situated in the southern part of the mound Ishin Aswad, not far from the southern town wall. In the rooms of the temple 146 clay tablets were unearthed. The mostly unpublished texts are the remains of at least one library with archive (**Babylon 11**). According to the little material available there are some hymns, lexical lists, and contracts. Texts in the temple seem to date to the reign of Nebuchadnezzar II and Nabonid (604–539 B.C.), except a few older ones possibly from lower levels.[69]

3.2.1.2 Archives in Private Houses

Although private houses have been excavated in different parts of Babylon, blocks of such houses have been uncovered only in the Merkes area in the middle of the central city. Several of the houses yielded archives representing a wide chronological range. The only private archive (**Babylon 12**) with known provenance, which to a large extent has been published so far, was found in Merkes 26h1 in two clay pots 30 meters south of the southwestern corner of the Ištar temple. The ca. 47 clay tablets dating from 660–627 B.C. during the reigns of Šamaš-šum-ukin and Kandalanu constituted the archive of Bel-ušallim. The texts are documents primarily concerning loans of silver made by Bel-ušallim.[70]

67. R. Koldewey, *Das wieder erstehende Babylon* (1981), 55–65; and R. Koldewey, *Die Tempel von Babylon und Borsippa*, WVDOG 15 (1911), 4–17, Bab 5372ff.

68. A. Cavigneaux, *Texts from Babylon: Textes scolaires du temple de Nabû ša ḫarê* 1 (1981).

69. R. Koldewey, *Die Tempel von Babylon und Borsippa*, WVDOG 15 (1911), 31, Bab 14217ff.

70. L. Jakob-Rost, "Ein neubabylonisches Tontafelarchiv aus dem 7. Jahrhundert v.u.Z.," *FuB* 10

A private house in the Persian Level was cut by the excavation trench in Merkes 26g2 50 meters southwest of the Ištar temple. In one of its rooms an archive (**Babylon 13**) of 164 clay tablets was unearthed. The tablets date to the reigns of Darius I and Xerxes I (521–465 B.C.), but other information about the contents have not been published.[71]

East of the Ištar temple, in the house on the other side of the road in Merkes 23/24l, an archive (**Babylon 14**) of clay tablets was unearthed. The texts are reported to be from the reign of Darius I (521–486 B.C.). No other information about the texts has been published, so we cannot decide whether this is a private archive or an archive that deals with matters concerning the temple.[72]

Early illicit excavations in Babylon produced the better-known archive (**Babylon 15**) belonging to the family of Egibi. It was reported that 3,000–4,000 clay tablets were found in several jars, each sealed with a brick and bitumen. Their findspot was probably correctly identified by R. Koldewey as being southeast of the Ninurta temple in Ishin Aswad in the southern part of Babylon. On the basis of content, almost 1,000 of these tablets have now been assigned to the archive of the family of Egibi. However, if the reported number of excavated tablets is even approximately correct, then a large quantity of tablets that remain unpublished or that do not refer to known members of the family was also found within the archive. The main Egibi family members spanned five generations: Šulaya, Nabû-aḫḫe-iddin, Itti-Marduk-balaṭu, Marduk-naṣir-apli (also called Širku), and Nidinti-Bel; there were also other members of the family (for example, Nuptaya, wife of Itti-Marduk-balaṭu and daughter of Iddin-Marduk) or associates, even some slaves who acted independently on behalf of the family. The texts date to the period 602–482 B.C., during the Neo-Babylonian period and early Persian rule. There are many documents relating to the purchase of slaves, fields and houses, leases of fields and houses, loans and investments in joint business ventures, legal settlements, marriages, adoption, and the division of inheritance.[73]

(1968), 39–62; L. Jakob-Rost, *FuB* 12 (1970), 58; and O. Reuther, *Die Innenstadt von Babylon (Merkes)*, WVDOG 47 (1926), 22, 64, pl. 3, Bab 38135f.

71. O. Reuther, *Die Innenstadt von Babylon (Merkes)*, WVDOG 47 (1926), 35, pl. 3, cf. pl. 44, Bab 38730ff.

72. O. Reuther, *Die Innenstadt von Babylon (Merkes)*, WVDOG 47 (1926), 35, pl. 33, cf. pl. 30 Bab 44709ff.

73. S. Weingort, *Das Haus Egibi in neubabylonischen Rechtsurkunden*, Diss. (1939); and J. Krecher, *Das Geschäftshaus Egibi in Babylon in neubabylonischer und achämenidischer Zeit*, Habilitationsschrift Münster (1970); a section of the archive has been treated in C. Wunsch, *Die Urkunden des babylonischen Geschäftsmannes Iddin-Marduk: Zum Handel mit Naturalien im 6. Jahrhundert v. Chr. I-II*, Cuneiform Monographs 3a–3b (1993). For the probable provenance south of the trenches east of the Ninurta temple, see R. Koldewey, *MDOG* 9 (1901), 3; cf. also J. Oelsner, *Materialien* (1986), 193 with n. 414; F. Delitzsch,

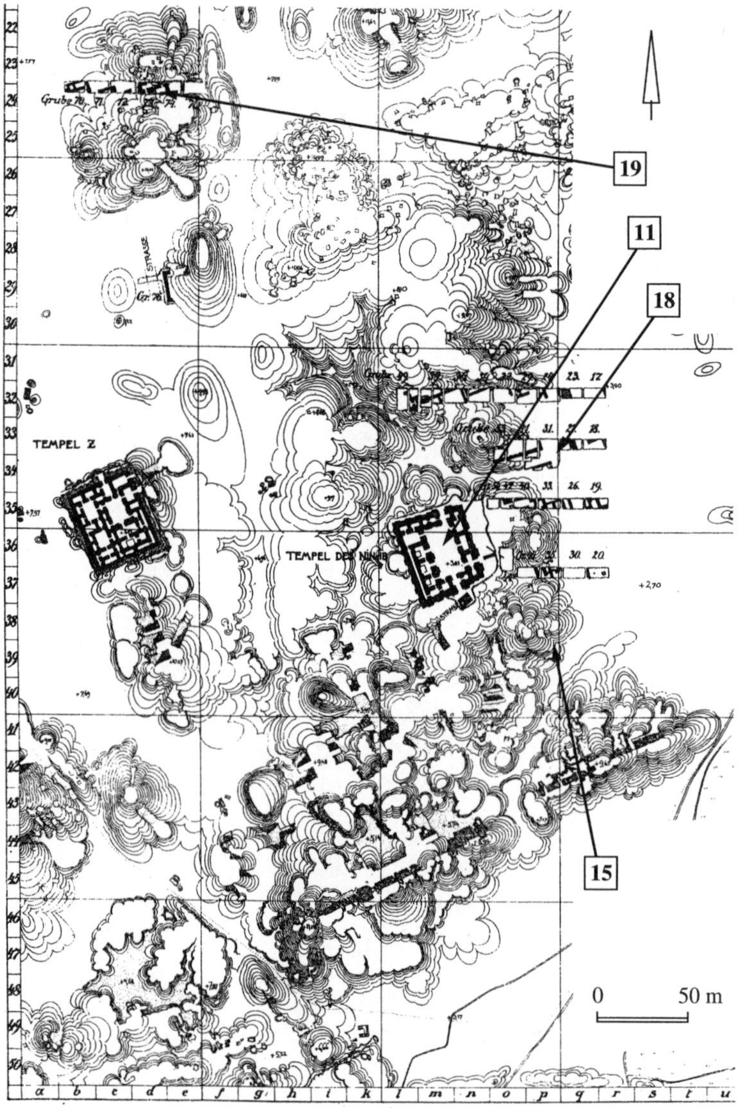

Plan 90. Babylon.
Plan of the Ishin Aswad area with temples and private houses, with archives and libraries **Babylon 11**, **Babylon 15**, and **Babylon 18-19**.
From R. Koldewey, *Die Tempel von Babylon und Borsippa*, WVDOG 15 (1911), pl. IV.

Iraqi archaeologists have excavated a large private house west of the Greek theatre. In Room 32 in the northwestern corner of the house, the excavators unearthed a number of clay tablets that probably are the remains of the archive (**Babylon 16**) of the owner of the house. The texts remain unpublished; one of them is reported to be a marriage document.[74]

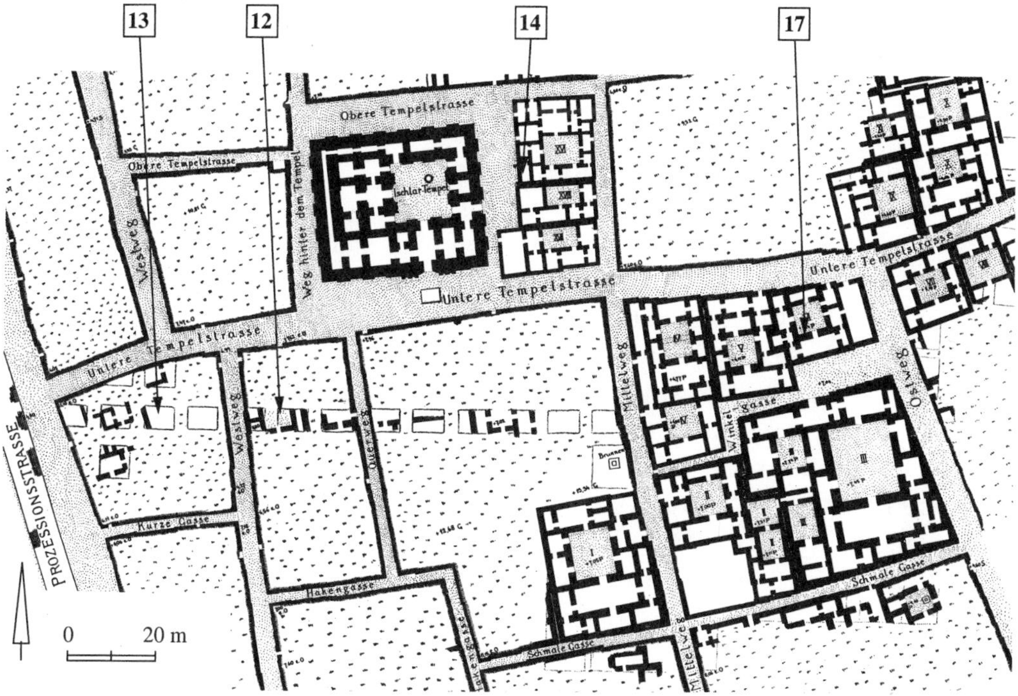

Plan 91. Babylon.
Plan of a section of the Merkes area with private houses, with archives and library **Babylon 12-14**, and **Babylon 17**.
From O. Reuther, *Die Innenstadt von Babylon*, WVDOG 47 (1926), pl. 17.

Babylon, Sendschrift der Deutschen Orient-Gesellschaft 1 (1901), 7–8; and S. M. Evers, "George Smith and the Egibi Tablets," *Iraq* 55 (1993), 107–117. One of the pots, evidently in secondary use, is referred to by C. B. F. Walker, "Some Mesopotamian Inscribed Vessels," *Iraq* 42 (1980), 85–86. For the family, cf. also C. Wunsch, "Die Frauen der Familie Egibi," *AfO* 42–43 (1995–1996), 33–63. For the end of the archive, cf. K. Abraham, "The End of Marduk-nāṣir-apli's Career as Business-man and Scribe: New Evidence from Unpublished Egibi Texts in the British Museum," *FS Lipinski* (1995), 1–9.

74. A. al-Bayati, "The Babylonian House," *Sumer* 41 (1985), 71–72, and 113–116 (Arabic section). Room 32 does not appear on the plan on p. 113. The plan reproduced by C. Castel, *Habitat urbain néo-*

3.2.1.3 Libraries in Private Houses

On the basis of the provenances of the literary texts, there may have existed several libraries with literary texts in different houses in the city. However, because so few literary texts have been published, the presentation of the libraries here is very preliminary.

House VI in the Merkes area has the entrance on "Untere Tempelstraße." In the center of the house is a courtyard. While examining the floors of the courtyard in Merkes 25o2, the excavators found that there were 27 clay tablets placed in the 20 cm fill between the two lowest floors. These remains of a library (**Babylon 17**) are dated to the reigns of Šamaš-šum-ukin and Nebuchadnezzar II (667–562 B.C.) The few published texts are medical and lexical.[75]

Northeast of the Ninurta temple a series of short excavation trenches cut through a rather limited area with private houses. Approximately 290 clay tablets have been unearthed in the trenches, with a heavy concentration of them (194 tablets) in trench 31, about 50 meters northeast of the temple. The tablets are the remains of a library with archive (**Babylon 18**); however, it is not clear whether all tablets belonged to just one library, whether some came from other houses or from other levels, or whether there may be any relation to the library in the temple. Most of the tablets remain unpublished, but it has been reported that among them, 31 tablets are lexical lists; 38 tablets are omens, rituals, incantations (partly Sumerian-Akkadian), god-lists, and other religious texts; five tablets are hymns (including a Sumerian-Akkadian hymn to Marduk); and some tablets are lists of cities, temples, and doors. In addition, there are 53 contracts and one tablet in old script. The latest available date is the succession year of Darius (I?) (522 B.C.).[76]

About 200 meters north of the Išḫara temple (during early research called Temple Z or the Gula temple) the short excavation trenches 70–76 cut one or more private houses. The excavators unearthed 19 clay tablets, the remains of a library with archive (**Babylon 19**). Among the texts, there are school texts, an astrological text, incantations, as well as contracts and a letter. The latest date is the second year of Alexander IV, 315 B.C.[77]

assyrien et néo-babylonien 2 (1992), pl. 36, shows a numbering of the rooms somewhat different from al-Bayati's—there, Room 32 is in the southwestern corner of the house.

75. O. Reuther, *Die Innenstadt von Babylon (Merkes)*, WVDOG 47 (1926), 112, pls. 3, 19, Bab 35824ff.

76. R. Koldewey, *Die Tempel von Babylon und Borsippa*, WVDOG 15 (1911), 35, Bab 13233ff.

77. R. Koldewey, *Die Tempel von Babylon und Borsippa*, WVDOG 15 (1911), 36, Bab 15420ff. Cf. for published texts, *LTBA* I (1933) 68, and VS 24 (1987) 10, 59.

A private house was unearthed 80 meters west of the Išḫara temple in Amran x35 (on later plans called Amran af35). The remains of a library (**Babylon 20**) were found with 36 clay tablets. Among the mostly unpublished texts are astronomical texts, hymns, incantations, lexical lists, and some contracts. They date to the Persian and Hellenistic periods; the latest is from year 106 of the Seleucid era, 206 B.C.[78]

3.2.2 Borsippa (Birs Nimrud)

Borsippa (modern Birs Nimrud and Tell Ibrahim al-Khalil northeast of it) was situated south of Babylon. Only brief excavations have been conducted on the site by H. Rassam in 1879–1882 and R. Koldewey in 1902. In recent years, an Austrian expedition, directed by E. Trenkwalder, has resumed excavations. The excavations have been concentrated on the Neo-Babylonian Levels of the Nabû temple and its zikkurrat in Birs Nimrud. The northeastern part of the city, Tell Ibrahim al-Khalil, was probably covered with private houses. It has essentially only been explored by the early excavations of Rassam, but it has been a preferred place for illicit excavations of clay tablets.[79]

3.2.2.1 Remains of Archives

No archaeologically well-established archives have, as yet, been studied from Borsippa. However, clay tablets were reported by Koldewey to have been unearthed in the precinct surrounding the courtyard with the zikkurrat and, northeast of it, the Nabû temple. Based upon the findspots, the tablets may be the remains of a temple administrative archive (**Borsippa 1**). Rassam reported a large collection of clay tablets on the southern limit of Tell Ibrahim al-Khalil. An archive (**Borsippa 2**) of the family of Ea-iluta-bani has recently been reconstructed from illicitly excavated tablets by means of internal criteria. Perhaps the tablets come from the latter tell, but proof is lacking.[80]

78. Bab 15534ff. Cf. R. Koldewey, *MDOG* 15 (1902), 6, where x34 should be changed to x35 according to the excavation inventory.

79. Cf. E. Unger, "Barsippa," *RLA* 1 (1932), 402–429; and R. Koldewey, *Die Tempel von Babylon und Borsippa*, WVDOG 15 (1911), 50–59.

80. Cf. L. Jakob-Rost, "Borsippa," *FuB* 27 (1989), 65–88; F. Joannès, *Archives de Borsippa, la famille Ea-ilûta-bâni: Étude d'un lot d'archives familiales en Babylonie du VIIIe au Ve siècle av. J.-C.*, École pratique des Hautes Études IVe section, II Hautes études orientales 25 (1989), with further references.

3.2.3 Nereb (Neirab)

Nereb (modern Neirab) is situated 6–8 kilometers east-southeast of Aleppo. A French expedition conducted excavations in 1926–1927. A number of trenches were cut, somewhat unsystematically, over the southeastern part of the tell. This may have been an area with private houses, but only a few remains of walls were reported by the excavators. The place where the two Aramaic stela are said to have been found in 1891 was in the western part of the excavated area.[81]

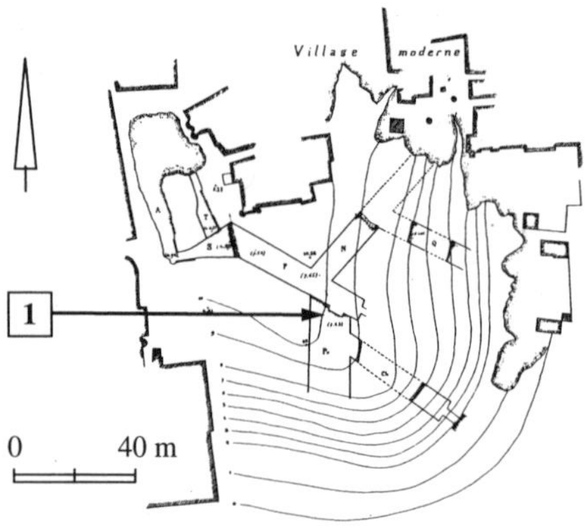

Plan 92. Nereb.
General plan of the southeast section of the tell with archive **Nereb 1**.
From B. Carrière and A. Barrois, *Syria* 8 (1927), pl. 31.

3.2.3.1 Archive Possibly from a Private House

In trench PR, about 60 meters southeast of the place where the two Aramaic stela are said to have been found, the excavators unearthed 25 clay tablets. They may be from a destroyed private house; their relation to a grave nearby is unclear. This is the family archive (**Nereb 1**) of the five sons of Nusku-gabbe: Mannaya, Sîn-aba-uṣur, Nusku-killani, Nuḫšaya/Nuḫsaya, and Sîn-uballiṭ, as well as Nusku-iddin, the son of Nusku-killani. The texts are written in Babylonian; five of the tablets include brief summaries in Aramaic. Due to the mention of king Nebuchadnezzar in two texts (II or IV), the archive dates between 604 and ca. 560, or between 556 B.C. and 522/521 B.C.

81. Cf. B. Carrière and A Barrois, "Fouilles de l'École archéologique française de Jérusalem effectuées a Neirab du 24 septembre au 5 novembre 1926," *Syria* 8 (1927), 126–142 and 201–212; M. Abel and A. Barrois, "Fouilles de l'École archéologique française de Jérusalem effectuées a Neirab du 12 septembre au 6 novembre 1927," *Syria* 9 (1928), 187–206 and 303–319; and R. P. Dhorme, "Note sur les tablettes de Neirab," *Syria* 8 (1927), 213–215. Cf. also D. M. Gropp, "Nerab Inscriptions," *OEANE* 4 (1997), 127–129, with bibliography concerning the Aramaic stela.

Most of the texts are loan documents or concern loans; there is also a marriage document. The loans are, as a rule, made to members of the family, not by them. There has been discussion whether the tablets concern local affairs or affairs in Babylonia.[82]

3.2.4 Sippar (Abu Habba)

Sippar (modern Abu Habba) was situated northwest of Babylon and southwest of modern Baghdad, along the Euphrates. Early British excavations directed by H. Rassam occurred in 1881–1882, and V. Scheil continued French work in 1894. Beginning in 1978, Iraqi expeditions headed by W. al-Jadir have excavated at Sippar. In connection with the Belgian explorations directed by L. de Meyer in the neighborhood, some excavation trenches were also made in Sippar 1972–1973. Possibly founded as early as the Uruk period, Sippar became important during the third millennium B.C., and flourished during the second and first millennia B.C.; a limited occupation existed until about A.D. 100 during Parthian rule. The city wall enclosed an area of ca. 1200 × 800 meters. The excavations of Neo-Babylonian Levels, of interest here, have been concentrated in the large Šamaš temple area, covering ca. 350 × 220 meters in the southwestern part of the city. The private houses unearthed north of the temple were of older, essentially Old Babylonian, date.[83]

3.2.4.1 Large Archive in the Šamaš Temple

It has been estimated that 60,000 to 70,000 clay tablets, most of them Neo-Babylonian, were excavated at Sippar during the nineteenth century. The provenances were only occasionally recorded, but about half of all texts are said to come from a large archive (**Sippar 1**) in Room 55, beside a courtyard in the southeastern precinct of the Šamaš temple. It will never be possible to sort out which texts were found in this room, in other rooms of the temple, or in other houses in the city. However, it may be possible to get a general view of the main archive from the catalogue of texts

82. R. P. Dhorme, "Les tablettes babyloniennes de Neirab," *RA* 25 (1928), 53–82; F. M. Fales, "Remarks on the Neirab texts," *OrAnt* 12 (1973), 131–142; I. Eph'al, "The Geographical and Historical Background of the Babylonian Documents from Neirab," *OrNS* 47 (1978), 84–87, 89–90; J. Oelsner, "Weitere Bemerkungen zu den Neirab-Urkunden," *AoF* 16 (1989), 68–77; and L. Cagni, "Considérations sur les textes babyloniens de Neirab près d'Alep," *Transeuphratène* 2 (1990), 169–185.

83. As an introduction to the site, cf. H. Gasche and C. Janssen, "Sippar," *OEANE* 5 (1997), 47–49, with bibliography. Cf., also e.g., W. al-Jadir and Z. R. Abdullah, "Preliminary Reports on the Baghdad University Excavations at Sippar (Abu Habba) 1978–1983," *Sumer* 39 (1983), 97–122 Arabic section, with a summary in W. al-Jadir, "Sippar, Ville du dieu soleil," *Dossiers histoire et archéologie* 103 (mars 1986), 52–54, as well as W. L. de Meyer, *Tell ed Dēr* I– (1971–), with further bibliography.

from Sippar now in the British Museum, which lists about 32,000 Neo-Babylonian tablets. Most of these date to the Neo-Babylonian and early Achaemenid periods, from the reign of Nabopolassar to the second year of Xerxes, ca. 625–486 B.C. In addition, there are a few Babylonian texts from the final years of the Neo-Assyrian period. The existence of some later texts is possible. Among the texts are large numbers of receipts, accounts, administrative lists, disbursements, ledgers, contracts, loan and purchase documents, letters, and school texts. Most of the administrative documents probably came from the archive room. It is impossible to establish how many of the private documents were also found in that room; some may have formed archives in private houses.[84]

3.2.4.2 Library Found on the Shelves in the Šamaš Temple

The 1985–1986 Iraqi excavations continued to unearth the northwestern part of the temple building. This section was dedicated probably to Aya, the consort of Šamaš. The Cella 369 (=155 of the old excavations) and the central Courtyard 358 (=151 of the old excavations) were re-excavated. Excavations were proceeding in a northeastern direction and a large Room 351 (courtyard?) was unearthed, southeast of which was Room 356 with a door in its southwest wall leading to Room 355, which served as a library (**Sippar 2**) of clay tablets with literary contents. Most of the tablets were still standing in their original places. This is the oldest library in history that was found essentially intact on its original shelves. The room, 4.40 × 2.70 meters, had niches for the storage of clay tablets, about 70 cm deep, built into the long wall in front of the door, as well as into both side walls. There were 14 tiers of niches, six in the long wall in the back and four in each of the side walls. The two tiers in the middle of the long wall had two niches above each other, the other tiers had three niches above each other, except the four tiers in the side wall to the right (and perhaps also the ones to the left), which had four niches above each other. This makes a total of 44 (possibly 48 or even 56) niches. Whereas the niches in the left side wall were well filled up with clay tablets, the niches in the right side wall were rather empty. The niches found

84. The catalogue of the Sippar collection in the British Museum is: E. Leichty, *Tablets from Sippar* 1 (with an introduction by J. E. Reade); E. Leichty and A. K. Grayson, *Tablets from Sippar* 2; E. Leichty, J. J. Finkelstein, and C. B. F. Walker, *Tablets from Sippar* 3, in the series Catalogue of the Babylonian Tablets in the British Museum VI-VIII (1986–1988). The publication of the catalogue has initiated a number of projects for the study and publication of texts from this site, including J. MacGinnis, *Letter Orders from Sippar and the Administration of the Ebabbara in the Late-Babylonian Period* (1995); M. Jursa, *Landwirtschaft in Sippar in neubabylonischer Zeit*, AfO Beih. 29 (1995); and A. C. V. M. Bongenaar, *The Neo-Babylonian Ebabbar Temple at Sippar: Its Administration and Its Prosopography*, Uitgaven van het Nederlands Historisch-Archaeologisch Instituut te Istanbul 80 (1997).

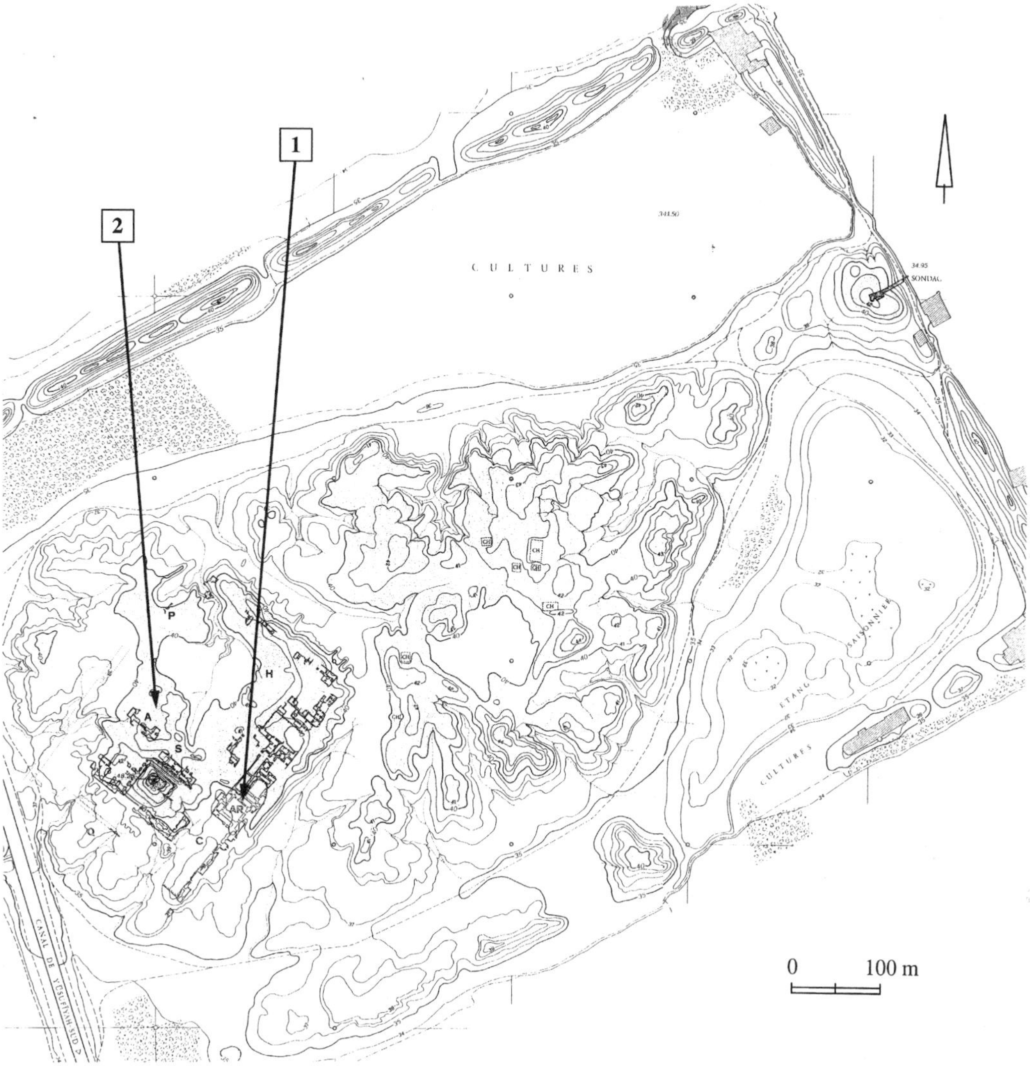

Plan 93. Sippar.
General plan with archive and library **Sippar 1-2**.
From L. de Meyer, *Tell ed-Dēr 3: Soundings at Abū Ḥabbah (Sippar)* (1980), plan 2.

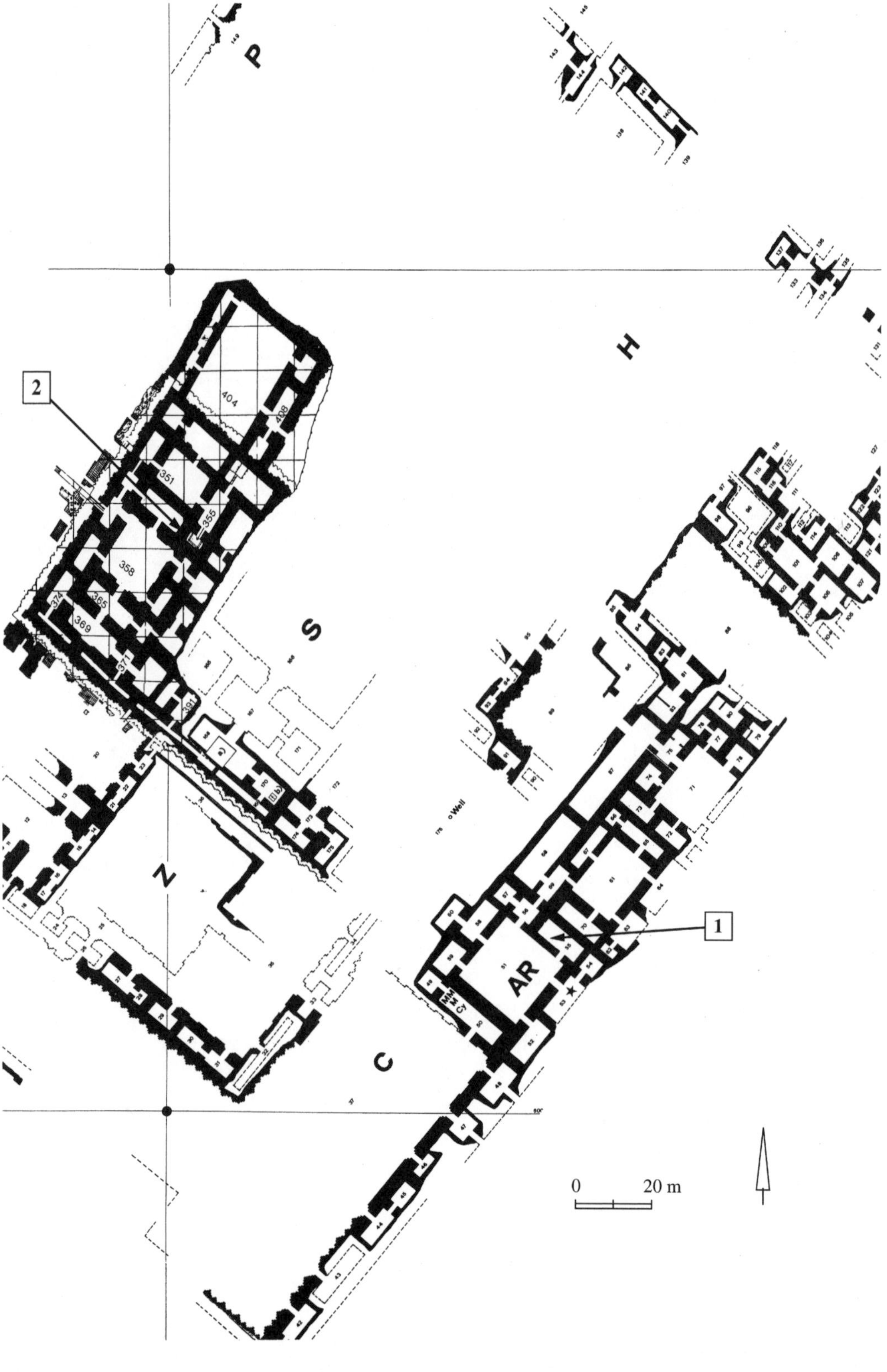
P
H
S
Z
C
AR
1
2
404
408
351
356
358
365
369
371
391
Well
0
20 m

empty may for some reason not have been in use during the final days of the library, or texts on perishable writing material, such as writing boards, papyri, or leather could have been placed there. The construction of the niches is similar to those found in the Nabû temple in Dur-Šarrukin (3.1.3.1). Room 356, where some lexical lists were found, may have served as a reading room (and scriptorium) for the library.

Approximately 800 clay tablets have been unearthed in the library temple. Only a handful of them have so far been published, and it can only be hoped that, when the texts are published, information about the exact location of each tablet on the shelves will also be presented, so that the organization of a large temple library can be studied. From the available information, many of the traditional literary works from Babylonia were represented. The texts were either Akkadian or bilingual Sumerian-Akkadian. There are a large number of different types of omens of the traditional series, as well as a number of incantations, hymns, prayers, and lamentations. Several of the traditional epics like Atraḫasis, Enuma elish, and Lugale have been reported. There are a number of lexical lists, mathematical, and astronomical texts. A collection of copies of royal inscriptions from previous periods of Mesopotamian history, including the prologue to Hammurabi's law, and some pseudo-biographical works has also been found. A small group of letters and economic texts have also been identified. The latest dated tablet is reported to be from the reign of Cambyses II (529–522 B.C.). When more texts have been studied, it may be possible from, for example, the colophons to give the names and professions of the persons responsible for creating the library.[85]

85. For brief surveys, see W. al-Jadir, "Une bibliothèque et ses tablettes dans le quartier sacre de Sippar," *Archéologia* 224 (mai 1987), 18–27; and W. al-Jadir, "Le quartier de l'É.BABBAR de Sippar (Sommaire des fouilles de 1985–1989, 8–11èmes campagnes)," *Mesopotamie et Elam*, CRRAI 36 (1991), 193–196; cf. "Excavations in Iraq 1985–1986, Sippar (Abu Habba)," *Iraq* 49 (1987), 248–249. For a few published texts, cf. F. N. H. al-Rawi, "Tablets from the Sippar Library I: A Supposititious Royal Letter concerning a Vision," *Iraq* 52 (1990), 1–13; F. N. H. al-Rawi and A. R. George, "Tablets from the Sippar Library II: Tablet II of the Babylonian Creation Epic," *Iraq* 52 (1990), 149–157; F. N. H. al-Rawi and A. R. George, "Tablets from the Sippar Library III: Two Royal Counterfeits," *Iraq* 56 (1994), 135–148; F. N. H. al-Rawi, "Tablets from the Sippar Library IV: Lugale," *Iraq* 57 (1995), 199–223; F. N. H. al-Rawi and A. R. George, "Tablets from the Sippar Library V: Mīs pî," *Iraq* 57 (1995), 225–228; and A. R. George and F. N. H. al-Rawi, "Tablets from the Sippar Library VI: Atra-ḫasīs," *Iraq* 58 (1996), 147–190. A facsimile edition of all tablets from the library is in preparation by A. Fadhil and W. Sommerfeld.

← *Plan 94*. Sippar.
Plan of Šamaš temple complex with archive and library **Sippar 1-2**.
Combined from L. de Meyer, *Tell ed-Dēr 3: Soundings at Abū Ḥabbah (Sippar)* (1980), pl. 3B, and from Walid al-Jadir, "Le quartier de l'É.BABBAR de Sippar (Sommaire des fouilles de 1985-1989, 8-11èmes campagnes)," *CRRAI* 36 (1991), 195.

3.2.5 Nippur

Nippur (modern Nuffar or Niffer), situated southeast of Babylon along an eastern branch of the Euphrates, during the third millennium B.C., had been the main Sumerian cult city, housing the Enlil temple, and had during the second millennium B.C. been an important center of administration and scholarly activity (cf. 2.4.3). During the late second and early first millennia B.C., occupation was much smaller (possibly due to a shift of the Euphrates during this period) and concentrated in the area around the Enlil temple. From the middle of the eighth century B.C., Nippur expanded again, and the excavations have unearthed the late levels of the temple, as well as areas with private houses and a possible administrative building or palace.[86]

3.2.5.1 Archives in Private Houses

The tablets from the Neo-Assyrian to the Persian period discussed here are documents found in several archives. The lack of clear provenances for the early excavations and the large amount of unpublished data from the later ones make it probable that additional archives were excavated in other private houses.

In the area with private houses in Tablet Hill, the excavators unearthed 28 clay tablets in a disturbed context, possibly discarded in a later pit above the reconstructed northwestern wall of Locus 70 of Area TA, Level III. This archive (**Nippur 6**) consists of Neo-Babylonian clay tablets dating to the end of the Neo-Assyrian period, 656 to 617 B.C. (one tablet dates to 702 B.C.). Ninurta-uballiṭ and some other men were the owners of the archive, which consisted of 11 loans, five real estate purchases (including the tablet from 702 B.C.), and nine concerning the purchase of children; the latter texts are all dated within a period of a few months during 617 B.C., the last year attested in the archive.[87]

86. See the references given in section 2.4.3.

87. J. A. Armstrong, *The Archaeology of Nippur from the Decline of the Kassite Kingdom until the Rise of the Neo-Babylonian Empire*, diss. University of Chicago (1989), 155, fig. 37. According to A. L. Oppenheim, "Siege-Documents from Nippur," *Iraq* 17 (1955), 69–89, the purchase of children, attested in the archive, took place during a siege; when the siege was over, there was such a strong reaction that the former business of the persons concerned, as well as their archive, was put to an end. Cf. also D. E. McCown, *Nippur* I: *Temple of Enlil, Scribal Quarter, and Soundings*, OIP 78 (1967), 76; and R. Zadok, "Archives from Nippur in the First Millennium B.C.," *Cuneiform Archives and Libraries*, CRRAI 30 (1986), 278–288. Most of the archives reconstructed by Zadok are without provenances and therefore not used here. It is rather questionable if they represent archives found in findgroups and not just dossiers of texts reconstructed by means of prosopography.

The archive (**Nippur 7**) belonging to the family of Murašû that was uncovered during the early excavations is rather well known. It was found in western Nippur near the later Area WA on the floor of a room in a private house that probably belonged to the family. The excavators unearthed about 730 clay tablets with Neo-Babylonian cuneiform writing, some of them with short summaries in Aramaic, as well as 20 uninscribed clay bullae with seal impressions—the bullae may once have been fastened to documents in Aramaic that were written on perishable materials. Most of the clay tablets bear a number of seal impressions, and several of the tablets have short notes in Aramaic, summarizing the content beside the cuneiform text. The texts date to the fifth century B.C., with a concentration in the years 440–415 B.C., the reigns of Artaxerxes I, Darius II, and the beginning of Artaxerxes II. Enlil-šum-iddin and his brother's son Rimut-Ninurta were the principal members of the family of Murašû, responsible for the transactions recorded in the archive of what may be called a family firm. They often acted through their subordinates who bore the title "slave," or "servant" (*ardu*). The texts are contracts on leases of land, canals, live-stock, or equipment by the Murašû firm to tenants, as well as (copies? of) leases of land and water to the firm. Moreover, there are receipts of the firm's payments of taxes to the state and of rents to landlords. The largest group of texts, representing about one-third the total number, consists of notes of obligation or loans made by the family against security (in mortgages), often for fields. The dates of these texts are concentrated in a few months during the first year in the reign of Darius II. Not one single letter has been assigned to this archive with certainty. The latest texts in the archive, which date from 413–404 B.C., show Enlil-suppê-muḫur, a former subordinate of the Murašû family, now working for the Persian prince (*mār bīti*) Aršam—perhaps the responsibility, and therefore the ownership, of the former Murašû belongings ended up in the hands of Aršam.[88]

3.2.5.2 Remains of Archive, Possibly from an Administrative Building

The remains of an archive (**Nippur 8**) of 128 clay tablets was unearthed in a secondary position (as packing around a clay pot containing a burial) in the western part of the city (Area WB), above the Kassite palace with the archive of the Kassite governor (*šandabakku*) of Nippur. The interpretation of the building that was situated

88. G. Cardascia, *Les archives des Murašû: Une famille d'hommes d'affaires babyloniens a l'époque perse (455–403 av. J.-C.)* (1951); M. W. Stolper, *Entrepreneurs and Empire: The Murašû Archive, the Murašû Firm, and Persian Rule in Babylonia*, Uitgaven van het Nederlands Historisch-Archaeologisch Instituut te Istanbul 54 (1985); and V. Donbaz and M. W. Stolper, *Istanbul Murašû Texts*, Uitgaven van het Nederlands Historisch-Archaeologisch Instituut te Istanbul 79 (1997), with further bibliography.

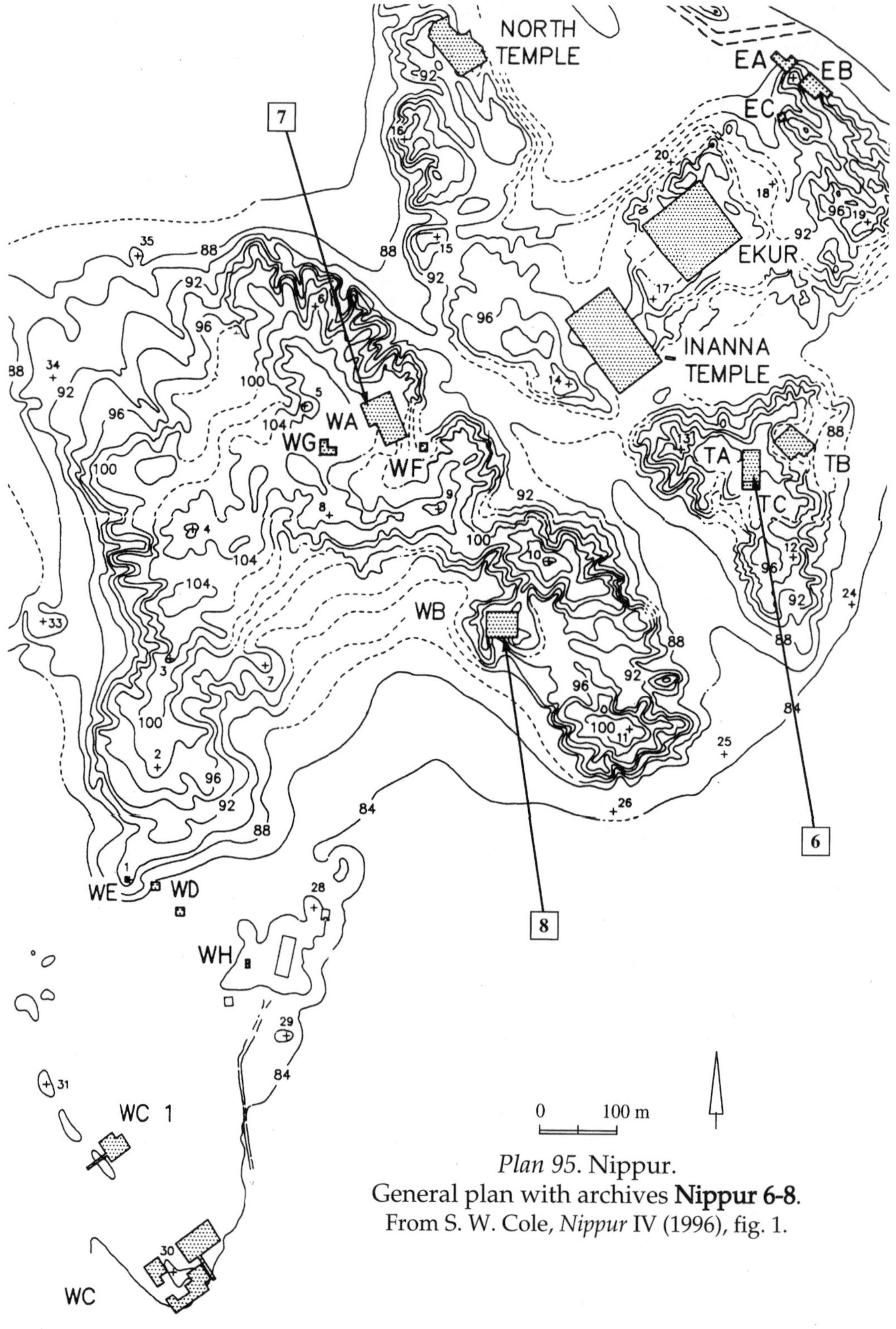

Plan 95. Nippur.
General plan with archives **Nippur 6-8**.
From S. W. Cole, *Nippur* IV (1996), fig. 1.

here as an administrative building or the governor's residence is a guess from the content of the archive. The texts include 113 letters, four administrative texts, one wisdom text, and ten school texts, such as lexical lists. This collection of texts seems to have been the remains of an archive of eighth-century B.C. governors (*šandabakku*) of Nippur. Among the persons mentioned in the archive, Kudurru, Erešu, and Eṭeru most probably acted as governors. All the texts are without date formulae, but, from their contents, it may be possible to date them to 754–732 B.C.[89]

3.2.6 Ur (Muqayyar)

Ur (modern Muqayyar), situated by an arm of the Euphrates southeast of Uruk, was an important Sumerian city and the center of the last Sumerian empire, the Third Dynasty of Ur (cf. 2.4.4). During the second millennium B.C., Ur had been an important city, and so it continued to be during the first millennium B.C. within the Neo-Babylonian culture. First millennium B.C. areas uncovered within the city wall encircling an oval-shaped urban area with axes measuring ca. 1200 × 700 meters included the Sîn temple that Nebuchadnezzar II enclosed within a temenos wall measuring ca. 200 × 400 meters, the palace at the north harbor, and an area with private houses in the southeast.[90]

3.2.6.1 Archive in the Sîn Temple

The archaeological reports indicate that only a few clay tablets were preserved in the temple area from the periods of interest. Northwest of the zikkurrat of the Sîn temple, not far from the temenos wall, a clay pot containing the remains of clay tablets was unearthed underneath the foundation wall of Room 3 of a building from Persian times. The mostly fragmentary clay tablets are said to date from the Persian period and to deal with offerings brought to the temple. They seem to be the remains of an administrative archive (**Ur 2**) of the temple, discarded just before the construction of the new building.[91]

89. S. W. Cole, *Nippur* IV: *The Early Neo-Babylonian Governor's Archive from Nippur*, OIP 114 (1996), and S. W. Cole, *Nippur in Late Assyrian Times, c. 755–612 BC*, SAAS 4 (1996).

90. See the references given in section 2.4.4, and for the period discussed here, cf. L. Woolley, *The Neo-Babylonian and Persian Periods*, Ur Excavations IX (1962).

91. Cf. L. Woolley, *The Neo-Babylonian and Persian Periods*, Ur Excavations IX (1962), 49, pl. 72. I have not been able to identify these texts in any publication of texts.

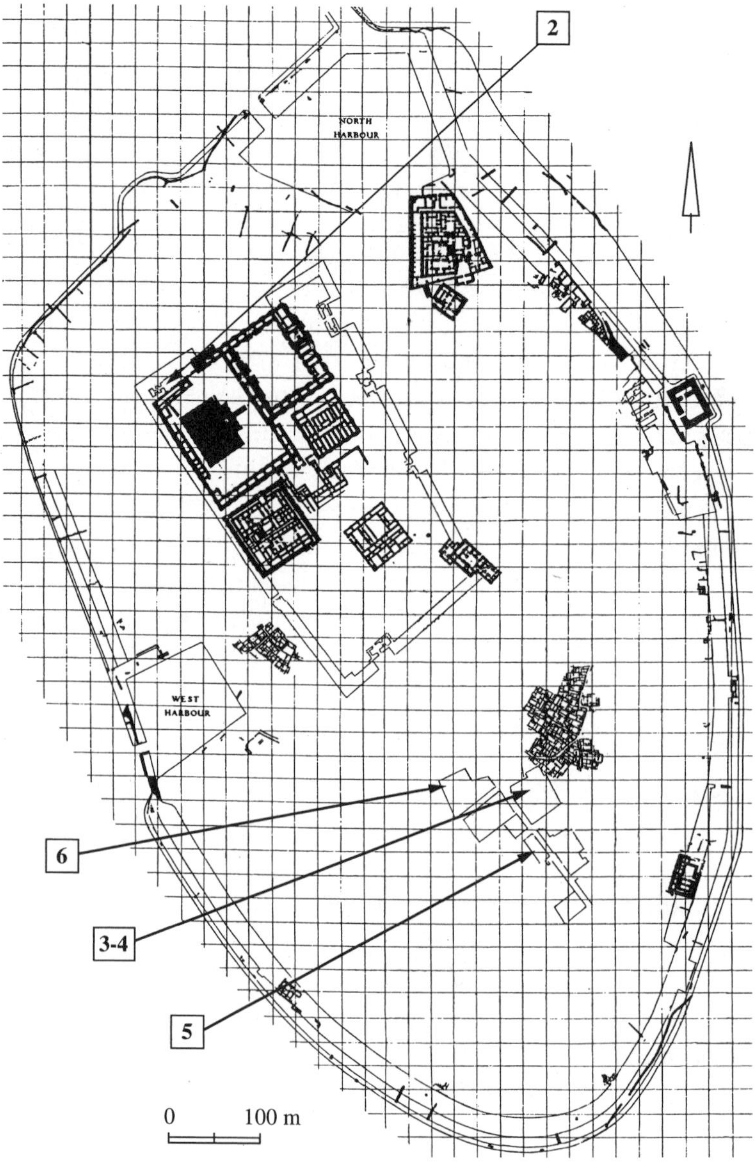

Plan 96. Ur.
General plan with archive **Ur 2-6**.
From L. Woolley, *Ur Excavations* VII (1976), pl. 116.

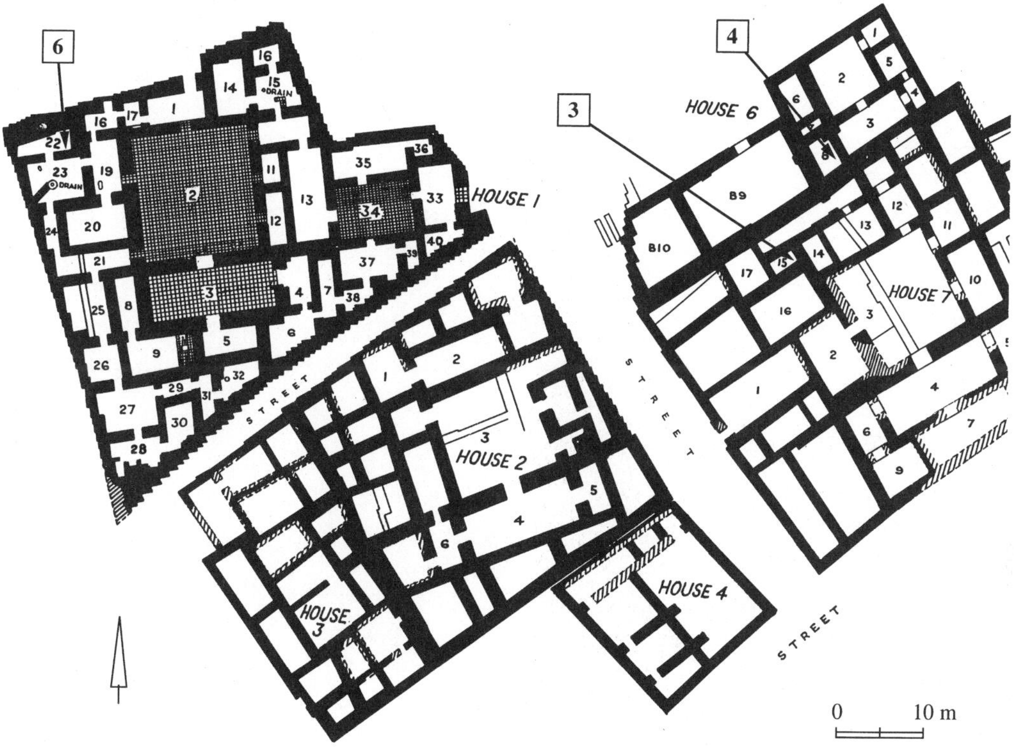

Plan 97. Ur.
Plan of area with private houses with archives and library **Ur 3-4** and **Ur 6**.
From L. Woolley, *Ur Excavations* IX (1962), pl. 71.

3.2.6.2 *Archives in Private Houses*

Two or three houses in a group of seven located southeast of the central city had archives, another had a library. Room 15 (originally built as a bathroom) in House 7 contained a clay pot with 61 clay tablets; above the pot were ten more clay tablets. The tablets are the archive (**Ur 3**) of Sîn-uballiṭ and other members of his family, and date to 624–616 B.C., during the reign of Nabopolassar. The ten tablets above the pot are letters from Sîn-uballiṭ, while the tablets in the pot are primarily documents about loans received by him. This is the reverse of customary storage procedures. Another remarkable feature is that most of the texts were written in Babylon, not in Ur, which may indicate that these are copies of letters he had sent and loan documents returned to him after he had repaid his debtors. Furthermore, it may be assumed that he had moved from Babylon to Ur. However, other explanations may also be possible. Room 8 of House 6 contained a clay pot with 51 clay tablets. The texts in this archive (**Ur 4**) concern a family of barbers (*gallābu*), and most date to the reigns of Darius II and Artaxerxes II, although there are some later texts (the latest from 317 B.C.), as well as a few older texts. Most of the documents concern date groves, fields, and houses, and often deal with purchases and leases, but a few deal with other matters, such as adoption. Another 15 clay tablets excavated next to House 5 may be the remains of an archive (**Ur 5**). Almost all of them date to 517–482 B.C., during the reigns of Darius I and Xerxes I, but there are also a few older texts. The texts represent a diverse range of topics; several concern obligations to deliver dates or other products.[92]

3.2.6.3 Library in Private House or School

A number of clay tablets were excavated in House 1, Room 22. These may be the remains of a library (**Ur 6**), possibly from a scribal school or represent the early training of some scribes. Syllabaries and different school texts with excerpts from traditional literature are common text types.[93]

3.2.7 Uruk (Warka)

Uruk (biblical Erech, modern Warka) was situated by an arm of the Euphrates in southern Babylonia. German excavations under the successive directorships of J. Jordan, A. Nöldeke, E. Heinrich, H. J. Lenzen, H. J. Schmidt, and R. M. Boehmer were conducted rather regularly from 1912–1989. Uruk was an important city as early as the Ubaid and Uruk Periods, with large groups of texts dating as early as ca. 3200 B.C. The city had its largest extent during the first third of the third millennium B.C., when it was a leading Sumerian city with a city wall that encompassed a rather circular area with a diameter of ca. 2.5 kilometers. In the following periods, only parts of the previous city was inhabited, so, for example, in the Neo-Babylonian period, it consisted essentially of only the central and southwestern parts. During the Seleucid period, once more it became a large city, almost covering the whole area of the previous Sumerian city. In the Parthian and Sasanian periods the city continued in a somewhat smaller scale. The excavations have been concentrated in the large temple complexes

92. H. H. Figulla, *Business Documents of the New-Babylonian Period*, Ur Excavations Texts IV (1949); cf. also J. Oelsner, *Materialien* (1986), 235–236.

93. Cf. L. Woolley, *The Neo-Babylonian and Persian Periods*, Ur Excavations IX (1962), 47. I have not been able to identify these texts in any publication of texts.

in the central part of the city. Eanna, the old temple of Ištar, seems to have been in use until at least the first part of the Persian rule. Bit Reš, the temple of Anu and his consort Antu, was reconstructed in the Seleucid period west of Eanna, and during the same period Irigal, the new temple of Ištar, was built south of Bit Reš. Excavations in several other areas of the city have unearthed buildings, many of which are private houses. Only selected texts or groups of texts have been published so far and when published their provenances have not always been included; these two circumstances render the following survey rather preliminary at times, especially the discussion of the temples.[94]

3.2.7.1 Archives with Libraries in the Ištar Temples

The main courtyard of the Eanna temple complex was situated northeast of the zikkurrat. At least 10,000 clay tablets, mostly of which are fragmentary, were unearthed during archaeological excavations in connection with several of the rooms in the precinct surrounding this courtyard. Fragment joins will reduce the actual number of tablets in these archives. Large numbers of the clay tablets were found in two small buildings inside the precinct at the northern and eastern corners of Courtyard A2. More precisely, main findspots are, in the north: the two northernmost rooms of the northwestern side of building K in area Qa XIV4; and in the east: Room 123 (= previously Room 11b) in area Qc XV1, as well as Room M (= previously Room 12) nearby in the precinct to its north in area Qc XIV5. Several tablets came from areas nearby. The tablets date to the Neo-Babylonian and early Persian periods, ca. 625–500 B.C., that is, until Darius I. Since only selected groups of tablets have been published, it cannot be determined whether all the tablets originally belonged to one archive (**Uruk 1**) or whether they had belonged to several distinct archives, for example, with specific text types in individual rooms. Many of the published texts are documents

94. As an introduction to the site, cf. R. M. Boehmer, "Uruk-Warka," *OEANE* 5 (1997), 294–298, with short bibliography. An index to most of the excavations in Uruk can be found in U. Finkbeiner, *Uruk, Analytisches Register zu den Grabungsberichten: Kampagnen 1912/13 bis 1976/77* (1993). For a preliminary survey of the excavated periods, cf. U. Finkbeiner, et al., "Die historische Topographie von Uruk-Warka," in U. Finkbeiner, et al., *Uruk, Kampagne 35–37, 1982–1984: Die archäologische Oberflächen-untersuchung (Survey)*, AUWE 4 (1991), 189–216. For publications, see J. Jordan, *Uruk-Warka*, WVDOG 51 (1928), and the preliminary reports in *Vorläufiger Bericht ... Uruk-Warka* (=*UVB*); *UVB* 1–11 were published within APAW 1929–1940, *UVB* 12/13 (1956) – 31/32 (1983) as a separate series. Many of the final publications of the excavations appear in the two series: Ausgrabungen der Deutschen Forschungs-gemeinschaft in Uruk-Warka (=ADFU) 1– (1936–), and Ausgrabungen in Uruk-Warka, Endberichte (=AUWE) 1– (1987–). For the later periods, cf. also J. Oelsner, *Materialien* (1986), 77–97.

concerning the administration of the Eanna temple, its property, and temple offerings, but there are also documents that, at present, cannot be connected directly to the temple. Among the texts published are lists of offerings delivered to the temple's four main goddesses, with information regarding delivery of incoming foodstuffs. Dates and emmer went to the bakers and barley to the brewers. In addition, there are receipts of different types, such as metals given to workers for manufacturing objects, documents concerning obligations, list of deliveries, and a few letters dealing with administrative matters. Another group of 2,000 published clay tablets comes from illicit excavations, but they have, from their contents, been assigned to the Eanna temple, and may be from the same archive. They are often the same types, but some text groups, for example, 400 letters, are better represented.[95]

Among the clay tablets from the Eanna are, at least, 250 literary texts, which, like the documents, can be dated to the Neo-Babylonian and early Persian periods. These remains of a library include many of the traditional Mesopotamian literary texts. There are a large number of omens, especially astrological and diagnostic ones, as well as incantations, prayers, hymns, epics, and lexical lists. In a few of the preserved colophons some exorcists (*āšipu*) are mentioned as the writers of the tablets, but how far this also applies to the other texts in the library cannot be determined.[96]

In Irigal, the newer Ištar temple, the excavators unearthed remains of an archive with a small library division (**Uruk 2**). They discovered at least about 55 cuneiform tablets and several clay bullae, once fastened to now missing Greek or Aramaic papyri. In a Room in area Lc XVIII1–2 in the precinct northwest of Forecourt II, several tablets and bullae were excavated; others came from Courtyard III to the northeast. The cuneiform tablets date to the Seleucid period, during the reign of Demetrius I (162–150 B.C.), with a few tablets just before or after his reign. Most are documents concerning purchases of, or other dealings with, houses or plots, or purchases of shares in the income of temple officials, such as butchers. There is also a

95. For the early excavations, cf. J. Jordan, *UVB* 1 (1930), 20, pls. 9–10; A. Schott, *UVB* 1 (1930), 45; and H. Lenzen, *UVB* 11 (1940), 15, pl. 8. For the later excavations, cf. H. Lenzen, et al., *UVB* 12/13 (1956), 13–19. Selections of the ca. 6,000 tablets or fragments from the early excavations were published by H. Freydank, *Spätbabylonische Wirtschaftstexte aus Uruk*, Institut für Orientforschung 71 (1971), and L. Jakob-Rost and H. Freydank, *Spätbabylonische Rechtsurkunden und Wirtschaftstexte aus Uruk*, VS 20 (1978). The ca. 400 tablets and 4,000 fragments from the later excavations come from Building K in the north corner of the courtyard. The first of the planned eight volumes of the publications of the latter texts is E. Gehlken, *Uruk, Spätbabylonische Wirtschaftstexte aus dem Eanna-Archiv* I: Texte verschiedenen Inhalts, AUWE 5 (1990), which contains a selection of the different types of texts in this group.

96. A. Falkenstein, *Literarische Keilschrifttexte aus Uruk* (1931).

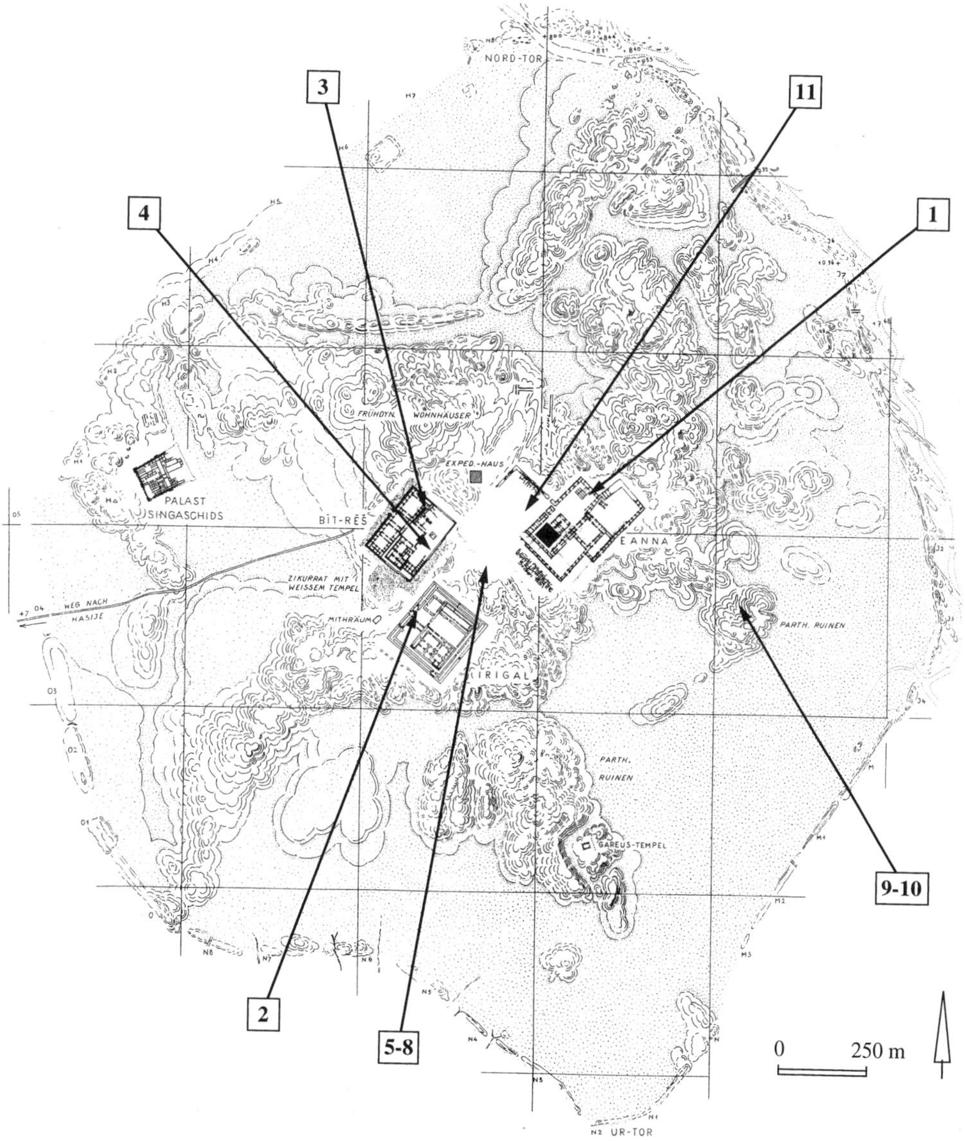

Plan 98. Uruk.
General plan with archives and libraries **Uruk 1-11**.
From H. Lenzen, *UVB* 21 (1965), pl. 27.

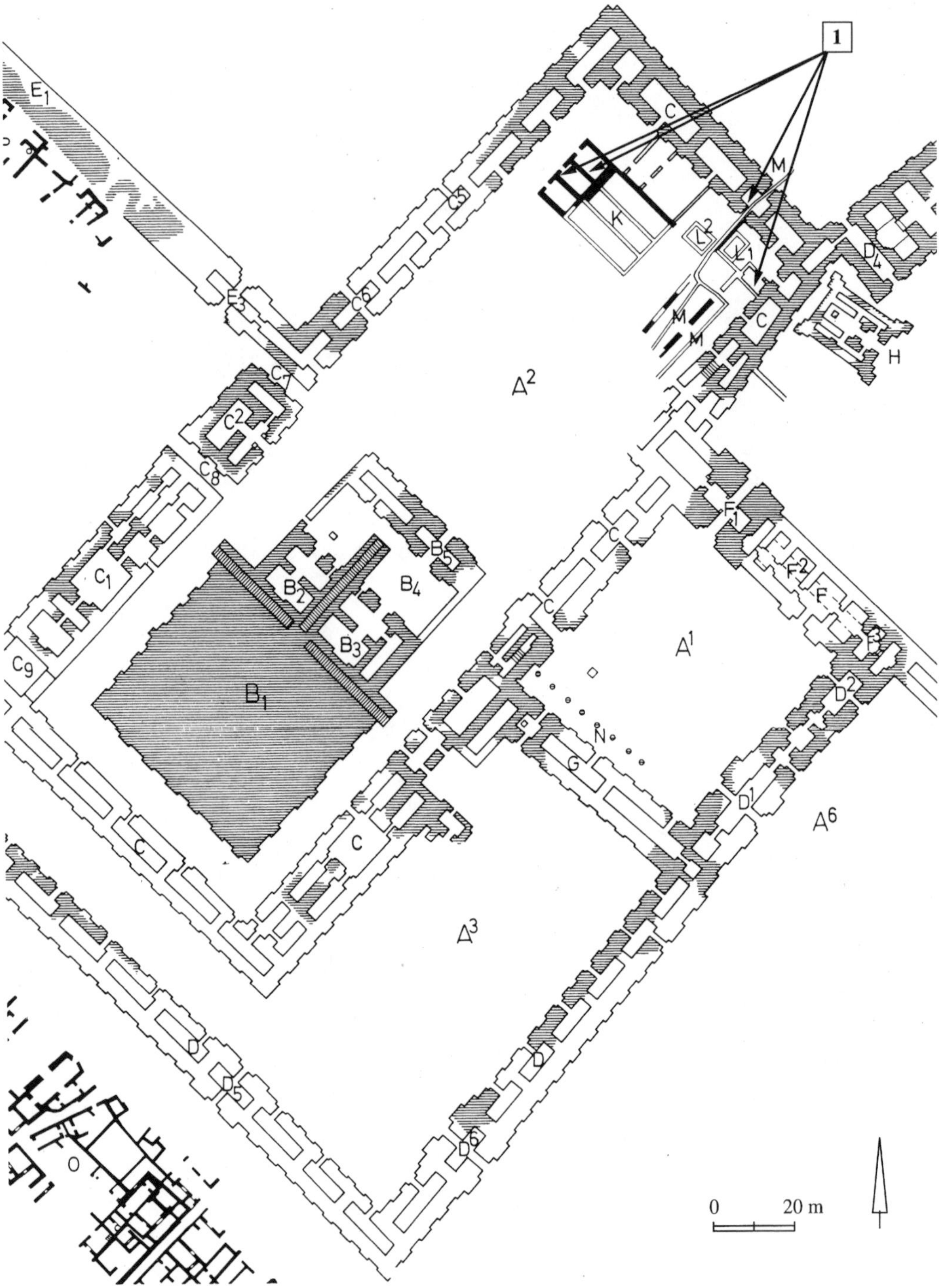
1
E1
E3
C
C5
C6
C7
C2
C8
C1
C9
K
L2
L1
M
M
M
C
D4
H
A2
B5
B4
B2
B3
B1
C
C
F1
F2
F
F3
A1
D2
N
G
D1
A6
C
C
A3
D
D5
D
D6
O
0
20 m

rather small library section with a few literary texts. Similar texts from illegal excavations may also originate from this archive.[97]

3.2.7.2 Archives and Library in the Anu Temple

The main remains of the upper levels of the Anu temple date to the Seleucid period. The double temple was surrounded by a precinct consisting of several courtyards with surrounding rooms. The main archive (**Uruk 3**) was excavated in the small Rooms 29c and 29d, which could only be entered through a door from the gate room at the northeast entrance of the precinct. In these rooms the excavators found numerous clay tablets and a large collection of bullae once fastened to now missing Greek or Aramaic papyri. The clay tablets date to the Seleucid period, during the third century and first half of the second century B.C., most of them being documents concerning purchases of, or other dealings with, houses or plots. Besides the main archive, there are also smaller collections of similar clay tablets and bullae in other rooms of the precinct.[98]

The southeast gate-building of the precinct of the Anu temple in area Le XVI3 had in its northeastern part a small brick-paved room, which had been previously used as a small additional gate, but later blocked from the outside to form a separate room. In this room, the excavators unearthed 158 clay tablets forming the remains of a library (**Uruk 4**), including some archival texts. Illicit diggers had previously been working in the same room as well as in adjoining sections of the precinct in a northeastern direction. The texts date to the years 120–150 of the Seleucid era (192–162 B.C.). Some of the colophons mention Anu-belšunu, son of Nidintu-Anu, and other lamentation-priests (*kalû*), of the famous family of Sîn-leqe-unninni; they may have created the

97. G. K. Sarkisian, "New Cuneiform Texts from Uruk of the Seleucid Period in the Staatliche Museen zu Berlin," *FuB* 16 (1975), 15–76, nos. 2–26, with additions in G. K. Sarkisian, *AoF* 5 (1977), 81–89; cf. J. Oelsner, *Materialien* (1986), 149–151. E. Heinrich, *UVB* 6 (1935), 30, pls. 10–11, and A. v. Haller, *UVB* 8 (1937), 56–57, pl. 24–25. For a reading of the temple name èš.gal instead of iri_{11}.gal, cf. A. R. George, *House Most High: The Temples of Ancient Mesopotamia* (1993).

98. J. Jordan, *Uruk-Warka*, WVDOG 51 (1928), 25, 63–66, pl. 18; O. Schroeder, *Kontrakte der Seleukidenzeit aus Warka*, VS 15, 1916; and M. Rostovtzeff, *Seleucid Babylonia: Bullae and Seals of Clay with Greek Inscriptions*, Yale Classical Studies 3 (1932), 1–114, pls. I-XI.

← *Plan 99*. Uruk.
Plan of Eanna with archive and library **Uruk 1**.
From E. Heinrich, *Die Tempel und Heiligtümer im Alten Mesopotamien* (1982), fig. 372.

library, or the library may have incorporated some texts written by them. Among the texts are rituals, cultic songs, omens, incantations, astronomical, and mathematical texts, as well as some economic documents. It has been suggested that several similar texts found during earlier excavations may also come from this library.[99]

3.2.7.3 Archives in Private Houses

Private houses with archives can be exemplified by what is probably a private house southwest of the Eanna temple, between that temple and the Anu temple. Here, clay tablets were unearthed in three different levels. In the lower level of area Nd XVI5, a clay pot contained 32 clay tablets from the years 700–593 B.C., from the reigns of Aššur-nadin-šumi until Nebuchadnezzar II. The owners of the archive (**Uruk 5**) were members of the family Šamšea: Nabû-ušallim, his children, and grandchildren, in particular the latest owner of the archive Nabû-šumu-lešir. The most frequent types of texts are loans, often made with rights on land tenure as security, and documents concerning the purchase of tenure. There are also a few documents concerning purchases of houses or plots, as well as those recording legal settlements.

In the middle level of the same area, Nd XVI5/Nd XVII1, 81 clay tablets and a large number of additional fragments were found in a clay pot. The documents date to 570–546 B.C., during the reigns of Nebuchadnezzar II and Nabonidus, with a concentration dating to the last ten years. Owners of the archive (**Uruk 6**) were the temple cook (*nuḫatimmu*) Bel-suppê-muḫur and a few related persons. Bel-suppê-muḫur is also referred to in the archive of the Eanna temple. The texts often concern the prebend of other temple cooks, for which Bel-suppê-muḫur took over the responsibility. There were more than 50 contracts about prebends, seven contracts of leases of slaves, six leases of houses, eight receipts, seven obligations or loans, and a few other documents, including a possible letter. Documents of other types and from later years of the career of Bel-suppê-muḫur were probably placed somewhere else.

In a higher level of area Nd XVI5, an archive (**Uruk 7**) with 202 unpublished clay tablets and a large number of additional fragments were excavated. They date from the reigns of Nabonidus until Darius. A member of the Egibi family, Nabû-eṭir-napšati, was the owner of the archive. Most of the texts are loan documents.

99. J. van Dijk and W. R. Mayer, *Texte aus dem Rēš-Heiligtum in Uruk-Warka*, BaM Beih. 2 (1980); cf. H. Lenzen, "Bīt Rēš," and J. van Dijk, "Die Inschriftenfunde, II. Die Tontafeln aus dem rēš-Heiligtum," in H. Lenzen, et al., *UVB* 18 (1962), 16–17 and 43–61, pl. 33; and J. Oelsner, *Materialien* (1986), 143–144. The texts in, e.g., F. Thureau-Dangin, *Tablettes d'Uruk à l'usage des prêtres du Temple d'Anu au temps des Sèleucides*, TCL VI (1922), dating from 90–100 of the Seleucid era may also be from this library.

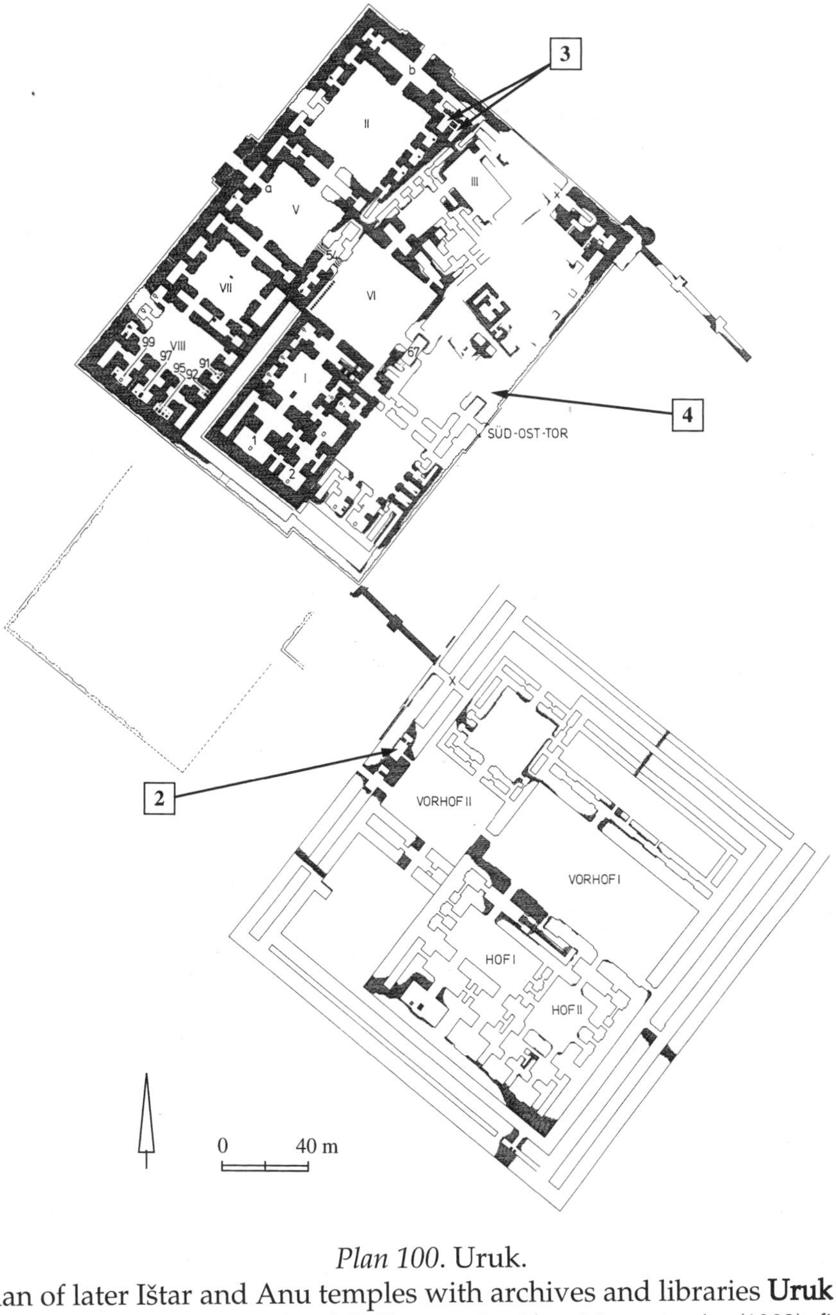

Plan 100. Uruk.

Plan of later Ištar and Anu temples with archives and libraries **Uruk 2-4**.

From E. Heinrich, *Die Tempel und Heiligtümer im Alten Mesopotamien* (1982), fig. 417.

The remains of another archive (**Uruk 8**) of seven clay tablets was found in a disturbed archaeological context just north of the findspots of the three other archives. It belonged to the sons of Bel-ušallim, of the Kuri family. The texts documented a number of loans and a division of inheritance, and date to 626–601 B.C., during the reigns of Nabopolassar and Nebuchadnezzar II.[100]

3.2.7.4 Libraries in Private Houses

In the eastern part of the city in area Ue XVIII1, the excavators unearthed some private houses. A few hundred clay tablets, essentially literary in content, were found in two (or three) archaeological levels—some subsequent mixing may have occurred. The clay tablets from the lower level (Level IV) come from one small room, where at least some were stored in clay pots. It is unclear whether the tablets were stored in the pots deliberately (for easy reference), or as a means for later discard. These tablets, together with about a hundred others from a less well-defined context in higher levels, seem to have been the remains of the library (**Uruk 9**) of Anu-ikṣur, an exorcist (*āšipu*) and his father Šamaš-iddina, as well as some other family members, probably all of whom bore the title *āšipu* and belonged to the family known as *šangû Ninurta*. Some of the tablets were written by the son of the owner mentioned in the tablet. There are many typically exorcistic texts, such as incantations and medical texts. In addition, there are lexical lists, omens, astronomical and astrological texts, as well as others belonging to typically literary genres, such as myths and hymns. One of the jars contained between 30 and 40 clay tablets that were essentially documents; only the forthcoming publication can prove whether they belonged to the same family. A higher level (Level III and also Level I in disturbed context) contained hundreds of clay tablets from the library (**Uruk 10**) of Iqiša, an *āšipu*, "exorcist," of the family of Ekur-zakir. Some of the texts that refer to him as the owner were written by his son Ištar-šuma-eriš or others. Some of these texts are dated to the years around 320 B.C., during early Greek rule. The texts from this level include incantations, medical texts, lexical lists, omens, astronomical and astrological texts, as well as myths, hymns, and similar texts. A few documents were also there, at least one of them concerning Iqiša.

100. Cf. J. van Dijk, "Die Inschriftenfunde, I. Die Tontafeln aus der Grabung in E-anna," in H. Lenzen, et al., *UVB* 18 (1962), 39–43; cf. the plan in *UVB* 21 (1965), pl. 28. The tablets from the lower level were published by H. Hunger, "Das Archive des Nabû-ušallim," *BaM* 5 (1970), 193–304. The texts from the middle level have been published together with a new discussion of those from the lower level in K. Kessler, *Uruk, Urkunden aus Privathäusern, Die Wohnhäuser westlich des Eanna-Tempelbereichs*, Teil I: *Die Archive der Söhne des Bēl-ušallim, des Nabû-ušallim und des Bēl-supê-muḫur*, AUWE 8 (1991); the texts from the upper level will be published in Teil II of that work.

The possibility cannot be excluded that some of the texts from the former library of Anu-ikṣur were taken over by Iqiša.[101] Another small library (**Uruk 11**) was excavated in a private house northwest of Eanna in area Oa/b XV3/4. In Room 38 and other rooms nearby, about 20 literary texts, including some lexical lists and two documents, were found.[102]

3.3 Persian Area

The archives with cuneiform texts from the main Persian area date to the period from the late Elamite to the Achaemenid Empire, ca. 646–458 B.C. The Neo-Elamite state was fatally struck by Assurbanipal with the destruction of Susa in 646 B.C. The area was, about a century later, annexed as part of the expanding Persian or Achaemenid state.

Archives of clay tablets have been unearthed in Susa, the old Elamite and later Achaemenid capital (3.3.1), in the lowland area, as well as in another of the Achaemenid capitals, Persepolis (3.3.2), in the highland. At Persepolis there appear to be remains of archives on perishable material. The archives from Susa seem to belong to the final interval of the Elamite period, whereas those from Persepolis date to the Achaemenid period.

In the main Persian and Elamite area, cuneiform script on clay tablets was used for writing Elamite. Akkadian is occasionally attested. Aramaic written on perishable material was in frequent use, but, due to the perishable writing material, very seldom preserved in this climate.

Outside the main Persian area, archives and libraries on clay tablets have been discovered from the Achaemenid period within the Neo-Babylonian area, in Babylon (3.2.1), Sippar (3.2.4), Nippur (3.2.5), Ur (3.2.6), and Uruk (3.2.7). In the Western Alphabetic area, remains of archives and libraries on perishable material from the same period have been excavated in Elephantine (3.4.1), Samaria (3.4.2), Arad (3.4.4), and Idalion (3.4.6).

101. H. Hunger, *Spätbabylonische Texte aus Uruk*, Teil I, ADFU 9 (1976); E. von Weiher, *Spätbabylonische Texte aus Uruk*, Teil II, ADFU 10 (1983); E. von Weiher, *Spätbabylonische Texte aus Uruk*, Teil III, ADFU 12 (1988); and E. von Weiher, *Uruk, Spätbabylonische Texte aus dem Planquadrat U 18*, Teil IV, AUWE 12 (1993); the forthcoming Teil V will complete the publication. Cf. E. von Weiher, "Die Tontafelfunde der XXIX. und XXX. Kampagne," in J. Schmidt, et al., *UVB* 29/30 (1979), 95–111.

102. A. Cavigneaux, "Texte und Fragmente aus Warka (32. Kampagne)," *BaM* 10 (1979), 111–140; cf. Cavigneaux, "II. Die Inschriften der XXXII. Kampagne," *UVB* 31/32 (1983), 54–57.

The dating systems on the tablets raise difficulties. The Susa texts are dated by month, not year. Although the Persepolis texts include also the regnal year of the king, the king is never named in the date-formula (although occasionally elsewhere).

In addition to the archives and libraries discussed below, individual tablets or small remains of archives have been found at numerous sites in the same area.[103]

3.3.1 Susa

Susa, the main Elamite capital and later one of the three Persian capitals alongside Persepolis and Ecbatana (for a short time also Pasargadae), was situated east of the Shaur River in the lowland of southwestern Iran. The city area east of Shaur covers ca. 1.4 × 2 kilometers. Founded before 4000 B.C., the city was a major capital in the Middle Elamite period, but had somewhat declined during the Neo-Elamite period until it was destroyed by Assurbanipal in 646 B.C. Its best-known and most magnificent period was when it was a Persian capital and Darius I (521–486 B.C.) adorned it with monumental buildings. Later, it was the Hellenistic Seleucia on the Eulaeus. The site was finally abandoned in the thirteenth century. After short English excavations in 1850–1853, and French excavations in 1884–1886, there were large-scale French excavations under the successive directorships of J. de Morgan, R. de Mecquenem, R. Ghirshman, and J. Perrot between 1897 and 1990. Work was concentrated on the fortified city, including the mounds with the modern names "Acropole" (ca. 500 × 350 meters), "Apadana," "Ville Royale," and "Donjon." Much less is known about the eastern lower city with the modern name "Ville des Artisans." Many of the old excavations were on the Acropole, where several temples, for example, those of Inšušinak and of Ninḫursag on the western and eastern sides of the zikkurrat, have been unearthed. In Apadana the excavators found the palace of Darius I. Another palace, of Artaxerxes II, has been unearthed on the western side of the Shaur River. Private houses have been excavated in the other areas of Susa.[104]

103. For a bibliography of Elamite texts from the period, cf. M.-J. Steve, *Syllabaire Elamite, histoire et paleographie*, CPOP 1 (1992), 21–24. For the problematic interpretation of the texts from Argištiḫenele (modern Armavir-Blur), cf. I. M. Diakonoff and N. B. Jankowska, "An Elamite Gilgameš Text from Argištihenele, Urartu (Armavir-Blur, 8th century B.C.)," *ZA* 80 (1990), 102–123; and H. Koch, "Elamisches Gilgameš-Epos oder doch Verwaltungstäfelchen?" *ZA* 83 (1993), 219–236.

104. As introductions to the site, cf. P. O. Harper, J. Aruz, and F. Tallon, eds., *The Royal City of Susa: Ancient Near Eastern Treasures in the Louvre* (1992); H. Pittman, "Susa," *OEANE* 5 (1997), 106–110; and P. de Miroschedji, "Susa (Place)," *The Anchor Bible Dictionary* VI (1992), 242–245, all with bibliographies. The main publications of the excavations have appeared in the series *MDP* with the somewhat changed names *Mémoires [de la] Délégation en Perse*, *Mémoires de la Mission Archéologique en Iran*, and *Mémoires de la Délégation Archéologique en Iran*, 1– (1900–). Preliminary publications of the later excavations have been

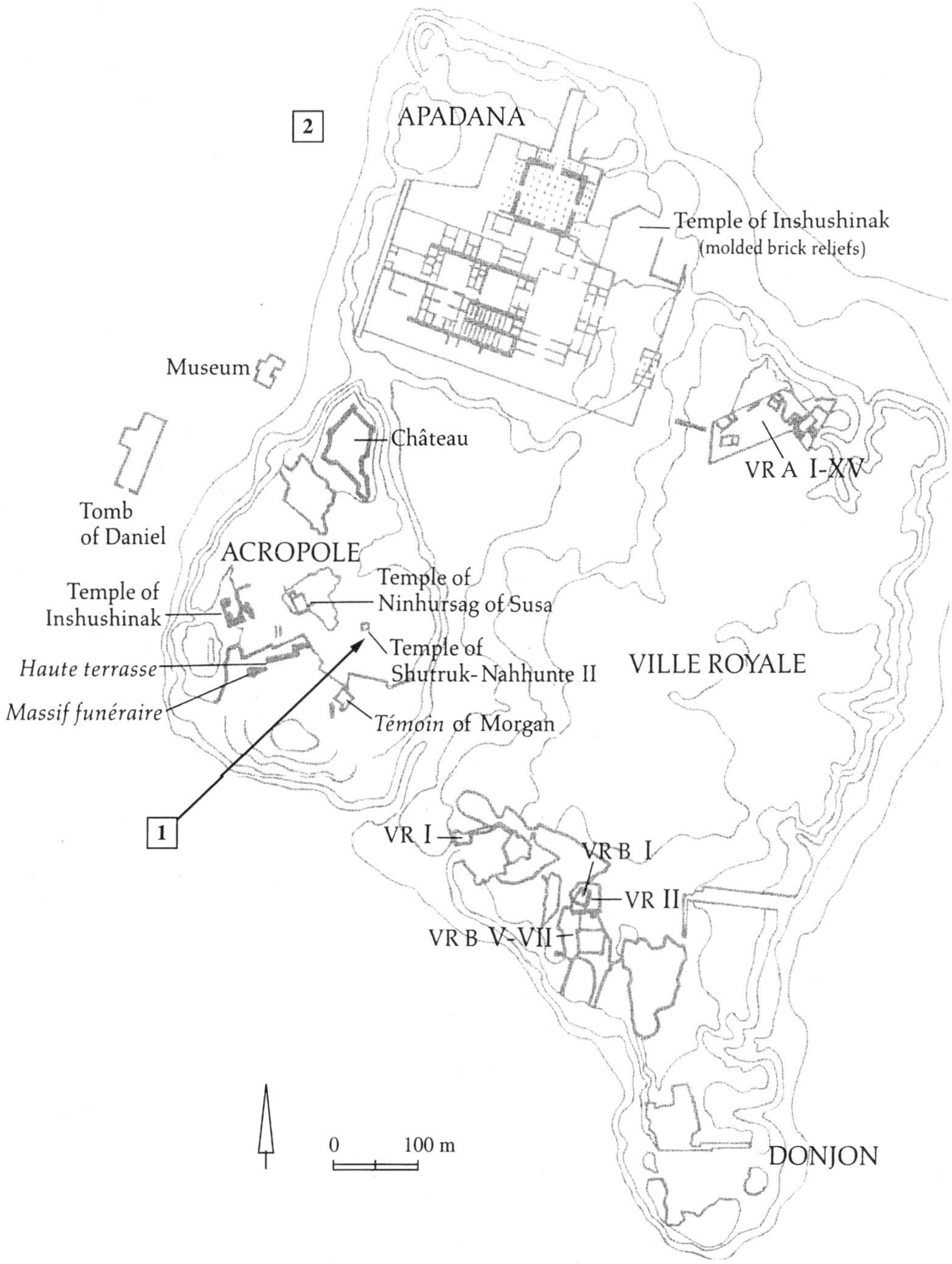

Plan 101. Susa.
General plan with archives **Susa 1-2**. The location of **Susa 2** is only approximative due to lack of detailed information.
From P. O. Harper, J. Aruz, and F. Tallon, *The Royal City of Susa* (1992), xvii fig. 3.

3.3.1.1 Administrative Archive

In Neo-Elamite times, a small temple of Inšušinak was erected by Shutruk-Nahhunte II on the eastern part of the Acropole, southeast of the temple of Ninḫursag. A few meters south of this temple, under a pavement, the excavators unearthed an archive (**Susa 1**) of about 300 Neo-Elamite clay tablets. They have been dated to the period between Assurbanipal's destruction of Susa and the Achaemenid occupation, or possibly the period ca. 605–539 B.C. The texts are administrative lists or notes documenting the delivery of textiles, weapons, and other objects or materials from an administrative unit. Kuddakaka, who bore the title superintendent (*araš hutlak*), was responsible for this unit.[105]

3.3.1.2 Possibly a Private Archive

Below the Apadana palace, built by Darius I, the excavators unearthed seven Neo-Elamite clay tablets. They are the remains of an archive (**Susa 2**) that belonged to Ummanunu and some other persons. The texts are loan documents often concerning silver, or other legal documents. This may be a private archive, but the available information about the finding circumstances is, unfortunately, quite unclear.[106] Also a few Neo-Elamite tablets have been unearthed in the Village Perse-Achéménide.[107]

3.3.2 Persepolis

Persepolis (Greek; Elamite, and probably Old Persian, Parsa; modern Takht-i Jamshid), one of the three Persian capitals, was situated on the Iranian high plateau, about 40 kilometers northeast of modern Shiraz. Darius I (521–486 B.C.) founded the city and Xerxes I (485–464 B.C.) adorned it with more monumental buildings. The American excavations were conducted between 1931 and 1934 under the leadership of E. Herzfeld, and 1935–1939 by E. F. Schmidt. They were concentrated in the citadel

published in *Arts Asiatiques* and *Cahiers de la Délégation Archéologique Française en Iran* (=*CDAFI*) 1 (1971) – 15 (1987).

105. V. Scheil, Textes Élamites-Anzanites, *MDP* 9 (1907), 1–298 and V. Scheil, Téxtes Élamites-Azanites, *MDP* 11 (1911), 309. The archive has been dated ca. 680 B.C. by W. Hinz and H. Koch, *Elamisches Wörterbuch* (1987), 552, and ca. 605–539 B.C. by M.-J. Steve, *Syllabaire elamite* (1992), 22. The statigraphy is problematic, and the later dating is essentially based on a reconstruction of seal types by P. Amiet. For a summary of the arguments for the later dating, cf. E. Carter, *Elam* (1984), 181–184.

106. V. Scheil, Téxtes Élamites-Azanites, *MDP* 11 (1911), 301–307.

107. H. H. Paper, "Note préliminaire sur la date des trois tablettes élamites du Suse," in R. Girshman, Village Perse-Achéménide, *MDP* 36 (1954), 79–82 pl. 24.

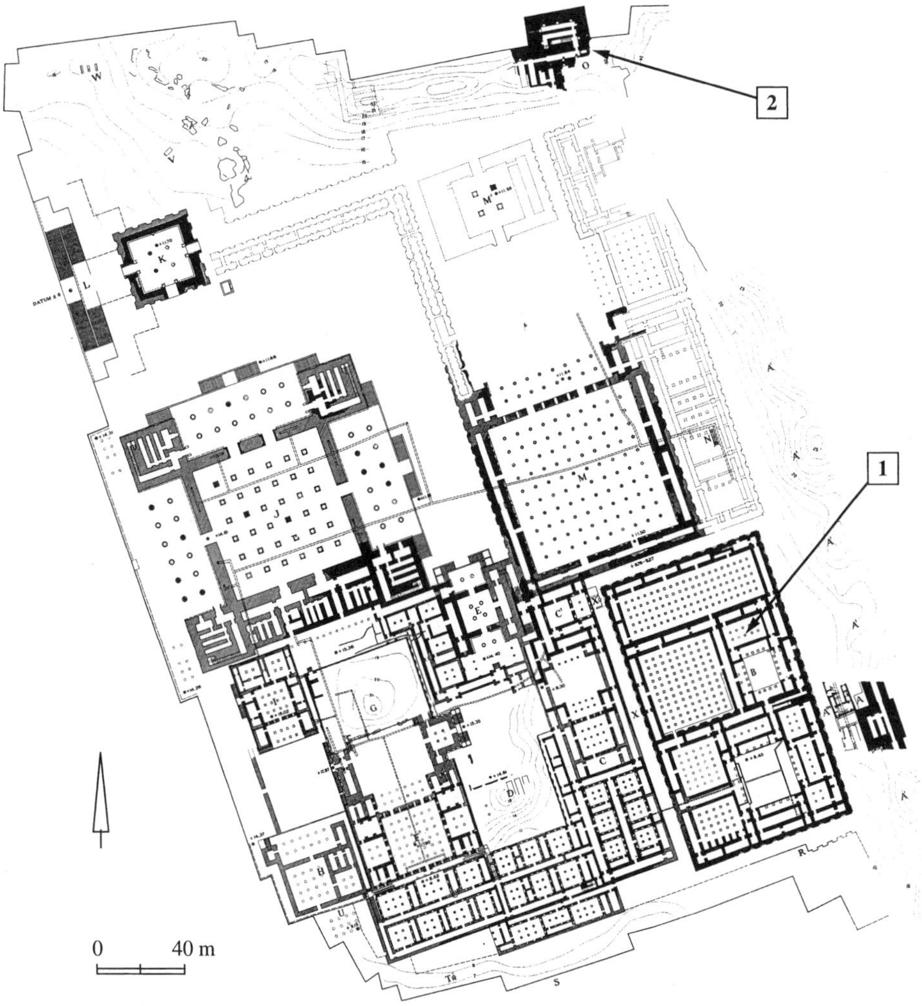

Plan 102. Persepolis.
Plan of palace area with archives **Persepolis 1-2**.
From E. F. Schmidt, *Persepolis* I, OIP 68 (1953), fig. 21.

area, which contained the fortified palace compound on a terrace with a number of magnificent buildings. The area below the terrace, where a lower city may have been situated, was only briefly examined. Since only palaces were excavated, a heavy concentration of texts from administrative archives was recovered. Many texts were written probably on perishable material, such as papyrus, and did not survive through time.[108]

3.3.2.1 Administrative Archives in the Palace Area

The royal treasury, situated in the southeast corner of the terrace, produced an archive (**Persepolis 1**) with more than 200 clay tablets written in cuneiform script in Elamite. The archive was discovered in Room 33, southeast of the main northernmost room of the treasury, with some tablets coming from adjacent areas. The excavators assumed that the archive had been located on an upper floor, from which the tablets had fallen down. Almost all the tablets are sealed dockets with traces of strings that once had been fastened either to Aramaic papyri or to other objects. The texts date to the years 492–458 B.C., from the reign of Darius I to Artaxerxes I, and record disbursements of silver from the treasury, chiefly in lieu of rations in kind. Two-thirds of the documents are written in the form of letter-orders. Five successive treasurers (*ganzabara*) were responsible for the administration. The same room also contained a collection of almost 200 clay labels (bullae) with seal impressions; on the back sides they show traces of strings that would have been fastened to containers of various goods or possibly to Aramaic papyri. In the northernmost room were a number of mortars, pestles, and plates made of green chert, with notes about their manufacture painted in Aramaic. A large number of texts on papyri, skins, or other perishable writing materials, now disintegrated, had probably once been placed in the palace.[109]

An archive (**Persepolis 2**) of thousands of clay tablets written in Elamite with cuneiform script was recovered from the fortification wall at the northeastern corner

108. As an introduction to the site, cf. D. Stronach and K. Codella, "Persepolis," *OEANE* 4 (1997), 273–277, with short bibliography. The main archaeological publications are E. F. Schmidt, *Persepolis* I-III, OIP 68, 69, 70 (1953–1970). For possible areas with private houses, cf. W. M. Sumner, "Achaemenid Settlement in the Persepolis Plain," *AJA* 90 (1986), 3–31.

109. G. G. Cameron, *Persepolis Treasury Tablets*, OIP 65 (1948); and R. A. Bowman, *Aramaic Ritual Texts from Persepolis*, OIP 91 (1970); cf. the reviews by B. A. Levin, *JAOS* 92 (1972), 70–79, and R. Degen, *BiOr* 31 (1974), 124–127. The existence of writing on perishable materials in Aramaic, sometimes perhaps to be read in Persian, in the Persian capital is rather probable, when, e.g., the Aramaic letters (see Section 3.4, Introduction) sent by the Persian prince Aršam, possibly from Babylon, to Egypt, are considered. Aramaic had a widespread use within the Persian Empire, and one of the capitals can hardly have been an exception.

of the terrace. More than 2,000 of these have been published, but many more remain unpublished. More than 80% of the tablets were sealed dockets with traces of strings as in the treasury archive. Forty-two of the tablets had additional short Aramaic notes written in ink. A small number of tablets were written in Aramaic, one in Neo-Babylonian, and one in Greek. The Elamite texts date to the years 509–494 B.C., during the reign of Darius I, and deal with administrative transfers of food commodities.[110]

3.4 Western Alphabetic Area

The archives and libraries with texts from the Levant and surrounding areas using the alphabet for West Semitic languages date to the period ca. 800–330 B.C. Texts on papyri, leather, and ostraca are preserved only during favorable climatic conditions. Therefore, the selection of such texts are much more limited than for cuneiform texts on clay tablets. This is especially true for documents made of papyri or leather, which can only be found well preserved in extremely dry areas in Egypt and near the Dead Sea, even if texts of such materials were in frequent use in a much wider area, and more and more increased in use also in the previously discussed areas. For this reason the remains of archives and libraries presented here are very limited in number and geographical distribution. Archives and libraries mainly with local scripts and languages from Egypt are not discussed here.

From the period of the Aramean, Israelite, and Phoenician states, the only remains of archives are a few in Samaria (3.4.2), Lachish (3.4.3), Arad (3.4.4), and Jerusalem (3.4.5) in the Israelite area. From the Persian period, archives have been found in Elephantine (3.4.1) in southern Egypt, and in Arad (3.4.4) and Samaria (3.4.2), as well as in Idalion (3.4.6) on Cyprus in the Phoenician area.

The languages used in these archives were Hebrew and Phoenician during the older periods and Aramaic during the Persian period. However, remains of archives with Aramaic alphabetic texts on papyri, leather, or ostraca have been found also at several sites in the Neo-Assyrian (3.1), Neo-Babylonian (3.2), and Persian areas (3.3). However, due to the climatic conditions in these areas, the clay tablets with cuneiform texts compose the great majority among the preserved artifacts.

Due possibly to the limited total amount of texts and the rather narrow types of texts preserved from Western Alphabetic area, the only texts with date formulae including the name of the king and the year of his reign are from the Persian Period.

110. R. T. Hallock, *Persepolis Fortification Tablets*, OIP 92 (1969).

The remains of Punic or Greek archives from Karthago from the end of this period or perhaps somewhat later have not been discussed.[111] The following four dossiers may actually have been archives, but there is not enough information as to their find-spots. A dossier of texts written on leather, found in a leather bag somewhere in Egypt, consists of 13 letters and additional fragments that date to the end of the fifth century B.C., and concern the administration of the Persian prince Aršam's property in Egypt (for other activities of probably the same Aršam, cf. 3.2.5.1 Nippur 7); the most frequently attested addressee is Neḥtiḥur, one of those responsible for Aršam's belongings.[112] A collection of 218 Aramaic ostraca, dated to 362–312 B.C., was found somewhere in Idumea.[113] There are also two collections of bullae from Israel; the bullae were previously fastened to papyrus documents.[114] In addition to the archives and libraries discussed below, individual texts or other remains of archives have been found at a number of other sites in the same area.[115]

111. For the ca. 3,600 clay bullae, from the late sixth to the middle second century B.C., once fastened to now missing papyri, found in a temple area in Karthago, cf. the preliminary report by D. Berges, "Die Tonsiegel aus dem Karthagischen Tempelarchiv," *Mitteilungen des Deutschen archäologischen Instituts*, Roemische Abteilung 100 (1993), 245–268, with further references.

112. G. R. Driver, *Aramaic Documents of the Fifth Century B.C.: Transcribed and Edited with Translations and Notes* (1954); G. R. Driver, et al., *Aramaic Documents of the Fifth Century B.C.: Abridged and Revised Edition* (1957); and B. Porten and A. Yardeni, *Textbook of Aramaic Documents from Ancient Egypt* 1: *Letters* (1986), 92–129

113. A. Lemaire, *Nouvelles inscriptions aramennes d'Idumee au musee d'Israel* (1996).

114. More than 70 bullae from the late sixth century B.C. during Persian rule are reported to have been found "in the Jerusalem region"; cf. N. Avigad, *Bullae and Seals from a Post-Exilic Judean Archive*, Qedem 4 (1976), and 225 bullae claimed to be find near Tell Beit Mirsim, cf. N. Avigad, *Hebrew Bullae from the Time of Jeremiah* (1986).

115. Especially Kuntillet 'Ağrud and Meṣad Ḥašavyahu have yielded almost archival-like findings; for these and other Hebrew texts from the period, cf. J. Renz and W. Röllig, *Handbuch der althebräischen Epigraphik* (=*HAHE*) I, II/1, and III (1995). For a bibliography of the Aramaic texts, cf. J. A. Fitzmyer and S. A. Kaufman, *An Aramaic Bibliography* I: *Old, Official, and Biblical Aramaic* (1992). A collection essentially of Demotic papyri from Saqqara contained also Aramaic texts, cf. J. B. Segal, *Aramaic Texts from North Saqqâra: With Some Fragments in Phoenician* (1983). Cf. also the Aramaic texts from Hermopolis, E. Bresciani and M. Kamil, *Le Lettere Aramaiche di Hermopoli*, Atti della Accademia Nazionale dei Lincei Memorie VIII 12:5 (1966). For Phoenician texts, cf. still H. Donner and W. Röllig, *Kanaanäische und aramäische Inschriften* I-III (1962–1964), but there are a number of later findings and additions, which are not listed here since they fall outside the intentions of the present work, e.g., A. Vanel, "Six 'ostraca' phéniciens trouvés au temple d'Echmoun, près de Saïda," *Bulletin du Musée de Beyrouth* 20 (1967), 45–95, pls. I–IV, tableau 1–2; and M. G. Guzzo Amadasi and V. Karageorghis, *Fouilles de Kition* III: *Inscriptions phéniciennes* (1977).

For the cuneiform texts from the area, cf., e.g., J. S. Cooper, "Cuneiform. E. Cuneiform in Palestine," *The Anchor Bible Dictionary* I (1992), 1217–1218, with further bibliography.

3.4.1 Elephantine

Elephantine (Greek rendering of the Egyptian *'ibw* or *'bw*, Aramaic *yb*) was situated on a small island with the same name opposite Asuan, just below the First Cataract at the southern border of mainland Egypt. German archaeological excavations were directed by O. Rubensohn in 1906–1908, and, partly contemporary with the German, French ones under the leadership of Clermont-Ganneau during 1907–1910. There followed several minor excavations until the joint German-Swiss expedition directed by W. Kaiser started new, long-term excavations in 1969. Occupation has been attested from prehistoric times (ca. 3500 B.C.) until the early Arab period. From the end of the Saite period and during the whole Persian period, the population in Elephantine consisted of, to a large extent, border-soldiers with families; among them were Egyptians and Jews who had settled there before the Persian conquest of Egypt by Cambyses II in 525 B.C. The excavated part of the city is situated in the southern section of the island, and consists of temples and private houses inside a town wall. A number of papyri belonging to archives and libraries has been unearthed during these excavations, as well as by papyrus robbers. The papyri are rather well preserved thanks to the climatic circumstances. As can be expected in Egypt, the archives and libraries in Elephantine consist of texts written on papyri and ostraca in Demotic, in Aramaic, or, after Alexander, in Greek. They belonged primarily to private families.[116]

3.4.1.1 Private and Communal Archives in Private Houses

Only a few important archives with Aramaic documents will be referred to below; other, less well-defined, Aramaic archives, as well as Demotic and Greek archives or libraries, will not be discussed. Several texts have date formulae naming the king and regnal year. Many of the papyri were in bad condition when unearthed, including the archive of Aramaic texts in the west room of the house below "House k" (called House G when re-excavated during the new excavations) ca. 7 meters northwest of the later enclosure wall of the Khnum temple (**Elephantine 1**). The substantial number of papyri in this archive disintegrated almost totally during the

116. As introductions to the site, cf. W. Kaiser, "Elephantine," *OEANE* 2 (1997), 234–23; and L. Habachi, "Elephantine," *Lexikon der Ägyptologie* I (1975), 1217–1225, both with bibliographical references. For excavation details of interest here, cf. W. Honroth, O. Rubensohn, and F. Zucker, "Bericht über die Ausgrabungen auf Elephantine in den Jahren 1906–1908," *ZÄS* 46 (1909), 14–61; W. Müller, *FuB* 20/21 (1980), 75–88; and W. Müller, *FuB* 22 (1982), 7–50. The new excavations have their preliminary reports published by W. Kaiser, et al., in MDAIK 26– (1970–); cf. P. Grossmann, MDAIK 36 (1980), 274–275, for the re-excavation of House k.

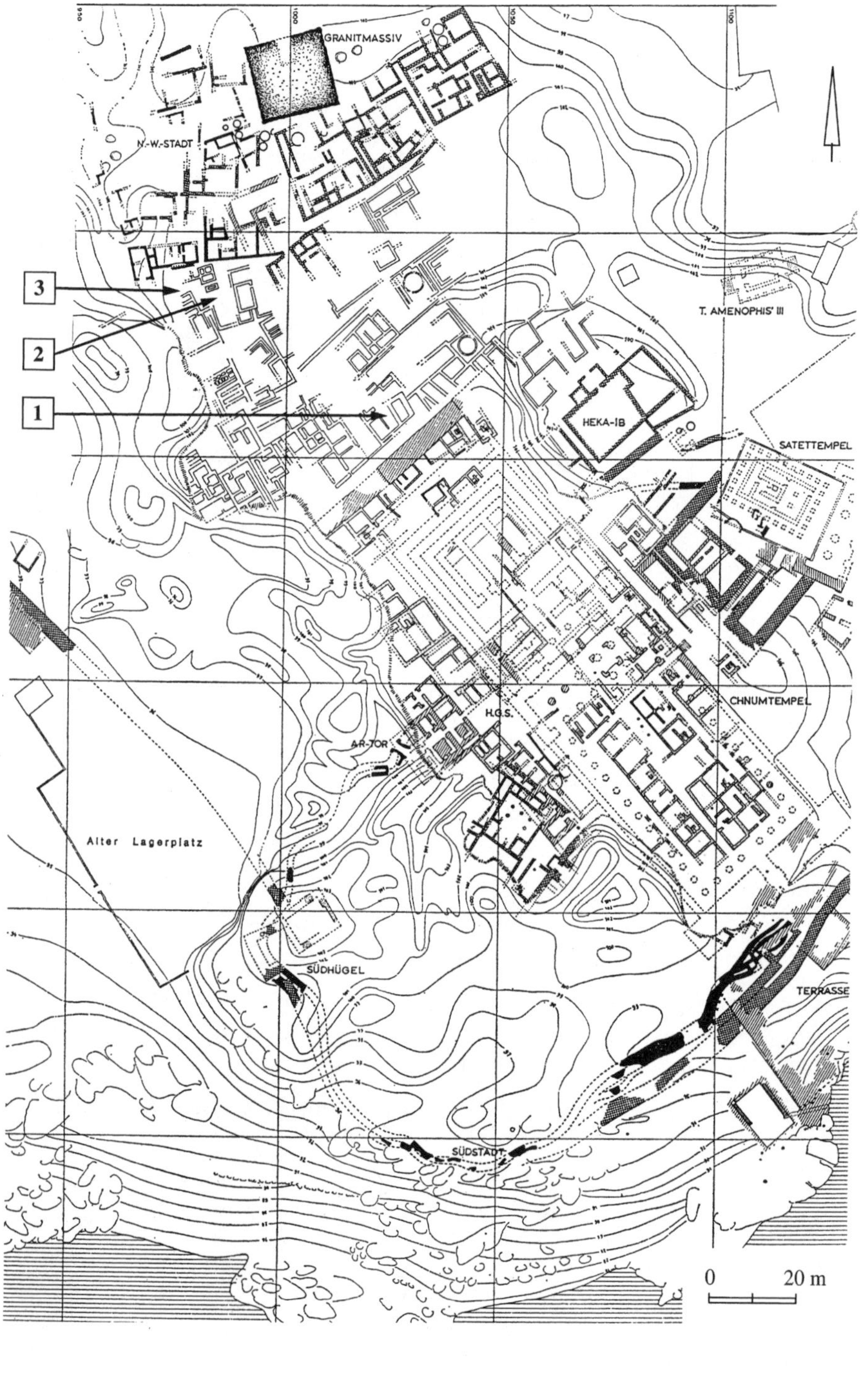
GRANITMASSIV
N.-W.-STADT
3
2
1
T. AMENOPHIS' III
HEKA-IB
SATETTEMPEL
CHNUMTEMPEL
H.G.S.
AR-TOR
Alter Lagerplatz
SÜDHÜGEL
TERRASSE
SÜDSTADT
0
20 m

process of excavation; however, a large number of jars with Aramaic, sometimes Phoenician, inscriptions were recovered from two other rooms of this house.

In "House m" ca. 50 meters northwest of the same enclosure wall of the Khnum temple, the papyri were better preserved even though the house was severely destroyed. This was the archive of the Jewish community under the leadership of Yedaniah, son of Gemariah (**Elephantine 2**); whether the destroyed house was the private residence of Gemariah or the community house cannot be established. The papyri are dated from 419 B.C. until at least 407 B.C. There are nine letters and one memorandum, all of which deal with the affairs of the Jewish community, especially relations with the Egyptians, with Aršam and other Persian leaders, as well as with the leaders in Judea in connection with the destruction of the Jewish sanctuary in Elephantine by priests of the god Khnum in 410 B.C. There are also some lists of persons, for example, a long roster listing those who had contributed to the rebuilding of the sanctuary. Finally, an Aramaic version of the inscription of Darius I and the book of Aḥiqar were found.

The archive of the woman Mibṭaḥiah (**Elephantine 3**) had been found by illicit diggers just before excavations started, but its provenance was pointed out to the Germans; it was in the house immediately west of "House m" or in a western part of "House m." Mibṭaḥiah was the sister of Yedaniah's father Gemariah, who probably was the leader of the Jewish community prior to his son. Mibṭaḥiah's archive consists of eleven papyri from three generations of her family, from 471–410 B.C. The oldest group of papyri are documents dealing with a house plot given to her by her father Maḥseiah. There are legal documents concerning one of her three marriages, as well as some court decisions. The two latest documents in the archive concern her children's dealing with property after her death.

In other archives, such as Anani's, which were not found during controlled excavations, there are documents concerning loans, purchases, marriages, adoptions, and legal settlements.[117]

117. B. Porten, *Archives from Elephantine* (1968), contains a good, basic reconstruction of the archives; the archaeological material, including the findspots of the texts, has however often not been fully integrated into the discussion. Cf. also B. Porten, "Elephantine Papyri," *The Anchor Bible Dictionary* II (1992), 445–455, with further bibliography. The texts now exist in new editions by B. Porten and A.Yardeni, *Textbook of Aramaic Documents from Ancient Egypt* 1: *Letters* (1986), 2: *Contracts* (1989), 3: *Literature, Accounts, Lists* (1993), and 4: *Ostraca* (to be published).

← *Plan 103*. Elephantine.
General plan with archives **Elephantine 1-3**.
From L. Habachi, "Elephantine," *Lexikon der Ägyptologie* I (1975), 1219–1220.

3.4.2 Samaria

In the beginning of the ninth century B.C., Omri made Samaria (modern Sebastia), in the highlands ca. 55 kilometers north of Jerusalem, the capital of Israel. In 722 B.C. the Assyrians conquered the city and turned Israel into the Assyrian province of Samerina (Samaria). The city became the seat of Assyrian, Babylonian, and Persian governors and continued in use at least into Roman times. Excavations were directed from 1908–1910 by G. Schumacher, G. A. Reisner, and C. S. Fisher, as well as 1931–1935 under the leadership of J. W. Crowfoot, with some more recent diggings in 1965–1968. Much of the work has been concentrated in the citadel (ca. 120 × 220 meters), whose palaces date from the time of the Israelite monarchy. The area also contains a number of later, mostly Roman, buildings. Except for a part of the city wall and the west gate, very little of the lower city, which probably was predominantly residential in nature, was excavated. Therefore, the size of the lower city has not been established with certainty for the periods before the Romans, when the area was encircled by a town wall of that period.[118]

3.4.2.1 Administrative Archives in the Palace Area

The remains of an administrative archive of about 102 ostraca in the Hebrew language were unearthed in the so-called "Ostraca House" in the western part of the palace area on the citadel (**Samaria 1**). The ostraca were found in the fill of the foundations and floors of a building complex that was used for a considerable time prior to the destruction of the city. The ostraca are dated to years 9, 10, and 15 in the reign of an unnamed king, assumed to be Jeroboam II, which would yield dates ca. 782–776 B.C. Alternatively, the first two years may have been during the reign of Jehoahaz, which would yield the dates ca. 796–795 and 776 B.C. These are administrative documents that concern the delivery of wine and oil to (or from?) persons from different places.

Eleven of the 15 clay bullae found in Samaria came from the northern part of the citadel, the same area as the famous findings of ivories. It has been suggested that they date to the eighth century B.C. They are the remains of an archive (**Samaria 2**) of papyri fastened with strings and sealed with the bullae. The papyri may have been

118. As introductions to the site, cf. R. Tappy, "Samaria," *OEANE* 4 (1997), 463–467; N. Avigad, "Samaria (city)," *NEAEHL* 4 (1993), 1300–1310; and J. D. Purvis, "Samaria (Place)," *The Anchor Bible Dictionary* V (1992), 914–921, all of them with bibliographies. The archaeological material has been published in G. A. Reisner, et al., *Harvard Excavations at Samaria 1908–1910*, vols. I-II (1924); and J. W. Crowfoot, et al., *Samaria-Sebaste*, vols. I-III (1938–1957); cf. also R. E. Tappy, *The Archaeology of Israelite Samaria* I: *Early Iron Age through the Ninth Century BCE*, HSS 44 (1992).

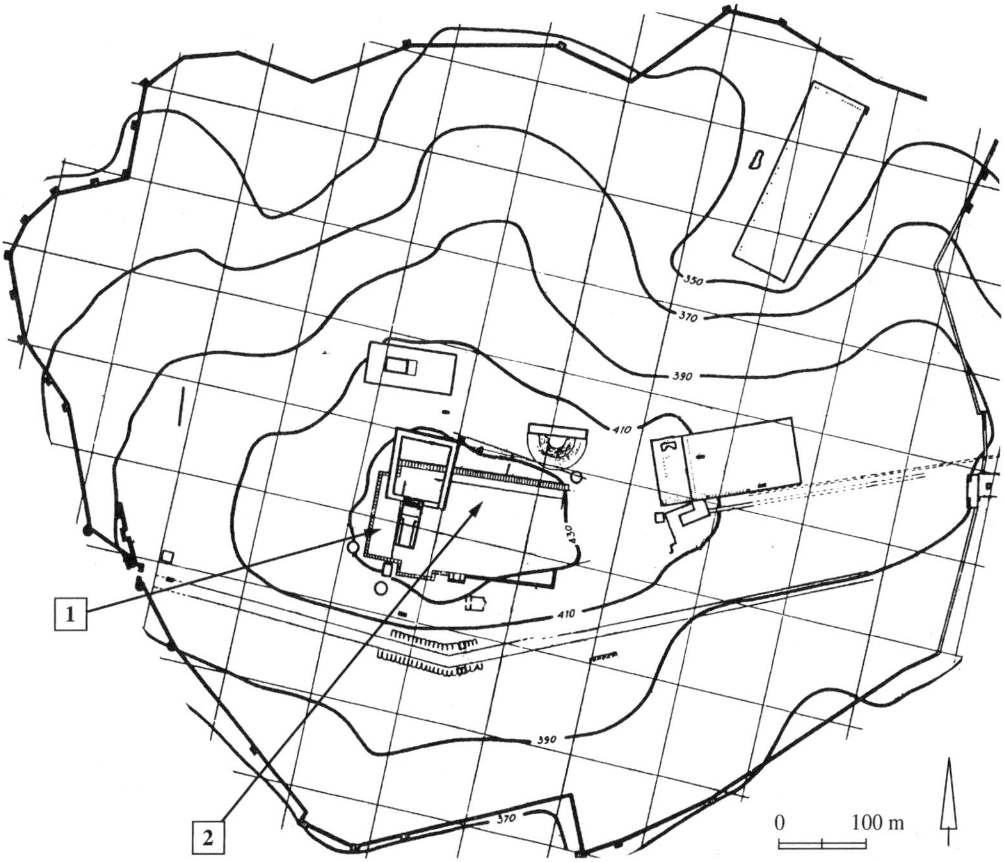

Plan 104. Samaria.
General plan with archives **Samaria 1-2**.
From J. W. Crowfoot, K. M. Kenyon, and E. L. Sukenik, *Samaria-Sebaste* I (1942), pl. I.

documents involving some kind of obligation or letters. Because of the provenance they were probably part of an administrative archive in the palace, but could also have been a private archive kept there. From the Assyrian period, the only remains of an archive is a single cuneiform clay document. Some Aramaic ostraca from the Persian period were also recovered in Samaria.[119]

119. J. Renz and W. Röllig, *HAHE* I (1995), 79–109, and A. Lemaire, *Inscriptions hébraïques* 1 (1977), 21–81, and 245–250, both with bibliographies. G. A. Reisner, et al., *Harvard Excavations at Samaria 1908–1910*, vol. I (1924), 247f.; vol. II, pl. 58. Cf. I. T. Kaufman, "Samaria Ostraca," *The Anchor Bible Dictionary* V (1992), 921–926, with further bibliography.

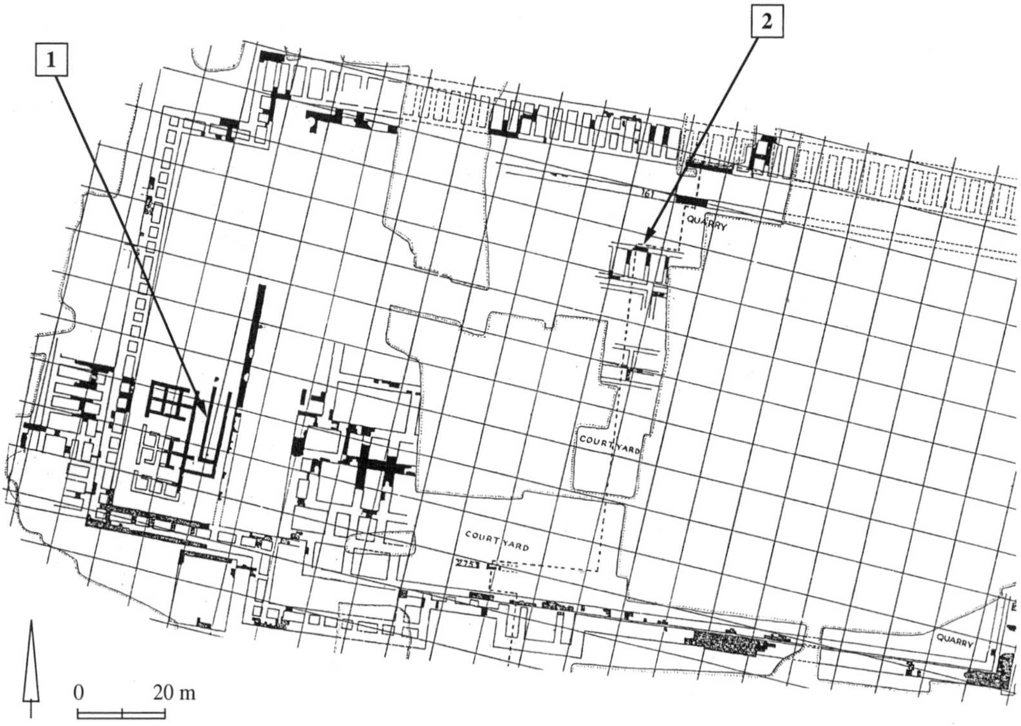

Plan 105. Samaria.
Plan of citadel with archives **Samaria 1-2**.
From J. W. Crowfoot, K. M. Kenyon, and E. L. Sukenik, *Samaria-Sebaste* I (1942), pl. II.

3.4.2.2 Private Archive from Wadi Daliyeh

In the Shinyeh cave in Wadi Daliyeh, about 37 kilometers southeast of Samaria and about 10 kilometers west of Jordan, the remains of an archive were found beside more than two hundred human skeletons. It may have been placed there by refugees fleeing from Samaria at the end of the Persian period. The archive includes 128 bullae and a number of fragmentary papyri written in Aramaic, some still rolled, tied with string, and sealed with one, four, or, in one case, seven bullae. These are the remains of an archive (or perhaps more than one) that possibly belonged to Yehonur and Neṭira' (**Samaria 3**). The papyri are legal documents from Samaria, dated to the last years of the Persian period, ca. 375–335 B.C. Many of them concern the purchase of slaves, but some also detail the purchase of houses. There are also documents concerning loans and marriages.[120]

3.4.3 Lachish

Lachish (modern Tel Lachish, Arabic Tell ed-Duwer) was situated on the coastal plain about 40 kilometers southwest of Jerusalem, about halfway along the road to Gaza. The city was occupied from the Chalcolithic period to the Persian and Hellenistic periods. A British excavation headed by J. L. Starkey was conducted 1932–1938. Israeli expeditions have continued the work, first directed by Y. Aharoni from 1966–1967, followed by the long-term excavations by D. Ussishkin beginning in 1973. The central palace, various buildings on the tell, the west gate, and the town wall enclosing an area ca. 300 × 350 meters date to the time of the Israelite monarchy.[121]

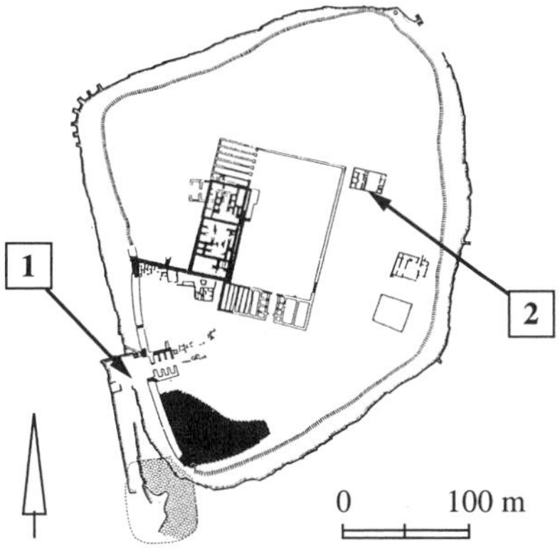

Plan 106. Lachish.
General plan with archives **Lachish 1-2**.
From D. Ussishkin, "Lachish," *NEAEHL* 3 (1993), 897.

120. A publication of the texts is in preparation by F. M. Cross. The largest group has been studied by D. M. Gropp, *The Samaria Papyri from the Wâdī ed-Dâliyeh: The Slave Sales*, Ph.D. diss. Harvard (1986); cf. D. M. Gropp, "Samaria (Papyri)," *The Anchor Bible Dictionary* V (1992), 931–932; and N. L. Lapp, "Daliyeh, Wadi ed-," *NEAEHL* 1 (1993), 320–323, both with further bibliographies. The circumstances of the finding are described in P. W. Lapp and N. Lapp, eds., *Discoveries in the Wâdī ed-Dâliyeh*, AASOR 41 (1974).

121. As introductions to the site, cf. D. Ussishkin, "Lachish," *OEANE* 3 (1997), 317–323; D. Ussishkin, "Lachish," *NEAEHL* 3 (1993), 897–911; and D. Ussishkin, "Lachish (Place)," *The Anchor Bible Dictionary* IV (1992), 114–126, all with further bibliographies. Main publications of the archaeological material can be found in the series Lachish II-V (1940–1975).

3.4.3.1 Administrative Archive in the City Gate

All 22 Hebrew ostraca registered at the excavations in Lachish were found in Level 2. Among them, 18 ostraca constitute the remains of an archive (**Lachish 1**) from the area of the city gate, as shown by the discovery of 16 of them in a small room immediately to the right of the outer gate, and the other two nearby. The ostraca were found in a burnt destruction layer together with hundreds of jar fragments. Since so many have been affected by fire, it is impossible to determine whether there originally were substantially more ostraca among them. The texts contain no date formulae, but have been assigned to the period immediately before the invasion of the Chaldeans in 589/586 B.C. The texts are letters to Yaosh, probably the military commander of the city, from some of his men stationed outside the city, as well as administrative lists of persons probably under the direction of the same man.[122]

3.4.3.2 Administrative or Private Archive

In the eastern part of the city, the remains of another archive (**Lachish 2**) were discovered in Level 2 in a house partly overlaid with the southern section of the later Hellenistic or possibly already Persian "Solar" shrine of Level 1. In Room 3, a small room with much pottery and six inscribed shekel weights, a Hebrew ostracon, and a clay pot containing 17 clay bullae were unearthed. The bullae were stamped with Hebrew seal impressions and bore traces of papyri and strings on the reverse sides. The broken ostracon is a list of persons (each with an amount of corn?). The now missing papyri, once sealed by means of strings fastened to clay bullae, may have been documents involving some kind of obligation, or letters. Too little is known to be able to say whether this was a private house with a family archive or an official building with an administrative archive.[123]

122. J. Renz and W. Röllig, *HAHE* I (1995), 405–438; H. Torczyner, *Lachish (Tell ed Duweir)* I: *The Lachish Letters* (1938); and A. Lemaire, *Inscriptions hébraïques* 1 (1977), 83–143; cf. D. Pardee, "Lachish Letters," *OEANE* 3 (1997), 323–324; and R. A. Di Vito, "Lachish Letters," *The Anchor Bible Dictionary* IV (1992), 126–128, both with bibliographies.

123. Y. Aharoni, *Investigations at Lachish: The Sancturary and the Residency*, Lachish V, (1975), 19–25, pls. 20–22, 57 (the excavator reports that the contents of the storeroom show that it served as an archive for the chancellery. However, the same content is to be expected in the home of a businessman); J. Renz and W. Röllig, *HAHE* I (1995), 437–438; and A. Lemaire, *Inscriptions hébraïques* 1 (1977), 136–137.

3.4.4 Arad

Arad (modern Tel Arad; 9 kilometers west-northwest of modern Arad) was situated about 55 kilometers south of Jerusalem in the eastern Negev. Israeli excavations were directed mainly by Y. Aharoni and R. Amiran. The citadel was unearthed during 1962–1967 and 1976, the lower city in a more long-term project from 1962–1984. During the Early and Middle Bronze Ages settlement spread over the whole lower city, ca. 300 × 400 meters. During the Israelite, Persian, and Roman periods, occupation was concentrated in the citadel in the northeastern part of the city. During these later times, which are of interest here, Arad served as a fortress, protecting the southern border of Israel or Judea against the essentially uninhabited areas to the south. The citadel was surrounded by a city wall of ca. 50 × 50 meters. Inside the wall were a number of houses belonging to the military garrison, including living houses, storerooms, and a sanctuary.[124]

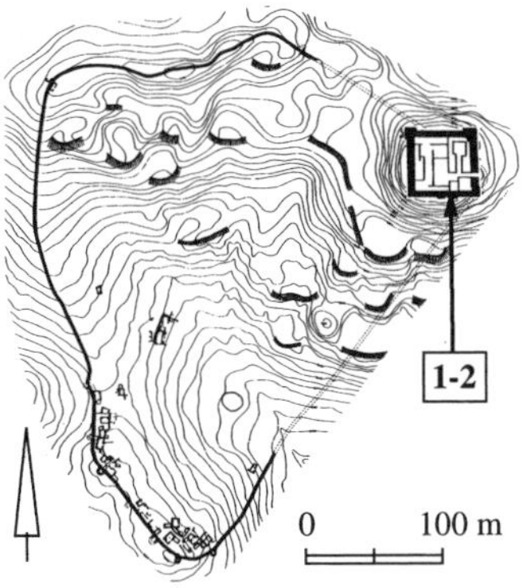

Plan 107. Arad.
General plan showing location of citadel with archives **Arad 1-2**.
From Y. Aharoni and R. Amiran, "Arad," *EAEHL* I (1975), 75.

124. As introductions to the site, cf. O. Ilan, R. Amiran, and Z. Herzog, "Arad," *OEANE* 1 (1997), 169–176; Y. Aharoni, R. Amiran, O. Ilan, and M. Aharoni, "Arad," *NEAEHL* 1 (1993), 75–87; and D. W. Manor and G. A. Herion, "Arad (Place)," *The Anchor Bible Dictionary* I (1992), 331–336, all with bibliographies.

3.4.4.1 *Administrative Archives from the Citadel*

The 90 or so Hebrew ostraca, which, according to the excavators, were found in Levels XII–VI in the citadel of Arad, may be the remains of the documentation from the administration of the citadel. Only the 18 ostraca unearthed in Locus 637 of Level VI, one of the rooms in the casemate at the south outer wall near the southeastern corner of the citadel, will here be treated as an archive (**Arad 1**). The remaining ones, found in various places and in different levels of the citadel, may be regarded as the remains of previous stages of the archival bookkeeping in the citadel. The texts from Locus 637 are without date formulae, but have been dated to the last Israelite period, around 597/586 B.C. or shortly before. The room belonged to what may have been the house of commander Elyašib. Almost all texts are letters or orders to Elyašib concerning the delivery of wine, oil, bread, and corn, apparently from the storerooms in the citadel, to various individuals (probably troops). Among those frequently named as recipients are some *ktym*, possibly Greeks or Cypriots. In Locus 779, a room nearby in Level VII, were a few more ostraca (one of them in hieratic writing) that are administrative lists of wheat given to various people. There were also three seals with

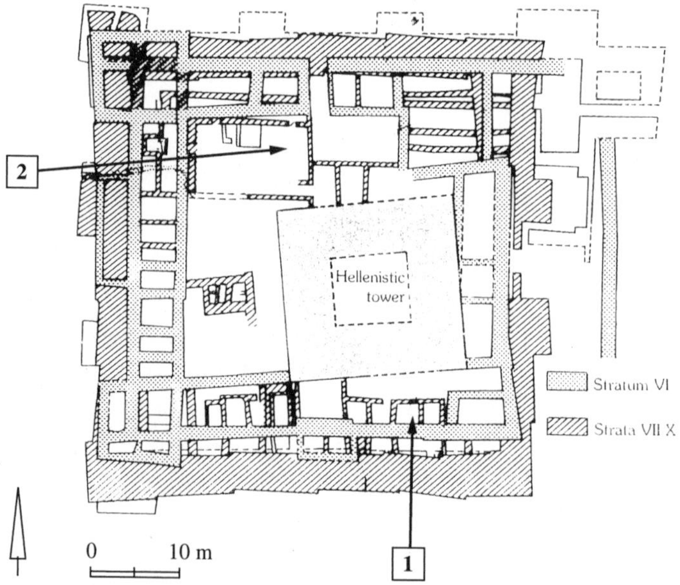

Plan 108. Arad.
Composite plan of different levels of citadel with archives **Arad 1-2**.
From M. Aharoni, "Arad," *NEAEHL* 1 (1993), 83.

Elyašib's name. This seems to be the remains of an earlier dossier of the archive of Elyašib, before the rebuilding of the citadel. Other Hebrew ostraca from various levels and provenances in connection with the citadel include letters, lists of persons, and deliveries of, for example, wheat to various individuals.

Some 85 Aramaic ostraca were discovered, mainly in pits, in Level V, dated to the Persian Period. No buildings have been unearthed from this period, but there probably existed a fortification where the Hellenistic tower was later built. The ostraca are the remains of an archive (**Arad 2**) from the administration of this fortification. The main group consists of the 67 ostraca found in Locus 325, located eight meters north of the northwestern corner of a Hellenistic tower. A man called Yaddua', possibly the commander of the fortification, was responsible for the delivery of barley to horsemen, horses, and donkeys, according to short notes in the archive. These notes, possibly to be dated to the middle of the fourth century B.C., are all without any date formulae, except their references to days 5 to 8, when the delivery was made.[125]

3.4.5 Jerusalem

In Jerusalem there have been many small excavations of varying quality. The most noteworthy was directed by K. Kenyon from 1961–1967. Thereafter, three major excavations headed by B. Mazar, N. Avigad, and Y. Shiloh explored large areas of the city. The city has been inhabited from the Chalcolithic period until the present time. In the first half of the first millennium B.C., Jerusalem was the capital of Israel and later of Judea. During the first half of the Israelite monarchy the city was concentrated south of the present temple mount, on the eastern ridge called the "City of David." It measured ca. 100 × 600 meters, excluding the temple area to the north. During the eighth and seventh centuries B.C., the city expanded towards the western hill, thereby increasing the width of the city.[126]

125. Y. Aharoni, *Arad Inscriptions* (1981); J. Renz and W. Röllig, *HAHE* I (1995), 40–47, 67–74, 111–122, 145–165, 290–306, and 347–403 (especially 347–384); as well as A. Lemaire, *Inscriptions hébraïques* 1 (1977), 145–235, with bibliographies; cf. A. Lemaire, "Arad Inscriptions," *OEANE* 1 (1997), 176–177, and R. B. Lawton, "Arad Ostraca," *The Anchor Bible Dictionary* I (1992), 336–337, with further bibliography. The number of ostraca reported from the excavations is 102, but this includes some inscribed jars, therefore giving the reduced number referred to above.

126. As short introductions to the site, cf. e.g., B. Mazar, Y. Shiloh, N. Avigad, and H. Geva, "Jerusalem: The Early Periods and the First Temple Period," *NEAEHL* 2 (1993), 698–716; D. Bahat, "Jerusalem," *OEANE* 3 (1997), 224–238; D. Tarler and J. M. Cahill, "David, City of," *The Anchor Bible Dictionary* II (1992), 52–67; and H. Geva, ed., *Ancient Jerusalem Revealed* (1994), all with further bibliography.

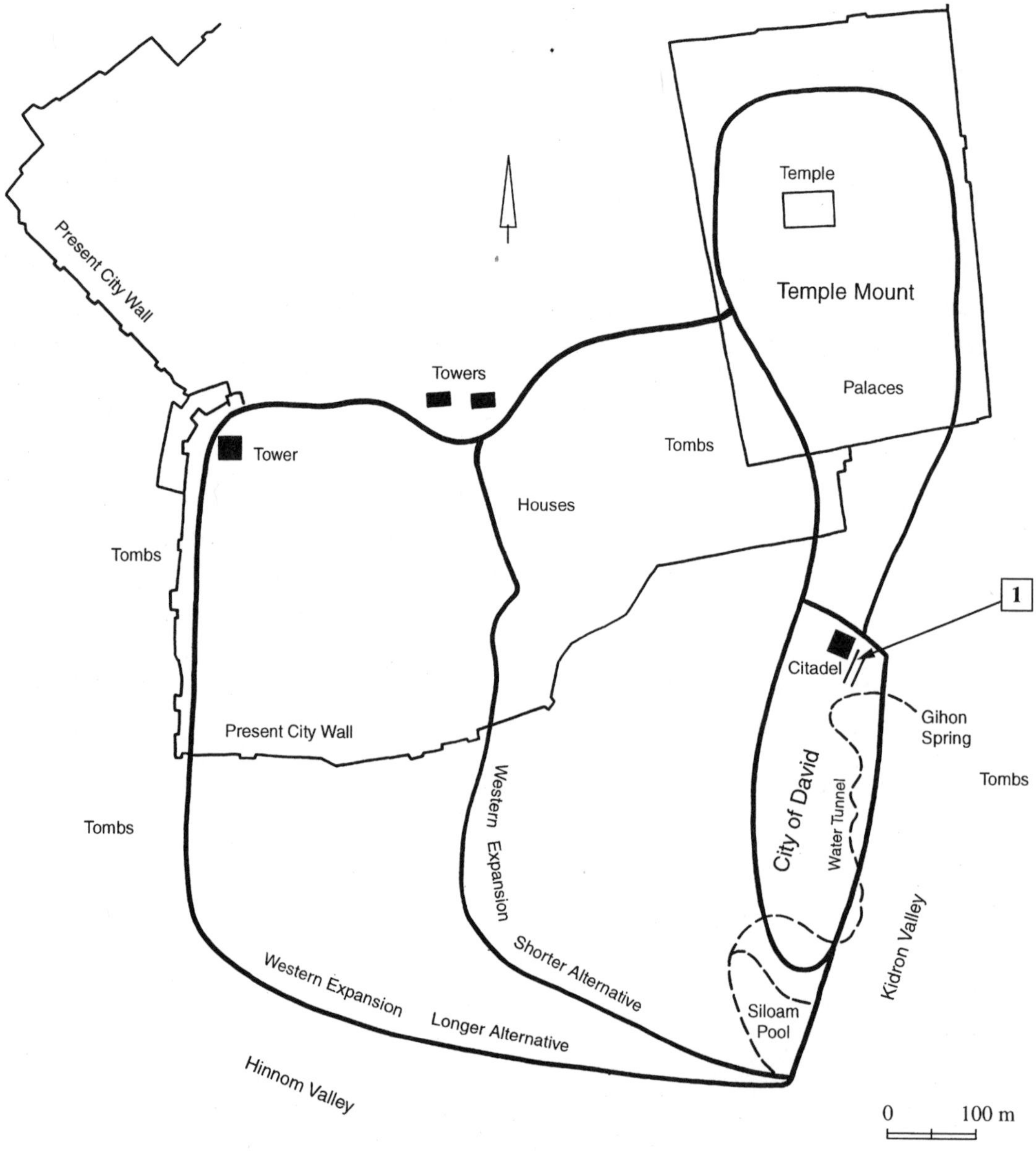

Plan 109. Jerusalem.
General plan of the oldest city in the east and possible expansions towards the west, with archive **Jerusalem 1**.
Courtesy D. Bahat.

3.4.5.1 Remains of Archive in a Probably Private House

When excavating Area G in the eastern slope of the "City of David" 200 meters south of the temple mound, Y. Shilo unearthed two terraces of Stratum 10 (Iron Age II) next to the eastern outer wall of the platform that possibly served as the base for the citadel. On the upper terrace, situated about five meters higher than the lower one, were private houses. Only a narrow strip, about one meter wide, of a house built on the lower terrace could be uncovered. This, too, was probably a private house, despite another interpretation by the excavator. In a destruction level on the floor of a room (Locus 967) of this house, 51 clay bullae were unearthed together with clay jars, arrowheads, and other metal objects. Most of the bullae are very well preserved. They are stamped with Hebrew seal impressions. Papyri that disintegrated long ago were once fastened with strings that were sealed with the clay bullae. In the conflagration during the destruction of Jerusalem in 586 B.C., the papyri were destroyed and the bullae burned. The seal impressions, as well as the stratigraphic context, point to a dating somewhat before 586 B.C. The destroyed papyri may have been documents involving some kind of obligation as well as letters, constituting an archive (**Jerusalem 1**) for the family living in this house (or alternatively for some administrative unit).[127]

3.4.6 Idalion (Dhali)

Idalion (modern Dhali) was situated in inland Cyprus, about 25 kilometers northwest of the main coastal city Kition, modern Larnaca. Following extensive Swedish excavations directed by E. Gjerstad (1927–1931) and American excavations headed by L. E. Stager and A. M. Walker (1971–1980), beginning in 1991 M. Hadjicosti has directed a Cypriote expedition. The city may have been occupied as early as the Late Bronze Age, but most of the unearthed buildings date from the Iron Age to the Hellenistic period. In this area—with Greek and Phoenician influences at least as early as the eighth century B.C.—the Persians had, after the Greek uprising probably in 470

127. Y. Shiloh, *Excavations of the City of David* I: *1978–1982, Interim Report of the First Five Seasons*, Qedem 19 (1984); Y. Shiloh, "A Group of Hebrew Bullae from the City of David," *IEJ* 36 (1986), 16–38; Y. Shiloh and D. Tarler, "Bullae from the City of David: A Hoard of Seal Impressions from the Israelite Period," *BA* 128.49 (1986), 196–209; and Y. Shoham, "A Group of Hebrew Bullae from Yigal Shiloh's Excavations in the City of David," in H. Geva, ed., *Ancient Jerusalem Revealed* (1994), 55–61. I have not been able to follow the preliminary interpretation by Y. Shilo that the multiplicity of ostensibly unrelated names appearing in the bullae corpus indicates the public nature of the archive. Even if this aspect of archive keeping has not been possible to study systematically here, my impression is that the opposite situation seems often to be typical.

B.C., placed Idalion under the control of the Phoenician city Kition. The Phoenician presence in the area ended probably after the conquest by Alexander in the early Hellenistic period. The city had two citadels; on the western citadel remains of a palace have been unearthed.[128]

3.4.6.1 Administrative Archive in the Palace

The palace on the western terrace was probably built around 475 B.C. In Level 4 (Phase 4), it was reorganized and remained the administrative center during the Phoenician occupation until the destruction, possibly by the Ptolemies, at the end of the fourth century B.C. A series of storerooms have been discovered in the northern part of the palace, probably from the final phase of Level 4. One of the storerooms contained large storage jars. Nearby, on the floor, an archive (**Idalion 1**) of ca. 75 ostraca, as well as limestone plaques, has been unearthed. The ostraca are economic documents, most of which are written in the Phoenician language with Phoenician alphabetic script, but some are in the Greek language with syllabic Cypriote script. With the exception of preliminary photos of an earlier finding of a few ostraca from the palace, they remain unpublished.[129]

128. As introductions to the site, cf., e.g., P. Gaber, "Idalion," *OEANE* 3 (1997), 137–138; and O. Masson, "Idalion," in E. Lipinski, ed., *Dictionnaire de la civilisation phénicienne et punique* (1992), 226–227, both with short bibliographies. The American expedition was published by L. E. Stager and A. M. Walker, *American Expedition to Idalion Cyprus 1973–1980*, OIC 24 (1989), 5–44, 459–466, especially 12, 21; the oldest excavations were published in the series *The Swedish Cyprus Expedition*.

129. Cf. provisionally C. Baurain and A. Destrooper-Georgiades, "Chypre," in V. Krings, ed., *La civilisation phénicienne & punique, Manuel de recherche*, HdO I 20 (1995), 618–619; D. Christou, *BCH* 117 (1993), 740–742; D. Christou, *BCH* 118 (1994), 667–678; and V. Karageorghis, "Cyprus and the Phoenicians: Achievement and perspectives," in *I Fenici: Ieri oggi domani, Richerche, scoperte, progetti* (Roma 3–5 marzo 1994) (1995), 327–334, especially 330–331. The study of the inscriptions is being done by M. Sznycer and O. Masson.

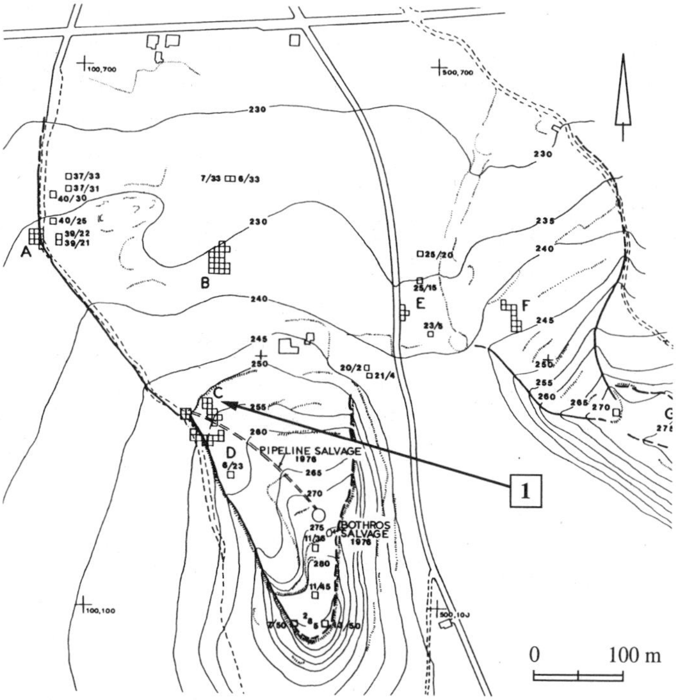

Plan 110. Idalion.
General plan with archive **Idalion 1**.
From L. E. Stager and A. M. Walker, *American Expedition to Idalion, Cyprus 1973–1980*, OIC 24 (1989), 4 fig. 2.

Chapter 4

Analysis and Conclusions: Archives and Libraries 1500–300 B.C.

In Chapters 2 and 3, the archives and libraries in the Near East from 1500–1000 B.C. and then from 1000–300 B.C. (including those continuing the cuneiform tradition in southern Mesopotamia into the following centuries) were presented with preliminary analyses, organized according to historical and geographical "areas." In this chapter we will try to arrive at general conclusions, on the basis of the data in the previous chapters, concerning archives and libraries in the Near East during these periods.

When making the following analysis and conclusions, the very different quality of the available material should be remembered. It should already be clear from the presentation in the pervious chapters that the information for most of the archives and libraries is quite preliminary, and important pieces of information that should have been known in order to place the following analysis on a well-established foundation is, for the time being, unavailable and may be so for many years to come or, in some cases, even forever. Despite such problems, as well as the recognition that future publications and finds may radically alter the nature of the data, and thus our perceptions, we, here, will attempt to reach general conclusions based on the available information. Because a large number of archives and libraries are being systematically collected in the previous chapters from these areas and time periods, we will attempt to use this material in order to achieve preliminary insights, often of a statistical nature. Although the information is frequently insufficient to provide secure statistics, we may, nonetheless, make some general observations about trends in the material presently at hand.

We will comment upon distribution, which involves: cities with archives and libraries, storage of archives and libraries, size of archives and libraries, the writing materials, scripts and languages in use, chronology and lifetime of archives and libraries. Then follow observations on the owners of the archives and libraries, in particular, their connections to the buildings used to store their text collections—both official and private. In the third section, we will summarize the types of texts in the archives and libraries, as well as survey the division of text collections into archives and libraries. Finally, we offer a brief discussion on the general principles used in the collection of archives and libraries, and to what degree there is a coherent application of such principles.

4.1 Distribution of Archives and Libraries

Fundamental issues concerning various aspects of the distribution of archives and libraries is discussed in this section. We will first comment upon the cities where archives and libraries have been found, then look at the appropriate rooms and storage facilities of the archives and libraries, and finally examine basic questions related to the texts in the archives and libraries, namely, size of the collections, the writing materials, scripts and languages in use, as well as absolute chronology and lifetime of the archives and libraries.

4.1.1 Cities with Archives and Libraries

This study of archives and libraries in the Near East 1500–300 B.C. has presented findings from 51 different cities (*Figure* 1), with a total of 253 archives and libraries. Six of the cities contain finds from both major periods (1500–1000 and 1000–300 B.C.) (indicated with * and ** after the city name). One hundred twenty-five archives and libraries date to the period 1500–1000 B.C., and 128 to the period 1000–300 B.C., (including a few later ones).

Since many of the very early excavations did not properly document the findspots of tablets, it is probable that some additional archives or libraries from this period have been unearthed. Moreover, a few archives or libraries from modern excavations may have been kept secret, or I may have overlooked some. Therefore, possibly between 260 and 300 (or even more) archives and libraries have been found from the period 1500 B.C. to 300 B.C.—this includes collections of cuneiform tablets down to the end of the use of cuneiform script, in the whole Near East, and excludes archives or libraries with local writing in Egypt. The number of archives and libraries from these periods still waiting to be discovered must be much larger, and thus those excavated probably are but a small fraction of all archives and libraries which had existed.

From the Mitannian and Egyptian areas there are 36 archives and libraries from seven cities. The most extensively excavated site in the Mitannian area is Nuzi, which

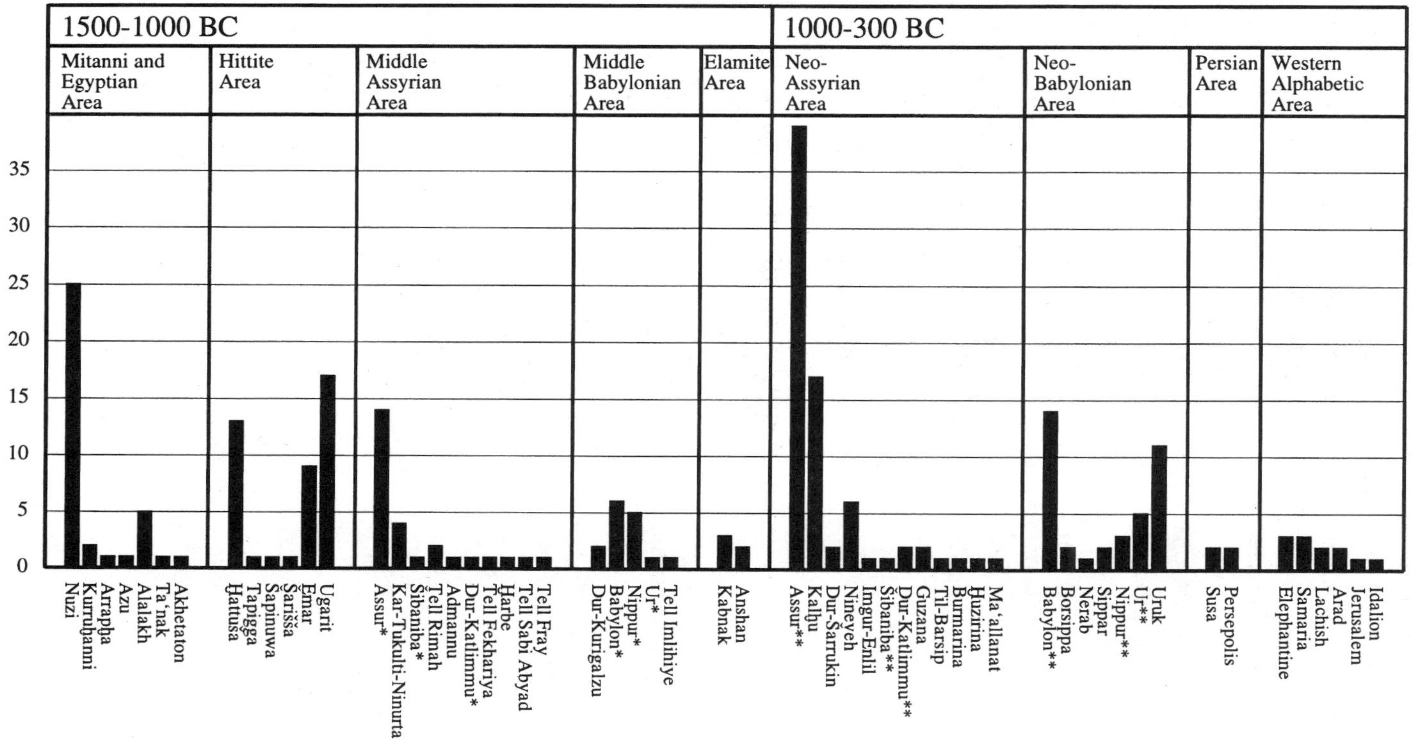

Figure 1.

Number of discussed archives and libraries in the Near East 1500–300 B.C.
City names followed by * have a chronological continuation with the same names followed by **.

yielded 25 archives, more than all others in this area together. The second best-attested city is Alalakh, with five archives and libraries. The Hittite area is the source of 42 archives and libraries from six cities. Four of the cities, with a total of 16 archives and libraries, are located in the central area of the Hittite state, where the most prominent city was the capital Ḫattuša with 13 archives and libraries. In the Syrian part of the Hittite area two cities with a total of 26 archives and libraries have been unearthed: Ugarit yielded 17 archives and libraries and Emar nine. Ten cities from the Middle Assyrian area have yielded 27 archives and libraries. From the capital Assur, we have 14 archives and libraries, and from the short-lived capital Kar-Tukulti-Ninurta, there are four archives. In the Middle Babylonian and Kassite area, 15 archives and libraries were found in five cities. Six archives and libraries were unearthed in Babylon, and five archives in Nippur. In two cities of the Elamite area, five archives and libraries have been discovered: three in Kabnak and two in Anshan.

From the Neo-Assyrian area there are 74 archives and libraries from 12 cities. The most extensively excavated site is the oldest capital, Assur, where 39 archives and libraries have been unearthed. The following capital, Kalḫu, has yielded 17 archives and libraries, and from the last capital, Nineveh, at least six archives and libraries have been defined. In the Neo-Babylonian area, excavations of seven cities have so far unearthed at least 38 archives and libraries. The largest collections consist of 14 archives and libraries in Babylon, 11 archives and libraries in Uruk, and five archives and libraries in Ur. Four archives have been identified during excavations in two cities in the Persian area, two in each city. Six cities in the Western Alphabetic area, or West-Semitic area, have yielded 12 archives. The largest number of archives, three in each city, comes from Elephantine and Samaria.

Most of the cities or towns where archives or libraries have been unearthed were cities of medium or major size. Only rarely has material been found in smaller towns (e.g., Tell Imlihiye 1); it is unclear whether this is due to lack of written documentation in rural areas or only a consequence of a limited number of excavations of smaller settlements.

The distribution of archives and libraries as presented here is, to a large extent, dependent on excavation activity. Excavations of an upper level in an area within which documents were frequently used have provided most of the sites containing the archives or libraries reported here. The cities with the highest number of attested archives and libraries are often the larger medium-sized cities where upper levels have been extensively excavated. This can be illustrated with the four cities producing the largest numbers of archives and libraries, Neo-Assyrian Assur**, Nuzi, Ugarit, and Kalḫu. The first three, during the periods of interest here, were politically dominated by larger cities, Nineveh, Arrapḫa, and Karkemish, respectively. These large cities were excavated to a smaller extent or with less proper methodology, and have, therefore, yielded fewer archives and libraries. In Assur most areas with private houses were cut only with about four-meters-wide excavation trenches each 100 meters of town area. A simple calculation of the areas between the trenches indicates that a great deal more private archives and libraries have been left unexcavated than so far unearthed. The ratio of unexcavated collections to excavated collections must be even greater for other cities where fewer private houses have been excavated.

4.1.2 Storage of Archives and Libraries

When in use, archives and libraries were maintained in buildings. If the archive or library was in use at the time of the destruction of the building, the texts were likely found in the archive or library room, or, due to the destruction, next to the original room, for example, in a room nearby on the same floor or on a lower floor. The material found is essentially only the final stage in the history of an archive or a library—during its earlier history texts may have been removed for study, discarded for various reasons, or placed in other archives or libraries. An archive (or library) no longer active at the time when the building was destroyed may have been put to the side in the previous archive room or stored in another room nearby for future reference (cf. Assur 5, 6, Babylon 15). Some archives and libraries were eventually discarded and the clay tablets or archival materials may have been used for other purposes, such as for building materials, e.g., fill under the floor (Babylon 4, Guzana 1), or recycled for the manufacture of new clay tablets (Babylon 6). But even in such circumstances the texts were probably often found near the original storage location of the archive or library. Sometimes clay tablets from one archive or library were spread over a large area (Ḫattuša 1, Assur 1). On the other hand, discarded texts from different archives or libraries may have been collected and thrown away in one single place, resulting in a mixing of different collections; however, this is difficult to prove and there is no certain evidence of such a habit in the material studied here.

Archives and libraries were placed in various types of official buildings, such as palaces and temples, as well as in private houses belonging to those not among the lowest social classes. Such houses with text collections, as noted above, have been found mainly in cities. In a private, family house there was, as a rule, only one archive or library, the archive often containing the dossiers for several members of the family. In larger, official buildings, such as palaces or temples, often there was more than one archive or library; several collections, each with a different purpose, could be found in different rooms.

The archives and libraries may have been placed either in rooms specifically set aside for text storage, or they may have been placed in rooms which served other functions as well. Due to the possible presence once of objects of a perishable nature in the rooms where clay tablets or bullae were found, the full original purpose(s) of these rooms, in most cases, cannot be completely known. It is reasonable, however, that in private houses, large rooms in which small collections were found probably served other functions and their use for storing archives or libraries may have been secondary. On the other hand, small rooms with large collections of texts may have functioned specifically for housing archives or libraries.

In several of the areas discussed here, houses often had rooms grouped around inner courtyards. This was in most areas the design for large building complexes, such as palaces and major temples, but also for private houses, especially in Babylonia or Assyria. If there was an archive or library in such a house, it was quite frequently placed in a room next to an inner courtyard (many examples)—easy access to good reading light in the courtyard may have been an important factor in placing archives or libraries nearby.

Sometimes administrative archives were located next to the main entrance of a building, often near a courtyard (Kurruḫanni 1, Alalakh 1, Ugarit 1). In Hellenistic Uruk, archives, as well as a library, were placed in rooms next to main gates of temples complexes (Uruk 2–4). Occasionally archives were placed in or next to town gates (Assur 8, Kar-Tukulti-Ninurta 4, Lachish 1). Archives have sometimes been unearthed in rooms with staircases or next to such rooms (e.g., Ugarit 4, Nineveh 2, Babylon 7).

In Assur, large areas with private houses have been examined at several archaeological levels. The placement of the family archives followed a general principle. In private houses with archives, often the archive was placed in the innermost room of the house, the room under whose floor were the family graves. To what extent this principle holds true for other cities and areas cannot be determined, due to a lack of extended excavations of areas with private houses.

Information as to the story on which archives and libraries were kept is often problematic, due to a lack of recorded evidence or insufficient archaeological methods (especially during early excavations). However, most of the archives and libraries have been found in a position that makes it probable that the original place of storage was on the ground floor of the building. This is especially true for private houses, but also for many of the palaces and temples.

Several of the buildings had a floor above the ground floor. This is well attested for larger official buildings. Some of the archives or libraries from palaces (e.g., Alalakh 2, Ḫattuša 1, 3 and 4, Tapigga 1, Šapinuwa 1, Ugarit 1, Dur-Katlimmu 1, Kalḫu

1, Nineveh 1, 4, Persepolis 1) had been, or may have had been, stored on the upper floor of the building or on a ground floor above the preserved basement. In a similar way, some of the libraries and archives from temples (e.g., Ḫattuša 1, Emar 1, Tell Rimah 1, 2, Assur 15) were on the upper floor. Other archives and libraries from several palaces and temples discussed may also have been placed on an upper floor, but the evidence is less conclusive. There is at least one archive (Dur-Katlimmu 3) from a private house found in a position indicating placement on an upper floor.

Most archives and libraries were found on the floor of rooms or in fill above the floor. Originally, texts were probably not placed directly on the floor of the rooms, but in boxes, in jars, or on shelves. Most boxes and shelves were probably made of wood or other perishable material, but remains may, in most cases, have been overlooked, except for the best, modern excavations. This may explain why more pots have been found as depositories than have boxes or shelves.

Among the 253 archives and libraries, 27 archives and possibly the remains of one small library (Ḫattuša 13) show evidence of having been stored in clay pots. There is about an equal number of archives stored in clay pots in both main periods: 14 archives were found in clay pots among the 125 archives and libraries dating to the period 1500–1000 B.C., and 13 archives came from clay pots among the 128 from the period 1000–300 B.C. This means that slightly more than 10 percent of the archives and libraries are archives found in clay pots—libraries in clay pots are much less attested.

During the period 1500–1000 B.C., eight of the 14 archives found in clay pots, that is, more than half of them, were preserved in official houses (Kurruḫanni 2?, Akhetaten 1 partly?, Emar 5, Assur 4, 6, 8, Tell Rimah 1, 2) and six of them concerned public matters (those listed first). The remaining eight archives concerned private matters and six of them came from private houses (Emar 6, Azu 1, Assur 12, Babylon 1, Nippur 5, Tell Imlihiye 1). The situation from 1000–300 B.C. is quite different. Twelve of the 13 clay pots containing texts were found in private houses. The pots contained archives (Assur 44, 51, Nineveh 6, Guzana 2, Babylon 12, 15, Ur 3, 4, Uruk 5, 6, Lachish 2) and a library (Uruk 9); administrative tablets were found in the only pot from an official building (Ur 2). It is not clear whether this difference in distribution represents an intentional change in administrative routine or is statistically insignificant due to the small number of attestations.

Clay pots may have been used for preservation of archives because they were an inexpensive and easy way to protect written material. In a limited number of cases, more elaborate bureaucratic or legal filing procedures are evident: one pot contained the bookkeeping for one year (Assur 6), some of the pots holding large archives had inscriptions indicating the content (Assur 4), and a large family archive was found in a number of sealed jars indicating a (temporary) end of it (Babylon 15).

Archives, and possibly libraries, may have been partly or completely preserved in boxes or baskets composed of perishable materials, which, as a rule, have not been preserved. Several references to such boxes can be found in a text from one of the archives (Assur 10).The remains of a library (Alalakh 5) may have been carried in what has been assumed to have been a basket. Boxes may, of course, also have been constructed of imperishable materials. In an archive room in an official building (Kalḫu 6), two rows of boxes made of bricks have been found on the floor. Clay tablets may have been placed in these boxes. Another archive has been found in a clay chest (Ta'nak 1), possibly an alternative to a clay pot.

In some of the official archives, brick benches have been unearthed. The benches may have been used for the preservation of clay tablets or for storage of valuable goods preserved in the archive rooms (Kurruḫanni 2?, Alalakh 3, Kalḫu 6, the last one also with brick boxes, cf. above).

Several of the archives and libraries, especially the larger ones, were apparently placed upon wooden shelves. Evidence of wooden shelves is purported to exist for a limited number of official archives (Tapigga 1, Ḫarbe 1), and has been assumed elsewhere (e.g., Nineveh 2). There is, however, a lack of evidence in many sites indicating the use of wooden shelves, probably due to the perishable nature of wood and a lack of sounder archaeological methodology during the earlier excavations. Sometimes the shelves were constructed of brick or designed as niches in the walls. Such imperishable shelves have been preserved in some libraries (Dur-Šarrukin 1 and 2, Sippar 2). The temple library in Sippar is the oldest library in history found with literary texts still standing in their original position on the shelves.

4.1.3 Size of Archives and Libraries

The size of the archives and libraries varies from tens of thousands to but a handful. The sizes reported for several archives and libraries are questionable, due to poor and inaccurate recording procedures during the early excavations, and a lack of information from later ones. Also, it is likely that future joins will dramatically reduce the count of texts in those archives or libraries which include many fragments; in others there will be no or very little change at all.

A general principle is that the larger the archive or library, the fewer of that size there are attested.

The largest archives and libraries consist of between 1,000 and 30,000 texts. There are at least 16, perhaps even 21, archives or libraries of such size. They represent six or eight percent of the total number of 253 archives and libraries discussed here. The largest archive is the Neo-Babylonian administrative archive from the Šamaš temple

(Sippar 1), comprising about 30,000 texts. Around 10,000 texts are from the administrative archive in the Neo-Babylonian Ištar temple (Uruk 1) and about the same size is reported for the administrative archive headed by the Middle Babylonian *šandabakku* governor (Nippur 1). Next in size is probably the largest of the libraries and archives in the Neo-Assyrian palaces (Nineveh 1, cf. also Nineveh 3–5).

Approximately 3,300 bullae may be the remains of a Hittite administrative archive (Ḫattuša 6). The largest private archive, the archive of the Egibi family, is said to have consisted of about 3,000 texts (Babylon 15). Other libraries and archives may have possibly 2,500 or less texts (Hattuša 3) or 2,000 (Hattuša 1, cf. also Hattuša 7, 8). More than 2,000 texts were found in a library and archive (Šapinuwa 1). Several thousand texts should be divided into three administrative archives (Kabnak 1–3), and more than 2,000 stem from another administrative archive (Persepolis 2). A Nabû temple was found with more than 1,500 school texts (Babylon 10). More than 1,000 texts are from the archive of the family of Teḫip-Tilla (Nuzi 19). The library with archive from Emar consisted of around 1,000 texts (Emar 1).

There are 213 archives and libraries documented as having less than 1,000 texts; in addition, there are 19 (perhaps 24, cf. above) having no clearly attested number of texts, but the original number was probably less than 1,000. The archives and libraries with less than 1,000 texts may therefore represent 92 percent (perhaps even 94 percent). *Figure* 2 graphically illustrates the 213 archives and libraries with less than 1,000 texts. Had the 16 to 21 archives and libraries with over 1,000 texts been included in the diagram, they would have been placed far to the right of the present end of the chart. Had it been possible to include the archives and libraries without a clearly attested number of texts, some of the numbers given in the diagram would be slightly higher. The inclusion of very small text collections not discussed in this work would increase the already high count of the smallest archives and libraries.

Within the archives and libraries consisting of less than 1,000 texts represented in the diagram, the fewer the number of tablets, the better the size is represented. There is one administrative archive (Babylon 8) of about 950 texts. A private library (Assur 20) and a library in a temple (Sippar 2) consist of about 800 texts each. The archive of the family of Murašû (Nippur 7) consists of 750 texts and the archive of the family of Šilwa-Teššup (Nuzi 24) of more than 700 texts. An administrative temple archive (Assur 4) consists of 650 texts and another administrative archive in a governor's palace of 600 texts (Dur-Katlimmu 1). Two administrative archives (Kurruḫanni 1 and 2) may possibly have consisted of 500 texts each; the exact size of the private library (Uruk 10) with hundreds of texts is not known. Administrative archives have been reported with 450 (bullae, Nineveh 2), 420 (Assur 7), and 400 texts (Kalḫu 6), as well as a private library with 400 texts (Ḫuzirina 1). There are the remains of an

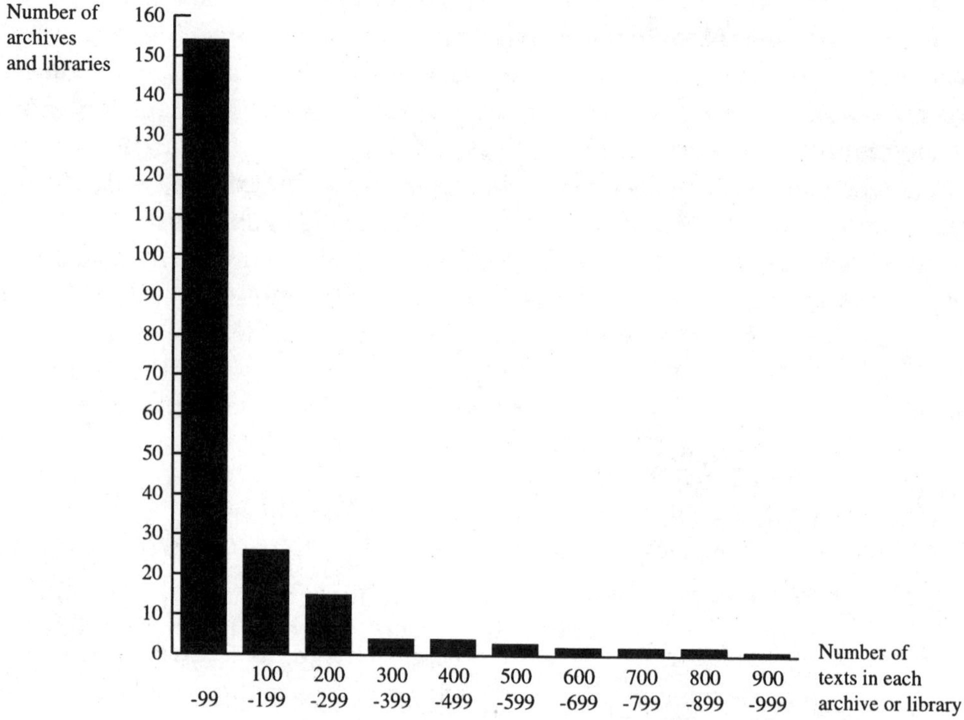

Figure 2.

Number of archives and libraries in the Near East 1500–300 B.C. with less than 1,000 texts within size-ranges of 100 texts. The addition of those with 1,000 or more texts would have given isolated attestations here and there to the right within the distance of 30 times the width of the present figure.

administrative archive with 376 texts (Akhetaten 1), a private archive with 343 texts (Ugarit 13), a library with archive comprising more than 300 texts in the Assur temple (Assur 15), and an administrative archive with 300 texts (Susa 1).

There are 15 archives or libraries with between 200 and 299 texts, 26 between 100 and 199, and at least 154 with less than 100. These three groupings, which comprise 77 percent of the 253 archives and libraries, contain private archives and libraries, as well as official, administrative archives and libraries.

According to this overview, most archives and libraries were small, although a limited number of larger collections existed. The largest archives (up to 30,000) are from administrative units in temples and other official buildings. Next in size are the libraries in palaces and temples. The largest archives in private houses are somewhat smaller (maximum 3,000), and the largest libraries in private houses are still smaller (up to 800).

4.1.4 Writing Materials, Scripts, and Languages

Texts in archives and libraries were, as a rule, written on the common writing material of the culture. In the archives and libraries from 1500–300 B.C. (including a few later ones), the texts were written on clay (clay tablets, clay dockets, and clay bullae), writing boards, ostraca, papyri, leather, and lead strips.

Most of the preserved texts in archives and libraries were written on clay tablets. This is partly due to the rather imperishable nature of clay tablets (when compared to other writing materials), but also due to clay being a cheap, plentiful, and practical writing medium. Among the 253 archives and libraries discussed here, 94 percent or 238 archives and libraries consisted completely, or at least to some extent, of clay tablets; the only exceptions are all 12 collections from the Western Alphabetic area, one uncertain one from the Hittite area (Ḫattuša 4), and two from the Neo-Assyrian area (Nineveh 2, Dur-Šarrukin 2). Clay tablets are of different shapes and sizes, one determining factor being the function of the text. (A systematic study of the physical characteristics of the tablets was, unfortunately, not possible due to the lack of availability of so many of the tablets.) Letters and documents with obligations often carry seal impressions in addition to the text on the clay tablet or on an additional surrounding envelope of clay. Seal impressions were placed also on clay dockets and clay bullae. Dockets and bullae were set about strings fastened to other objects, either writing materials or objects without texts.

The clay dockets are from the Neo-Assyrian area (Assur 16, 24, 32, 33, 42, Kalḫu 16, 17, Dur-Katlimmu 2, 3, Guzana 2) and the Persian area (Persepolis 1, 2). They were formed like tablets, but often more triangular shaped, and bore, in most cases, an inscription. The dockets were often hung without direct contact with the other object, thereby limiting our ability to reconstruct its exact purpose. However, during the last decades it has been often suggested that the associated objects, at least in most cases, were documents written on scrolls of papyri or leather, even small writing boards cannot be excluded. A copy of the document is to be find on the clay docket.

The clay bullae were small pieces of clay put around a string, often directly on the object to which the string was attached. Bullae were used to seal documents, each area using them with a particular medium. The bullae from the Western Alphabetic area (Samaria 2, 3, Lachish 2, Jerusalem 1) and from later periods in the Babylonian area (Uruk 2, 3, possibly Nippur 7) were used to seal papyrus documents. In the Hittite area bullae were placed on wooden writing boards (Ḫattuša 4, 6, 9, 10, more questionable Tapigga 1?, and Šariššа 1?). So too, bullae from the Neo-Assyrian area may have been used to seal writing boards (Kalḫu 3, Nineveh 2), although the traditional interpretation of one group (Nineveh 2) has associated the bullae with papyri. The association of bullae with writing materials in other areas, such as in the Middle Assyrian area (Dur-Katlimmu 1, Tell Fekhariya 1), the Neo-Assyrian area (Dur-Katlimmu 3) and the Persian area (Persepolis 1), is unclear.

Writing boards were usually made of wood; occasionally other materials, such as ivory, were used. The text was written on a thin layer of wax that covered the writing surface of the board. The only surviving writing boards are from the remains of a palace library (Kalḫu 10), some fragments from a temple library (Kalḫu 14), and a single writing board found outside a private library of clay tablets (Assur 20)—all are from the Neo-Assyrian area. However, there are references to writing boards in numerous texts from the Hittite, Middle Assyrian, Neo-Assyrian and Neo-Babylonian areas.[1] It is, therefore, reasonable to assume that several of the archives and libraries discussed here also contained writing boards, even if there are no remains. So too, bullae or dockets, as discussed above, may serve as indirect evidence of the occurrence of writing boards.

Remains of papyrus or leather as a writing material have been found under extremely good climatological conditions in the Western Alphabetic area (Elephantine 1, 2, 3, Samaria 3). As already mentioned, inspections of the back side of bullae from the Western Alphabetic area (Samaria 2, 3, Lachish 2, Jerusalem 1) and from later periods in the Babylonian area (Uruk 2, 3, possibly Nippur 7) testify to the use of papyrus documents, even when the papyrus is no longer preserved. The dockets may, as mentioned above, have been fastened to papyrus or leather documents, but, due to the construction of the dockets, evidence is lacking.

Ostraca were a cheap alternative to papyrus or leather as a writing material. Ostraca were used in the Western Alphabetic area (Samaria 1, Lachish 1, 2, Arad 1, 2, Idalion 1, Elephantine), but limited evidence also comes from other sites (Assur 38, Kalḫu 5).

In one archive, in the Neo-Assyrian area, the texts were written on rolled strips of lead (Assur 28).[2]

1. Cf. Chapter 1, n. 8; as noticed there, writing boards have also been found in the Late Bronze Age shipwreck at Ulu Burun, next to the south coast of Turkey.

2. Cf. also the lead strips from Kululu referred to in Chapter 3, n. 2.

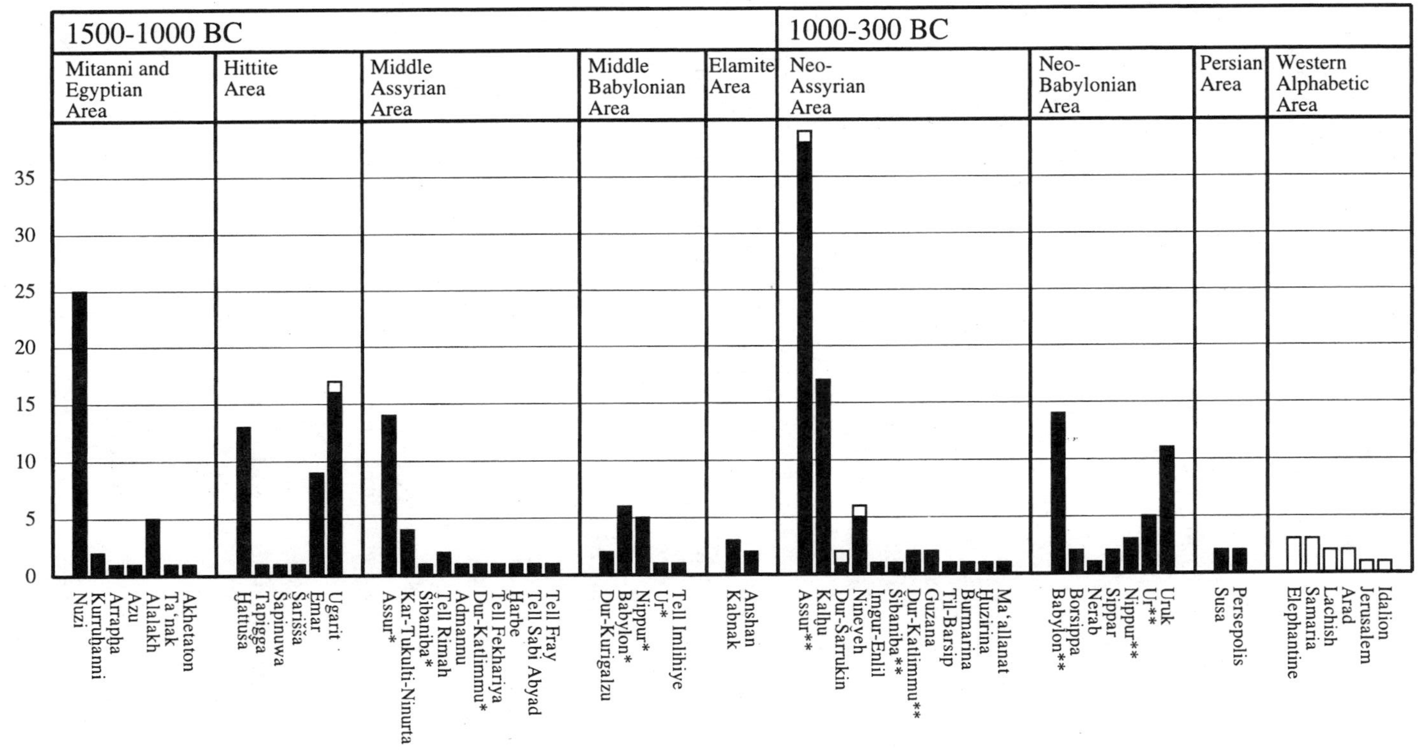

Figure 3.

Number of archives and libraries containing non-alphabetic, cuneiform texts (black) in comparison with the total number of archives and libraries (the whole columns) in the Near East 1500–300 B.C.

Empty shelves in libraries (Dur-Šarrukin 2, partly Dur-Šarrukin 1, Sippar 2) may indicate that, for some reason, the texts had been removed so that the shelves were empty during the final days of the library. An alternative possibility is that texts on perishable writing materials, such as writing boards, papyri, or leather, had been stored there.

The best-attested writing system in the archives and libraries is the cuneiform script from Mesopotamia. Among the 253 archives and libraries in this study, 236 contain cuneiform texts written with the Mesopotamian syllabic-logographic script (*Figure* 3). The writing materials used with cuneiform script in the archives and libraries were in most cases clay tablets, but wax-covered writing boards, sometimes clay dockets, and occasionally bullae made of clay are also attested.

The most frequent language in use for cuneiform script in the archives and libraries was the Semitic Akkadian language in its Babylonian and Assyrian dialects. During the period 1500–1000 B.C., the Middle Assyrian dialect dominated in the Middle Assyrian area, even though Babylonian was occasionally used, especially for literary texts. In the other areas, Babylonian dialects were either the most frequently used or at least the second language from the point of view of number of texts. Middle Babylonian dominated in the Middle Babylonian area and had an important position also in the Elamite area. More or less heavily influenced by local languages, such as Hurrian or West Semitic, Middle Babylonian was also the dominant language in the Mitannian and Egyptian areas, and dominated in the inland of the Syrian part of the Hittite area, even having an important role in the Hittite homeland. During the period 1000–300 B.C., the Neo-Assyrian dialect dominated for ordinary texts in the Neo-Assyrian area, but Babylonian was used, especially for literary texts. In the Neo-Babylonian area, Neo-Babylonian dominated for cuneiform texts.

The Indo-European Hittite language was used with cuneiform script at all sites within the Hittite area during the period 1500–1000 B.C. At the sites within the central part of that area, a majority of the texts in the archives and libraries were in the Hittite language. Sometimes texts were written in the related Luwian or Palaic dialects. In the Syrian part of the Hittite area (Emar, Ugarit), the number of Hittite texts was much more limited.

The Sumerian, Hurrian, Hattic, and Elamite languages (all ergative and agglutinative but without relation to each other) are attested in archives and libraries. The Sumerian language, so closely related to the origin of cuneiform writing, was sometimes used for literary or scientific texts in many areas. Hurrian, the spoken language in the Mitannian area, is attested in individual texts or text groups in archives and libraries from the Mitannian and Egyptian, as well as Hittite, areas. Hattic is limited to some texts from libraries in the mainland Hittite area. The Elamite language is the

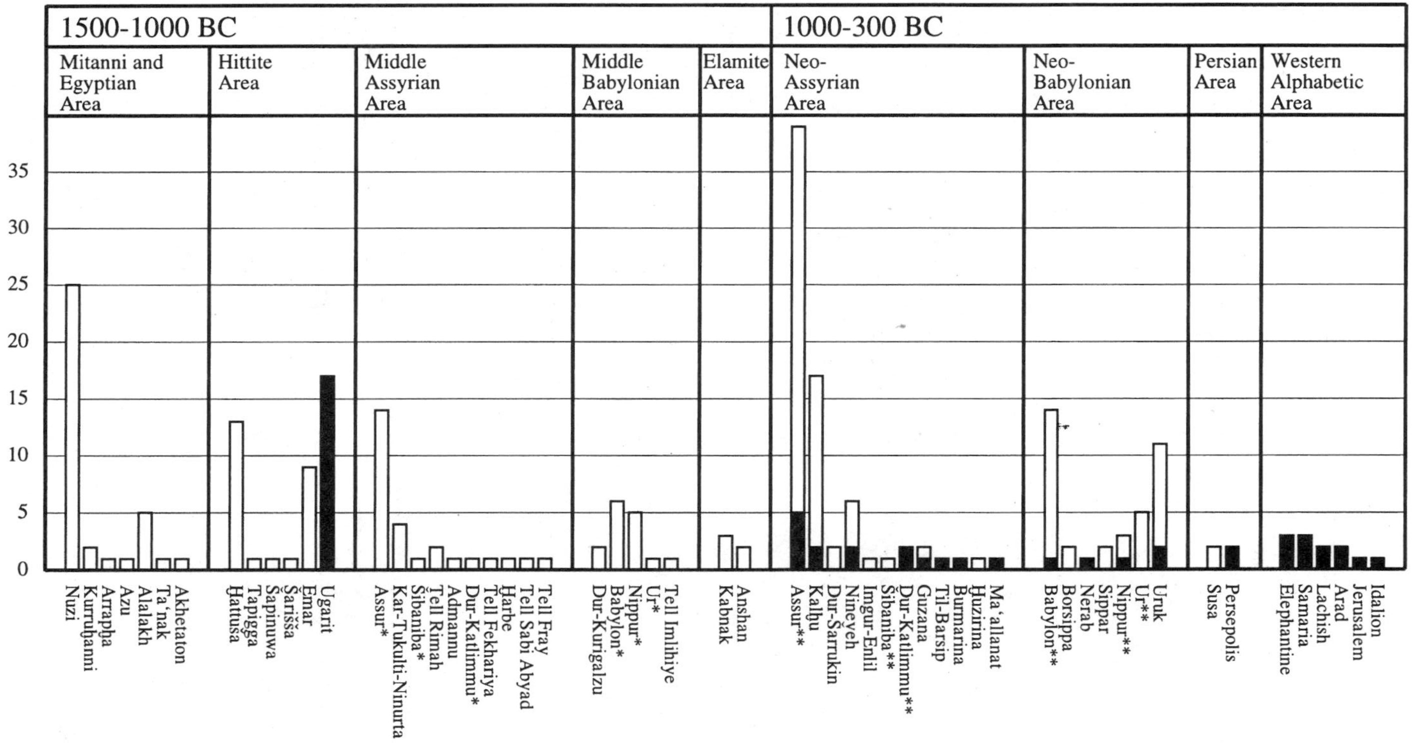

Figure 4.

Number of archives and libraries containing alphabetic texts (black) in comparison with the total number of archives and libraries (the whole columns) in the Near East 1500–300 B.C.

dominant language in some of the archives in the Elamite area, as well as in all attested archives from the Persian area.

Forty-eight of the 253 archives and libraries contained alphabetic texts or testify to the preservation of such texts (*Figure* 4). Among them are 17 archives and libraries with the special alphabetic-cuneiform script on clay tablets from Ugarit in the Hittite area, and at least 31 with the common alphabetic script from the Neo-Assyrian, Neo-Babylonian, Persian, and Western Alphabetic areas. Usually the material used for writing the common alphabetic script was perishable, namely papyrus or leather, but ostraca and, on occasion, clay tablets or clay dockets were used.

The alphabetic cuneiform script from Ugarit in the Hittite area was used for a Semitic language, Ugaritic, and sometimes for the Hurrian. In the Neo-Assyrian, Neo-Babylonian, Persian, and Western Alphabetic areas, alphabetic texts were often written with ink on perishable writing materials, thus causing some uncertainty about the language. However, most or all of the alphabetic texts from these areas were probably written in the West Semitic languages: Hebrew, Aramaic, and Phoenician. In the Western Alphabetic area, Hebrew was, during the first part of the period, in frequent use in the archives; in the later archives from the same area Aramaic and Phoenician are attested. Aramaic appears to have been used with perishable materials and occasionally also on clay tablets or clay dockets in the Neo-Assyrian, Neo-Babylonian, and Persian areas.

There is extremely little direct evidence for the use of alphabetically written Indo-European Greek texts during the periods and in the areas discussed, but the numerous bullae from the Hellenistic period (Uruk) may indicate frequent use on now destroyed papyri, if the script and language was not Aramaic. Other large findings of bullae from the Hellenistic period have usually been interpreted as remnants of Greek archives.[3]

Scripts other than cuneiform and alphabetic are sometimes attested. One archive in the Neo-Assyrian area consists of texts written in hieroglyphic Luwian script on lead strips (Assur 28). The language used is the Indo-European Luwian. In the western part of the discussed area, there are occasional attestations of Cypro-Minoan texts on clay tablets in a few archives (Ugarit 12, 13, 14) from the first of the two discussed main periods. From the latest period from the Western Alphabetic area, there are some examples of Greek texts (cf. above for alphabetic ones) written with syllabic Cypriote script (Idalion 1).

3. Cf. Chapter 1, n. 6.

4.1.5 Chronology and Lifetime

Establishing the correct chronological sequence for the archives and libraries depends greatly on the dating system used in the texts themselves and how well this dating can be converted to absolute dates. The quality of the chronological schema in use for some areas is better than for others. The Middle Assyrian and the Neo-Assyrian areas, as well as the Middle Babylonian and the Neo-Babylonian areas, used well-established dating systems. The Assyrians used eponyms and the Babylonians used regnal years. Unfortunately, the Middle Assyrian eponym list is very poorly preserved. Therefore, many of the Middle Assyrian texts can be dated to a specific ruler, but not to the exact year in his reign. The Neo-Assyrian eponym list is better preserved, yielding secure dating, with the exception of the beginning and the final years in the period 650–612 B.C. Within a margin of error of a few years, the chronology is fixed for the Middle Babylonian period. The Neo-Babylonian chronology is well established and many of the texts can be assigned a secure dating.

Establishing a correct chronology in the other areas is much more difficult. The texts from the Mitannian and Egyptian areas, as well as the Hittite-dominated area and the Elamite area, do not have any standardized method of dating. This fact and the general unsecured absolute datings of these areas have resulted in several problems in dating the archives and libraries. Dates, therefore, usually have not been expressed in absolute years, but in approximate years, sometimes related to the reigns of named kings. So too, the dating systems used for tablets in the Persian area are problematic for absolute dating. The Susa texts are dated by month, not year. The Persepolis texts include the regnal year of the king; however the king is never named in the date-formula (although occasionally elsewhere). In the Western Alphabetic area, the only texts with date formulae including the name of the king and the year of his reign are from the Persian Period; thus the earlier texts are difficult to date precisely.

Despite these problems, it has, in most cases, been possible to give at least an approximate dating of the archives and libraries. Some of the datings given here, as a result of future studies and finds, will need to be adjusted, but for general issues, the dates given here, despite the imperfections, may be useful.

The archives and libraries may be arranged according to the century to which the latest texts in each collection date (*Figure* 5). Isolated, much later texts, which seem to be the result of a text being misplaced, have not been considered. It is apparent that the archives and libraries are not evenly distributed over the discussed periods. We have two main groups with archives and libraries, from the fifteenth to eleventh centuries and from the ninth to fourth (or second) centuries B.C. The lack of material

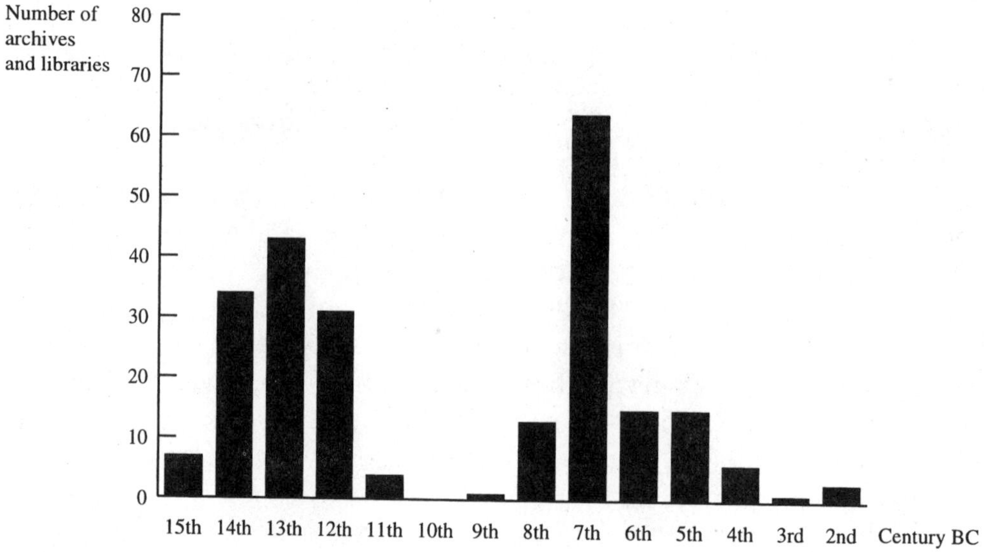

Figure 5.

Number of archives and libraries in the Near East 1500–300 B.C., with a few later ones continuing the older tradition. The date of each archive and library used here is the date of its latest text if this is not an isolated text, but falls within a main part of the texts of the collection. A few archives and libraries also contained texts from one or several previous centuries.

from the tenth century B.C. and rather little from the eleventh and ninth centuries B.C. has already been considered in the main disposition of this work, with its division into two chronologically separated main chapters. Due to the life span of the archives or libraries (cf. below), some also include material from an earlier century (occasionally even more than one earlier century), thereby modifying the picture to some extent.

The distribution of archives and libraries for each century will now be considered in detail. From the fifteenth century B.C., there are seven archives from the Mitannian area (Alalakh, Azu, and Ta'nak). However, several of the Mitannian and Hittite archives terminating during following centuries contain numerous texts from this period. There are 34 archives and libraries terminating during the fourteenth century B.C. Among them, 29 are from the Mitannian and Egyptian areas (Nuzi, Kurruḫanni, Arrapḫa in Mitanni, and Akhetaten in Egypt). Three archives and libraries are from the Elamite area (Kabnak), one from the Hittite area (Tapigga), and one from the Assyrian area (Assur). Several archives and libraries from the next century, especially in the Hittite area (Ḫattuša), contain texts from this period. From the thirteenth century B.C., there are 43 archives and libraries: from the central part of the Hittite area (Ḫattuša, Šapinuwa, and Šariššа) there are 15; from the Middle Assyrian area there are 20 archives, namely, the majority of the Middle Assyrian ones (Assur, Kar-Tukulti-Ninurta, Šibaniba, Tell Rimah, Admannu, Dur-Katlimmu, Tell Fekhariya, Ḫarbe, Tell Sabi Abyad, and Tell Fray); and from the Middle Babylonian area there are eight archives (Dur-Kurigalzu, Babylon, Nippur, and Tell Imlihiye). Many of the archives and libraries terminating during the next century contain texts from the thirteenth century B.C. There are 31 archives and libraries terminating during the twelfth century B.C. Among them, 26, terminating during the beginning of the century, are from the Syrian part of the Hittite area (Emar and Ugarit). There are also two archives and libraries from the Middle Assyrian area (Assur), and three from the Middle Babylonian area (Dur-Kurigalzu, Babylon, and Ur). At least one of the archives from the eleventh century contains texts from the twelfth century B.C. Only four archives date to the eleventh century B.C. Among them are two from the Middle Assyrian area (Assur), and two from the Elamite area (Anshan). The tenth century B.C. has not produced any archive or library in the analyzed material (if not, the two archives from Anshan alternatively may be placed here).

After a chronological hiatus, archives reappear in the ninth century B.C., when one archive from the Neo-Assyrian area (Šibaniba) terminated. In addition, a few of the later archives and libraries contain texts from this century. From the eighth century B.C. there are 13 archives and libraries. Among them, there are ten from the Neo-Assyrian area (Kalḫu and Guzana), one from the Neo-Babylonian area (Nippur), and two from the Western Alphabetic area (Samaria). Some of the later archives and libraries had texts from this century. There are 64 archives and libraries terminating during the seventh century B.C. Among them, there are 60 from almost all the cities in the Neo-Assyrian area, and four from the Neo-Babylonian area (Babylon, Nippur, Ur, and Uruk). Texts from the seventh century were found also in archives and libraries from the following century. From the sixth century B.C., there are 15 archives and libraries. Among them, there are ten from the Neo-Babylonian area (Babylon, Uruk, Nereb, and Sippar), one from the Persian area (Susa), and four from the Western Alphabetic area (Lachish, Arad, and Jerusalem). Several of the archives terminating during the fifth century contain texts also from the sixth century B.C. From the fifth century B.C., there are 15 archives and libraries. Among them, there are ten from the Neo-Babylonian area (Babylon, Ur, Borsippa, Sippar, Nippur, and Uruk), two from the Persian area (Persepolis), and three from the Western Alphabetic area (Elephantine). Texts from the fifth century also were found in archives and libraries from the following century. From the fourth century B.C., there are six archives: three from the Neo-Babylonian area (Babylon, Ur, and Uruk), and three from the Western Alphabetic area (Samaria, Arad, and Idalion).

After the lower chronological limit, 300 B.C., for the main part of this work, archives and libraries continuing the older traditions, especially the cuneiform tradition, have been followed for some centuries. We therefore have considered one library with archive (Babylon) terminating in the third century B.C. and three archives and libraries (Uruk) from the second century B.C.; the remains of Greek archives from other sites during the Hellenistic period have not been considered.[4]

Due to chronological uncertainties, it has not been possible to assign 16 archives to a particular century; these unassigned ones consist of two from the Middle Assyrian area, four from the Middle Babylonian area, three from the Neo-Assyrian area, six from the Neo-Babylonian area, and one from the Persian area.

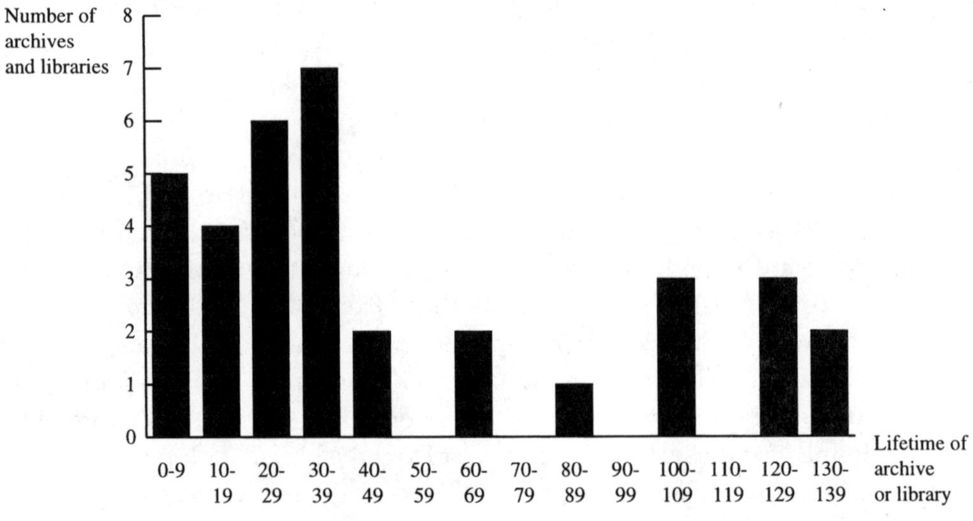

Figure 6.

Number of archives and libraries with different lifetimes. Only 35 archives and libraries with secured lifetime out of a total of 253 have been used here. The rest of the archives and libraries with less-secured datings would probably had given a similar picture with a concentration of archives and libraries within 0–49 years, but with several archives and libraries up to about 140 years, and a few with even larger lifetimes.

4. Cf. Chapter 1, n. 6.

The life span of most of the archives or libraries is unfortunately impossible to determine with any precision, due to the lack of established dating practices for several of the areas and the unavailability of much of the relevant detailed information. Despite these problems, some preliminary remarks are offered, focusing on the 35 archives and libraries with the most secure, detailed chronological information. These archives and libraries are the best-documented ones in the Middle Babylonian and Neo-Babylonian areas, in the middle part of the Neo-Assyrian area, and in the later part of the Western Alphabetic area (cf. 4.2 for generations of owners).

The life span of archives and libraries may vary greatly and may be between hundreds of years and a single year or less. *Figure* 6 graphically shows this variation for the 35 chronologically best-documented archives and libraries. Only four are libraries, spanning from 30 to 125 years.

The five archives with the shortest time span, namely, from one year (or less) up to nine years, are administrative archives (Kalḫu 15, Assur 6, Kalḫu 8, and Samaria 1) and one private archive (Ur 3). The four archives between 10 and 19 years consist of two private (Nippur 5 and Elephantine 2) and two official administrative (Uruk 2 and Persepolis 2) archives. The six archives between 20 and 29 years consist of at least three from official buildings (Nippur 8, Babylon 7, and Imgur-Enlil 1) and possibly three from private houses (Uruk 6 and 8, and Šibaniba 2?). The largest group of archives and the first library, a total of seven, had a lifetime of 30 to 39 years. They consist of five private archives (Babylon 12, Nereb 1, Ur 5, and Nippur 6 and 7), one official administrative archive (Persepolis 1), and one library from an official building (Uruk 4). There is one private archive (Samaria 3) and one archive from an official building (Kalḫu 16) that spanned from 40 to 49 years. No collections fall within the range of 50 to 59. Between 60 and 69, there is one private archive (Elephantine 3) and one official administrative archive (Kalḫu 9). There is no archive or library with a lifetime of 70 to 79 years. Between 80 to 89 years, there is one official archive (Nippur 2). There is no archive or library with a life span of 90 to 99 years. Between 100 and 109 years, there are two private archives (Ur 1 and Uruk 5) and one private library (Babylon 17). A life span of 110 to 119 years is not attested. Between 120 and 129 years, there is one large private archive (Babylon 15), one large administrative archive (Uruk 1), and one medium-sized administrative archive (Kalḫu 12). The two archives between 130 and 139 years are both large official administrative archives (Nippur 1 and Sippar 1). No archive or library with a life span of 140 years or more is attested in the selected group of best-dated archives and libraries.

In many private archives or libraries several generations of a family are attested, for example, three generations during 61 (Elephantine 3) or 107 (Uruk 5) years, as well as five generations under 120 years (Babylon 15). This yields a generation every

26 years for multi-generational archives and libraries. With understandable reservations based on the small sampling available for this calculation, as well as for possible individual situations in other archives or libraries, such a number of years may be used for general calculations in the chronologically less secure areas where the number of generations is known. Also, official archives may sometimes cover several generations of successive officials, for example, the 125 years with five successive governors (Kalḫu 12).

Sometimes a few texts in an archive or a library may be much older than the main group of texts. These older texts can often be of special types, for example, acquisition of houses or other immovable property. Such texts were the oldest texts in several of the private archives and could sometimes come from older generations than the main section of the collection of texts.

Had the perspective been enlarged outside the 35 archives and libraries with best-established datings, the results would had been rather similar. The Middle Assyrian and late Neo-Assyrian archives and libraries substantiate these results. So too, the other areas with less-established chronological schemata seem to follow the same general tendency. With more material, it would, however, have been possible to get statistically more secure results. However, there seem to be several archives and libraries with larger life spans than in the better-established group, some of which contain texts 300 years old or even older. A detailed assessment of the life span must await more detailed analysis of the individual archives and libraries, as well as solutions to some of the general chronological problems.

4.2 Owners of Archives and Libraries

Palaces, temples, and other public buildings have, in the previous chapters, been classified as official buildings, whereas living quarters have been classified as private houses. We will try to determine the extent to which this division also applies to the owners of the archives and libraries, namely, how often official institutions are the owners of archives and libraries placed in official buildings, and how often private families or persons are the owners of archives and libraries found in private houses. Also the cases when this does not seem to be the situation will be discussed. The owners of the archives and libraries discussed here include both the eventual owners and the persons responsible for storing the archives and libraries. For some archives or libraries found in disturbed or unclear circumstances establishing the house of preservation as a private or official building may be difficult and open to discussion. Therefore, there is a margin of error in the numbers presented here, and future detailed research may, in some cases, reach somewhat different conclusions.

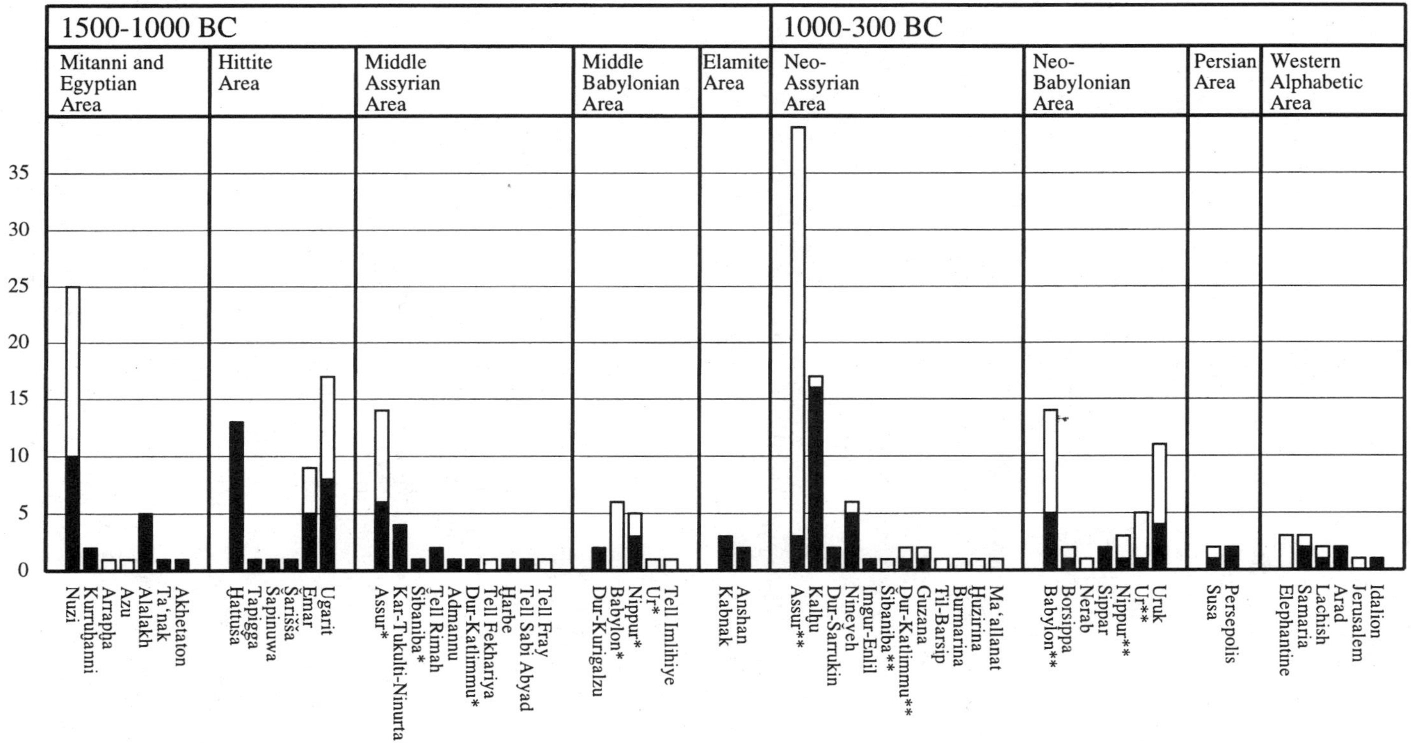

Figure 7.

Number of archives and libraries from official buildings (black) in comparison with the total number of archives and libraries (the whole columns) in the Near East 1500–300 B.C.

4.2.1 Official Houses and Official Owners

This section contains a brief survey of cities with official buildings containing archives or libraries. Official buildings will be analyzed in two groups: religious (temples) and secular (palaces, fortifications, administrative, etc.) buildings and an attempt will be made to establish the ownership in each case.

Among the 253 archives and libraries discussed in this study, 127, that is, slightly more than the half, are from houses that have been classified as official buildings, namely, palaces, temples, fortifications, and other public buildings. Distribution of the archives and libraries in official buildings is shown in *Figure* 7.

Seventy-five (=59 percent) of the 127 archives and libraries from official buildings date to the period 1500–1000 B.C. From the Mitannian and Egyptian areas there are 19 archives and libraries from official buildings: ten archives from Nuzi, five from Alalakh, two from Kurruḫanni, one each from Ta'nak and Akhetaten. The Hittite area has 29 archives and libraries from official buildings: 13 from Ḫattuša, eight from Ugarit, five from Emar, and one each from Tapigga, Šapinuwa, and Šariššа. In the Middle Assyrian area, excavations revealed 17 archives and libraries from official buildings: six from Assur, four from Kar-Tukulti-Ninurta, two from Tell Rimah, and one each from Šibaniba, Admannu, Dur-Katlimmu, Ḫarbe, and Tell Sabi Abyad. In the Middle Babylonian area five archives and libraries were unearthed in official buildings: three from Nippur and two from Dur-Kurigalzu. There are five archives and libraries from official buildings in the Elamite area: three from Kabnak and two from Anshan.

Fifty-two (=41 percent) of the 127 archives and libraries from official buildings date to the period 1000–300 B.C., with a few even later. There are 29 archives and libraries from official buildings in the Neo-Assyrian area: 16 from Kalḫu, five from Nineveh, three from Assur, two from Dur-Šarrukin, and one each from Imgur-Enlil, Dur-Katlimmu, and Guzana. The Neo-Babylonian area has 14 archives and libraries in official buildings: five from Babylon, four from Uruk, two from Sippar, and one each from Borsippa, Nippur, and Ur. In the Persian area, excavations have unearthed three archives in official buildings: two from Persepolis and one from Susa. Finally, there are six known archives and libraries from official buildings found in the Western Alphabetic area: two each from Samaria and Arad, and one each from Lachish and Idalion.

We can now consider in more detail the archives and libraries from different types of official buildings, such as temples and palaces, including some uncertain examples. Also, we will propose to identify the owners of the archives and libraries, especially when it is not clear if the building is an official institution.

4.2.1.1 Temples

There are ca. 36 archives and libraries unearthed in temples or buildings related to temples among the total of 127 archives and libraries from official buildings. The number is approximate, because, on the one hand, there is a possibility that one of the buildings, here regarded as a temple, may actually have been a private house (Emar 1), and, on the other hand, some buildings here classified as palaces could possibly have been temples (Kabnak 1–2, Susa 1).

Half (18) of the archives and libraries found in temples date to the period 1500–1000 B.C. In the Mitannian area one archive with private legal documents (Nuzi 10) was found in the Ištar-Šawuška temple in Nuzi. In the Hittite area, 11 archives and libraries were found in temples in two cities. In Ḫattuša, two large libraries including state archival sections are from the central temple area (Ḫattuša 7) and the possibly associated "House on the Slope" (Ḫattuša 8); five smaller archives or libraries (Ḫattuša 9–13) were found in other temples. One large library combined with archive (Emar 1) under the responsibility of a family of diviners (*bārû*) was found in the so-called temple M1 in Emar. Three small administrative archives were placed in other temples in that city, one (including private texts) in temple M2, one in the Ba'al temple, and another one in the Astarte temple (Emar 2–4). In the Middle Assyrian area, five archives were unearthed in temples in three cities. Two large administrative archives (Assur 4–5) were unearthed in the area of the Assur temple in Assur, one of which concerns offerings under the responsibility of four successive supervisors of offerings (*ša muḫḫi ginā'e* or *rab ginā'e*). An administrative archive (Kar-Tukulti-Ninurta 3) is from the Assur temple in Kar-Tukulti-Ninurta. Two family archives (Tell Rimah 1–2) were placed in the temple in Tell Rimah. One archive is from a temple in the Middle Babylonian area. An administrative archive (Nippur 2) was unearthed in the Gula temple in Nippur. Two archives and libraries from Kabnak are treated, below, together with the palaces, although we cannot exclude the possibility that the building may have been a temple (Kabnak 1–2).

The other half, that is, another 18, of the archives and libraries from temples date to the period 1000–300 B.C., including a few later ones. In the Neo-Assyrian area, seven archives and libraries have been found in temples in four cities. In the Assur temple in Assur, a library including archival texts (Assur 15) was unearthed; a substantial part of the library was originally part of another several-hundred-year-old library. In the Nabû temple in Kalḫu, archaeologists unearthed a library (Kalḫu 14) created by scribes (*ṭupšarru*) and exorcists (*āšipu*), as well as two small archives (Kalḫu 15–16). The two libraries (Dur-Šarrukin 1–2) in the Nabû temple in Dur-Šarrukin were found almost completely empty of texts. The archive (Imgur-Enlil 1) in the Mamu temple in Imgur-Enlil consists of private documents, possibly for a priest (*šangû*). In the Neo-Babylonian area 11 archives and libraries were unearthed in five cities. In Babylon there was an administrative archive from the rebuilding (Babylon 9) of the Ninmaḫ temple, a large collection of school texts (Babylon 10) in the temple of Nabû *ša ḫarê*, and a library combined with an archive (Babylon 11) in the Ninurta temple. The remains of an archive (Borsippa 1) come from the Nabû temple in Borsippa. In the Šamaš temple in Sippar there was one large administrative archive and a library (Sippar 1–2), in which the texts were still standing on the shelves. An administrative archive (Ur 2) has been found in the Sîn temple in Ur. In Uruk, excavations have revealed one large administrative archive with a library section (Uruk 1), at least partly for an exorcist (*āšipu*), in the Neo-Babylonian Ištar temple, an archive with private documents (Uruk 2) from the later Ištar temple, as well as another archive with private documents in the late Anu temple (Uruk 3), where also a library for a lamentation-priest (*kalû*) (Uruk 4) was unearthed. For an archive under the floor in the temple area in Susa, see below under palaces (Susa 1).

The owners of these archives or libraries found in temples may often be the temples themselves. This is reasonable, especially for the archives consisting of documents dealing with the administration of the property of the temples in which the texts were found or with more general matters of administration for the state. Occasionally, such ownership is explicitly stated in the text, and, in a few instances, it is stated that the god of the temple is the ultimate owner. For such official archives there can often be established at least one responsible administrator, for example, the supervisor of offerings. The archives with private documents in the temples may often have been placed there because they belonged to persons working for the temple, such as priests. There may have been other reasons to deposit documents in temples, but they are not readily discernible in the material at hand. The libraries found in temples were, as far as known, created by members of learned professions. To what extent the temples or the members of these learned professions may be regarded as the rightful owners of the texts is more complicated. Learned professionals, such as exorcists, diviners, and lamentation-priests, were, at least, responsible for creating and maintaining the libraries, since they were the main users of the texts.

4.2.1.2 Palaces and Other Official Secular Buildings

Among the 127 archives and libraries from official buildings, ca. 91 were unearthed in palaces and similar official buildings. The number is approximate, because two buildings with archives and libraries (Kabnak 1–2, Susa 1) here considered to be palaces may have been temples. More serious is the blurry distinction between palaces and large private houses: several houses for governors have here been treated as palaces or other official buildings, whereas other large buildings (e.g., Ugarit 12) are here regarded as private houses.

Fifty-seven (=63 percent) of the archives and libraries discovered in palaces and similar official buildings date to the period 1500–1000 B.C. In the Mitannian and Egyptian areas, 18 archives and libraries have been found in palaces and similar buildings in five cities. In Nuzi, eight administrative archives (Nuzi 1–8) were unearthed in different sections of the palace; among these archives one concerns military matters, and another the duties of the palace manager (*šakin bīti*); one administrative archive (Nuzi 9) is from the arsenal. Two administrative archives (Kurruḫanni 1–2) come from the palace in Kurruḫanni. Two administrative archives (Alalakh 1–2), an archive with private documents (Alalakh 3), and the remains of a library (Alalakh 4) were unearthed in the palace in Alalakh; in the nearby fortress another administrative archive (Alalakh 5) under the supervision of royal administrators (*šatam šarri*) was found. In Ta'nak are the remains of an administrative archive (Ta'nak 1) in what may have been an official building. An archive with royal international correspondence and a small library section (Akhetaten 1) was found in a building next to the palace area in Akhetaten.

In the Hittite area, 18 archives and libraries have been unearthed in palaces and similar buildings in six cities. In Ḫattuša there were five archives or libraries (Ḫattuša 1–5) in the palaces on the citadel, and another archive in a related building on another mound (Ḫattuša 6). An administrative archive (Tapigga 1) under the supervision of a military commander (UGULA NIMGIR.ÉRIN.MEŠ) was unearthed in Tapigga. A library with archive (Šapinuwa 1) was found in the palace in Šapinuwa, and another library (Šarišša 1) in a palace in Šarišša. The palace or *ḫilānu*-building in Emar contained an archive (Emar 5) with essentially private documents, but with some unusual traits. In the palace in Ugarit, the excavators unearthed eight administrative archives (Ugarit 1–8).

In the Middle Assyrian area, 11 archives and libraries have been unearthed in palaces and similar buildings in seven cities. In Assur, a small library (Assur 2) for the royal exorcist (*āšip šarri*) was found in the Old Palace, and three administrative archives elsewhere: one west of the Old Palace for an animal fattener (*zāriqu* or *ša kurissi'e*), one in a central administrative building with a large courtyard under the responsibility of at least four successive stewards (*abarakku*), and one in the area of a western city gate (Assur 6–8). Two administrative archives (Kar-Tukulti-Ninurta 1–2) were found in the palace in Kar-Tukulti-Ninurta, and one smaller in a city gate (Kar-Tukulti-Ninurta 4). An administrative archive (Šibaniba 1) for the district chief (*ḫassiḫlu*) was found in a possibly administrative building in Šibaniba. From Admannu there is an administrative archive (Admannu 1) for a shepherd. A large administrative archive (Dur-Katlimmu 1) under the responsibility of a leading governor (*sukkallu rabiu*) was found in what probably was the palace in Dur-Katlimmu. Other archives for governors were found in Ḫarbe (Ḫarbe 1), and in Tell Sabi Abyad (Tell Sabi Abyad 1).

In the Middle Babylonian area four archives have been unearthed in palaces in three cities. Two administrative archives (Dur-Kurigalzu 1–2) are from the palace in Dur-Kurigalzu. In Nippur there was a large administrative archive (Nippur 1) under the responsibility of the governor (*šandabakku*), as well as another mainly administrative archive (Nippur 3).

In the Elamite area five archives have been unearthed in palaces or similar buildings in two cities. In what may have been palaces (or perhaps partly temples) in Kabnak, there were three administrative archives (Kabnak 1–3), one of them including library texts. Two administrative archives (Anshan 1–2) were found in the palace in Anshan.

Thirty-four (=37 percent) of the archives and libraries discovered in palaces and similar official buildings date to the period ca. 1000–300 B.C. In the Neo-Assyrian area, 22 archives and libraries have been unearthed in palaces in five cities. A library with archive (Assur 16) was found in the Prince's Palace and a small administrative archive (Assur 17) for military personal in the Old Palace. In Kalḫu, five archives (Kalḫu 1–5) were found in Fort Shalmaneser; three of them were administrative and concerned military matters, wine, and the duties of the palace manager (*rab ekalli*). The remaining two archives in that building contained texts of a private nature; one of these archives was for the queen and her female manager (*šakintu*). Five archives and a library (Kalḫu 6–11) were unearthed in the Northwest Palace; among them were three administrative archives, one of them royal, and two other archives, one of them for the palace scribe (*ṭupšar ekalli*) and other palace personnel, with essentially private documents. An archive (Kalḫu 12) for successive governors (*šaknu* and *bēl pāḫiti*) was found in the Governors Palace, and the remains of a royal archive (Kalḫu 13) in the Burnt Palace. In Nineveh, one royal library with archive (Nineveh 1), as well as two other archives (Nineveh 2–3), come from the Southwest Palace, and an archive as well as a library (Nineveh 4–5) were found in the North Palace. The archives contained administrative documents, including royal documents, as well as private documents for persons related to the palace; library texts were noted as belonging to the king (Assurbanipal's library). The archive (Dur-Katlimmu 2) from the so-called palace in the lower city of Dur-Katlimmu consisted of private documents. An administrative archive (Guzana 1) of the governor was unearthed next to the northeastern palace in Guzana.

In the Neo-Babylonian area three archives have been unearthed in palaces in two cities. One of the two administrative archives (Babylon 7) in the palaces in Babylon concerned the administration of prisoners, the other one (Babylon 8) belonged to an administrative unit possibly responsible to a governor (*pīḫātu*). An administrative archive (Nippur 8) in Nippur involved the governor (*šandabakku*). In the Persian area, three archives have been unearthed in palaces and similar buildings in two cities. An administrative archive (Susa 1) found under a floor in the later temple area in Susa was under the supervision of a superintendent (*araš hutlak*). In Persepolis there were two administrative archives (Persepolis 1–2), one in the palace area for the treasurers (*ganzabara*) and the other in the nearby fortification.

In the Western Alphabetic area six archives have been unearthed in palaces and similar buildings in four cities. In the palace area of Samaria two archives (Samaria 1–2) were found; at least one of them is administrative in nature. An archive (Lachish 1) of a military commander was discovered in the city gate of Lachish. In Arad two administrative archives (Arad 1–2) of commanders of the fortification were unearthed. One administrative archive (Idalion 1) has been unearthed in the palace of the west citadel of Idalion.

The owners of these archives and libraries from palaces and other secular buildings may often have been the official institutions, in which buildings the archives and libraries were discovered. Eventually the king may be regarded as the owner not only of royal archives with royal letters and documents, but in a less direct way, of most of the administrative archives located in royal palaces. However, immediately responsible for the archives were other officials, such as palace managers, royal administrators, and the queen's female managers. Stewards, superintendents, military commanders, animal fatteners, and several other officials were also responsible for administrative archives in palaces or other official buildings. Often attested are administrative archives in provincial centers under the supervision of different types of provincial governors or district chiefs. Administrative archives are occasionally found in buildings connected with city gates; such archives were sometimes the responsibility of military or police officers. Some of the archives in palaces consisted partly or completely of private documents. The owners of these archives or dossiers of archives were members of the royal family or, more often, officials involved in the palace or military. Also libraries or library sections in archives are sometimes attested in palaces, particularly in the Hittite area. Direct evidence of their ownership is often missing but is sometimes available, for example, in Nineveh, the king Assurbanipal was said to be the owner of the library in the palace, but in Assur a royal exorcist seems to have been responsible.

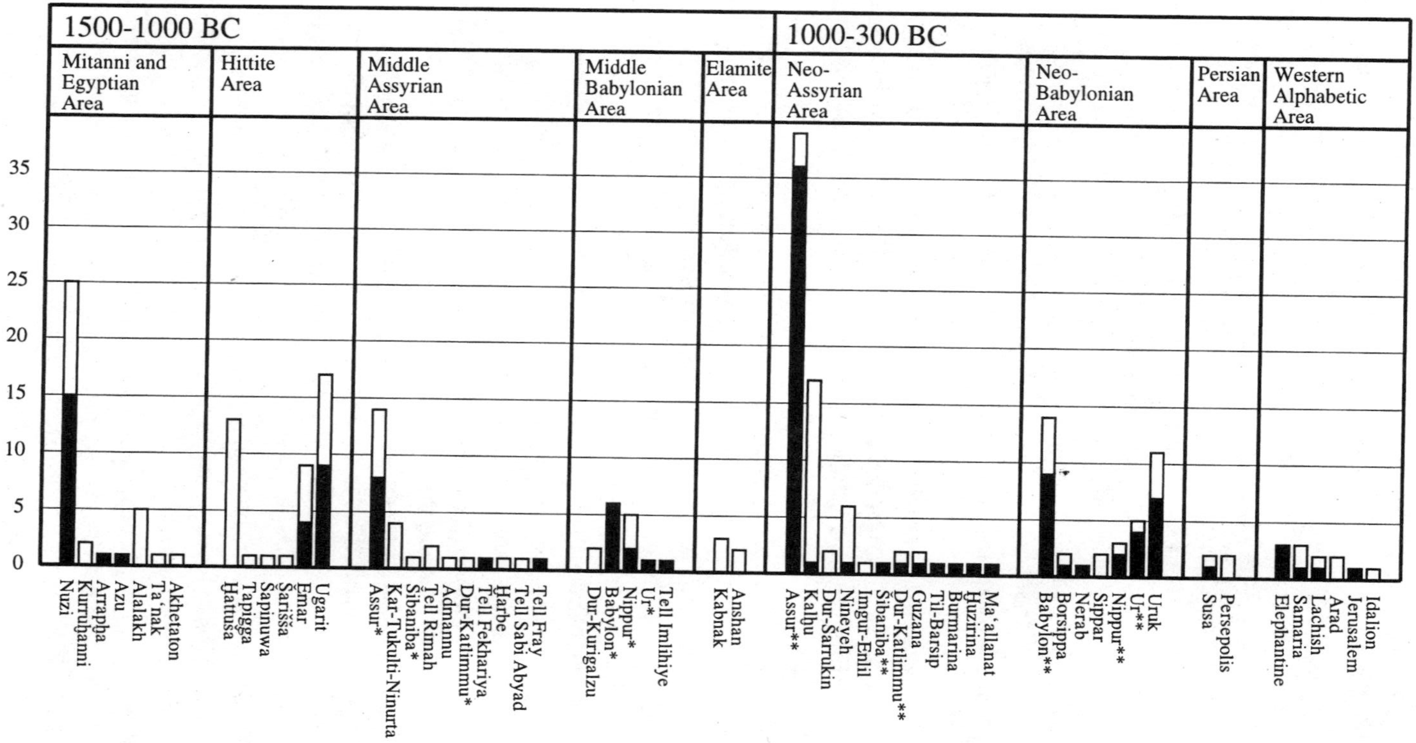

Figure 8.

Number of archives and libraries from private houses (black) in comparison with the total number of archives and libraries (the whole columns) in the Near East 1500–300 B.C.

4.2.2 Private Houses and Private Owners

Among the 253 archives and libraries, 126, that is, slightly less than half, come from houses, which have been classified as private family houses. We will look at the distribution of archives and libraries from private houses in different cities and consider the archives and libraries from some buildings in more detail, including, when possible, the names and/or professions of the owners of the archives and libraries, especially when it is not clear that it is the person or family living in the house. The profession of most owners of archives or libraries is not usually explicitly stated in the texts, since, in most cases, it is unnecessary to mention one's profession in private documents or letters to be included in one's own archive. See *Figure* 8 for the distribution.

Fifty (=40 percent) of the archives and libraries from private houses date to the period 1500–1000 B.C. In the Mitannian area 17 archives have been unearthed in private houses in three cities. In Nuzi, 15 archives (Nuzi 11–25) were unearthed in areas with private houses. Among the owners are families with from one to five (e.g., Teḫip-Tilla) generations attested. Only a few have documented professions, for example, Šilwa-Teššup son of the king (*mār šarri*), and a representative (*amumiḫḫuru*) of another son of the king (*mār šarri*). A private archive (Arrapḫa 1) from Arrapḫa was found without a well-defined findspot, but was probably originally from a private house. An archive (Azu 1) was also found in a private house in Azu.

In the Hittite area 13 archives and libraries have been unearthed in private houses in two cities. In Emar four archives (Emar 6–9) were found in different private houses. Ugarit delivered nine archives and libraries from private houses: three libraries (Ugarit 9–11) from Ugarit were unearthed in private homes; one of the owners was the high priest (*rb khnm*). Six archives (Ugarit 12–17) were found in private houses in the same city; among the owners were the high official *šatammu rabû*, a supervisor of the harbor (*akil kāri*), and a governor (*sākinu*).

In the Middle Assyrian area ten archives and libraries have been unearthed in private houses in three cities. In Assur eight archives and libraries were found in private houses: two libraries (Assur 1, 3) may be from such houses, even if the archaeological evidence is lacking; one of the libraries was created by a family of scribes (*ṭupšarru*). In the same city, six archives (Assur 9–14) were found in private houses; the owners were members of different families for which one to three generations are attested. Some of the owners were leading persons of the state, such as Babu-aḫa-iddina and a family serving in the provinces as governors, but the only documented professions are shepherd (*nāqidu*) and governor (*bēl pāḫete*) (both documented for the same person), and *alaḫḫinu*. One archive (Tell Fekhariya 1) was found in a possibly private house in Tell Fekhariya, and another archive (Tell Fray 1) in a private house in Tell Fray.

In the Middle Babylonian area ten archives and libraries have been unearthed in private houses in four cities. In Babylon the excavators unearthed six archives and libraries in private houses. Among them are: three libraries (Babylon 4–6); one of the libraries belonged to diviners (*bārû*). In the same city, there were also three archives (Babylon 1–3) found in private houses. Two archives (Nippur 4–5) were unearthed in private houses in Nippur. In an area with private houses in Ur, excavations revealed an archive (Ur 1) for a family of brewers (*sirašû*). Next to a destroyed private house in the small town Tell Imlihiye, an archive (Tell Imlihiye 1) was found for individuals involved in agriculture.

Seventy-six (=60 percent) of the archives and libraries from private houses date to the period ca. 1000–300 B.C., as well as a few later ones. In the Neo-Assyrian area 45 archives and libraries have been unearthed in private houses in ten cities. In Assur, as a result of extensive excavation of private houses, 36 archives and libraries were unearthed. There were six libraries (Assur 18–23); among the owners were scribes (*ṭupšarru*), chief singers (*nargallu*), and exorcists (*āšipu*). Thirty archives (Assur 24–53) were unearthed in other private houses owned by different families. Among all the owners of these archives only a few have attested professions, for example, door-keepers (*atû*), tanners (*ṣāripu*), gold- and silversmiths (*ṣarrāpu, kutimmu*), and *ḫundu-raya*. An archive (Kalḫu 17) was found in the house of a eunuch (*ša rēši*) in Kalḫu. In a secondary position, an archive (Nineveh 6) of a son of the palace (*mār ekalli*) was unearthed in Nineveh; it may originally have been placed in a private house. In Šibaniba an archive (Šibaniba 2) was found in what may have been an area with private houses, but the texts seem to be official administrative documents. An archive (Dur-Katlimmu 3) was found in a large private house in Dur-Katlimmu. Other archives were unearthed in private houses in Guzana (Guzana 2), Til-Barsip (Til-Barsip 1), and Burmarina (Burmarina 1). A library (Ḫuzirina 1) belonging to priests (*šangû*) was found just outside what was probably their house in Ḫuzirina. The private archive (Ma'allanat 1) of a palace steward (*šaknu ša ekalli*) is without recorded findspot; it may be from the private house of the owner, or perhaps from the palace where he served.

In the Neo-Babylonian area 24 archives and libraries have been unearthed in private houses in six cities. In Babylon nine archives and libraries were unearthed in private houses: five archives (Babylon 12–16) were found; one of the archives belonged to the Egibi family. Four libraries (Babylon 17–20) were unearthed in other private homes. A family archive (Borsippa 2) has been reconstructed from findings from illicit excavations probably in a private house in Borsippa. An archive (Nereb 1) spanning two generations of a family was found in what was probably a private house in Nereb. Two archives (Nippur 6–7) were unearthed in private houses in Nippur; the largest of the archives belonged to the Murašû family. In Ur the excavators unearthed four archives and libraries in private houses. They consist of three archives (Ur 3–5), one of which belonged to a family of barbers (*gallābu*), as well as a library (Ur 6) with numerous school texts. In Uruk were found seven archives and libraries in private houses. They are four archives (Uruk 5–8) belonging to families of between one and three generations, one of them a temple cook (*nuḫatimmu*). In the same city three libraries (Uruk 9–11) were unearthed; two of them belonging to exorcists (*āšipu*). In the Persian area, in Susa, a possibly private archive (Susa 2) was found in a poorly defined archaeological context, perhaps originally a private house.

In the Western Alphabetic area six archives have been unearthed in private houses in four cities. In Elephantine, three archives (Elephantine 1–3) were discovered in the area with private houses; one of the archives was for a religious leader and another one was for three generations of another branch of his family. Remains of private archives were also unearthed outside Samaria (Samaria 3), and possibly also in Lachish (Lachish 2) and Jerusalem (Jerusalem 1).

The owners of these archives and libraries from private houses were, as a rule, those living in the houses. Archives in private houses concern, in most cases, economic and legal matters of importance for those living there. The documentation might cover one generation of a family, but often included documents from several earlier generations, sometimes up to five generations. The professions of the archive owners are only occasionally explicitly stated, and when attested, the professions represent a wide range of persons working for the king, for a temple, or with matters concerning other private persons. Private archives could be owned by people of various professions—there is no concentration of private archives in any specific group of professions. Beside high- or middle-ranking persons with titles explicitly mentioned, there were many others who, according to the archives, conducted business or acquired property. In some of the private archives, there were also dossiers of documents from the official careers of the owners. In this way, documents from official institutions may sometimes be found in the houses of officials, a situation to be compared with the occasional findings of private documents in official buildings. The libraries placed in private houses were created and owned by families with learned professions living in the houses, such as exorcists, priests, scribes, diviners, and singers. As a rule these professionals seem to have connections with temples or with the king. The professionals with private libraries are essentially of the same professions as those responsible for creating libraries in official buildings (cf. 4.2.1).

4.3 Archives and Libraries according to Types of Texts

In the first of the two following sections, the types of texts in archives and libraries will be discussed. In the second section, the division of the text collections into archives and libraries will be considered. We have defined archives as consisting of different types of documents (including letters) in a broad sense of the word. Libraries consist of literary texts, including religious, historical, and scientific texts. Some collections of texts may be called both archive and library. The frequency and extent of such mixed collections will be discussed.

4.3.1 Types of Texts

Many texts in the archives and libraries remain inaccessible—unpublished or known only through preliminary studies by various scholars using different classifications. As a consequence, too many texts have been assigned classification types that provide a general description, but cannot be used for detailed comparison. Therefore, there will not be any statistics by text type; the presentation will be limited to main types of texts in the archives and libraries, according to categories used throughout this work.

The most common types of texts in official archives may be called administrative documents. They document persons, materials, and objects belonging to or being under the responsibility of official institutions. Main administrative processes are reflected in documentation of receipt, inventory, and delivery of these belongings. Administrative lists may be used as inventories, but also as documentation of deliveries or disbursements, or as records of goods received—tables may perform the same function. The many types of documents include: administrative notes, which are short documents, e.g., a delivery note; contracts, often formulated as loans; receipts and other documentation concerning leases; letters received or copies of letters sent—sometimes of the letter-order type; astrological reports and queries; and, in special cases, treaties and royal grants.

The different types of texts in private archives document the interests, often economic, of the owners. The most frequently attested text-types are loan documents and purchase documents. Documents formulated as loans may, beside their obvious use for loans made by the archive owner, document investments, and carry obligations or security in the interest of the archive owner. Purchase documents usually concern the archive owner's acquisition of houses, lands, and slaves. There are documents concerning gifts or donations; contracts, for example, about leases, prebends, or work; and documents about rent, exchange, receipt, or payment. Records of legal settlements, litigation, adoption, sale-adoption, marriage, inheritance, and wills are attested. Lists or accounts for the administration of the private belongings of the archive owner are found. Letters occur with business or legal information, sometimes including information about private matters (these letters had been sent to family members of the archive owner, even if copies of dispatched letters sometimes existed).

Libraries contain literary, historical, and scientific texts. Most of these text types are found in both official and private libraries. The best-attested types of texts are omens, incantations, and lexical lists. Omens, so frequently found in libraries, like the oracles and hemerologies, were used for forecasting. Also well attested are incantations and incantation rituals, which were used to counteract evil, sickness, and bad omens. Medical texts and prescriptions were used for the treatment of sickness. Religious, or more strictly speaking, literary texts included epics, myths, hymns, prayers, and lamentations. There are also rituals or descriptions of festivals, as well as cultic inventories.

Objects with historical texts were normally built into the walls of monumental buildings. Historical texts were, on occasion, placed in libraries; there are royal annals, treaties, laws, and occasionally special types, such as regulations of palace and harem life.

Frequently attested are the different types of lexical lists in use for the proper writing of cuneiform. Related categories are the grammatical lists and, among the Ugaritic alphabetic texts, the alphabets. Other lists include god-lists and several scientific texts. Mathematical, astronomical, and astrological texts are attested in some of the libraries. Some school or exercise texts many be preserved in libraries, and large amounts of such texts have been found in buildings used as schools.

Models of livers and lungs, as well as different kinds of figure drawings on clay tablets, have been unearthed in libraries. In order to keep track of collection contents, library catalogues were written.

4.3.2 Archives and Libraries

In this survey of the division of text collections into archives and libraries, archives and the archival sections of libraries will be reviewed. Then, the libraries, including the library sections of archives, will be analyzed. Finally, the combined archives and libraries will be considered in further detail.

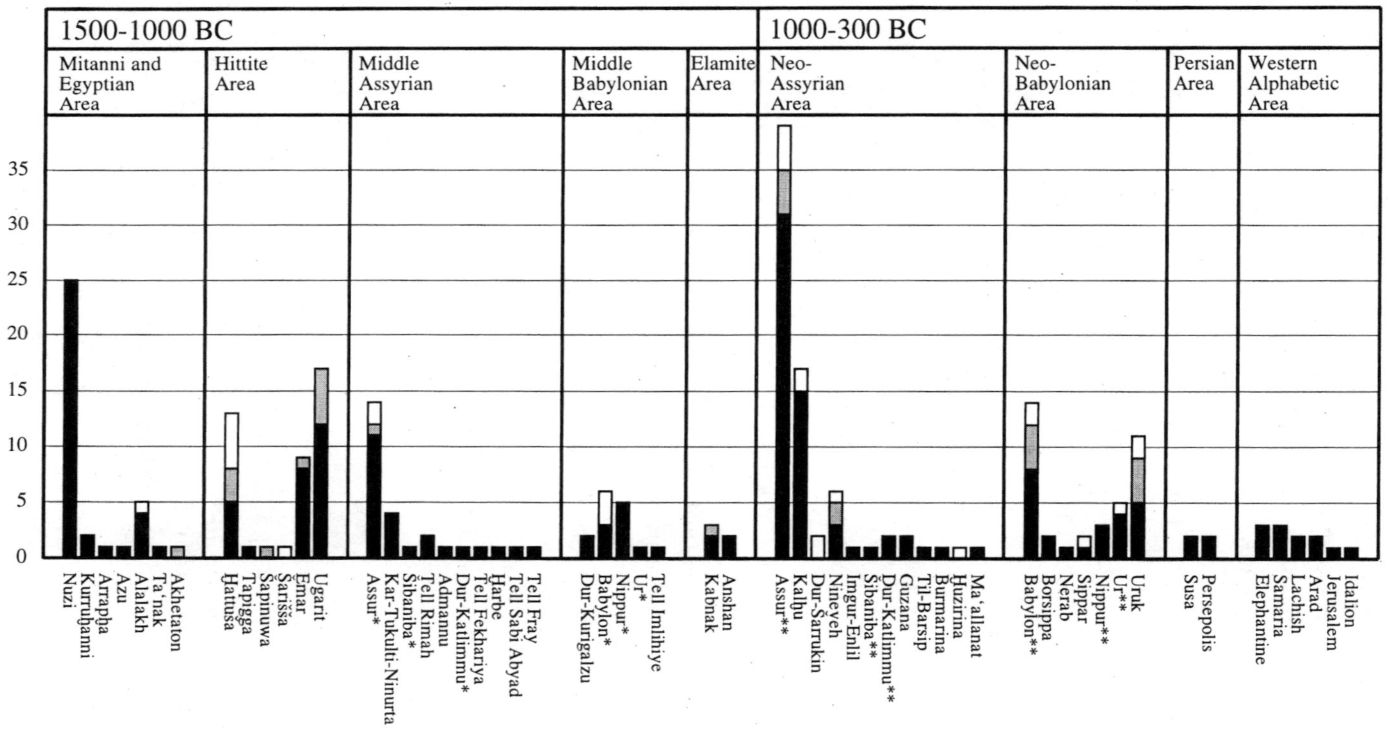

Figure 9.

Number of archives (black) and all combinations of archives and libraries (gray) containing documents in comparison with the total number of archives and libraries (the whole columns) in the Near East 1500–300 B.C.

4.3.2.1 Archives

Of the 253 archives and libraries, most of them, 225 (=89 percent) may, on the basis of text type, be classified as archives or archives combined with libraries (*Figure* 9). One hundred thirteen archives, approximately one half of these 225, date from the period 1500–1000 B.C. Among the 36 archives and libraries from the Mitannian and Egyptian areas, there are 35 archives, including an archive with library section. Most of the archives (25), are from Nuzi: ten from official buildings and 15 from private houses. Two archives were found in an official building in Kurruḫanni. One archive is from a private house in Arrapḫa, and another one from a private house in Azu. In Alalakh, four archives were unearthed in official buildings. One archive is from an official building in Ta'nak and an archive with a small library section comes from an official building in Akhetaten.

Among the 42 archives and libraries in the Hittite area, there are 36 archives or archival sections of libraries. In Ḫattuša eight archives have been unearthed: five archives and three archival sections in libraries, all from official buildings; one found in an official building in Tapigga; and one library combined with an archive was unearthed in Šapinuwa. In Emar, nine archives were found: one archival section (ca. 25 percent of total number of texts in collection) of a library in a possibly official building; four archives in other such buildings; and four archives in private homes. In Ugarit 17 archives were unearthed: eight archives (one of them included a library section) are from an official building; six archives (one of them including a library section) were found in private houses; and three consist of archival sections (each ca. 25 percent of the total collection) in libraries in private houses.

Among the 27 archives and libraries from the Middle Assyrian area, there are 25 archives or archival sections of libraries. In Assur 12 archives were unearthed: five archives were found in official buildings; six archives in private houses; and there may have been an archival section of a library perhaps in a private house. Four archives were unearthed in official buildings in Kar-Tukulti-Ninurta: one archive is from an official building in Šibaniba; two from an official building in Tell Rimah; one probably from an official building in Admannu; and one from an official building in Dur-Katlimmu. One archive was unearthed in what is probably a private house in Tell Fekhariya. One archive comes from an official building in Ḫarbe and another archive from such a building in Tell Sabi Abyad. One archive was unearthed in a private house in Tell Fray.

Among the 15 archives and libraries from the Middle Babylonian area, there are 12 archives: two are from an official building in Dur-Kurigalzu; three were unearthed in private houses in Babylon; in Nippur, three archives were found in official buildings and two in private houses; one archive comes from a private house in Ur; and another archive is from a private house in Tell Imlihiye.

In the Elamite area excavations have revealed five archives: in Kabnak three archives have been unearthed in official buildings—one of these archives included a library section; two archives were found in an official building in Anshan.

One hundred twelve of the 225 archives date from the period 1000–300 B.C. or later. Among the 74 archives and libraries from the Neo-Assyrian area, there are 64 archives or archival sections of libraries. Most of the archives (35) are from Assur: one archive and two libraries with archival sections in official buildings and 30 archives and two libraries with archival sections in private houses. Among the 15 archives found in Kalḫu, 14 archives were unearthed in official buildings and one archive in a private house. In Nineveh, at least five archives have been found: three archives (one of them possibly with a library section) and one library combined with archive have been documented in official buildings; and an archive may originally have come from a private house. One archive was found in an official building in Imgur-Enlil, and one archive may possibly be from a private house in Šibaniba. Two archives were unearthed in Dur-Katlimmu, one of them in an official building, the other in a private house. Two archives were found in Guzana, one from an official building and one from a private house. One archive was from a private house in Til-Barsip; one archive was found in a private house in Burmarina; and one archive probably comes from a private house in Ma'allanat.

Among the 38 archives and libraries from the Neo-Babylonian area, there are 32 archives or archival sections of libraries. The largest number of archives (12) was found in Babylon: three archives and one archival section in a library all unearthed in official buildings and eight archives (including three archival sections in libraries) from private houses. In Borsippa one archive has been found in an official building and another one possibly in a private house. One archive is probably from a private house in Nereb. A quite large archive was found in an official building in Sippar. Among the three archives found in Nippur, one is from an official building and two from private homes. In Ur four archives have been unearthed: one in an official building and three in private houses. Among the nine archives excavated in Uruk: four archives (among them two archives with library sections, and one archive section of a library) unearthed in official buildings and four archives and an archival section of a library in private houses.

Only archives—no libraries at all—were found in the Persian and Western Alphabetic areas. In the Persian area four archives have been unearthed: in Susa two archives were found, one in an official building and the other possibly in a private house; and two archives are from official buildings in Persepolis. In the Western

Alphabetic area excavations have revealed 12 archives: in Elephantine, three archives were found in private houses; three archives were connected with Samaria, two unearthed in official buildings in the city, another may originally have been placed in a private house in the city, but was found secondarily hidden in a cave far away from the city; two archives from Lachish, one from an official building and the other possibly from a private house; in Arad, two archives were found in connection with official buildings; one archive was from a possibly private house in Jerusalem; and one in an official building in Idalion.

In both main periods and in all areas discussed, there were clearly more archives (225) than libraries. There have been found slightly more archives (115) in official buildings, such as palaces and temples, than archives (110) in private houses. In four of the five cities with the largest number of archives, namely, Assur, Nuzi, Ugarit, and Babylon, excavations have been conducted both in extensive areas with private houses and in official buildings. The result is, that in these four cities, the majority of the text collections consists of archives found in private houses. In other cities excavations have often been more concentrated in official buildings, which have yielded their archives. Thus, due to preferences by excavators, archives from privates houses are underrepresented in the material at hand, when compared to those from official buildings. There is a basic division between the often administrative archives in the official buildings and the archives in private houses, since the latter obviously concern the owner's personal needs. Twenty-seven of the 225 archives were combined with library sections (see below).

4.3.2.2 Libraries

Among the 253 archives and libraries, 55 (=22 percent) have, in this work, been categorized as libraries or library divisions of archives, on the basis of the types of texts in the collections (*Figure* 10). Twenty-five (=45 percent) of the 55 libraries date from the period 1500–1000 B.C. Among the 36 archives and libraries from the Mitannian and Egyptian areas, two libraries have been found: the remains of one small library from an official building in Alalakh and one library section (7 percent of the total number of texts in the collection) of the archive from such a building in Akhetaten.

Among the 42 archives and libraries in the Hittite area, there are 16 libraries or library sections of combined archives and libraries. In Ḫattuša eight libraries have been found in official buildings; three of these libraries seem to have been combined with archives. One library combined with an archive was found in official building in Šapinuwa, and one library in an official house in Šarišša. One library with ca. 25

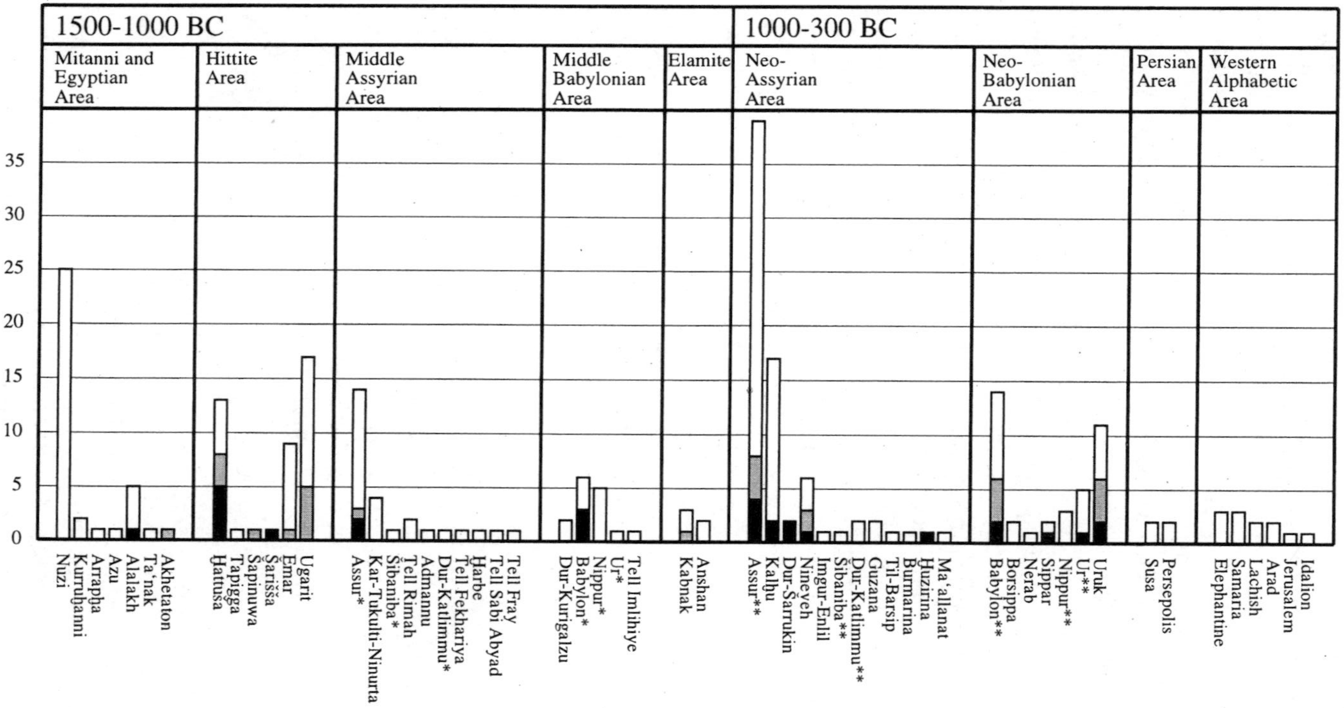

Figure 10.

Number of libraries (black) and all combinations of libraries and archives (gray) containing literary texts in comparison with the total number of archives and libraries (the whole columns) in the Near East 1500–300 B.C.

percent archival material was unearthed in a possibly official building in Emar. In Ugarit, three libraries, with ca. 25 percent archival section in each, as well as a small library section of an archive, were discovered in private houses, and one library section of an archive was found in an official building.

Among the 27 archives and libraries from the Middle Assyrian area, three libraries have been identified. They are all from Assur: one is from an official building and the others are possibly from private houses, one of which may have contained an archival section. Among the 15 archives and libraries from the Middle Babylonian area, three libraries have been unearthed—all from private houses in Babylon. Among the five archives and libraries from the Elamite area, one library has been identified; this is a sections of an archive in an official building from Kabnak.

Thirty (=55 percent) of the 55 libraries date from the period 1000–300 B.C. or later. Among the 74 archives and libraries from the Neo-Assyrian area, there are 15 libraries or library section in archives. Eight of the libraries are from Assur: two libraries with archival sections from official buildings and six libraries (two of them with archival sections, the others with only one or two archival tablets) from private houses. Remains of two libraries have been unearthed in official buildings in Kalḫu. Two almost empty library rooms were discovered in an official building in Dur-Šarrukin. In official buildings in Nineveh, at least two libraries were discovered (one of these libraries was combined with an archive), and in one of the archives there, it is possible that a library section may have existed—the existence of another library or library section of an archive in an official building cannot be excluded, but has not been accounted for here. One library was found in connection with a private house in Ḫuzirina.

Among the 38 archives and libraries from the Neo-Babylonian area, there are 15 libraries or library sections of archives. In Babylon six libraries have been found: two libraries (one of them combined with an archive) in official buildings and four libraries (three of them combined with archival texts) in private houses. One library was excavated with most of the texts still standing on the shelves in an official building in Sippar. One library has been found in a private house in Ur. Six libraries have been found in Uruk: two library sections in archives and one library (with a small archival section), all in official buildings; and four libraries (one of them combined with an archival section) in private houses. In both the Persian and the Western Alphabetic areas, no libraries have as yet been excavated. The lack of unearthed libraries from the Persian and the Western Alphabetic areas is probably the result of the use of perishable writing materials; libraries are attested from earlier periods in these same geographical areas.

It is clear that, for all periods and areas, there are fewer libraries (55) than archives. Thirty libraries were discovered in official buildings, whereas 25 libraries were found in private homes. In the cities with the largest number of libraries, namely, Assur, Babylon, Ḫattuša, and Uruk, almost all cities had more libraries recovered from private houses than from official buildings. The only exception is Ḫattuša, where all libraries are from official buildings (the main thrust of the excavations). The libraries may contain representative collections of literary or scientific texts or simple collections of school texts with such content. There is no clear difference in type of texts between libraries in official buildings and private houses. Twenty-seven of the 55 libraries were combined with archive sections (see below).

4.3.2.3 Combinations of Archives and Libraries

It has been relatively easy to classify the great majority of text collections as either archives or libraries on the basis of the types of texts in each. However, 27 (=11 percent) of the 253 collections of texts could not be classified as either an archive *or* a library, but rather as archive *and* library, or, for example, library with archive section (or the opposite, depending on whether the archive or the library section was the larger portion). These combined collections have been previously discussed, first among the archives and then among the libraries. The details of the placement of most of these collections are often unknown, that is, it is only occasionally possible to determine whether the archival section was stored together and mixed with the library section, or whether it was only stored next to it.

Among the 27 collections of texts classified as both archives and libraries, there are seven archives with library sections: six found in official buildings and one in a private house. The library section of the archive (Akhetaten 1) from Akhetaten consists of 27 texts (=7 percent of the collection), and the library section of an archive (Ugarit 5) from Ugarit contains 25 texts (=15 percent of the collection). The sizes of the library sections of archives (Kabnak 2, Nineveh 4) from Kabnak and possibly from Nineveh are not known. One of the library sections from archives (Uruk 1) in Uruk is limited in comparison with the archival part (250 texts compared to 10,000), the other example is quite small (Uruk 2). In Ugarit an archive with a library section (Ugarit 16) was discovered in a private house.

Among the 27 combined collections, there are ten libraries with archival sections found in official buildings. The contents of the archival sections of three libraries (Ḫattuša 1, 3, 7) in Ḫattuša and the one library (Šapinuwa 1) in Šapinuwa need to be clarified. The archival section of a library (Emar 1) in an official building (or possibly a private house) in Emar was about 25 percent of the complete collection. The sizes and contents of archival sections of two libraries (Assur 15, 16) in Assur are as yet unknown. The number of texts in the archival sections of a library (Nineveh 1) in Nineveh and of another library (Babylon 11) in Babylon has not been possible to establish. The archival section of a library (Uruk 4) in Uruk consists of just a few texts.

Another ten libraries with archival sections have been found in private houses. All the archival sections of the libraries (Ugarit 9–11) in private houses in Ugarit were approximately 25 percent of each complete collection. Two libraries (Assur 19, 20) from private houses in Assur had archival sections—one of these archives had been placed in a room other than the library. Another library (Assur 1), possibly from a private house in Assur, may have contained an archival section (depending on the original placement of the texts). Three of the libraries (Babylon 18, 19, 20) in private houses in Babylon had archival sections; the only one of them where the number of texts is known is about 18 percent of the library. One library (Uruk 9) in a private house in Uruk has an archival section which had been stored in a separate clay jar.

In addition to archives with library section and libraries with archive section, there may be one or two texts of archival character in libraries or of library character in archives. These few texts have not caused any change in the classification of the text collection as a library or archive, nor has it been always possible to treat them systematically here (e.g., Ugarit 1, 2, 6, Assur 18, 21, 22, 23, Kalḫu 6, 12, 14, Uruk 10, 11, Sippar 2).

As seen from the above numbers, only 27 archives and libraries (=11 percent of the total) contain a substantial number of texts of the other category. These divided archive and libraries represent 12 percent of the 225 archives. There are only seven archives with library sections (=3 percent)—six of these archives are from official houses and one from a private house. We may, therefore, conclude that the overwhelming majority of the archives are normally without literary texts. Only quite seldom is there a library division of an archive.

The libraries present another picture. The 27 divided archives and libraries represent 49 percent of the 55 libraries. There are 28 libraries without accountable archive section and 20 libraries with an archive division—ten in private houses and ten in official buildings. There have been several problems with those from official buildings, but the libraries with archive sections from private houses seem to be well established. Apparently an owner of a library often included his archival texts among the literary ones, but sometimes texts of different categories are reported to have been found in different rooms or in separate jars.

This mixing of archival collections with library collections raises the issue as to whether there is, in fact, a valid reason to differentiate between the two. However, this division conveys information about the type of texts in a collection and about the different uses of the collection by different professionals. This division becomes particularly clear, if we focus upon the buildings with archives and libraries—at least for official buildings. Several of the large palaces and temples had more than one archive or library in different rooms, often with specialized functions (Nuzi, Kurruḫanni, Alalakh, Ḫattuša, Ugarit, Assur, Kar-Tukulti-Ninurta, Tell Rimah, Dur-Kurigalzu, Kabnak, Anshan, Kalḫu, Nineveh, Sippar, and Uruk). Where relevant excavation documentation is available, a tendency to separate the archive and the library can be noticed in large palaces and temples (Alalakh 2–5, Assur 1, 4, 5, Kabnak 1–2, Kalḫu 6–11, Kalḫu 14–16, Sippar 1–2, and Uruk 2–4). In the private houses, there was normally only one collection of texts, but a division into archive and library sections has sometimes been reported (e.g., Assur 20, Uruk 9). Due to a lack of information regarding the circumstances of many finds, it has not been possible to determine whether within a "mixed collection" of texts there may have been an internal division according to types or texts, e.g., in different parts of the room or on different shelves.

In the overwhelmingly number of cases, archives were not combined with libraries, whereas the more rarely attested libraries with literary texts often contained archival sections. The clear separation of archives and libraries occurred more often in official buildings than in private houses.

4.4 General Principles

Our knowledge of archives and libraries from 1500–300 B.C. is dependent upon four main factors: (1) the extent written documentation was used during the periods and areas under consideration; (2) the proportion of texts preserved, which is dependent on, for example, the durability of the writing material; (3) the extent and quality of excavations in the appropriate buildings within suitable levels of sites; and (4) the availability and completeness of information about the excavations and the text collections unearthed.

Archives and libraries were collected and kept according to the needs and within the abilities of the owners. According to the definitions used in this work, archives consisted of a broad range of documents, including letters. Libraries consisted of literary texts, including religious, historical, and scientific texts. The number of texts in a collection may range from a handful of texts up to 30,000. The smaller collections are far better attested than the larger ones.

Within the time-span of our study, there are two distinct periods with a number of attested archives and libraries, separated by a lacuna during the tenth century B.C.

The largest number of archives and libraries date to or cease functioning in the seventh and thirteenth centuries B.C.

Two hundred fifty-three archives and libraries from 51 cities have been surveyed. Remains of a few additional archives and libraries from these areas have been referred to, but their reconstruction was not possible. A group of well-excavated cities of upper medium size account for the largest number of archives and libraries. The highest number of archives and libraries, 53 in all, have been unearthed in Assur. Twenty-five cities have yielded only one archive or library each. And all these unearthed archives and libraries are only a fraction of those once in use.

A wide range of Semitic, Indo-European, and different types of unrelated agglutinative languages were in frequent use. The choice of writing material varied according to each culture and its resources. Cuneiform texts were written on clay tablets, which allowed for excellent preservation, or on writing boards, usually of wood and thus prone to poor preservation. Alphabetic texts were, as a rule, written on perishable materials, such as papyrus or leather, but sometimes on ostraca and, on rare occasion, clay tablets; writing boards may also have been in use. The preservation of other writing systems on other materials, such as hieroglyphic Luwian on lead strips, is rare.

Seal impressions occur on archival clay tablets, but for texts written on other materials sealings had to be placed on attached bullae or dockets made of clay—for alphabetic texts written on perishable material, these bullae or dockets are sometimes all that have survived of the archive.

Archives and libraries were normally in use for one, two, or three generations of a family, or for some successive administrative officials. Collections covering no more than a year as well as those in use for several hundreds of years are seldomly attested.

Archives and libraries have been found in both official buildings, such as palaces and temples, and in private houses. They were originally stored in a room with shelves, boxes, or jars. In major palaces or temples, a single building complex could house more than one archive or library, each collection fulfilling a special function. Usually there was only one archive or library in a private house. The owner of an archive located in an official buildings might be the king, officials of that institution, or the institution itself. The owner of an archive or library kept in a private home was the owner of the house, who lived there.

Most collections of texts were archives: often administrative archives in official buildings and private ones in private houses. There are occasional exceptions, when texts of a personal nature were stored in official buildings (presumably to meet the needs of the owner/official working there) or official texts were taken home by the officials using them.

Only 55 (=22 percent) of the text collections should be categorized as libraries. The types of texts in libraries stored in official buildings were often the same as those stored in private houses. Rarely did an archive contain literary material, texts typically found in a library. Yet almost half of the more poorly attested libraries contained more or less substantial archival sections.

I have endeavored to analyze the large textual findings within their archaeological setting. For reasons enumerated above, our conclusions must be quite broad and, perhaps, preliminary. The unearthing of new archives and libraries, further publication of excavated material, and more detailed study of archives and libraries will add to, and may, to some extent, change the observations and conclusions offered here. I await these new finds, publications, and studies eagerly.

Indices

The personal and geographical names used in this work involve some standardization and sometimes simplification, as well as adjustment to name forms in common usage. Ancient professions are always given in the singular. The index of personal names is limited to persons of immediate importance to the archives and libraries—usually the owners. The indices of professions and their modern equivalents treat the professions for the same persons as the index of personal names. The indices of ancient city names and their modern equivalents list the cities with archives and libraries discussed in this work, as well as some other sites referred to in this work as having texts.

Personal Names

PROFESSIONS

Modern Equivalents of Professions

Ancient City Names

Modern Site Names